THE
RA
CONTACT

TEACHING THE
LAW OF ONE

VOLUME I

Source: Ra, an Humble Messenger of the Law of One
Instrument: Carla L. Rueckert
Questioner: Don Elkins
Scribe: Jim McCarty

Relistening Project: Tobey Wheelock
Production and Editing: Gary Bean and Austin Bridges

The Ra Contact: Teaching the Law of One – Volume 1

Second printing.

Copyright © 2018 L/L Research, Tobey Wheelock

ISBN: 978-0-945007-94-4

Published by L/L Research
Box 5195
Louisville, Kentucky 40255-0195, USA
www.llresearch.org
contact@llresearch.org

Cover art by Aaron Maret

DEDICATION

It would have been an honor for me to work with Don and Carla even without the Ra Contact. The harmony between the three of us was so obvious and easy that it felt like old friends coming together again for another adventure in consciousness. Whatever we did felt like what we should be doing to be of service in the way that our hearts knew best. Don was like a big brother who knew the secrets of how to play the game of life that Carla and I were just learning.

After the Ra contact, and Don's passing, Carla and I shared a life together for 28 years as husband and wife, and she became the dearest, sweetest love of my life. Now that she is also gone, I, with my present-day companions Gary Bean and Austin Bridges, carry on the work that she and Don began in 1968 as Love & Light Research.

For all of these reasons this book is dedicated to Donald T. Elkins, whose intelligence, intuition, and experience with the paranormal perfectly prepared him to carry on an astounding conversation with those of Ra, and to Carla L. Rueckert who fearlessly offered her life in service to planet Earth as she served as the instrument for the Ra contact. Don's wisdom and Carla's love blazed a trail through the veil of forgetting for any who would become a seeker of truth.

Jim McCarty

TABLE OF CONTENTS

Foreword.. 6
Acknowledgments................................... 8
How These Books Came to Be 13
Introduction 14
Note to the Reader................................. 23

Ra Contact Sessions
Session 1.. 24
Session 2.. 31
Session 3.. 37
Session 4.. 43
Session 5.. 51
Session 6.. 54
Session 7.. 63
Session 8.. 71
Session 9.. 80
Session 10... 86
Session 11... 94
Session 12... 102
Session 13... 111
Session 14... 118
Session 15... 127
Session 16... 136
Session 17... 150
Session 18... 164
Session 19... 173
Session 20... 182
Session 21... 192
Session 22... 201
Session 23... 209
Session 24... 217
Session 25... 224
Session 26... 229
Session 27... 240
Session 28... 247
Session 29... 254
Session 30... 262
Session 31... 269

Session 32 278
Session 33 285
Session 34 293
Session 35 300
Session 36 305
Session 37 313
Session 38 318
Session 39 323
Session 40 329
Session 41 335
Session 42 345
Session 43 354
Session 44 361
Session 45 366
Session 46 369
Session 47 374
Session 48 381
Session 49 388
Session 50 394
Session 51 401
Session 52 407
Session 53 414
Session 54 422
Session 55 433
Session 56 440

Photo Gallery 444
The Relistening Report 460
Glossary 478
Index 500
Afterword 539

FOREWORD

There has never been, nor can there ever be, a single unproblematic definition of what it means to seek the truth. The pathways to knowledge and to human perfection are as numerous as the stars, and as resistant to synoptic characterization. If one may speak, therefore, of a unity of truth, a *one* truth, one must have opened a gateway to a way of relating to this problem that transcends all known limitations, and in fact leaves behind all readily delineated requirements of knowledge itself. From any point of view achievable to experience, such a gateway can only be hard won; and to win one's way to assimilation and integration of such experience is surely that much harder.

It is thus always something of a miracle—and in any case certainly an inspiration—when the thick veil that surrounds our human consciousness thins even a little to afford the most fleeting glimpse of glory. And when there comes through that veil a finely constellated light so bright that it positively penetrates, in discretely articulated points, the entire fog of incarnate existence, that is an occasion worthy of the utmost attention. To a growing number of seekers of the way, the *Ra Contact* is just such a light.

To be sure, the communications contained in this work have a cultural genre into which they have long since been fitted. They belong to the category of channeled communication. There is indeed a good supply of channeled material already available to the seeker of truth, and more discerning seekers have long since realized that a great deal of careful discrimination is required when surveying what is on offer. Yet, to report only on my own experience, the *Ra Contact* stands alone in this genre as a source that has stood every test I have been able to put to it. In terms of scope, in terms of consistency, in terms of depth, and in terms of inexhaustibility it is without parallel and without peer. But all of these judgments are merely evaluations from one reader. Each of us must reach our own conclusions. Let me therefore simply commend to you the text, conveying to any earnest reader my sincere blessings.

Viewed from the outside, the gatherings of those whose interest in the Law of One is deep and abiding are somewhat remarkable. Hardly anywhere else does one find scientists, engineers, philosophers, poets, mystics, economists, farmers and office managers collected into one circle of seeking and able to find common ground in what is brought forward.

That speaks to a multivalence of the material that is quite striking. I know of no other way to enter into this multivalence than a careful reading of the text, pondering, one after another, so many turns of phrase that offer openings onto a cosmic landscape that is staggering in its scope, even while at the same time they give clues to possibilities for further exploration.

The story of the three brave adventurers whose collective efforts made this communication possible is itself a narrative well worth hearing. This narrative is told in considerable detail, and with as complete a fidelity to the actual truth of events as I have ever encountered, in Gary L. Bean's *Tilting at Windmills*. The story, it must be admitted, is genuinely poignant. One learns that an undertaking of the kind necessary to bring forth the *Law of One* was not without cost. And that the cost was, indeed, great for all concerned. I therefore wish to conclude this brief preface by expressing my gratitude to those intrepid travelers who have gone before me, and have played a decisive role in opening a clearing filled with love and light. It is a clearing in which I have learned to stand with others of like mind, like spirit, and like commitment to seeking that truth which beckons ever from a place just beyond the reach of the grasping mind, but not at all remote from the open heart.

Stephen Tyman, PhD
Murphysboro, Illinois
October 10, 2016

ACKNOWLEDGMENTS

There are some people without whom this book would not have been possible, and others without whom this book would not have reached its full potential.

Thanking the **One Infinite Creator** may seem unusual, but as Ra mentioned many times, the One Creator has made all that is made out of Itself, so this is where I shall start. Thank you, Infinite Creator. Every word in this book speaks about you as the Author of everything, everyone, everywhere—in ways mysterious and awesome beyond our imagining.

Thank you, **Ra**—all 6.5 million souls that make up your unified consciousness—for caring enough about each one of us on Earth to speak with such love, wisdom, power and precision in answering our call for assistance as we move into the fourth density of love and understanding. Your words inspire and inform me every day of my life.

As I return my focus to the human realm, there are two giants who pass through the halls of my heart each and every day. These two heard the call of the Ra contact and bent every effort, risked everything, and gave themselves to service just to have this conversation, just to bring a little clarity, a little illumination, a little perspective to the thirsty seeker and to this often troubled world.

Don Elkins's vast intellect, uncanny intuition, and decades of experience in researching all facets of the paranormal made him the perfect questioner for carrying on a conversation with the social memory complex of Ra. He was the wisest person I have ever met. I have not found an end to the marvel I feel every time I read the questions he asked Ra.

Carla L. Rueckert's stunning spiritual fearlessness in risking far more than her life every time she left her physical body in order to open the door to the universe, receiving in turn a perspective or philosophy that may be unique in human history. I thank you and admire you beyond words for everything you gave the world, and more so, everything you personally gave me with each smile and every moment of your life shared with me. I can't believe I had the privilege of being your companion during the Ra contact and your husband in our many years together afterward. Though you are no longer here, I walk everyday with you.

I owe a tremendous debt of gratitude to **Tobey Wheelock**, who initiated the Relistening Project many years ago. In this effort he spent years listening to the cassette recordings of all 106 sessions of the Ra contact—transcribing, editing, refining, and eventually working with volunteers on a Re-Relistening Project until he had produced for the world the Lightly Edited Version, that which is the basis for the text of this book. His dedication to the integrity of the material is total. Without Tobey's Relistening Project this book would not exist. And without his tireless effort the world would not have the best study tool for the Law of One in the world, something Gary, Austin, and I have called upon countless times in our own studies: www.lawofone.info.

And speaking of those volunteers on the Re-Relistening Project, I send my gratitude to **Terry Hsu** and a couple others who wished to remain anonymous. I know the tedious hours you spent on this project made a more perfect text representation of the great conversation captured on those cassettes.

I can't thank **Gary Bean** enough for all that he has done to make this book a reality. Starting with the Lightly Edited Version and culminating in the *The Ra Contact*, he has led our team in producing, coordinating, editing, contributing to, and shepherding this material through each stage of its journey. L/L Research would not function today if not for Gary Bean. You will not be surprised to hear that I love him dearly, as did Carla before me.

A long sequence of thanks and love to **Austin Bridges**, who is an inseparable and vital part of L/L Research and this book's journey. From the thousand decisions needing to be made, to contributions of creativity and composition, to undertaking the months-long intensive final editing with Gary and me, to formatting the entire work, managing its printing, and structuring the Index, Austin's energy has been an invaluable and guiding aid to *The Ra Contact's* development.

Thank you to **Steve Tyman** for providing assistance in editing the Introduction to this book, authoring its Foreword, and helping me to reignite the channeling service after Carla's passing.

Thank you a thousand-fold to **Joseph Dartez** who turned his methodical mind to systematic reading of the 106 sessions, in turn producing a list of 202 terms. Those terms combined with Carla's and my own formed the basis of the extraordinary index accompanying this material.

And, oh, the glorious Index. Over 9,000 catalogued Q&As! From the initial list of terms, Gary coordinated a supreme volunteer effort that literally spanned the globe, from friends in Kentucky, Washington, Ohio, Colorado, Virginia, and Tennessee, to China, Germany, and Italy. This treasure of study would not have succeeded were it not for the truly intensive efforts of **Jade Norby**, **Jochen Blumenthal**, **Sean Hsu**, **Fox Hutt**, **Joseph Dartez** (for yet another round of contributions), **Erez Batat**, **Gianluca Mosaico**, **Lana Autio**, and **Ken Wendt**. Thanks also to **Jeremy Weiland** who offered technical assistance in automating a part of the process. And a deep bow to Austin who expended enormous energy innovating the formatting and building the structure that brought the Index into its present state of clarity, precision, and perfection.

I would also like to give a double hearty thanks to **Sean Hsu**. In addition to his work on the Index, he somehow found time to contribute to insightful edits to the 106 sessions and yet one more project. Then in the 11th hour I discovered the possibility of adding footnotes to instances when Ra or Don mentioned "previously covered" information that would identify where that information was previously covered. The indefatigable Sean attacked that project with alacrity, finding the right Q&As to the 17 we identified, and then going on to find another 94 instances where Ra or Don points to previously mentioned material.

I am most grateful to **Aaron Maret** (lead of the Asheville Law of One Study Group), who created powerfully evocative covers for all three books of *The Ra Contact*. What imagery is best to associate with Ra's words? Or would an image-less, solid color cover be most appropriate? Aaron helped answer these questions by doing what the artist does best: manifesting a beautiful something from seeming nothing, invoking themes that bespeak the universality and cosmic, but Earth-centered scope of this philosophy. He also generously offered some modifications to the books' interior layout that makes it shine.

My gratitude extends also to my dear friend **Beatriz Gonzales** for her contributions to the Introduction that Gary, Austin, and I wrote, as she gave me critically important suggestions as how to organize the content of the thoughts that I wanted to discuss, and to the gifted **Diana Roy** for last-minute but critical edits to the same piece.

And then to those band of beings who generously offered to review the printed proofs of this book, including **Fox Hutt, Mary Allen, Jade Norby, Jeremy Weiland, Sean Hsu,** and **Garry Fung.**

Gary, Austin, and I could not have had better people for these most tedious and time-consuming jobs—all done with love and devotion to service to others. As you can tell, this book exists thanks primarily to the efforts of many volunteers. For any individual we forgot to include in the above list, please accept our apologies and our sincere gratitude.

And, finally, thank you to all the individuals unnamed here who have written to L/L Research or Tobey with questions and thoughts about possible refinements to the text. Though the majority of the work on the 106 sessions was completed by the small number of people listed above, the whole scope of the project was essentially crowdsourced. It is you, the reader, who kept Carla and me going after Don's passing. It is you, the reader, who shared your enthusiasm and personal testimony of the transformative and healing effects that this material had upon you, inspiring and fueling our work to make it available to all.

Jim McCarty
Louisville, KY

Along with many other devoted students of this information, both of our lives were utterly and irrevocably transformed by Ra's perspective. The Law of One philosophy has come to serve as the foundation and framework of our worldviews and spiritual seekings. Indeed, Gary likes to say that he would be scraping his knuckles somewhere were it not for this work.

We obviously have **Ra** to thank for their singular insight, but it is to **Don Elkins, Carla Rueckert,** and, despite his protest, **Jim McCarty** that we turn. We have lived with and worked with two of those three. We know well their history, their personalities, and their energies. We know that Don, Carla, and Jim gave themselves completely to the contact with Ra not for the purpose of fame, status, wealth, or acquisition of personal power, but entirely for the purpose of service. They simply desired to bring light into this darkened place, to allow love a space to speak to our hearts. It is still mind-bending to consider what Carla risked in order to perform this service. Indebtedness is not ultimately a viable concept, yet we, and many other spiritual seekers, remain in their debt for the gift that quenches the thirst of many lifetimes of searching and seeking. Thank you Carla, Don, and Jim for taking up the mantle of your incarnational missions with such integrity, steadfast dedication, and purity of heart.

Though Carla participated in the early stages of this book, she had moved on from this incarnation by the time this work really got underway. So it was Jim who, for the purposes of creating (and naming) *The Ra Contact: Teaching the Law of One*, read through all 106 sessions more times than we have fingers on our hands. In each step of this book's development described above, Jim McCarty graciously lent his input, insight, support, and joy. And most notably, his friendship.

Gary L. Bean

Austin Bridges

Louisville, KY

HOW THESE BOOKS CAME TO BE

Beginning in the fall of 2004, Tobey Wheelock commenced what would come to be called "The Relistening Project." As the name implies, he, along with the help of volunteers, methodically *re-listened* to the original recordings of the 106 sessions of the contact with Ra three times over the course of eight years. From this effort emerged a brand new transcript that would become the basis of this book.

After completing the project in March of 2012, Tobey wrote the "Relistening Report," meticulously cataloguing the many changes to the text and sharing something of his journey in the great effort that would produce what he called The Relistened and the Lightly Edited Versions. The former is an exact transcript of what is on the audio, all syllables and sounds included. The latter is a *lightly edited* version of the same. The Relistened and Lightly Edited Versions are not derivative of or based upon the original five published books; instead, they are entirely new manuscripts taken directly from the source material (i.e., the audio tapes).

The text of *The Ra Contact* book comes directly from the Lightly Edited Version. Therefore the great majority of the changes to the Relistened and Lightly Edited Version (itemized in the "Relistening Report") have been carried into this book. However, additional refinements were made to the text for *The Ra Contact*. Consequently, the reader may discover slight discrepancies between the changes catalogued in the report and the material as it appears in this book.

The Ra Contact is meant to serve as a continuation of the Lightly Edited project. And in that regard its mission is to provide, as best as possible, an exact transcript of the actual audio with minor, mostly grammatical edits in order to improve readability. The two volumes of *The Ra Contact* neither negate nor supersede the original five published books. Both sets will continue to be offered side by side for the reader to choose their form of reading, each having its own merits.

You may read Tobey's "Relistening Report" at the end of this book, along with an Addendum summarizing our additional refinements. His website, www.lawofone.info, is the single best study tool for this work. We extend our infinite and heartfelt gratitude to Tobey for his singular dedication to this project and opening the way to this book.

Introduction

From January 15, 1981, through March 15, 1984, three dedicated seekers of truth received the spoken communication in this book. The messages, as you will discover, came from a civilization of extraterrestrial beings who identified themselves as Ra. *The Ra Contact: Teaching the Law of One* contains the whole, rectified, and now unified record of this three-year period of contact with Ra.

This introduction does not intend to thoroughly explain the contact or its philosophy. The purpose of this section is simply to offer the reader a little context regarding how this contact happened, some background about the source with whom Don Elkins, Carla Rueckert, and Jim McCarty were communicating, and a thumbnail sketch of what this source says about metaphysical reality. This introduction is not essential to reading and understanding this book; it is offered as a means of orientation and preparation for the journey to come.

About Ra

In Earth's ancient history, Ra is known as the Egyptian god of the sun. They state, however, that when they visited the Egyptians they came as brothers and sisters, not as gods. They came because that civilization had developed a culture and a belief system that prepared them to comprehend the concepts of the Law of One. This readiness for the Law of One drew those of Ra to them to serve as teachers of these principles.

Ra reports that their efforts to aid that particular culture were misunderstood and distorted. The Egyptians, particularly the royal elite who reserved the message only for themselves, robbed the message of its inherent compassion, distorting the philosophy of the oneness of all things. Ra consequently removed themselves from the Egyptian experience, but they continued from then until now to observe Earth's development from a distance. It was Ra's longstanding desire to correct the distortions introduced to the Law of One during that time period that led them to make contact with our group.

But that was not their only reason. Ra also made contact with our group because Earth is nearing the end of a 75,000 year master cycle of evolution, and many of its population are ready to graduate to the next evolutionary stage, what Ra calls the fourth density, the density of love and understanding. They wished to be of aid in this time of transition and thus responded to the call for service issuing forth from this planet.

Ra said that they are from the sixth density and they are, in their words, a "social memory complex." This is what a planetary population becomes in the densities of evolution beyond our own. In this arrangement, the thoughts, memories, and experiences of every individual are known and available to the whole group. The entire social body, then, consists of many unique individuals who also have access to a shared group repository of memory and identity.

According to Ra, the population of Earth will birth its own social memory complex after its graduation to the fourth density is complete. Just as individuals evolve over time, the social memory complex likewise evolves, transforming and becoming more unified as the lessons of each higher density of evolution are successfully grasped. To Ra, as a social memory complex, there is no distinction between an individual and the whole group. Thus when we communicated with those of Ra we spoke to one individualized entity of the social memory complex. Since everyone in this group accesses a shared mind, it was as if we were communicating with all 6.5 million entities of the Ra social memory complex.

Ra is also part of a larger group called the Confederation of Planets in the Service of the One Infinite Creator that consists of many other social memory complexes from other planets in our local portion of the Milky Way Galaxy. According to Ra, members of the Confederation have been offering their services through channeling and other means to various individuals and groups around the world for some time, their interaction with this planet stretching back into our deep pre-historical past. Our group has been in contact with assorted members of this Confederation since we began in 1962.

The Confederation's primary message has always been that we live in a universe of unity, that the world *as we perceive it* is an illusion, that we are here to learn how to give and receive love, and that meditation is one of the principal means of discovering the Creator that exists in all of us.

In the course of this conversation, Ra certainly took responsibility for their perspective but renounced any authority, indicating that what they had to share was their perspective only—what they described as a "somewhat different slant upon the information which is always and ever the same." They wished not to be identified as the *source* of this information. Instead, they asked specifically that they be described as "humble messengers of the Law of One." In this statement they acknowledge their limitations and honor their relationship to the one truth which transcends (but includes) every seeming portion of identity throughout the universe:

> *[We encourage the seeker not to remove] the focus from the One Infinite Source of love and light, of which we are all messengers, humble and knowing that we, of ourselves, are but the tiniest portion of the Creator, a small part of a magnificent entirety of infinite intelligence.*

The Law of One and its Cosmology
This is how Ra described the Law of One:

> *In truth there is no right or wrong. There is no polarity, for all will be, as you would say, reconciled at some point in your dance through the mind/body/spirit complex which you amuse yourself by distorting in various ways at this time. This distortion is not in any case necessary. It is chosen by each of you as an alternative to understanding the complete unity of thought which binds all things. You are not speaking of similar or somewhat like entities or things. You are every thing, every being, every emotion, every event, every situation. You are unity. You are infinity. You are love/light, light/love. You are. This is the Law of One.*

In this book, Ra brings us face to face with the same basic truth that has been reported by mystics from all quarters of the world throughout the ages: the astounding realization that the One Infinite Creator is within us and is within everything, everywhere. In fact, the Law of One asserts there is nothing that is not the Creator; there is nothing that is *outside of* this underlying unity. Ra reports that the Creator has made the infinite creation out of Itself for the purpose of knowing and experiencing Itself. This "intelligent infinity," as Ra calls it, generates out of its own being the galaxies, stars, planets, entities such as ourselves, darkness and light, love and fear, every shade of meaning and experience, every mode of thought and activity, and everything else real and imagined on every plane of existence. And It has endowed each and every seeming portion of this creation with a foundation of free will: the capacity to learn, to grow, to intend, to adapt, to make evolutionary choices, to chart a return path of experience to the Creator.

As we travel on our spiritual journeys we exercise free will, choosing to gradually know ourselves more clearly, and sooner or later we grow into unity with the One Creator. As all of the infinity of entities in the infinite creation travel this path, the One Creator comes to know Itself in ways that are unimaginable and endless through every free will choice that is ever made by each portion of the creation.

The journey that each soul takes, according to Ra, moves through an infinite system of "octaves," each octave divided into seven ascending densities (or concentrations) of light. In the **first density** of our current octave, fire and wind teach earth and water to be formed in such a way as to produce the foundation for subsequent biological life.

The **second density** is the level of consciousness inhabited by bacteria and single-celled organisms in the lower stages to plants and animals in the higher stages. This density's lessons involve transforming from the random change of first density to a more coherent awareness that facilitates growth and directed movement. As entities progress through the second density, they begin to strive toward the next density of self-consciousness; and as the spirit complex becomes awakened, graduation to the third density becomes possible.

Earth and its human population are currently approaching the end of the third-density cycle, according to the Confederation. In this **third density**, the density of choice, we have a more highly developed self-awareness that includes the mind, the body, and, for the first time, a fully activated spirit. The function of this density is to polarize our consciousness and to choose our form of love, our form of service. On one end of the spectrum of polarization is **service to self**: an exclusive love of self which rejects *universal* love and seeks to control, manipulate, exploit, and even enslave others for the benefit of the self. On the other end of the spectrum is **service to others**: a love of not only the self, but of all other-selves. Service to others seeks and embraces universal, unconditional love, sees the Creator in all things, and supports the free will of all. Our lived lives are not so black and white, however, as we strive toward either end of the spectrum of polarity in consciousness.

In congruency with various wisdom traditions of Earth, Ra communicates that we are moving toward a "new age," or what Ra would call a harvest to the **fourth density** of love and understanding. This is where the social memory complex is born, where thoughts become things, love becomes visible, and the positive and negative polarities separate from each other to inhabit environments more suited to their respective and divergent courses of evolution.

The **fifth density** is the density of light, wherein wisdom becomes the focus and criterion for graduation to the next density. The **sixth density** balances and unifies the love learned in fourth density with the light (wisdom) learned in fifth density and produces a power to serve others that is more effective than that of love or wisdom alone. The **seventh density** reaches a realm of experience even more difficult to describe. According to Ra it is the density of "foreverness," and here we begin to move into total harmony with the One Creator. The eighth density represents the complete coalescence of all of the creation with the One Creator and can be viewed as the first density of a new octave, similar in arrangement to the notes on a musical scale. The fruits of this octave will eventually give birth to another octave of densities, whose fruits will give birth to another octave of densities, and so on, infinitely.

How the Ra Contact Came to Be

Don Elkins started asking the big questions about life when he was in junior high school. Amidst the everyday reading, writing, and arithmetic he was thinking to himself: *What is the meaning of life? How big is the universe, and how does it work? What don't we know?* That desire to understand and put the puzzle pieces together would persist unabated throughout his incarnation. In his professional life Elkins would go on to become a professor of both Mechanical Engineering and Physics, and in his personal life a determined investigator of UFOs, reincarnation, and other areas of inquiry that might be cobbled together under the heading of the paranormal. He realized that modern science fell short of revealing the fundamental workings and purpose of the universe, so he turned to these fields for answers that science could not provide.

Carla L. Rueckert was a person gifted since childhood with a soaring intellect and a profoundly deep and personal faith. On the latter point she called herself a "cradle Episcopalian" and, eventually, a mystical Christian. On the former, Carla was a precocious child who excelled in school, mastering any test offered her. And most centrally, despite tough circumstances growing up, Carla vibrated with a love of life. She lived to dance, to sing, to interact with nature, and to embody a life of devotion and service. She was so committed to the loving viewpoint that people often took her as innocent or naïve, compelling from some a desire to protect and guard Carla against a world they felt was less pure than she was.

In late 1961 Don was given a small, brown volume, creatively titled *The Brown Notebook*, which had been compiled by Walt Rogers of Detroit, Michigan, a fellow who previously experienced a face-to-face encounter with a UFO entity. After the encounter, Mr. Rogers displayed "lingering telepathic contact" with this entity, a phenomenon that frequently was reported in similar encounters from the 1950s. Rogers's compiled brown notebook contained information about the metaphysical nature of reality from alleged extraterrestrial sources. It also described how a group of people who meditated together on a frequent basis could receive this sort of information via telepathic contact with extraterrestrial entities. Elkins was so thoroughly impressed with the correlations between the channeled material in the notebook and his own work that, based on this information, he decided to try an experiment with a dozen of his physics students in Louisville, Kentucky.

News of that reached the ears of a girlfriend of one of those students. She had recently developed a driving interest in silence and love of meditation, so she asked to attend. Her name was Carla L. Rueckert.

Don didn't tell the group what might happen, only that something interesting could possibly occur if they meditated together. He was actually attempting to conduct a scientific experiment to see if the students would receive extraterrestrial telepathic contact without prompting. After some time had elapsed, and no definitive results were produced, Walt Rogers visited the group and channeled from his source, Hatonn, the entity with whom he had experienced the face-to-face encounter. Hatonn said that they had been trying to channel through some of Don's group, but the students were not aware that the impressions they had been receiving—but not verbalizing—were from extraterrestrials. Elkins felt that this event nullified the scientific validity of the experiment, but it did begin producing results. After this visit everyone in the group, except Carla, learned how to channel; she preferred silent meditation.

Carla's and Don's respective courses after this meeting took them on different paths for some time, but they would eventually reunite and officially join together upon a shared mission of research and seeking in 1968. Two years later they would form the L/L Company, changing its name to L/L Research in 1976. And it was in 1974—twelve years after Carla attended Don's first channeling experiment—that Don asked Carla to take up the channeling service herself. Not coincidentally this was the same year that Elkins began to actually preserve (not throw away or recycle) the cassette recordings of the channelings. The messages took a qualitative leap forward thanks to Carla's aptitude in channeling coupled with the refinements she made to Don's rudimentary channeling protocols. Among these refinements, Carla developed the crucial procedures of tuning the instrument and challenging the contact that became hallmarks of L/L Research's style of channeling.

In 1978, Jim McCarty was living off the grid in a log cabin that he built on his 132 acres of land in the woods of central Kentucky. One evening, while he was listening on his battery-powered radio to station WKQQ broadcasting from Lexington, Kentucky, he heard an interview with Don Elkins and Carla L. Rueckert on the topic of UFOs. Fascinated, Jim hoped to meet them one day. A year later, his wish came true when he was introduced to Don and Carla by fellow homesteaders who knew them. After driving to Louisville each Sunday night for a year to attend their channeling meditations, Don and Carla invited Jim to join them to help with their research. Jim moved in with them on December 23, 1980.

Twenty-three days later, on January 15, 1981, while Carla was teaching a student how to channel, a voice spoke through Carla and said, "I am Ra." Prior to this session all of Carla's channeling had been done consciously, but when serving as an instrument to channel Ra, she went completely unconscious. In a way that was never fully understood by Don, Carla, or Jim, she left her body for the Ra contact. Ra was then able to remotely and mechanically operate Carla's vocal chords to produce replies to Don's questions. For every subsequent of the 105 sessions following the first one, Carla would slip into unconsciousness, completely unaware of what was coming through her. It wasn't until session 23 that Don began showing her the transcripts of Ra's words. He had previously kept them from her to preserve the scientific viability of the contact.

The Ra contact was such a quantum leap forward in depth of insight and breadth of vision that Don, Carla, and Jim devoted themselves completely to this contact for the next three years and two months. [1]

---

[1] To read a more in-depth account of the events that led up to the contact with Ra, see the Resource Series.

The Conversation with Ra

Ra's style of contact was question-and-answer only. They felt that this format was the best to ensure that the free will of each person in the group was not abridged. Ra described their contact as "narrow band," which meant a few things: one, that considerable focus and discipline were required to maintain their contact; two, that the quality of the information was of much greater precision and depth than was available through conscious channeling; and three, that they wished to focus principally upon philosophy and timeless spiritual principles, which meant avoiding transient information that had no lasting value.

Ra chose Don, Carla, and Jim to communicate with because, of course, Don and Carla had been practicing and refining the process of channeling for years. But more fundamentally they chose these three seekers because, as a group, they enjoyed significant, sustained, almost effortless harmony. Of equal importance was Carla's absolute purity of desire and total dedication to be of service to the One Infinite Creator, especially through communication, and more especially through channeling. These factors supported the Ra contact in a stable manner that would eventually produce 106 sessions exploring the Law of One.

The preparations for contact with Ra began the night before each session was to be held. Don, Carla, and Jim would meditate together and then go over the previous session, fashioning new questions to pose to Ra. It was discovered that sexual energy transfers lengthened the Ra sessions by increasing Carla's vital energies, so Carla and Jim, having already developed an intimate relationship, would dedicate this transfer to the One Creator and to the Ra contact. On the morning of the session, Don, Carla, and Jim would have a light breakfast, and then Jim would give Carla a back massage to stave off the arthritic pain that would eventually come from her lying motionless for about an hour.

Between breakfast and the session, they would meditate together in the living room, and during this meditation Don would often receive another question or two to ask Ra. They would then retire to the Ra room and situate Carla on the bed in the middle of the room. Jim would set up the three tape recorders to ensure a successful recording. Don would measure what Ra called the "appurtenances"—the Bible, incense, chalice of water and candle—to be sure that they were in the optimal placement, per Ra's instructions. (These items were chosen by Ra due to their personal significance to Carla, as she had served on her church's altar guild and had dressed the altar with these items each Sunday. They were a great comfort to her as she left her body.)

Ra gave the group a ritual of protection called the Circle of One in which Don and Jim would walk around Carla while repeating the words that reflected their desire to be of service to others. Then Don would take his chair and review the questions for Ra, and Jim would take his chair and begin a meditation that would last for the duration of the session. He would visualize light moving through Carla's energy centers from the top of her head through the bottoms of her feet. Within a minute or two after completing the Circle of One, Ra would begin the session.

During the three year contact with Ra, Don was able to ask over 2,600 questions of Ra. Their replies allowed him to fit together many of the puzzle pieces that he needed to finally answer his biggest, most pressing questions.

The Seeker Seeks the One

Ra said that each of us is a seeker of truth. As we strengthen our will to seek the truth and our faith that we shall find love in ourselves and in the world around us, we also will surely find our true nature, which is another way of saying, the One Infinite Creator. As Ra said:

> *The seeker seeks the One. This One is to be sought, as we have said, by the balanced and self-accepting self, aware both of its apparent distortions and its total perfection. Resting in this balanced awareness, the entity then opens the self to the universe which it is. The light energy of all things may then be attracted by this intense seeking, and wherever the inner seeking meets the attracted cosmic prana, realization of the One takes place.*

During our channeling sessions, the Confederation almost always prefaces each session by advising seekers to consider the messages carefully and to then use their own discernment to determine what is helpful and true for oneself, and leave the rest behind. We echo this sentiment to readers of this book, encouraging all who read Ra's words to approach them with an open yet discerning mind. We used the word "true" above but remind you that *you* are the truth that you seek; no message, philosophy, or any combination of words can ever equal or substitute for who you are.

Blessings on your journey of seeking the One Infinite Creator in yourself, in your friends and family, and in the world around you.

NOTE TO THE READER

When Don, Carla and I were having these sessions with Ra back in the early '80s we knew that we were living the best days of our lives. We knew that this work was the primary reason that we were on this Earth. We could hardly believe our good luck to be involved with extraterrestrial entities who spoke so eloquently, so precisely, and so profoundly about the nature of creation, how we all evolve through it, the meaning of life, and how love, light, and unity are the basic building blocks of all things. Quite simply, Ra spoke the language of our hearts and our souls, and we vibrated in harmony with everything that they had to say.

Over the years we have found that there is a small community of seekers of truth who also have this powerful sympathetic vibration with Ra's information. If you are one of these people, welcome to our family. Even if we never meet, it's good to know that you are here. In our shared service to the One Infinite Creator we are always together, no matter what the appearance of our physical realities may seem to be. So we send our love and light to you and ask that you share your love and light with everyone that you meet in all present and future life experiences.

Jim McCarty

SESSION 1

1.0 **RA** I am Ra. I have not spoken through this instrument before. We had to wait until she was precisely tuned, as we send a narrow-band vibration. We greet you in the love and in the light of our Infinite Creator.

We have watched your group. We have been called to your group, for you have a need for the diversity of experiences in channeling which go with a more intensive, or as you might call it, advanced approach to the system of studying the patterns of the illusions of your body, your mind, and your spirit, which you call seeking the truth. We hope to offer you a somewhat different slant upon the information which is always and ever the same.

The Confederation of Planets in the Service of the Infinite Creator has only one important statement. That statement, my friends, as you know, is: "All things, all of life, all of the creation is part of One Original Thought."

We will exercise each channel if we are able to. The reception of our beam is a somewhat more advanced feat than some of the more broad vibration channels opened by other members for more introductory and intermediate work.

Let us for a moment consider thought. What is it, my friends, to take thought? Took you then thought today? What thoughts did you think today? What thoughts were part of the Original Thought today? In how many of your thoughts did the creation abide? Was love contained? And was service freely given?

You are not part of a material universe. You are part of a thought. You are dancing in a ballroom in which there is no material. You are dancing thoughts. You move your body, your mind, and your spirit in somewhat eccentric patterns, for you have not completely grasped the concept that you are part of the Original Thought.

We would at this time transfer to an instrument known as Don. I am Ra.

[*Two-minute pause.*]

I am Ra. I am again with this instrument. We are close to initiating a contact but are having difficulty penetrating a certain mental tension and distraction that is somewhat characteristic of this channel. We will, therefore, describe the type of vibration which is being sent. The instrument will find us entering the energy field at a slight angle towards the back of the top of the head in a narrow but strong area of intensity. We are not able to offer any conditioning due to our own transmitting limitations. Therefore, if the instrument can feel this particular effect he may then speak our thoughts as they come to him. We will again attempt this contact. I am Ra.

[*Ninety-second pause.*]

This instrument is resisting our contact. However, we assure her that we are satisfied that contact with the one known as Don is not at this time preferable to that instrument. We will, therefore, move on to the one known as Leonard. Again we caution the instrument that it is a narrow-band communication which is felt as a vibration entering the aura. We will now transfer this contact. I am Ra.

[*Ninety-second pause.*]

I am Ra. We greet you once more in the love and the light of our Infinite Creator. We ask that you be patient with us, for we are a difficult channel to receive. However, we may perhaps add some dimensions to your understanding.

At this time we would be glad to attempt to speak to any subject or question which those entities in the room may have potential use in the requesting.

1.1   QUESTIONER It seems members of the Confederation have a specific purpose. Is this true with you, and if so, what is your purpose?

RA I am Ra. We communicate now. We, too, have our place. We are not those of the Love [density] or of the Light [density].[1] We are those who are of the Law of One. In our vibration the polarities are harmonized, the

---

[1] The word "density" was added here to add clarity to what we believe to be Ra's intended meaning. The fourth density is the density of love and understanding. The fifth density is the density of light. Ra is of the sixth density where love and light are unified.

complexities are simplified, and the paradoxes have their solution. We are one. That is our nature and our purpose.

We are old upon your planet and have served with varying degrees of success in transmitting the Law of One, of Unity, of Singleness to your peoples. We have walked your earth. We have seen the faces of your peoples. This is not so with many of the entities of the Confederation. We found it was not efficacious.

However, we then felt the great responsibility of staying in the capacity of removing the distortions and powers that had been given to the Law of One. We will continue in this until your, shall we say, cycle is appropriately ended. If not this one, then the next. We are not a part of time, and thus are able to be with you in any of your times.

Does this give you enough information from which to extract our purpose, my brother?

1.2   **QUESTIONER**   Yes, it does. Thank you.

RA   We appreciate your vibration. Is there another query?

1.3   **QUESTIONER**   I've heard of the name "Ra" in connection with the Egyptians. Are you connected with that Ra in any way?

RA   I am Ra. Yes, the connection is congruency. May we elucidate?

1.4   **QUESTIONER**   Please do.

RA   What do you not understand?

1.5   **QUESTIONER**   Could you give me a little more detail about your role with the Egyptians?

RA   I am Ra. The identity of the vibration Ra is our identity. We as a group, or what you would call a social memory complex, made contact with a race of your planetary kind which you call Egyptians. Others from our density made contact at the same time in South America, and the so-called "lost cities" were their attempts to contribute to the Law of One.

We spoke to one who heard and understood and was in a position to decree the Law of One. However, the priests and peoples of that era quickly distorted our message, robbing it of the, shall we say, compassion with which unity is informed by its very nature. Since it contains all, it cannot abhor any.

When we were no longer able to have appropriate channels through which to enunciate the Law of One, we removed ourselves from the now hypocritical position which we had allowed ourselves to be placed in. And other myths, shall we say, other understandings having more to do with polarity and the things of your vibrational complex, again took over in that particular society complex.

Does this form a sufficient amount of information, or could we speak further?

1.6 QUESTIONER [*Inaudible*]

RA Is there another query?

1.7 QUESTIONER [*The question was lost because the questioner was sitting too far from the tape recorder to be recorded.*]

RA I am Ra. Consider, if you will, that the universe is infinite. This has yet to be proven or disproven, but we can assure you that there is no end to your selves, your understanding, what you would call your journey of seeking, or your perceptions of the creation.

That which is infinite cannot be many, for many-ness is a finite concept. To have infinity you must identify or define that infinity as unity; otherwise, the term does not have any referent or meaning. In an Infinite Creator there is only unity. You have seen simple examples of unity. You have seen the prism which shows all colors stemming from the sunlight. This is a simplistic example of unity.

In truth there is no right or wrong. There is no polarity, for all will be, as you would say, reconciled at some point in your dance through the mind/body/spirit complex which you amuse yourself by distorting in various ways at this time. This distortion is not in any case necessary. It is chosen by each of you as an alternative to understanding the complete unity of thought which binds all things.

You are not speaking of similar or somewhat like entities or things. You are every thing, every being, every emotion, every event, every situation. You are unity. You are infinity. You are love/light, light/love. You are. This is the Law of One.

May we enunciate this law in more detail?

1.8 QUESTIONER [*Inaudible*]

RA Is there another query at this time?

1.9 **QUESTIONER** Can you say anything about the coming planetary changes?

RA I am Ra. I preferred to wait until this instrument had again reached the proper state of depth of singleness or one-pointedness before we spoke.

The changes are very, very trivial. We do not concern ourselves with the conditions which bring about harvest.

1.10 **QUESTIONER** Another question. Is it possible to create any acceleration of understanding [in] other entities [or are] all efforts . . . efforts by the individual on himself accelerating his understanding? In other words, if an individual tries to act as a catalyst in general to increase the awareness of planetary consciousness, is he doing nothing but acting upon himself, or is it possible [*inaudible*]?

RA I am Ra. We shall answer your question in two parts, both of which are important equally.

Firstly, you must understand that the distinction between yourself and others is not visible to us. We do not consider that a separation exists between the consciousness-raising efforts of the distortion which you project as a personality, and the distortion which you project as an other personality. Thus, to learn is the same as to teach unless you are not teaching what you are learning; in which case you have done you/they little or no good. This understanding should be pondered by your mind/body/spirit complex as it is a distortion which plays a part in your experiences at this nexus.

To turn to the second part of our response, may we state our understanding, limited though it is. Group-individuated consciousness is that state of sharing understanding with the other distortions of mind/body/spirit complexes, which are within the evident reach of the mind/body/spirit complex individual or group. Thus, we are speaking to you and accepting both our distortions and your own in order to enunciate the laws of creation, more especially the Law of One.

We are not available to many of your peoples, for this is not an easily understood way of communication or type of philosophy. However, our very being is hopefully a poignant example of both the necessity and the near-hopelessness of attempting to teach.

Each of those in this group is striving to use, digest, and diversify the information which we are sending this instrument into the channels of the mind/body/spirit complex without distortion. The few whom you will illuminate by sharing your light are far more than enough reason for the greatest possible effort. To serve one is to serve all.

Therefore, we offer the question back to you to state that indeed it is the only activity worth doing: to learn/teach or teach/learn. There is nothing else which is of aid in demonstrating the Original Thought except your very being, and the distortions that come from the unexplained, inarticulate, or mystery-clad being are many. Thus, to attempt to discern and weave your way through as many group mind/body/spirit distortions as possible among your peoples in the course of your teaching is a very good effort to make. We can speak no more valiantly of your desire to serve.

May we speak in any other capacity upon this subject?

1.11   **QUESTIONER** Will you be available for communication? Can we call on you in the future?

RA I am Ra. We have good contact with this instrument because of her recent experiences with trance. She is to be able to communicate our thoughts in your future. However, we advise care in disturbing the channel for a few moments, and then the proper procedure for aiding an instrument who has, to some extent, the need of re-entering the mind/body/spirit complex which the instrument has chosen for the life experience of this time/space. Do you understand how to nurture this instrument?

1.12   **QUESTIONER** No. Could you explain it?

RA We suggest first a brief period of silence.

Then the repetition of the instrument's vibratory complex of sound in your density which you call name. Repeat until an answer is obtained.

Then the laying on of the hands at the neck region for a brief period so that the instrument may recharge batteries which are not, shall we say, full of the essence of this particular field at this time.

And finally, a gift of water into which the love of all present has been given. This will restore this entity, for her distortions contain great sensitivity towards the vibrations of love, and the charged water will effect comfort.

Do you now understand?

1.13 QUESTIONER Not completely.

RA I am Ra. We search your mind to find the vibration "Alrac." It is this vibration from you which contains the largest amount of what you would call love. Others would call this entity "Carla."

The charging of the water is done by those present placing their hands over the glass and visualizing the power of love entering the water. This will charge that very effective medium with those vibrations.

This instrument is, at this time, quite fatigued. However, her heart is such that she continues to remain open to us and useful as a channel. This is why we have spent the time/space explaining how the distortions of what you may call fatigue may be ameliorated.

Under no circumstances should this instrument be touched until she has responded to her name. I do not wish to take this instrument beyond her capacity for physical energy. It grows low. Therefore, I must leave this instrument.

I leave you in the glory and peace of unity. Go forth in peace, rejoicing in the power of the One Creator. I am Ra.

SESSION 2

2.0   **RA**   I am Ra. I greet you in the love and the light of our Infinite Creator. I am with this mind/body/spirit complex which has offered itself for a channel. I communicate with you.

Queries are in order in your projections of mind-distortion at this time/space. Thusly would I assure this group that my own social memory complex has one particular method of communicating with those few who may be able to harmonize their distortions with ours, and that is to respond to queries for information. We are comfortable with this format. May the queries now begin.

2.1   **QUESTIONER**   I'm guessing that there are enough people who would understand what you are saying, interested enough, for us to make a book of communications with it, and I wondered if you would agree to this, us making a book. And if so, I was thinking that possibly a bit of historical background on yourself would be in order.

RA   I am Ra. The possibility of communication, as you would call it, from the One to the One through distortion acceptable for meaning, is the reason we contacted this group. There are few who will grasp, without significant distortion, that which we communicate through this connection with this mind/body/spirit complex.

However, if it be your desire to share our communications with others, we have the distortion towards a perception that this would be most helpful in regularizing and crystallizing your own patterns of vibration upon the levels of experience which you call the life. If one is illuminated, are not all illuminated? Therefore, we are oriented towards speaking for you in whatever supply of speakingness you may desire. To teach/learn is the Law of One in one of its most elementary distortions.

2.2   **QUESTIONER**   Could you tell us something of your historical background, your earlier times in the illusion, possibly your incarnation on this planet that you spoke of before, and contact with earlier races on this planet? Then we would have something to start with in writing this book.

RA   I am Ra. We are aware that your mind/body is calculating the proper method of performing the task of creating a teach/learning instrument.

We are aware that you find our incarnate, as you call it, state of interest. We waited for a second query so as to emphasize that the time/space of several thousand of your years creates a spurious type of interest. Thus in giving this information, we ask the proper lack of stress be placed upon our experiences in your local space/time. The teach/learning which is our responsibility is philosophical rather than historical. We shall now proceed with your request which is harmless if properly evaluated.

We are those of the Confederation who, eleven thousand of your years ago, came to two of your planetary cultures which were at that time closely in touch with the creation of the One Creator. It was our naïve belief that we could teach/learn by direct contact, and the free-will distortions of individual feeling or personality were in no danger, we thought, of being disturbed, as these cultures were already closely aligned with a[n] all-embracing belief in the live-ness or consciousness of all.

We came and were welcomed by the peoples whom we wished to serve. We attempted to aid them in technical ways having to do with the healing of mind/body/spirit-complex distortions through the use of the crystal, appropriate to the distortion, placed within a certain appropriate series of ratios of time/space material. Thus were the pyramids created.

We found that the technology was reserved largely for those with the effectual mind/body distortion of power. This was not intended by the Law of One. We left your peoples. The group that was to work with those in the area of South America, as you call that portion of your sphere, gave up not so easily. They returned. We did not. However, we have never left your vibration due to our responsibility for the changes in consciousness we had first caused and then found distorted in ways not relegated to the Law of One. We attempted to contact the rulers of the land to which we had come, that land which you call Egypt, or in some areas, the Holy Land.

In the Eighteenth Dynasty, as it is known in your records of space/time distortions, we were able to contact a pharaoh, as you would call him. The man was small in life-experience on your plane and was a . . . what this instrument would call, wanderer. Thus, this mind/body/spirit complex received our communication-distortions and was able to blend his distortions with our own.

This young entity had been given a vibratory complex of sound which vibrated in honor of a prosperous god, as this mind/body complex, which we call instrument for convenience, would call "Amun." The entity decided that this name, being in honor of one among many gods, was not acceptable for inclusion in his vibratory sound complex. Thus, he changed his name to one which honored the sun disc. This distortion, called "Aten," was a close distortion to our reality as we understand our own nature of mind/body/spirit-complex distortion. However, it does not come totally into alignment with the intended teach/learning which was sent. This entity, Akhenaten, became convinced that the vibration of One was the true spiritual vibration, and thus decreed the Law of One.

However, this entity's beliefs were accepted by very few. His priests gave lip service only, without the spiritual distortion towards seeking. The peoples continued in their beliefs. When this entity was no longer in this density, again the polarized beliefs in the many gods came into their own, and continued so until the one known as Muhammad delivered the peoples into a more intelligible distortion of mind/body/spirit relationships.

Do you have a more detailed interest at this time?

2.3   **QUESTIONER** We are very interested in the entire story that you have to tell and in getting into the Law of One in quite some detail. There will be several questions that I'll ask as we go along that may or may not be related directly to understanding the Law of One. However, I believe that the proper way of presenting this as a teach/learning vehicle to the population of the planet that will read it, at this time, is to investigate different facets of what you tell us.

You spoke of crystal healing. (One other thing I might mention is that when the instrument becomes fatigued we want to cut off communication and resume it at a later time after the instrument is recharged.) And if the instrument is suitable at this time I would like a little discussion of the crystal healing that you mentioned.

RA I am Ra. The principle of crystal healing is based upon an understanding of the hierarchical nature of the structure of the illusion which is the physical body, as you would call it. There are crystals which work upon the energies coming into the spiritual body; there are crystals which work upon the distortions from spirit to mind; there are crystals which balance the distortions between the mind and the body. All of these crystal healings are charged through purified channels. Without the relative crystallization of the healer working with the crystal, the crystal will not be properly charged.

The other ingredient is a proper alignment with the energy fields of the planet upon which you dwell, and the holistic or cosmic distortions or streamings which enter the planetary aura in such a manner that an appropriate ratio of shapes and placement within these shapes is of indicated aid in the untangling or balancing process.

To go through the various crystals to be used would be exhaustive to this instrument, although you may ask us if you wish in another session. The delicacy, shall we say, of the choosing of the crystal is very critical and, in truth, a crystalline structure such as a diamond or ruby can be used by a purified channel who is filled with the love/light of One in almost any application.

This, of course, takes initiation, and there have never been many to persevere to the extent of progressing through the various distortion leavings which initiation causes.

May we further inform you in any fairly brief way upon this or another subject?

2.4   **QUESTIONER** Yes. You mentioned that the pyramids were an outgrowth of this. Could you expand a little bit on— Were you responsible for the building of the pyramid, and what was the purpose of the pyramid?

RA I am Ra. The larger pyramids were built by our ability using the forces of One. The stones are alive. It has not been so understood by the mind/body/spirit [complex] distortions of your culture. The purposes of the pyramids were two:

Firstly, to have a properly oriented place of initiation for those who wished to become purified or initiated channels for the Law of One.

Two, we wished then to carefully guide the initiates in developing a healing of the people whom they sought to aid and the planet itself. Pyramid after pyramid, charged by the crystal and initiate, were designed to balance the incoming energy of the One Creation with the many and multiple distortions of the planetary mind/body/spirit. In this effort we were able to continue work that brothers within the Confederation had effected through building of other crystal-bearing structures and thus complete a ring, if you will, of these about the earth's, as this instrument would have us vibrate it, surface.

This instrument begins to lose energy. We ask for one more query or subject, and then we shall take our leave for this time/space.

2.5   **QUESTIONER** You might mention that . . . there was originally a capstone on the pyramid at the top, what was it made of, and how you moved the heavy blocks to build the pyramid. What technique was used for that?

RA I am Ra. I request that we be asked this question in our next worktime, as you would term the distortion sharing that our energies produce.

If you have any questions about the proper use of this mind/body/spirit [complex], we would appreciate your asking them now.

2.6   **QUESTIONER** Consider them asked. I mean, I don't have anything to go on. What is the proper use of this instrument? What should we do to maximize her ability to . . . comfort, rejuvenation, etc.?

RA I am Ra. We are pleased that you asked this question, for it is not our understanding that we have the right/duty to share our perceptions on any subject but philosophy without direct question. However, this mind/body/spirit [complex] is not being correctly used and therefore is experiencing unnecessary distortions of body in the area of fatigue.

The vibrations may well be purified by a simple turning to the Circle of One and the verbal vibration while doing so of the following dialogue:

Question: "What is the Law?"

Answer: "The Law is One."

Question: "Why are we here?"

Answer: "We seek the Law of One."

Question: "Why do we seek Ra?"

Answer: "Ra is an humble messenger of the Law of One."

Both together: "Rejoice then, and purify this place in the Law of One. Let no thought-form enter the circle we have walked about this instrument, for the Law is One."

The instrument at this time should be in trance. The proper alignment is the head pointed twenty degrees north-by-northeast. This is the direction from which the newer, or New Age, distortions of love/light, which are less distorted, are emanating from, and this instrument will find comfort therein. This is a sensitive instrument, by which we mean the distortions which enter her mind/body/spirit complex come from any of her senses. Thus, it is well to do the following:

Place at the entity's head a virgin chalice of water.

To the center, the book most closely aligned with the instrument's mental distortions which are allied most closely with the Law of One, that being the Bible that she touches most frequently.

To the other side of the Bible, a small amount of cense, or incense, in a virgin censer.

To the rear of the book symbolizing One, opened to the Gospel of John, Chapter One, a white candle.

The instrument would be strengthened by the wearing of a white robe. The instrument shall be covered and prone, the eyes covered.

We feel that, though this is a complex of activity/circumstance and may seem very distorted from a purposeful teach/learning experience, these elaborations on the technique of trance will ease the mind distortions of those about the instrument as they perceive improvement in the instrument's distortions with regard to fatigue. We add only that if these teach/learning sessions are held during time/space during which your sun-body does not light your room that it is best to call the instrument before the lighting of the illuminatory mechanism.

I am Ra. I leave you in the glory and the peace of the One Creator. Rejoice in the love/light, and go forth in the power of the One Creator. In joy, we leave you. Adonai.

SESSION 3

3.0　**RA** I am Ra. I greet you in the love and the light of the One Infinite Creator. I communicate with you now.

3.1　**QUESTIONER** My first question is, did we correctly perform the ritual for starting the communication?

RA I am Ra. The placement of the artifacts designed to balance the instrument should be placed at the instrument's head for the least distortion of effect. The remainder of the beginning account of purpose is quite acceptable, for those speaking desire to serve. Otherwise, the attendant emphasis in mind complexities would not have been effected properly.

We caution you to guard against those who are not wishing to serve others above all else from taking part in the beginning, or in lending their distortions of mind/body/spirit complex to any session, as we should then be unable to properly blend our distortions with those of this instrument.

3.2　**QUESTIONER** Should I move the Bible, candle, and incense at this time?

RA I am Ra. This would be appropriate.

3.3　**QUESTIONER** [*After moving the items.*] Is this the proper position?

RA I am Ra. Please correct the angle of the incense so that it is perpendicular to the plane of twenty degrees north-by-northeast.

3.4　**QUESTIONER** [*After making the correction.*] Is this satisfactory?

RA Please check [by] your eye to make fine correction. We will explain the process by which this becomes a significant distortion balancer.

The incense acts as energizer to the physical body of this instrument, signifying its humanity. This is, therefore, a necessity that the wafted smoke is perceived from the same relative angle as the instrument perceives the opened Bible, balanced by the lighted candle signify[ing] love/light and light/love and, therefore, give the mental and emotional, shall we call it, distortion complex of this instrument the sight of paradise and peace which it seeks. Thus energized from the lower to the higher, the instrument becomes balanced and does not grow fatigued.

We appreciate your concern, for this will enable our teach/learning to proceed more easily.

3.5   **QUESTIONER** Does it appear correctly aligned now?

RA I judge it within limits of acceptability.

3.6   **QUESTIONER** At the last session we had two questions we were saving for this session: one having to do with the possible capstone of the Great Pyramid at Giza; the other with how you moved the heavy blocks. I know these questions are of no importance at all with respect to the Law of One, but it was my judgment, which you may correct, that this would provide an easy entry for the reader of the material. We are very grateful for your contact and will certainly take suggestions about how we should proceed with this. This is just one guess.

RA I am Ra. I will not suggest the proper series of questions. This is your prerogative as free agent of the Law of One, having learn/understood that our social memory complex cannot effectually discern the distortions of the societal mind/body/spirit complex of your peoples. We wish now to fulfill our teach/learning honor/responsibility by answering what is asked. This only will suffice, for we cannot plumb the depths of the distortion complexes which infect your peoples.

The first question, therefore, is the capstone. We iterate the unimportance of this type of data.

The so-called Great Pyramid had two capstones. One was of our design and was of smaller and carefully contrived pieces of the material upon your planet which you call "granite." This was contrived for crystalline properties and for the proper flow of your atmosphere via a type of what you would call "chimney."

At a time when we as a people had left your density, the original was taken away and a more precious one substituted. It consisted, in part, of a golden material. This did not change the properties of the pyramid, as you call it, at all, and was a distortion due to the desire of a few to mandate the use of the structure as a royal place only.

Do you wish to query further upon this first question?

3.7 **QUESTIONER** What did you mean by chimney? What was its specific purpose?

RA There is a proper flow of your atmosphere which, though small, freshens the whole of the structure. This was designed by having air-flow ducts, as this instrument might call them, situated so that there was a freshness of atmosphere without any disturbance or draft.

3.8 **QUESTIONER** How were the blocks moved?

RA I am Ra. You must picture the activity within all that is created. The energy is, though finite, quite large compared to the understanding-distortion of your peoples. This is an obvious point well known to your peoples, but little considered.

This energy is intelligent. It is hierarchical. Much as your mind/body/spirit complex dwells within an hierarchy of vehicles and retains, therefore, the shell, or shape, or field, and the intelligence of each ascendingly intelligent or balanced body, so does each atom of such a material as rock. When one can speak to that intelligence, the finite energy of the physical, or chemical, rock/body is put into contact with that infinite power which is resident in the more well-tuned bodies, be they human or rock.

With this connection made, a request may be given. The intelligence of infinite rock-ness communicates to its physical vehicle, and that splitting and moving which is desired is then carried out through the displacement of the energy field of rock-ness from finity to a dimension which we may conveniently call, simply, infinity.

In this way, that which is required is accomplished due to the cooperation of the infinite understanding of the Creator indwelling in the living rock. This is, of course, the mechanism by which many things are accomplished which are not subject to your present means of physical analysis of action at a distance.

3.9 **QUESTIONER** I am reminded of the statement, approximately, if you had enough faith, you could say to a mountain to move and the mountain would move. I assume this is approximately what you are saying, and I am assuming that if you are fully aware of the Law of One, then you are able to do these things. Is that correct?

RA I am Ra. The vibratory distortion of sound, "faith," is perhaps one of the stumbling blocks between those of what we may call the infinite path and those of the finite proving-understanding.

You are precisely correct in your understanding of the congruency of faith and intelligent infinity; however, one is a spiritual term, the other more acceptable perhaps to the conceptual-framework distortions of those who seek with measure and pen.

3.10 **QUESTIONER** Then if an individual is totally informed with respect to the Law of One, and lives and is the Law of One, such things as the building of a pyramid by direct mental effort would be commonplace. Is that what I am to understand? Am I correct?

RA I am Ra. You are incorrect in that there is a distinction between the individual power through the Law of One and the combined, or societal memory complex mind/body/spirit understanding of the Law of One.

In the first case, only the one individual, purified of all flaws, could move a mountain. In the case of mass understanding of unity, each individual may contain an acceptable amount of distortion and yet the mass mind could move mountains.

The progress is normally from the understanding which you now seek to a dimension of understanding which is governed by the Laws of Love, and which seeks the Laws of Light. Those who are vibrating with the Law of Light seek the Law of One. Those who vibrate with the Law of One seek the Law of Foreverness.

We cannot say what is beyond this dissolution of the unified self with all that there is, for we still seek to become all that there is, and still are we Ra. Thus our paths go onward.

3.11 **QUESTIONER** Was the pyramid then built by the mutual action of many of your people?

RA I am Ra. The pyramids which we thought/built were constructed from thought-forms created by our social memory complex.

3.12 **QUESTIONER** Then the rock was created by thought in place rather than moved from somewhere else? Is that correct?

RA I am Ra. We built with everlasting rock the Great Pyramid, as you call it. Other of the pyramids were built with stone moved from one place to another.

3.13 **QUESTIONER** What is everlasting rock?

RA I am Ra. If you can understand the concept of thought-forms you will realize that the thought-form is more regular in its distortion than the energy fields created by the materials in the rock which has been created, through thought-form, from thought to finite energy and beingness in your, shall we say, distorted reflection of the level of the thought-form.

May we answer you in any more helpful way?

3.14 **QUESTIONER** This is slightly trivial, but I was wondering why, in that case, the pyramid was made of many blocks rather than the whole thing being created at once.

RA I am Ra. There is a law which we believe to be one of the more significant primal distortions of the Law of One. That is the Law of Confusion. You have called this the Law of Free Will.

We wished to make an healing machine, or time/space ratio complex which was as efficacious as possible. However, we did not desire to allow the mystery to be penetrated by the peoples in such a way that we became worshiped as builders of a miraculous pyramid. Thus it appears to be made, not thought.

3.15 **QUESTIONER** Well, then you speak of the pyramid—especially the Great Pyramid, I assume—as primarily a healing machine, and also spoke of it as a device for initiation. Are these one and the same concepts?

RA They are part of one complex of love/light intent/sharing. To use the healing aspects properly it was important to have a purified and dedicated channel, or energizer, for the love/light of the Infinite Creator to flow through; thus the initiatory method was necessary to prepare the mind, the body, and the spirit for service in the Creator's work. The two are integral.

3.16 **QUESTIONER** Does the shape of the pyramid itself . . . is that a key function in the initiation process?

RA This is a large question. We feel that we shall begin and ask you to re-evaluate and ask further at a later session this somewhat, shall we say, informative point.

To begin, there are two main functions of the pyramid in relation to the initiatory procedures. One has to do with the body. Before the body can be initiated, the mind must be initiated. This is the point at which most adepts of your present cycle find their mind/body/spirit complexes distorted from.

When the character and personality that is the true identity of the mind has been discovered, the body then must be known in each and every way. Thus, the various functions of the body need understanding and control with detachment. The first use of the pyramid, then, is the going down into the pyramid for purposes of deprivation of sensory input so that the body may, in a sense, be dead and another life begin.

We advise, at this time, any necessary questions and a fairly rapid ending of this session. Have you any query at this time/space?

3.17 QUESTIONER The only question is, is there anything that we have done wrong, or anything that we could do to make the instrument more comfortable?

RA We scan this instrument.

This instrument has been much aided by these precautions. We suggest only some attention to the neck which seems in this body-distortion to be distorted in the area of strength/weakness. More support, therefore, to the neck area may be an aid.

3.18 QUESTIONER Should we have her drink the water from the chalice behind her head after we charge it, or should we use a different glass of water?

RA That and only that chalice shall be the most beneficial as the virgin material living in the chalice accepts, retains, and responds to the love vibration activated by your beingness.

I am Ra. I will now leave this group rejoicing in the power and peace of the One Creator. Adonai.

SESSION 4

4.0   **RA** I am Ra. I greet you in the love and the light of the Infinite Creator. I communicate now.

4.1   **QUESTIONER** Finishing the last session, I had asked a question that was too long to answer. It had to do with the shape of the pyramid and its relationship to the initiation. Is this an appropriate time to ask this question?

RA I am Ra. Yes, this is an appropriate time/space to ask that question.

4.2   **QUESTIONER** Does the shape of the pyramid have effect upon the initiation?

RA I am Ra. As we began the last session question, you have already recorded in your individual memory complex the first use of the shape having to do with the body complex initiation. The initiation of spirit was a more carefully designed type of initiation as regards the time/space ratios about which the entity to be initiated found itself.

If you will picture with me the side of the so-called pyramid shape and mentally imagine this triangle cut into four equal triangles, you will find the intersection of the triangle which is at the first level on each of the four sides forms a diamond in a plane which is horizontal. The middle of this plane is the appropriate place for the intersection of the energies streaming from the infinite dimensions and the mind/body/spirit complex's various interwoven energy fields.

Thus it was designed that the one to be initiated would, by mind, be able to perceive and then channel this, shall we say, gateway to intelligent infinity. This, then, was the second point of designing this specific shape.

May we provide a further description of any kind to your query?

4.3   **QUESTIONER** As I understand it then, the initiate was to be on the center line of the pyramid, but at an altitude above the base as defined by the intersection of the four triangles made by dividing each side into four triangles. Is that correct?

RA This is correct.

4.4   **QUESTIONER** Then at this point there is a focusing of energy that is extra-dimensional in respect to our dimensions. Am I correct?

RA You may use that vibratory sound complex. However, it is not totally and specifically correct as there are no "extra" dimensions. We would prefer the use of the term "multi" dimensions.

4.5   **QUESTIONER** Is the size of the pyramid a function in effectiveness of the initiation?

RA I am Ra. Each size pyramid has its own point of streaming in of intelligent infinity. Thus a tiny pyramid that can be placed below a body, or above a body, will have specific and various effects depending upon the placement of the body in relationship to the entrance point of intelligent infinity.

For the purposes of initiation, the size needed to be large enough to create the expression of towering size so that the entrance point of multi-dimensional intelligent infinity would completely pervade and fill the channel, the entire body being able to rest in this focused area. Furthermore, it was necessary for healing purposes that both channel and the one to be healed be able to rest within that focused point.

4.6   **QUESTIONER** Is the large pyramid at Giza still usable for this purpose, or is it no longer functioning?

RA I am Ra. That, like many other pyramid structures, is like the piano out of tune: it, as this instrument would express, plays the tune, but oh so poorly. The disharmony jangles the sensitive. Only the ghost of the streaming still remains due to the shifting of the streaming points which is, in turn, due to the shifting electromagnetic field of your planet; due also to the discordant vibratory complexes of those who have used the initiatory and healing place for less compassionate purposes.

4.7   **QUESTIONER** Would it be possible to build a pyramid and properly align it and use it today with materials we have available?

RA I am Ra. It is quite possible for you to build a pyramid structure. The material used is not critical, merely the ratios of time/space complexes. However, the use of the structure for initiation and healing depends completely upon the inner disciplines of the channels attempting such work.

4.8   **QUESTIONER** My question then would be, are there individuals incarnate upon the planet today who would have the necessary inner disciplines to, using your instructions, construct and initiate in a pyramid they built and then possibly do it again? Is this within limits of what anyone can do on the planet today, or is there no one available for this?

RA I am Ra. There are people, as you call them, who are able to take this calling at this nexus. However, we wish to point out once again that the time of the pyramids, as you would call it, is past. It is indeed a timeless structure. However, the streamings from the universe were, at the time we attempted to aid this planet, those which required a certain understanding of purity. This understanding has, as the streamings revolve and all things evolve, changed to a more enlightened view of purity. Thus, there are those among your people at this time whose purity is already one with intelligent infinity. Without the use of structures, healer/patient can gain healing.

May we further speak to some specific point?

4.9   **QUESTIONER** Is it possible for you to instruct healing techniques if we could make available these individuals that have the native ability?

RA I am Ra. It is possible. We must add that many systems of teach/learning the healing/patient nexus are proper given various mind/body/spirit complexes. We ask your imagination to consider the relative simplicity of the mind in the earlier cycle and the less distorted, but often overly complex, views and thought/spirit processes of the same mind/body/spirit complexes after many incarnations.

We also ask your imagination to conceive of those who have chosen the distortion of service and have removed their mind/body/spirit complexes from one dimension to another, thus bringing with them in sometimes totally latent form many skills and understandings which more closely match the distortions of the healing/patient processes.

4.10   **QUESTIONER** I would very much like to continue investigation into the possibility of this healing process, but I'm a little lost as to where to begin. Can you tell me what my first step would be?

RA I am Ra. I cannot tell you what to ask. I may suggest that you consider the somewhat complex information just given and thus discover several avenues of inquiry. There is one "health," as you call it, in your polarized environment, but there are several significantly various distortions of types of mind/body/spirit complexes. Each type must pursue its own learn/teaching in this area.

4.11 **QUESTIONER** I would assume that the first step would be to find an individual with ability brought with him into this incarnation? Is this correct?

RA I am Ra. This is correct.

4.12 **QUESTIONER** Once I have selected an individual to perform healing, it would be helpful to receive instruction from you. Is this possible?

RA I am Ra. This is possible given the distortions of vibratory sound complexes.

4.13 **QUESTIONER** I'm assuming, then, that the selected individual would necessarily be one who was very much in harmony with the Law of One. Though he may not have any intellectual understanding of it, he should be living the Law of One. Is this correct?

RA I am Ra. This is both correct and incorrect. The first case, that being correctness, would apply to one such as the questioner itself who has the distortion towards healing, as you call it.

The incorrectness, which shall be observed, is the healing of those whose activities in your space/time illusion do not reflect the Law of One but whose ability has found its pathway to intelligent infinity regardless of the plane of existence from which this distortion is found.

4.14 **QUESTIONER** [*Aside*: Jim, did you understand?] I'm a little confused. I partially understood you; I'm not sure that I fully understood you. Could you restate that in another way?

RA I can restate that in many ways, given this instrument's knowledge of your vibratory sound complexes. I will strive for a shorter distortion at this time.

Two kinds there are who can heal: those such as yourself who, having the innate distortion towards knowledge-giving of the Law of One, can heal but do not; and those who, having the same knowledge but showing no significant distortion consciously towards the Law of One in mind, body, or spirit, yet and nevertheless, have opened a channel to the same ability.

The point being that there are those who, without proper training, shall we say, nevertheless, heal.

It is a further item of interest that those whose life does not equal their work may find some difficulty in absorbing the energy of intelligent infinity and thus become quite distorted in such a way as to cause disharmony in themselves and others, and perhaps even find it necessary to cease the healing activity. Therefore, those of the first type, those who seek to serve and are willing to be trained in thought, word, and action are those who will be able to comfortably maintain the distortion towards service in the area of healing.

4.15   **QUESTIONER** Then would it be possible for you to train us in healing practice?

RA I am Ra. It is possible.

4.16   **QUESTIONER** Will you train us?

RA We will.

4.17   **QUESTIONER** I have no idea of how long this would take or if you can even tell anything about that. Is it possible for you to give me a synopsis of the program of training required? I have no knowledge of what questions to ask at this point. I'll ask that question in the hopes that it makes sense.

RA I am Ra. We consider your request for information, for as you noted, there are a significant number of vibratory sound complexes which can be used in sequence to train the healer.

The synopsis is a very appropriate entry that you might understand what is involved.

Firstly, the mind must be known to itself. This is perhaps the most demanding part of healing work. If the mind knows itself then the most important aspect of healing has occurred, for consciousness is the microcosm of the Law of One.

The second part has to do with the disciplines of the body complexes. In the streamings reaching your planet at this time, these understandings and disciplines have to do with the balance between love and wisdom in the use of the body in its natural functions.

The third area is the spiritual, and in this area the first two disciplines are connected through the attainment of contact with intelligent infinity.

4.18 **QUESTIONER** I believe I have some idea of the accomplishment—a little idea, anyway, of the accomplishment—of the first step. Can you elaborate the steps? The other two steps I am not at all familiar with.

RA I am Ra. Imagine the body. Imagine the more dense aspects of the body. Proceed therefrom to the very finest knowledge of energy pathways which revolve and cause the body to be energized. Understand that all natural functions of the body have all aspects from dense to fine and can be transmuted to what you may call sacramental. This is a brief investigation of the second area.

To speak to the third: imagine, if you will, the function of the magnet. The magnet has two poles. One reaches up. The other goes down. The function of the spirit is to integrate the upreaching yearning of the mind/body energy with the downpouring instreaming of infinite intelligence. This is a brief explication of the third area.

4.19 **QUESTIONER** Then would this training program involve specific things to do, specific instructions and exercises?

RA I am Ra. We are not at this time incarnate among your peoples; thus, we can guide and attempt to specify, but cannot, by example, show. This is an handicap. However, there should indeed be fairly specific exercises of mind, body, and spirit during the teach/learning process we offer.

It is to be once again iterated that healing is but one distortion of the Law of One. To reach an undistorted understanding of that law, it is not necessary to heal or, indeed, to show any manifestation but only to exercise the disciplines of understanding.

We would ask that one or two more questions be the ending of this session.

4.20 **QUESTIONER** My objective is primarily to discover more of the Law of One, and it would be very helpful to discover techniques of healing. I am aware of your problem with respect to free will. Can you make— You cannot make suggestions, so I will ask you if you can state the Law of One and the laws of healing to me?

RA I am Ra. The Law of One, though beyond the limitations of name, as you call vibratory sound complexes, may be approximated by stating that all things are one, that there is no polarity, no right or wrong, no disharmony, but only identity. All is one, and that one is love/light, light/love, the Infinite Creator.

One of the primal distortions of the Law of One is that of healing. Healing occurs when a mind/body/spirit complex realizes, deep within itself, the Law of One; that is, that there is no disharmony, no imperfection; that all is complete and whole and perfect. Thus, the intelligent infinity within this mind/body/spirit complex re-forms the illusion of body, mind, or spirit to a form congruent with the Law of One. The healer acts as energizer or catalyst for this completely individual process.

One item which may be of interest is that a healer asking to learn must take the distortion understood as responsibility for that ask/receiving, thus healing. This is a[n] honor/duty which must be carefully considered in free will before the asking.

4.21 **QUESTIONER** I assume that we should continue tomorrow.

RA I am Ra. Your assumption is correct unless you feel that a certain question is necessary. This instrument is best nurtured by approximately this length of work.

4.22 **QUESTIONER** One short question. Is this instrument capable of two of these sessions per day, or should we remain with one?

RA I am Ra. This instrument is capable of two sessions a day. However, she must be encouraged to keep her bodily complex strong by the ingestion of your foodstuffs to an extent which exceeds this instrument's normal intake of your foodstuffs, this due to the physical material which we use to speak.

Further, this instrument's activities must be monitored to prevent over-activity, for this activity is equivalent to a strenuous working on the physical level.

If these admonitions are considered, the two sessions would be possible. We do not wish to deplete this instrument.

4.23 **QUESTIONER** Thank you, Ra.

RA I am Ra. I leave you in the love and the light of the One Infinite Intelligence which is the Creator. Go forth rejoicing in the power and the peace of the One. Adonai.

SESSION 5

JANUARY 23, 1981

5.0   RA   I am Ra. I greet you in the love and the light of the Infinite Creator. I communicate now.

5.1   QUESTIONER   The last time we communicated we were speaking of learning of healing. It is my impression that from what you gave to us in the earlier session that it is necessary to first purify the self by certain disciplines and exercises. Then in order to heal a patient, it is necessary, by example, and possibly certain exercises, to create a mental configuration in the patient that allows him to heal himself. Am I correct?

RA   I am Ra. Although your learn/understanding-distortion is essentially correct, your choice of vibratory sound complex is not entirely as accurate as this language allows.

It is not by example that the healer does the working. The working exists in and of itself. The healer is only the catalyst, much as this instrument has the catalysis necessary to provide the channel for our words, yet, by example or exercise of any kind, can take no thought for this working.

The healing working is congruent in that it is a form of channeling some distortion of the intelligent infinity.

5.2   QUESTIONER   We have decided to accept, if offered, the honor/duty of learning/teaching the healing process. I would ask as to the first step which we should accomplish in becoming effective healers.

RA   I am Ra. We shall begin with the first of the three teachings/learnings.

We begin with the mental learn/teachings necessary for contact with intelligent infinity. The prerequisite of mental work is the ability to retain silence of self at a steady state when required by the self. The mind must be opened like a door. The key is silence.

Within the door lies an hierarchical construction you may liken unto geography and in some ways geometry, for the hierarchy is quite regular, bearing inner relationships.

To begin to master the concept of mental discipline it is necessary to examine the self. The polarity of your dimension must be internalized.

Where you find patience within your mind you must consciously find the corresponding impatience and vice versa. Each thought that a being has, has in its turn an antithesis. The disciplines of the mind involve, first of all, identifying both those things of which you approve and those things of which you disapprove within yourself, and then balancing each and every positive and negative charge with its equal. The mind contains all things. Therefore, you must discover this completeness within yourself.

The second mental discipline is acceptance of the completeness within your consciousness. It is not for a being of polarity in the physical consciousness to pick and choose among attributes, thus building the roles that cause blockages and confusions in the already-distorted mind complex. Each acceptance smooths part of the many distortions that the faculty you call judgment engenders.

The third discipline of the mind is a repetition of the first but with the gaze outward towards the fellow entities that it meets. In each entity there exists completeness. Thus, the ability to understand each balance is necessary. When you view patience, you are responsible for mirroring in your mental understanding patience/impatience. When you view impatience, it is necessary for your mental configuration of understanding to be impatience/patience. We use this as a simple example. Most configurations of mind have many facets, and understanding of either self polarities, or what you would call other-self polarities, can and must be understood as subtle work.

The next step is the acceptance of the other-self polarities, which mirrors the second step.

These are the first four steps of learning mental discipline. The fifth step involves observing the geographical and geometrical relationships and ratios of the mind, the other mind, the mass mind, and the infinite mind.

The second area of learn/teaching is the study/understanding of the body complexes. It is necessary to know your body well. This is a matter of using the mind to examine how the feelings, the biases—what you would call the emotions—affect various portions of the body complex. It shall be necessary to both understand the bodily polarities and to accept them, repeating in a chemical/physical manifestation the work you have done upon the mind bethinking the consciousness.

The body is a creature of the mind's creation. It has its biases. The biological bias must be first completely understood and then the opposite bias allowed to find full expression in understanding. Again, the process of acceptance of the body as a balanced, as well as polarized, individual may then be accomplished.

It is then the task to extend this understanding to the bodies of the other-selves whom you will meet. The simplest example of this is the understanding that each biological male is female; each biological female is male. This is a simple example. However, in almost every case wherein you are attempting the understanding of the body of self or other-self, you will again find that the most subtle discernment is necessary in order to fully grasp the polarity complexes involved.

At this time we would suggest closing the description until the next time of work so that we may devote time to the third area commensurate with its importance.

We can answer a query if it is a short one before we leave this instrument.

5.3   **QUESTIONER** Is the instrument comfortable? Is there any other thing that would increase the instrument's comfort? That's all.

RA I am Ra. The candle could be rotated clockwise approximately 10° each session to improve the flow of spiraled energy through the being's receiving mechanisms. This particular configuration is well otherwise. But we ask that the objects described and used be centered with geometric care and checked from time to time. Also that they not be exposed to that space/time in which work is not of importance.

I am Ra. I leave this instrument in the love and light of the One Infinite Creator. Go forth rejoicing in the power and the peace of the One Creator. Adonai.

SESSION 6

6.0   **RA** I am Ra. I greet you in the love and the light of the Infinite Creator. I communicate now.

6.1   **QUESTIONER** We would like to continue the material from yesterday. We had to cease before [*inaudible*].

RA I am Ra. This is well with us.

We proceed now with the third area of teach/learning concerning the development of the energy powers of healing.

The third area is the spiritual complex which embodies the fields of force and consciousness which are the least distorted of your mind/body/spirit complex. The exploration and balancing of the spirit complex is indeed the longest and most subtle part of your learn/teaching. We have considered the mind as a tree. The mind controls the body. With the mind single-pointed, balanced, and aware, the body comfortable in whatever biases and distortions make it appropriately balanced for that instrument, the instrument is then ready to proceed with the great work.

That is the work of wind and fire. The spiritual body energy field is a pathway, or channel. When body and mind are receptive and open, then the spirit can become a functioning shuttle, or communicator, from the entity's individual energy of will upwards and from the streamings of the creative fire and wind downwards.

The healing ability, like all other, what this instrument would call paranormal abilities, is effected by the opening of a pathway, or shuttle, into intelligent infinity. There are many upon your plane who have a random hole or gateway in their spirit energy field, sometimes created by the ingestion of chemicals such as, what this instrument would call LSD, who are able, randomly and without control, to tap into energy sources. They may or may not be entities who wish to serve. The purpose of carefully and consciously opening this channel is to serve in a more dependable way, in a more commonplace or usual way, as seen by the distortion complex of the healer. To others there may appear to be miracles. To the one who has carefully opened the door to intelligent infinity this is ordinary; this is commonplace; this is as it should be. The life experience becomes somewhat transformed and the great work goes on.

At this time we feel these exercises suffice for your beginning. We will, at a future time, when you feel you have accomplished that which is set before you, begin to guide you into a more precise understanding of the functions and uses of this gateway in the experience of healing.

6.2   QUESTIONER I've been asked if it is possible for Tom Flaherty to attend one of these communication sessions tomorrow. Are you familiar with the entity, Tom Flaherty?

RA I am Ra. This mind/body/spirit complex, sound vibration of "Tom Flaherty," is acceptable. We caution you to carefully instruct this entity in the frame of mind and various appurtenances which it must understand before it is conducted into the circle.

6.3   QUESTIONER I'm not quite sure what you meant by appurtenances.

RA I was referring to the symbolic objects which trigger this instrument's distortions towards love/light. The placement and loving acceptance of them by all present is important in the nurturing of this instrument. Therefore, the appurtenances involved must be described and their presence explained in your own words of teach/learning, for you have the proper attitude for the required results.

6.4   QUESTIONER He'll understand me. We'll be very careful to totally inform Tom before he attends. Thank you very much.

It seems to me that it might be an appropriate time to include a little more historical background of yourself, possibly information having to do with where you came from prior to involvement with planet Earth, if this is possible.

RA I am Ra. I am, with the social memory complex of which I am a part, one of those who voyaged outward from another planet within your own solar system, as this entity would call it. The planetary influence was that you call Venus. We are a race old in your measures. When we were at the sixth dimension our physical beings were what you would call golden. We were tall and somewhat delicate. Our physical body complex covering, which you call the integument, had a golden luster. [1]

In this form we decided to come among your peoples. Your peoples at that time were much unlike us in physical appearance, as you might call it. We, thus, did not mix well with the population and were obviously other than they. Thus, our visit was relatively short, for we found ourselves in the hypocritical position of being acclaimed as other than your other-selves. This was the time during which we built the structures in which you show interest.

6.5   **QUESTIONER** How did you journey from Venus to this planet?

RA We used thought.

6.6   **QUESTIONER** Would it be possible to take one of the people at that time from our planet and place him on Venus? Would he survive? Were conditions much [*inaudible*]?

RA The third-density conditions are not hospitable to the life-forms of your peoples. The fifth and sixth dimensions of that planetary sphere are quite conducive to growing/learning/teaching.

6.7   **QUESTIONER** How were you able to make the transition from Venus, and I assume the sixth dimension, which—would that be invisible when you reached here? Did you have to change your dimensions to walk on the earth?

RA You will remember the exercise of the wind. The dissolution into nothingness is the dissolution into unity, for there is no nothingness. From the sixth dimension, we are capable of manipulating, by thought, the intelligent infinity present in each particle of light, or distorted light, so that we were able to clothe ourselves in a replica visible in the third density of our mind/body/spirit complexes in the sixth density. We were allowed this experiment by the Council which guards this planet.

6.8   **QUESTIONER** Where is this Council located?

---

[1] A number of clues seem to indicate that Ra intended to say third dimension here instead of sixth, including the information given in 6.7 and because they speak of the "physical body complex" and the "integument," which we know from other transmissions that in the sixth density they have become light (e.g., 8.20).

RA This Council is located in the octave, or eight[h] dimension, of the planet Saturn, taking its place in an area which you understand in third-dimensional terms as the rings.

6.9 **QUESTIONER** Are there any people such as you find on Earth on any of the other planets in this solar system?

RA Do you request space/time present information or space/time continuum information?

6.10 **QUESTIONER** Both.

RA At one time/space, in what is your past, there was a population of third-density beings upon a planet which dwelt within your solar system. There are various names by which this planet has been named. The vibratory sound complex most usually used by your peoples is Maldek. These entities, destroying their planetary sphere, thus were forced to find room for themselves upon this third density, which is the only one in your solar system at their time/space present which was hospitable and capable of offering the lessons necessary to decrease their mind/body/spirit distortions with respect to the Law of One.

6.11 **QUESTIONER** How did they come here?

RA They came through the process of harvest and were incarnated through the processes of incarnation from your higher spheres within this density.

6.12 **QUESTIONER** How long ago did this happen, in our years?

RA I am having difficulty communicating with this instrument. We must deepen her state.

This occurred approximately five hundred thousand [500,000] of your years ago.

6.13 **QUESTIONER** Thanks. Is all of the earth's population then—human population of the earth—are all of them originally from Maldek?

RA I am Ra. This is a new line of questioning and deserves a place of its own. The ones who were harvested to your sphere from the sphere known before its dissolution as other names, but to your peoples as Maldek, incarnated, many within your earth's surface rather than upon it. The population of your planet contains many various groups harvested from other second-dimension and cycled third-dimension spheres. You are not all one race or background of beginning. The experience you share is unique to this time/space continuum.

6.14   **QUESTIONER** I think it would be appropriate to discover how the Law of One acts in this transfer of beings to our planet and the action of harvest.

RA I am Ra. The Law of One states simply that all things are one, that all beings are one. There are certain behaviors and thought-forms consonant with the understanding and practice of this law. Those who, finishing a cycle of experience, demonstrate various grades of distortion of that understanding of thought and action will be separated by their own choice into the vibratory distortion most comfortable to their mind/body/spirit complexes.

This process is guarded, or watched, by those nurturing beings who, being very close to the Law of One in their distortions, nevertheless have the distortion towards active service.

Thus, the illusion is created of Light, or more properly but less understandably, light/love. This is in varying degrees of intensity. The spirit complex of each harvested entity moves along the line of light until the light grows too glaring, at which time the entity stops. This entity may have barely reached third density or may be very, very close to the ending of the third-density light/love distortion vibratory complex. Nevertheless, those who fall within this octave of intensifying light/love then experience a major cycle during which the opportunities are many for the discovery of the distortions which are inherent in each entity and, therefore, the lessening of these distortions.

6.15   **QUESTIONER** What is the length, in our years, of one of these cycles currently?

RA One major cycle is approximately twenty-five thousand [25,000] of your years. There are three cycles of this nature during which those who have progressed may be harvested. At the end of three major cycles—that is, approximately between seventy-five and seventy-six thousand [75–76,000] of your years—all are harvested regardless of their progress, for during that time the planet itself has moved through the useful part of that dimension and begins to cease being useful for the lower levels of vibration within that density.

6.16 **QUESTIONER** What is the position of this planet with respect to progression of the cycle at this time?

RA I am Ra. This sphere is at this time in fourth-dimension vibration. Its material is quite confused due to the society memory complexes embedded in its consciousness. It has not made an easy transition to the vibrations which beckon. Therefore, it will be fetched with some inconvenience.

6.17 **QUESTIONER** Is this inconvenience imminent within a few years?

RA I am Ra. This inconvenience, or disharmonious vibratory complex, has begun several of your years in the past. It shall continue unabated for a period of approximately three oh, thirty [30], of your years.

6.18 **QUESTIONER** After this thirty-year period I am assuming we will be a fourth-dimension or fourth-density planet. Is this correct?

RA I am Ra. This is so.

6.19 **QUESTIONER** Is it possible to estimate what percentage of the present population will inhabit the fourth-density planet?

RA The harvesting is not yet, thus estimation is meaningless.

6.20 **QUESTIONER** Does the fact that we are in this transition period now have anything to do with the reason that you have made your information available to the population?

RA I am Ra. We have walked among your people. We remember. We remember sorrow. We have seen much. We have searched for an instrument of the proper parameters of distortion in mind/body/spirit complex and supporting and understanding group of mind/body/spirit complexes to accept this information with minimal distortion and maximal desire to serve for some of your years.

The answer, in short, is yes. However, we wished you to know that in our memory we thank you.

6.21 **QUESTIONER** The disc-shaped craft we call UFOs have . . . some have been said to come possibly from the planet Venus. Would any of these be your craft?

RA I am Ra. We have used crystals for many purposes. The craft of which you speak have not been used by us in your space/time present memory complex. However, we have used crystals and the bell shape in the past of your illusion.

6.22 **QUESTIONER** How many years ago in the past did you use the bell-shaped craft to come here?

RA I am Ra. We visited your peoples eighteen thousand [18,000] of your years ago and did not land; again, eleven thousand [11,000] years ago.

6.23 **QUESTIONER** The photographs of the bell-shaped craft and reports of contact from Venus exist from less than thirty years ago. Do you have any knowledge of these reports?

RA I am Ra. We have knowledge of oneness with these forays of your time/space present. We are no longer of Venus. However, there are thought-forms created among your peoples from our time of walking among you. The memory and thought-forms created therefrom are a part of your society-memory complex. This mass consciousness, as you may call it, creates the experience once more for those who request such experience. The present Venus population is no longer sixth-density.

6.24 **QUESTIONER** Do any of the UFOs that are presently reported come from other planets here at this time, or do you have this knowledge?

RA I am one of the members of the Confederation of Planets in the Service of the Infinite Creator. There are approximately fifty-three civilizations comprising approximately five hundred planetary consciousness complexes in this Confederation. This Confederation contains those from your own planet who have attained dimensions beyond your third. It contains planetary entities within your solar system, and it contains planetary entities from other galaxies. It is a true Confederation in that its members are not alike, but allied in service according to the Law of One.

6.25 **QUESTIONER** Do any of them come here at this time in spacecraft? In the past, say, thirty years?

RA I am Ra. We must state that this information is unimportant. If you will understand this, we feel that the information may be acceptably offered. The Law of One is what we are here to express. However, we will speak upon this subject.

Each planetary entity which wishes to appear within your third-dimensional space/time-distortion requests permission to break quarantine, as you may call it, and appear to your peoples. The reason and purpose for this appearance is understood and either accepted or rejected. There have been as many as fifteen of the Confederation entities in your skies at any one time; the others available to you through thought.

At present there are seven which are operating with craft in your density. Their purposes are very simple: to allow those entities of your planet to become aware of infinity which is often best expressed to the uninformed as the mysterious or unknown.

6.26 **QUESTIONER** I am fully aware that you are primarily interested in disseminating the Law of One. However, it is my judgment—could be wrong—that in order to disseminate this material it will be necessary to include questions such as the one I have just asked for the purpose of creating the widest possible dissemination of the material. If this is not the objective, I could limit my questions only to the application of the Law of One. But I understand that at this time it is the objective to widely disseminate this material. Is this correct?

RA I am Ra. This perception is only slightly distorted in your understand/learning. We wish you to proceed as you deem proper. That is your place. We, in giving this information, find our distortion of understanding of our purpose to be that not only of the offering of information, but the weighting of it according to our distorted perceptions of its relative importance. Thus, you will find our statements, at times, to be those which imply that a question is unimportant. This is due to our perception that the given question is unimportant. Nevertheless, unless the question contains the potential for answer-giving which may infringe upon free will, we offer our answers.

6.27 **QUESTIONER** Thank you very much. We do not want to overtire the instrument. It's now considerably over the normal working time. Could you tell me the condition of the instrument?

RA The instrument is balanced due to your care. However, her physical vehicle is growing stiff.

6.28   **QUESTIONER** In that case perhaps we should continue at a later time.

RA We shall agree. Therefore, unless you have a short question we will take our leave.

6.29   **QUESTIONER** The only question I have is that I must assume since Leonard was here when you first made contact, it'd be as suitable for him to be here as Tom. Is this correct?

RA This is correct and completes the number of those at this time able to come who are suitable. Again, remember the instructions given for the preparation of the vibratory sound complex, Tom.

I am Ra. I leave you in the love and the light of the One Infinite Creator. Go forth rejoicing in the power and the peace of the One Creator. Adonai.

7.0 RA I am Ra. I greet you in the love and the light of our Infinite Creator. I communicate now.

7.1 QUESTIONER You mentioned that you were a member of the Confederation of Planets. What avenues of service, or types of service, are available to members of the Confederation? Would you describe some of them?

RA I am Ra. I am assuming that you intend the service which we of the Confederation can offer, rather than the service which is available to our use.

The service available for our offering to those who call us is equivalent to the square of the distortion/need of that calling divided by, or integrated with, the basic Law of One in its distortion indicating the free will of those who are not aware of the unity of creation.

7.2 QUESTIONER From this I am assuming that the difficulty you have contacting this planet at this time is the mixture of people here—some being aware of the unity, some not, and for this reason you cannot come openly or give any proof of your contact. Is this correct?

RA I am Ra. As we just repeated through this instrument, we must integrate all of the portions of your social memory complex in its illusory disintegration form. Then the product of this can be seen as the limit of our ability to serve.

We are fortunate that the Law of Service squares the desires of those who call. Otherwise, we would have no beingness in this time/space at this present continuum of the illusion. In short, you are basically correct. The thought of not being able is not a part of our basic thought-form complex towards your peoples, but rather is a maximal consideration of what is possible.

7.3 QUESTIONER By squared, do you mean that if ten people call you can count that, when comparing it to the planetary ratio of people, as 100 people, squaring ten, getting 100? Is that correct?

RA I am Ra. This is incorrect. The square is sequential — one, two, three, four, each squared by the next number.

7.4 **QUESTIONER** [*Inaudible*] use an example. If ten, only ten, entities on Earth required your services, how would you compute their call using this square rule?

RA We would square one ten sequential times, raising the number to the tenth square.

7.5 **QUESTIONER** What would be the result of this calculation?

RA [*24-second pause*] The result is difficult to transmit. It is one thousand and twelve [1,012], approximately. The entities who call are sometimes not totally unified in their calling, and thus the squaring is slightly less. Thus, there is a statistical loss over a period of call. However, perhaps you may see by this statistically corrected information the squaring mechanism.

7.6 **QUESTIONER** About how many entities at present are calling from planet Earth for your services?

RA I am called personally by three hundred fifty-two thousand [352,000]. The Confederation, in its entire spectrum of entity-complexes, is called by six hundred thirty-two millions [632,000,000] of your mind/body/spirit complexes. These numbers have been simplified.

7.7 **QUESTIONER** Can you tell me what the result of the application of the Law of Squares is to those figures?

RA The number is approximately meaningless in the finite sense as there are many, many digits. It, however, constitutes a great calling which we of all creation feel and hear as if our own entities were distorted towards a great and overwhelming sorrow. It demands our service.

7.8 **QUESTIONER** At what point would this calling be enough for you to openly come among the people on Earth? How many entities on Earth would have to call the Confederation?

RA I am Ra. We do not calculate the possibility of coming among your peoples by the numbers of calling, but by a consensus among an entire societal-memory complex which has become aware of the infinite consciousness of all things. This has been possible among your peoples only in isolated instances.

In the case wherein a social memory complex which is servant of the Creator sees this situation and has an idea for the appropriate aid which can only be done among your peoples, the social memory complex desiring this project lays it before the Council of Saturn. If it is approved, quarantine is lifted.

7.9   **QUESTIONER** I have a question here, I believe, about that Council from Jim. Who are the members, and how does the Council function?

RA I am Ra. The members of the Council are representatives from the Confederation and from those vibratory levels of your inner planes bearing responsibility for your third density. The names are not important because there are no names. Your mind/body/spirit complexes request names, and so, in many cases, the vibratory sound complexes which are consonant with the vibratory distortions of each entity are used. However, the name concept is not part of the Council. If names are requested, we will attempt them. However, not all have chosen names.

In number, the Council that sits in constant session—though varying in its members by means of balancing which takes place, what you would call, irregularly—is nine. That is the Session Council. To back up this Council, there are twenty-four entities which offer their services as requested. These entities faithfully watch and have been called the Guardians.

The Council operates by means of, what you would call, telepathic contact with the oneness or unity of the nine, the distortions blending harmoniously so that the Law of One prevails with ease. When a need for thought is present, the Council retains the distortion-complex of this need, balancing it as described, and then recommends what it considers as appropriate action. This includes: one, the duty of admitting social memory complexes to the Confederation; two, offering aid to those who are unsure how to aid the social memory complex requesting aid in a way consonant with both the call, the Law, and the number of those calling (that is to say, sometimes the resistance of the call); three, internal questions in the Council are determined.

These are the prominent duties of the Council. They are, if in any doubt, able to contact the twenty-four who then offer consensus judgment/thinking to the Council. The Council then may reconsider any question.

7.10 **QUESTIONER** Is the Council of Nine the same nine that was mentioned in this book? [*Questioner gestures to* Uri *by Andrija (Henry) Puharich.*]

RA I am Ra. The Council of Nine has been retained in semi-undistorted form by two main sources: that known in your naming as Mark, and that known in your naming as Henry. In one case, the channel became the scribe. In the other, the channel was not the scribe. However, without the aid of the scribe, the energy would not have come to the channel.

7.11 **QUESTIONER** The names you spoke of, are they Mark Probert and Henry Puharich?

RA I am Ra. This is correct.

7.12 **QUESTIONER** I am interested in the application of the Law of One as it pertains to free will and what I would call the advertising done by UFO contact with the planet. That is, the Council has allowed the quarantine to be lifted many times over the past thirty years. This seems to me to be a form of advertising for what we are doing right now, so that more people will be awakened. Am I correct?

RA I am Ra. It will take a certain amount of untangling of conceptualization of your mental complex to reform your query into an appropriate response. Please bear with us.

The Council of Saturn has not allowed the breaking of quarantine in the time/space continuum you mentioned. There is a certain amount of landing taking place. Some of these landings are of your peoples. Some are of the entities known to you as the group of Orion.

Secondly, there is permission granted, not to break quarantine by dwelling among you, but to appear in thought-form capacity for those who have eyes to see.

Thirdly, you are correct in assuming that permission was granted at the time/space in which your first nuclear device was developed and used for Confederation members to minister unto your peoples in such a way as to cause mystery to occur. This is what you mean by advertising and is correct.

The mystery and unknown quality of the occurrences we are allowed to offer have the hoped-for intention of making your peoples aware of infinite possibility. When your peoples grasp infinity, then, and only then, can the gateway be opened to the Law of One.

7.13 **QUESTIONER** You mentioned both our people and those of Orion coming here. Can you expand on that?

RA I am Ra. Your thought complexes did not match your vibratory sound complexes. We are unable to respond. Please restate your query.

7.14 **QUESTIONER** I'll just ask about Orion. You mentioned Orion as a source of some of the contacts of UFOs. Can you tell me something of that contact, its purpose?

RA I am Ra. Consider, if you will, a simple example of intentions which are bad/good. This example is Adolf. This is your vibratory sound complex. The intention is to presumably unify by choosing the distortion complex called elite from a social memory complex, and then enslaving, by various effects, those who are seen as the distortion of not-elite. There is then the concept of taking the social memory complex thus weeded and adding it to a distortion thought of by the so-called Orion group as an empire.

The problem facing them is that they face a great deal of random energy released by the concept of separation. This causes them to be vulnerable as the distortions amongst their own members are not harmonized.

7.15 **QUESTIONER** What is the density of the Orion group?

RA I am Ra. Like the Confederation, the densities of the mass consciousnesses which comprise that group are varied. There are a very few third density, a larger number of fourth density, a similarly large number of fifth density,[1] and very few sixth-density entities comprising this organization. Their numbers are perhaps one-tenth ours at any point in the space/time continuum as the problem of spiritual entropy causes them to experience constant disintegration of their social memory complexes.

---

[1] It is unclear and subject to interpretation, but this information about the number of fifth-density entities comprising the Orion group may contradict information given in 48.6.

Their power is the same as ours. The Law of One blinks neither at the light or the darkness but is available for service to others and service to self. However, service to others results in service to self, thus preserving and further harmonizing the distortions of those entities seeking intelligent infinity through these disciplines.

Those seeking intelligent infinity through the use of service to self create the same amount of power but, as we said, have constant difficulty because of the concept of separation which is implicit in the manifestations of the service to self which involve power over others. This weakens and eventually disintegrates the energy collected by such mind/body/spirit complexes who call the Orion group and the social memory complexes which comprise the Orion group.

It should be noted, carefully pondered, and accepted, that the Law of One is available to any social memory complex which has decided to strive together for any seeking of purpose, be it service to others or service to self. The laws, which are the primal distortions of the Law of One, then are placed into operation, and the illusion of space/time is used as a medium for the development of the results of those choices freely made.

Thus all entities learn, no matter what they seek. All learn the same, some rapidly, some slowly.

7.16   **QUESTIONER** Using as an example a fifth-density group or social memory complex of the Orion group, what was their previous density before they became fifth density?

RA I am Ra. The progress through densities is sequential. A fifth-density social memory complex would be comprised of mind/body/spirit complexes harvested from fourth density. Then the conglomerate or mass mind/body/spirit complex does its melding, and the results are due to the infinitely various possibilities of combination of distortions.

7.17   **QUESTIONER** I'm trying to understand how a group such as the Orion group would progress. I was of the opinion that a closer understanding of the Law of One created the condition of acceptability moving, say, from our third density to the fourth in our transition now. And I'm trying to understand how it would be possible—if you were in the Orion group and pointed toward self-service—how you would progress, say, from the third density to the fourth. What learning would be necessary for that?

RA I am Ra. This is the last question of length for this instrument at this time.

You will recall that we went into some detail as to how those not oriented towards seeking service for others yet, nevertheless, found and could use the gateway to intelligent infinity. This is true at all densities in our octave. We cannot speak for those above us, as you would say, in the next quantum, or octave, of beingness.

This is, however, true of this octave of densities. The beings are harvested because they can see and enjoy the light/love of the appropriate density. Those who have found this light/love, love/light without benefit of a desire for service nevertheless, by the Law of Free Will, have the right to the use of that light/love for whatever purpose.

Also, it may be inserted that there are systems of study which enable the seeker of separation to gain these gateways. This study is as difficult as the one which we have described to you, but there are those with the perseverance to pursue the study just as you desire to pursue the difficult path of seeking to know in order to serve.

The distortion lies in the fact that those who seek to serve the self are seen by the Law of One as precisely the same as those who seek to serve others, for are all not one? To serve yourself and to serve other is a dual method of saying the same thing, if you can understand the essence of the Law of One.

At this time we would answer any brief questions you may have.

7.18 **QUESTIONER** Is there anything we can do to make the instrument more comfortable?

RA I am Ra. There are small adjustments you may make. However, we are now able to use this instrument with minimal distortion and without depleting the instrument to any significant extent.

Do you wish to ask further?

7.19 **QUESTIONER** We do not wish to overly tire the instrument. Thank you very much. That was very helpful. We will continue in the next session taking up this point. I believe that I'm beginning to understand the progression. Thank you very much.

RA I am Ra. I leave you in the love and the light of the One Infinite Creator. Go forth then rejoicing in the power and the peace of the One Creator. Adonai.

SESSION 8

8.0   **RA** I am Ra. I greet you in the love and the light of the Infinite Creator. I communicate now.

8.1   **QUESTIONER** I have a question about what I call the advertising of the Confederation. It has to do with free will. There have been certain contacts allowed, as I understand, by the Council, but this is limited because of free will of those who are not oriented in such a way that they could maybe want contact. This material that we are doing now will be disseminated. Dissemination of this material will be dependent upon the wants of a relatively small number of people on the planet. Many people on the planet now want this material, but even though we disseminate it, they will not be aware it is available. Is there any possibility of creating some effect which I would call advertising, or is this against the principle of free will?

RA I am Ra. Consider, if you will, the path your life-experience complex has taken. Consider the coincidences and odd circumstances by which one thing flowed to the next. Consider this well. Each entity will receive the opportunity that each needs.

This information source-beingness does not have uses in the life-experience complex of each of those among your peoples who seek. Thus the advertisement is general and not designed to indicate the searching out of any particular material but only to suggest the noumenal aspect of the illusion.

8.2   **QUESTIONER** There was a portion of the material yesterday which I will read where you say, "There is a certain amount of landing taking place. Some of these landings are of your peoples; some are of the entities known to you as the group of Orion." My first question is what did you mean by the "landings are of your peoples"?

RA I am Ra. Your peoples have, at this time/space present, the technological achievement, if you would call it that, of being able to create and fly the shape and type of craft known to you as unidentified flying objects. Unfortunately for the social memory complex vibratory rate of your peoples, these devices are not intended for the service of mankind but for potential destructive use. This further muddles the vibratory nexus of your social memory complex, causing a situation whereby neither those oriented towards serving others nor those oriented towards serving self can gain the energy/power which opens the gates to intelligent infinity for the social memory complex. This in turn causes the harvest to be small.

8.3   **QUESTIONER** Are these craft that are of our peoples from what we call planes that are not incarnate at this time? Where are they based?

RA I am Ra. These of which we spoke are of third density and are part of the so-called military complex of various of your peoples' societal divisions or structures.

The bases are varied. There are bases, as you would call them, undersea in your southern waters near the Bahamas as well as in your Pacific seas in various places close to your Chilean borders on the water. There are bases upon your moon, as you call this satellite, which are at this time being reworked. There are bases which move about your lands. There are bases, if you would call them that, in your skies. These are the bases of your peoples, very numerous and, as we have said, potentially destructive.

8.4   **QUESTIONER** Where do the people who operate these craft come from? Are they affiliated with any nation on Earth? What is their source?

RA These people come from the same place as you or I. They come from the Creator.

As you intend the question, in its shallower aspect, these people are those in your and other-selves' governments responsible for what you would term national security.

8.5   **QUESTIONER** Am I to understand then that the United States has these craft in undersea bases?

RA I am Ra. You are correct.

8.6   **QUESTIONER** How did the United States learn of the technology to build these land [*inaudible*]?

RA I am Ra. There was a mind/body/spirit complex known to your people by the vibratory sound complex, Nikola. This entity departed the illusion, and the papers containing the necessary understandings were taken by mind/body/spirit complexes serving your security of national divisional complex. Thus your people became privy to the basic technology.

In the case of those mind/body/spirit complexes which you call Russians, the technology was given from one of the Confederation in an attempt, approximately twenty-seven of your years ago, to share information and bring about peace among your peoples. The entities giving this information were in error, but we did many things at the end of this cycle in attempts to aid your harvest from which we learned the folly of certain types of aid. That is a contributing factor to our more cautious approach at this date, even as the need is power-upon-power greater, and your people's call is greater and greater.

8.7   QUESTIONER I'm puzzled by these craft that we have undersea bases for. They are [*inaudible*]. Is this technology sufficient to overshadow all other armaments? Do we have just the ability to fly in these craft, or are there any weapons like there are— Were they given to us [*inaudible*] or are they just craft for transport? What is the basic mechanism of their [*inaudible*]? It's really hard to believe is what I'm saying.

RA I am Ra. The craft are perhaps misnamed in some instances. It would be more appropriate to consider them as weaponry. The energy used is that of the field of electromagnetic energy which polarizes the earth sphere. The weaponry is of two basic kinds: that which is called by your peoples psychotronic, and that which is called by your peoples particle beam. The amount of destruction which is contained in this technology is considerable, and the weapons have been used in many cases to alter weather patterns and to enhance the vibratory change which engulfs your planet at this time.

8.8   QUESTIONER How have they been able to keep this a secret? Why aren't these craft in use for transport?

RA The governments of each of your societal division illusions desire to refrain from publicity so that the surprise may be retained in case of hostile action from what your peoples call enemies.

8.9   QUESTIONER How many of these craft does the United States have?

RA I am Ra. The United States has five hundred seven three, five seven three [573] at this time. They are in the process of adding to this number.

8.10   **QUESTIONER** What is the maximum speed of one of these craft?

RA I am Ra. The maximum speed of these craft is equal to the earth energy squared. This field varies. The limit is approximately one-half the light speed, as you would call it. This is due to imperfections in design.

8.11   **QUESTIONER** Wouldn't this type of craft totally solve, or come close to solving, a lot of the energy problems as far as transport goes? That we're used to transporting [*inaudible*] . . . transporting [*inaudible*].

RA I am Ra. The technology your peoples possess at this time is capable of resolving each and every limitation which plagues your social memory complex at this present nexus of experience. However, the concerns of some of your beings with distortions towards what you would call powerful energy cause these solutions to be withheld until the solutions are so needed that those with the distortion can then become further distorted in the direction of power.

8.12   **QUESTIONER** At the same time you mentioned that some of the landings were of our peoples, you also mentioned that some were of the Orion group. We talked a little about the Orion group, but why do the Orion group land here? What is their purpose?

RA I am Ra. Their purpose is conquest. Unlike those of the Confederation who wait for the calling, the so-called Orion group calls itself to conquest.

8.13   **QUESTIONER** Specifically, what do they do when they land?

RA There are two types of landings. In the first, entities among your peoples are taken on their craft and programmed for future use. There are two or three levels of programming. First, the level that will be discovered by those who do research. Second, a triggering program. Third, a second and most deep triggering program crystallizing the entity thereby rendering it lifeless and useful as a kind of beacon. This is a form of landing.

The second form is that of landing beneath the earth's crust which is entered from water. Again, in the general area of your South American and Caribbean areas and close to the so-called northern pole. The bases of these people are underground.

8.14   **QUESTIONER** What do the Orion group have . . . what's the objective with respect to the conquest of the Orion group?

RA I am Ra. As we have said previously, their objective is to locate certain mind/body/spirit complexes which vibrate in resonance with their own vibrational complex, then to enslave the un-elite, as you may call those who are not of the Orion vibration.

8.15   **QUESTIONER** Was the landing at Pascagoula in 1973 when Charlie Hickson was taken on board this type of landing?

RA I am Ra. The landing of which you speak was what you would call an anomaly. It was neither the Orion influence nor our peoples in thought-form but rather a planetary entity of your own vibration which came through quarantine in all innocence in a random landing.

8.16   **QUESTIONER** What did they do to Charlie Hickson when they took him on board?

RA I am Ra. They used his mind/body/spirit complex's life experience, concentrating upon the experience of the complexes of what you call war.

8.17   **QUESTIONER** How did they use them?

RA I am Ra. The use of experience is to learn. Consider a race who watches a movie. It experiences a story and identifies with the feelings, perceptions, and experiences of the hero.

8.18   **QUESTIONER** Was Charlie Hickson originally of the same social memory complex as the ones who picked him up?

RA I am Ra. This entity of vibratory sound complex did not have a connection with those who used him.

8.19   **QUESTIONER** Did those who used him use his war experiences to learn more of the Law of One?

RA I am Ra. This is correct.

8.20   **QUESTIONER** Were the entities that picked him . . . is that the normal configuration of these entities? They [*inaudible*] rather unusual.

RA I am Ra. The configuration of their beings is their normal configuration. The unusualness is not remarkable. We ourselves, when we chose a mission among your peoples, needed to study your peoples, for had we arrived in no other form than our own, we would have been perceived as light.

8.21 **QUESTIONER** Well, what density did the entities who picked up Charlie Hickson come from? What was their density?

RA I am Ra. The entities in whom you show such interest are third-density beings of a fairly high order. We should express the understanding to you that these entities would not have used the mind/body/spirit complex, Charlie, except for the resolve of this entity before incarnation to be of service.

8.22 **QUESTIONER** What was the home or origin of the entities that took Charlie?

RA I am Ra. These entities are of the Sirius galaxy.

8.23 **QUESTIONER** The most startling information that you've given me, which I must admit I'm having difficulty believing, is that the United States has 573 craft like you describe. How many people in our government are aware that we have these? How many total people of United States designation are aware of this, including those who operate the craft?

RA I am Ra. The number of your peoples varies, for there are needs to communicate at this particular time/space nexus so that the number is expanding at this time. The approximate number is one five oh oh [1,500]. It is only approximate, for as your illusory time/space continuum moves from present to present at this nexus many are learning.

8.24 **QUESTIONER** Where are these craft constructed?

RA These craft are constructed one by one in two locations: in the desert or arid regions of your so-called New Mexico and in the desert or arid regions of your so-called Mexico, both installations being under the ground.

8.25 **QUESTIONER** Do you say the United States actually has a manufacturing plant in Mexico?

RA I am Ra. I spoke thusly. May I, at this time, reiterate that this type of information is very shallow and of no particular consequence compared to the study of the Law of One. However, we carefully watch these developments in hopes that your peoples are able to be harvested in peace.

8.26 **QUESTIONER** I am totally aware how this line of questioning is of no consequence at all, but this particular information is so startling to me that it makes me question your validity on this. Up until this point, I was in agreement with everything. This is very startling, and it does not seem possible that this secret could have been kept twenty-seven years and that we are operating these craft. I apologize for my attitude, but I thought I would be very honest about this. It is unbelievable to me that we would operate a plant in Mexico, outside of the United States, to build these craft. Maybe I'm mistaken. These craft are physical craft built by our physical people? I could go get in one and ride in one? Is that correct?

RA I am Ra. This is incorrect. You could not ride one. The United States, as you call your society divisional complex, creates these as a type of weapon.

8.27 **QUESTIONER** There are no occupants then? No pilot, shall I say?

RA I am Ra. This is correct.

8.28 **QUESTIONER** How are they controlled?

RA I am Ra. They are controlled by computer from a remote source of data.

8.29 **QUESTIONER** Why do we have a plant in Mexico?

RA I am Ra. The necessity is both for dryness of the ground and for a near total lack of population. Therefore, your so-called government and the so-called government of your neighboring geographical vicinity arranged for an underground installation. The government officials who agreed did not know the use to which their land would be put but thought it a governmental research installation for use in what you would call bacteriological warfare.

8.30 **QUESTIONER** Is this the type of craft that Dan Frye was transported in?

RA I am Ra. The one known as Daniel was, in thought-form, transported by Confederation thought-form vehicular illusion in order to give this mind/body/spirit complex data so that we might see how this type of contact aided your people in the uncovering of the intelligent infinity behind the illusion of limits.

8.31   **QUESTIONER** Would it be possible for any of us to have some type of contact with the Confederation in a more direct way?

RA I am Ra. In observing the distortions of those who underwent this experiential sequence we decided to gradually back off, shall I say, from direct contact in thought-form. The least distortion seems to be available in mind-to-mind communication. Therefore, the request to be taken aboard is not one we care to comply with. You are most valuable in your present orientation.

8.32   **QUESTIONER** The reason that I have questioned you so much upon the craft which you say the United States government operates is that if we include this in the book it will create numerous problems. It is something that I am considering leaving out of the book entirely, or I am going to have to question you in considerable detail about it. It's difficult to even question in this area, but I would like maybe to ask a few more questions about it, with still the possible option of leaving it out of the book. What are the diameter of these craft the United States [*inaudible*]?

RA I am Ra. I suggest that this be the last question for this session. We will speak as you deem fit in further sessions, asking you to be guided by your own discernment only.

The approximate diameter, given several model changes, is twenty-three of your feet, as you measure.

May we ask at this time if you have a needed short query before we end this session?

8.33   **QUESTIONER** Is there anything that we can do to make the instrument more comfortable?

RA I am Ra. The instrument is well balanced. It is possible to make small corrections in the configuration of the spine of the instrument that it be straighter. Continue also to carefully monitor the placement and orientation of the symbols used. This particular session the censer is slightly off and, therefore, this instrument will experience a slight discomfort.

8.34   **QUESTIONER** Is the censer off with respect to angle or with respect to lateral displacement?

RA There is an approximate three degree displacement from proper perpendicularity.

I am Ra. I leave you in the love and the light of the One Infinite Creator. Go forth, therefore, rejoicing in the power and the peace of the One Creator. Adonai.

SESSION 9

9.0 **RA** I am Ra. I greet you in the love and the light of our Infinite Creator. We communicate now.

9.1 **QUESTIONER** We are definitely going to make the Law of One the primary portion of this book. I apologize for getting sidetracked on these subjects. We're in the position of, shall we say, beating around as to what direction to go with the book to begin with. For this reason I have asked a few questions, and probably will ask a few more questions in the early part of these sessions, that will be somewhat meaningless with respect to application of the Law of One because my own ignorance of what I'm doing. However, I expect to become more proficient rapidly while we go on.

There are a couple of questions that are probably meaningless, but if I could get them out of the way . . . they're bothering me a little bit.

Is it possible for you to suggest a publisher for this book?

RA I am Ra. No.

9.2 **QUESTIONER** Is it possible for you to tell us of anything in our past incarnations, our past experiences before this incarnation?

RA I am Ra. It is possible. However, such information as this is carefully guarded by your mind/body/spirit being totality so that your present space/time experiences will be undiluted.

Let us scan for harmless material for your beingness. [20-second pause.] I am, in the distortion of desire for your freedom from preconception, able to speak only generally.

There have been several times when this group worked and dwelt together. The relationships varied. There is balanced karma, as you call it; each thus the teacher of each. The work has involved healing, understanding the uses of the earth energy, and work in aid of civilizations which called, just as your sphere has done, and we have come. This ends the material which we consider harmless.

9.3   **QUESTIONER** The healing exercises that you gave to us are of such a nature that it is best to concentrate on a particular exercise at a time. I would like to ask at this time what exercise I should concentrate on. Possibly a little exercise change . . . should concentrate on [*inaudible*], say tonight?

RA I am Ra. Again, to direct your judgment is an intrusion upon your space/time-continuum distortion called future. To speak of past or present within our distortion/judgment limits is acceptable. To guide rather than teach/learn is not acceptable to our distortion in regards to teach/learning. We instead can suggest a process whereby each chooses the first of the exercises given in the order in which we gave them, which you, in your discernment, feel is not fully appreciated by your mind/body/spirit complex.

This is the proper choice—building from the foundation, making sure the ground is good for the building. We have assessed for you the intensity of this effort in terms of energy expended. You will take this in mind and be patient, for we have not given a short or easy program of consciousness learn/teaching.

9.4   **QUESTIONER** The way I understand the process of evolution of a planetary population is that a population has a certain amount of time to progress. This is generally divided into three 25,000-year cycles. At the end of 75,000 years, the planet progresses itself. What caused this situation to come about? The preciseness of the years, 25,000 years, etc. What set this up to begin with?

RA I am Ra. Visualize, if you will, the particular energy which, outward flowing and inward coagulating, formed the tiny realm of the creation governed by your Council of Saturn. Continue seeing the rhythm of this process. The living flow creates a rhythm which is as inevitable as one of your timepieces. Each of your planetary entities began the first cycle when the energy nexus was able in that environment to support such mind/body experiences. Thus, each of your planetary entities is on a different cyclical schedule, as you might call it. The timing of these cycles is a measurement equal to a portion of intelligent energy.

This intelligent energy offers a type of clock. The cycles move as precisely as a clock strikes your hour. Thus, the gateway from intelligent energy to intelligent infinity opens regardless of circumstance on the striking of the hour.

9.5   **QUESTIONER** The original, the first entities on this planet . . . what was their origin? Where were they before they were on this planet?

RA I am Ra. The first entities upon this planet were water, fire, air and earth.

9.6   **QUESTIONER** The people that we now have—the first people, [*inaudible*] like us—where did they come from? How did they evolve?

RA I am Ra. You speak of third-density experience. The first of those to come here were brought from another planet in your solar system called by you the Red Planet, Mars. This planet's environment became inhospitable to third-density beings. The first entities, therefore, were of this race, as you may call it, manipulated somewhat by those who were Guardians at that time.

9.7   **QUESTIONER** What race is that, and how did they get from Mars to here?

RA I am Ra. The race is a combination of the mind/body/spirit complexes of those of your so-called Red Planet and a careful series of genetical adjustments made by the Guardians of that time. These entities arrived, or were preserved, for the experience upon your sphere by a type of birthing which is non-reproductive, but consists of preparing genetic material for the incarnation of the mind/body/spirit complexes of those entities from the Red Planet.

9.8   **QUESTIONER** Then I'm assuming what you're saying is that the Guardians transferred the race here after the race had died from the physical as we know it on Mars. Is that correct?

RA I am Ra. This is correct.

9.9   **QUESTIONER** The Guardians obviously were acting with an understanding of the Law of One in doing this. Can you explain the application of the Law of One in this process?

RA I am Ra. The Law of One was named by these Guardians as the bringing of the wisdom of the Guardians in contact with the entities from the Red Planet, thus melding the social memory complex of the Guardian race and the Red Planet race. It, however, took an increasing amount of distortion into the application of the Law of One from the viewpoint of other Guardians, and it is from this beginning action that the quarantine of this planet was instituted, for it was felt that the free will of those of the Red Planet had been abridged.

9.10 **QUESTIONER** Were the entities of the Red Planet following the Law of One prior to leaving the Red Planet?

RA The entities of the Red Planet were attempting to learn the Laws of Love which form one of the primal distortions of the Law of One. However, the tendencies of these people towards bellicose actions caused such difficulties in the atmospheric environment of their planet that it became inhospitable for third-density experience before the end of its cycle. Thus, the Red Planet entities were unharvested and continued in your illusion to attempt to learn the Law of Love.

9.11 **QUESTIONER** How long ago did this transfer occur from the Red Planet to Earth?

RA I am Ra. In your time this transfer occurred approximately seven five zero zero zero [75,000] years ago.

9.12 **QUESTIONER** 75,000 years ago?

RA I am Ra. This is approximately correct.

9.13 **QUESTIONER** Were there any entities of this form that I am now—two arms, two legs—on this planet before this transfer occurred?

RA I am Ra. There have been visitors to your sphere at various times for the last four million of your years, speaking approximately. These visitors do not effect[1] the cycling of the planetary sphere. It was not third-density in its environment until the time previously mentioned.

9.14 **QUESTIONER** Then there were second-density entities here prior to approximately 75,000 years ago. What type of entities were these?

RA The second density is the density of the higher plant life and animal life which exists without the upward drive towards the infinite. These second-density beings are of an octave of consciousness just as you find various orientations of consciousness among the conscious entities of your vibration.

---

[1] Ra carefully enunciated the initial long "e," thus the spelling "effect" instead of "affect."

9.15 **QUESTIONER** Did any of these second-density entities have shapes like ours: two arms, two legs, head, and walk upright on two feet?

RA I am Ra. The two higher of the sub-vibrational levels of second-density beings had the configuration of the biped, as you mentioned. However, the erectile movement which you experience was not totally effected in these beings who were tending towards the leaning forward, barely leaving the quadrupedal position.

9.16 **QUESTIONER** Where did these beings come from? Were they a product of evolution as it is understood by our scientists? Were they evolved from the original material of the earth that you spoke of?

RA I am Ra. This is correct.

9.17 **QUESTIONER** Do these beings then evolve from second density to third density?

RA I am Ra. This is correct, although no guarantee can be made of the number of cycles it will take an entity to learn the lessons of consciousness of self which are the prerequisite for transition to third density.

9.18 **QUESTIONER** Is there any particular race of people on our planet now who were incarnated here from second density?

RA I am Ra. There are no second-density consciousness complexes here on your sphere at this time. However, there are two races which use the second-density form. One is the entities of the planetary sphere you call Maldek. These entities are working their understanding complexes through a series of what you would call karmic restitutions. They dwell within your deeper underground passageways and are known to you as "Bigfoot."

The other race is that being offered a dwelling in this density by Guardians who wish to give the mind/body/spirit complexes of those who are of this density at this time appropriately engineered physical vehicles, as you would call these chemical complexes, in the event that there is what you call nuclear war.

9.19 **QUESTIONER** I didn't understand what these vehicles or beings were for that were appropriate in the event of nuclear war.

RA I am Ra. These are beings which exist as instinctual second-density beings which are being held in reserve to form what you would call a gene pool in case these body complexes are needed. These body complexes are greatly able to withstand the rigors of radiation which the body complexes you now inhabit could not do.

9.20 **QUESTIONER** Where are these body complexes located?

RA I am Ra. These body complexes of the second race dwell in uninhabited deep forest. There are many in various places over the surface of your planet.

9.21 **QUESTIONER** Are they Bigfoot-type creatures?

RA I am Ra. This is correct although we would not call these Bigfoot, as they are scarce and are very able to escape detection. The first race is less able to be aware of proximity of other mind/body/spirit complexes, but these beings are very able to escape due to their technological understandings before their incarnations here. These entities of the glowing eyes are those most familiar to your peoples.

9.22 **QUESTIONER** Then there are two different types of Bigfoot. Correct?

RA I am Ra. This will be the final question.

There are three types of Bigfoot, if you will accept that vibratory sound complex used for three such different races of mind/body/spirit complexes. The first two we have described.

The third is a thought-form.

9.23 **QUESTIONER** We plan to do a second session later today if the instrument is capable, and I'd like to ask if there is anything we can do to aid the instrument's comfort.

RA I am Ra. This instrument will require some adjustment of the tender portions of her body complex. The distortions are due to the energy center blockage you would call pineal.

I leave you in the love and the light of the One Infinite Creator. Go forth, therefore, rejoicing in the power and the peace of the One Creator. Adonai.

10.0 **RA** I am Ra. I greet you in the love and the light of the Infinite Creator. I communicate now.

10.1 **QUESTIONER** I think it would clarify things for us to go back to the time just before the transfer of souls from Maldek to see how the Law of One operated with respect to this transfer, and why this was necessary. What happened to Maldek, or the people on Maldek, to cause them to lose their planet? How long ago did this occur?

RA I am Ra. The peoples of Maldek had a civilization somewhat similar to that of the societal complex known to you as Atlantis in that it gained much technological information and used it without care for the preservation of their sphere, following to a majority extent the complex of thought, ideas, and actions which you may associate with your so-called negative polarity, or the service to self.

This was, however, for the most part, couched in a sincere belief/thought structure which seemed to the perception of the mind/body complexes of this sphere to be positive and of service to others. The devastation that wracked their biosphere and caused its disintegration resulted from what you call war.

The escalation went to the furthest extent of the technology this social complex had at its disposal in the space/time present of the then time. This time was approximately seven oh five oh oh oh, seven hundred and five thousand [705,000] of your years ago. (The cycles had begun much, much earlier upon this sphere due to its relative ability to support the first-dimensional life forms at an earlier point in the space/time continuum of your solar system.) These entities were so traumatized by this occurrence that they were in what you may call a social complex knot, or tangle, of fear. Some of your time passed. No one could reach them. No beings could aid them.

Approximately six hundred thousand [600,000] of your years ago, the then-existing members of the Confederation were able to deploy a social memory complex and untie the knot of fear. The entities were then able to recall that they were conscious. This awareness brought them to the point upon what you would call the lower astral planes where they could be nurtured until each mind/body/spirit complex was able, finally, to be healed of this trauma to the extent that each entity was able to examine the distortions it had experienced in the previous life-illusion complex.

After this experience of learn/teaching, the group decision was to place upon itself a type of what you may call karma alleviation. For this purpose they came into incarnation within your planetary sphere in what were not acceptable human forms. This, then, they have been experiencing until the distortions of destruction are replaced by distortions towards the desire for a less distorted vision of service to others.

Since this was the conscious decision of the great majority of those beings in the Maldek experience, the transition to this planet began approximately five hundred thousand [500,000] of your years ago, and the type of body complex available at that time was used.[1]

10.2   **QUESTIONER** Was the body complex available at that time what we refer to as the ape type?

RA That is correct.

10.3   **QUESTIONER** And have any of the Maldek entities transformed now? Are they now still second-density, or are they forming some third-density planet now?

RA The consciousness of these entities has always been third-density. The alleviation mechanism was designed by the placement of this consciousness in second-dimensional physical chemical complexes which are not able to be dexterous or manipulative to the extent which is appropriate to the workings of the third-density distortions of the mind complex.

10.4   **QUESTIONER** Well, have any of these entities moved on now, made a, shall we say, graduation at the end of a seventy-five thousand year cycle and gotten out of the second-density body into third-density-type bodies?

RA I am Ra. Many of these entities were able to remove the accumulation of what you call karma, thus being able to accept a third-density cycle

---

[1]   The dates given in this answer seem to conflict with those given in 21.5.

within a third-density body. Most of those beings so succeeding have incarnated elsewhere in the creation for the succeeding cycle in third density. As this planet reached third density, some few of these entities became able to join the vibration of this sphere in the third-density form. There remain a few who have not yet alleviated, through the mind/body/spirit coordination of distortions, the previous action taken by them. Therefore, they remain.

10.5 **QUESTIONER** Are these the Bigfoot you spoke of?

RA I am Ra. These are one type of Bigfoot.

10.6 **QUESTIONER** Then our present race is formed of a few who originally came from Maldek and quite a few who came from Mars. Are there entities here from other places?

RA I am Ra. There are entities experiencing your time/space continuum who have originated from many, many places, as you would call them, in the creation, for when there is a cycle change those who must repeat then find a planetary sphere appropriate for this repetition. It is somewhat unusual for a planetary mind/body/spirit complex to contain those from many, many various loci, but this explains much, for, you see, you are experiencing the third-dimensional occurrence with a large number of those who must repeat the cycle. The orientation, thus, has been difficult to unify even with the aid of many of your teach/learners.

10.7 **QUESTIONER** When Maldek was destroyed, did all people of Maldek have the problem, or were some advanced enough to transfer to other planets?

RA I am Ra. In the occurrence of planetary dissolution none escaped, for this is an action which redounds to the social complex of the planetary complex itself. None escaped the knot or tangle.

10.8 **QUESTIONER** Is there any danger of this happening to Earth at this time?

RA I am Ra. We feel this evaluation of your planetary mind/body/spirit complex's so-called future may be less than harmless. We say only the conditions of mind exist for such development of technology and such deployment.

It is the distortion of our vision/understanding that the mind and spirit complexes of those of your people need orientation rather than the "toys" needing dismantlement, for are not all things that exist part of the Creator? Therefore, freely to choose is your honor/duty.

10.9 **QUESTIONER** When a graduation occurs and an entity or entities move at the end of a cycle from one planet to another, by what means do they go from one planet to the other?

RA I am Ra. In the scheme of the Creator, the first step of the mind/body/spirit totality beingness is to place its mind/body/spirit complex-distortion in the proper place of love/light. This is done to ensure proper healing of the complex and eventual attunement with the totality-beingness complex. This takes a very variable length of your time/space.

After this is accomplished, the experience of the cycle is dissolved and filtered until only the distillation of distortions in its pure form remains. At this time, the harvested mind/body/spirit totality beingness evaluates the density needs of its beingness and chooses the more appropriate new environment for either a repetition of the cycle or a moving forward into the next cycle. This is the manner of the harvesting, guarded and watched over by many.

10.10 **QUESTIONER** When the entity is moved from one planet to the next, is he moved in thought or in a vehicle?

RA I am Ra. The mind/body/spirit totality beingness is one with the Creator. There is no time/space distortion. Therefore, it is a matter of thinking the proper locus in the infinite array of time/spaces.

10.11 **QUESTIONER** While an entity is incarnate in this third density at this time he may either learn without consciously knowing what he's doing, or he may learn after he is consciously aware that he is learning in the ways of the Law of One. The second way, it is possible for the entity to greatly accelerate his growth. Is not this correct?

RA I am Ra. This is correct.

10.12 **QUESTIONER** Then although many entities are not aware of this, what they really desire is to accelerate their growth, and it is their job to discover this while incarnate. Is it correct that they can accelerate their growth much more while incarnate in third density than in between incarnations of this density?

RA I am Ra. This is correct. We shall attempt to speak upon this concept.

The Law of One has, as one of its primal distortions, the Free Will distortion. Thus each entity is free to accept, reject, or ignore the mind/body/spirit complexes about it and ignore the creation itself. There are many among your social memory complex-distortion who, at this time/space, engage daily, as you would put it, in the working upon the Law of One in one of its primal distortions; that is, the Ways of Love.

However, if this same entity—being biased from the depths of its mind/body/spirit complex towards love/light—were then to accept responsibility for each moment of the time/space accumulation of present moments available to it, such an entity can empower its progress in much the same way as we described the empowering of the call of your social complex-distortion to the Confederation.[2]

10.13 **QUESTIONER** Would you state in a little different way how you empower this call?

RA I am Ra. We understand you to speak now of our previous information. The call begins with one. This call is equal to infinity and is not, as you would say, counted. It is the cornerstone. The second call is added. The third call empowers or doubles the second, and so forth, each additional caller doubling or granting power to all the preceding call. Thus, the call of many of your peoples is many, many-powered and overwhelmingly heard to the infinite reaches of the One Creation.

10.14 **QUESTIONER** For general development of the reader of this book, could you state some of the practices or exercises to perform to produce an acceleration toward the Law of One?

RA I am Ra.

Exercise One. This is the most nearly centered and usable within your illusion complex. The moment contains love. That is the lesson/goal of this illusion or density. The exercise is to consciously seek that love in awareness and understanding-distortions. The first attempt is the cornerstone. Upon this choosing rests the remainder of the life-experience of an entity. The second seeking of love within the moment begins the addition. The third seeking powers the second, the fourth powering or

---

2 Described in 7.3–5.

doubling the third. As with the previous type of empowerment, there will be some loss of power due to flaws within the seeking in the distortion of insincerity. However, the conscious statement of self to self of the desire to seek love is so central an act of will that, as before, the loss of power due to this friction is inconsequential.

Exercise Two. The universe is one being. When a mind/body/spirit complex views another mind/body/spirit complex, see the Creator. This is an helpful exercise.

Exercise Three. Gaze within a mirror. See the Creator.

Exercise Four. Gaze at the creation which lies about the mind/body/spirit complex of each entity. See the Creator.

The foundation or prerequisite of these exercises is a predilection towards what may be called meditation, contemplation, or prayer. With this attitude, these exercises can be processed. Without it, the data will not sink down into the roots of the tree of mind, thus enabling and ennobling the body and touching the spirit.

10.15 **QUESTIONER** I was wondering about the advent of the civilization called Atlantis and Lemuria, the way these civilizations occurred, and where did they come from [*inaudible*] civilizations?

RA I am Ra. This is the last question of this work. The civilizations of Atlantis and Lemuria were not one but two. Let us look first at the Mu entities.

They were beings of a somewhat primitive nature, but those who had very advanced spiritual distortions. The civilization was part of this cycle, experienced early within the cycle at a time of approximately five three oh oh oh, fifty-three thousand [53,000] of your years ago. It was an helpful and harmless place which was washed beneath the ocean during a readjustment of your sphere's tectonic plates through no action of their own.

They set out those who survived and reached many places in what you call Russia, North America, and South America. The Indians of whom you have come to feel some sympathy in your social complex-distortions are the descendants of these entities. Like the other incarnates of this cycle, they came from elsewhere. However, these particular entities were largely drawn from a second-density planet which had some difficulty, due to the age of its sun, in achieving third-density life conditions. This planet was from the galaxy Deneb.

The Atlantean race was a very conglomerate social complex which began to form approximately three one oh oh oh, thirty-one thousand [31,000] years in the past of your space/time continuum illusion. It was a slow-growing and very agrarian society until approximately one five oh oh oh, fifteen thousand [15,000] of your years ago. It reached quickly a high technological understanding which caused it to be able to use intelligent infinity in a less informative manner.

We may add that they used intelligent energy as well, manipulating greatly the natural influxes of the indigo or pineal ray from divine or infinite energy. Thus they were able to create life forms. This they began to do instead of healing and perfecting their own mind/body/spirit complexes, turning their distortions towards what you may call the negative.

Approximately eleven thousand [11,000] of your years ago, the first of the, what you call, wars, caused approximately forty percent of this population to leave the density by means of disintegration of the body. The second and most devastating of the conflicts occurred approximately one oh eight two one, ten thousand eight hundred twenty-one [10,821] years in the past according to your illusion. This created an earth-changing configuration and the large part of Atlantis was no more, having been inundated. Three of the positively oriented of the Atlantean groups left this geographical locus before that devastation, placing themselves in the mountain areas of what you call Tibet, what you call Peru, and what you call Turkey.

Do you have any brief questions before we close this meeting?

10.16 **QUESTIONER** Only one, other than what we can do to make the instrument more comfortable. I have only one other question. I would like to have brief information of the word you use, "galaxy."

RA I am Ra. We use the term known to your people by the sound vibration complex "galaxy." We accept that some galaxies contain one system of planetary and solar groups, others containing several. However, the importance of the locus in infinite time/space dimensionality is so little that we accept the distortion implicit in such an ambiguous term.

10.17 **QUESTIONER** Then would nine planets and our sun we have here in our system, would you refer to that as a solar galaxy?

RA We would not.

10.18 **QUESTIONER** How many stars, approximately, would be in a galaxy?

RA It depends upon the galactic system. Your own, as you know, contains many, many millions of planet entities and star bodies.

10.19 **QUESTIONER** I was just trying to get to the definition you were using for galaxy. You mentioned them a couple of times and it seemed to me that [*inaudible*] what you call a galaxy we call a planetary system. Is there any way to make the instrument more comfortable?

RA I am Ra. This instrument could be made somewhat more comfortable if more support were given the body complex. Other than this, we can only repeat the request to carefully align the symbols used to facilitate this instrument's balance. Our contact is narrow-banded and thus the influx brought in with us must be precise.

I am Ra. I leave you in the love and the light of the One Infinite Creator. Go forth, therefore, rejoicing in the power and the peace of the One Creator. Adonai.

SESSION 11

11.0 **RA** I am Ra. I greet you in the love and the light of the Infinite Creator. I communicate now.

11.1 **QUESTIONER** Should we include the ritual that you have suggested that we use to call you in the book that will result from these sessions?

RA I am Ra. This matter is of small importance, for our suggestion was made for the purpose of establishing contact through this instrument with this group.

11.2 **QUESTIONER** Is it of any assistance to the instrument to have [*name*] and [*name*] present during these sessions? Does the number in the group make any difference in these sessions?

RA I am Ra. The most important of the entities are the questioner and the vibratory sound complex, Jim. The two entities additional aid the instrument's comfort by energizing the instrument with their abilities to share the physical energy complex which is a portion of your love vibration.

11.3 **QUESTIONER** You said yesterday that Maldek was destroyed due to warfare. If Maldek hadn't destroyed itself due to warfare, would it have become a planet that evolved with self-service? And would the entities have increased in density, gone on to, say, the fourth, fifth density in the negative sense or the sense of self-service?

RA I am Ra. The planetary social memory complex, Maldek, had in common with your own sphere the situation of a mixture of energy direction. Thus it, though unknown, would most probably have been a mixed harvest—a few moving to fourth density, a few moving towards fourth density in service to self, the great majority repeating third density. This is approximate due to the fact that parallel possibility/probability vortices cease when action occurs and new probability/possibility vortices are begun.

11.4 **QUESTIONER** Is there a planet behind our sun, opposite to us in orbit, that we do not know about?

RA I am Ra. There is a sphere in the area opposite your sun of a very, very cold nature but large enough to skew certain statistical figures. This sphere should not properly be called a planet as it is locked in first density.

11.5 QUESTIONER You said that entities from Maldek might go to . . . some may go to fourth-density negative. Are there people who go out of our present third density to places in the universe and serve, which are fourth-density self-service or negative type of planets?

RA I am Ra. Your question is unclear. Please restate.

11.6 QUESTIONER As our cycle ends and graduation occurs, is it possible for anyone to go from this third density to a fourth-density planet that is a self-service type, or negative type?

RA I am Ra. We grasp now the specificity of your query. In this harvest the probability/possibility vortex indicates an harvest, though small, of this type. That is correct.

11.7 QUESTIONER Can you tell us what happened to Adolf Hitler?

RA I am Ra. The mind/body/spirit complex known [as] Adolf is at this time in an healing process in the middle astral planes of your spherical force field. This entity was greatly confused and, although aware of the circumstance of change in vibratory level associated with the cessation of the chemical body complex, nevertheless, needed a great deal of care.

11.8 QUESTIONER Is there anyone in our history that is commonly known who went to a fourth-density self-service or negative type planet, or who will go there?

RA I am Ra. The number of entities thus harvested is small. However, a few have penetrated the eighth level, which is only available from the opening up of the seventh through the sixth. Penetration into the eighth, or intelligent infinity, level allows a mind/body/spirit complex to be harvested, if it wishes, at any time/space during the cycle.

11.9 QUESTIONER Are any of these people known in the history of our planet by name?

RA I am Ra. We will mention a few. The one known as Taras Bulba, the one known as Genghis Khan, the one known as Rasputin.

11.10 **QUESTIONER** How did they accomplish this? What was necessary for them to accomplish this?

RA All of the aforementioned entities were aware, through memory, of Atlantean understandings having to do with the use of the various centers of mind/body/spirit complex energy influx in attaining the gateway to intelligent infinity.

11.11 **QUESTIONER** Did this enable them to do what we refer to as magic? Do paranormal things while they were incarnate here?

RA I am Ra. This is correct. The first two entities mentioned made little use of these abilities consciously. However, they were bent single-mindedly upon service to self, sparing no efforts in personal discipline to double, re-double, and so empower this gateway. The third was a conscious adept and also spared no effort in the pursuit of service to self.

11.12 **QUESTIONER** Where are these three entities now?

RA I am Ra. These entities are in the dimension known to you as fourth. Therefore, the space/time continua are not compatible. An approximation of the space/time locus of each would net no actual understanding. Each chose a fourth-density planet which was dedicated to the pursuit of the understanding of the Law of One through service to self: one in what you know as the Orion group, one in what you know as Cassiopeia, one in what you know as Southern Cross. However, these loci are not satisfactory. We do not have vocabulary for the geometric calculations necessary for transfer of this understanding to you.

11.13 **QUESTIONER** Who went to the Orion group?

RA I am Ra. The one known as Genghis Khan.

11.14 **QUESTIONER** What does he presently do there? What is his job or occupation? What does he do?

RA I am Ra. This entity serves the Creator in its own way.

11.15 **QUESTIONER** Is it impossible for you to tell us precisely how he does this service?

RA I am Ra. It is possible for us to speak to this query. However, we use any chance we may have to reiterate the basic understanding/learning that all beings serve the Creator.

The one you speak of as Genghis Khan, at present, is incarnate in a physical light body which has the work of disseminating material of thought control to those who are what you may call crusaders. He is, as you would term this entity, a shipping clerk.

11.16 **QUESTIONER** What do the crusaders do?

RA I am Ra. The crusaders move in their chariots to conquer planetary mind/body/spirit social complexes before they reach the stage of achieving social memory.

11.17 **QUESTIONER** At what stage does a planet achieve social memory?

RA I am Ra. A mind/body/spirit social complex becomes a social memory complex when its entire group of entities are of one orientation or seeking. The group memory lost to the individuals in the roots of the tree of mind then become[s] known to the social complex, thus creating a social memory complex. The advantages of this complex are the relative lack of distortion in understanding the social beingness and the relative lack of distortion in pursuing the direction of seeking, for all understanding-distortions are available to the entities of the society.

11.18 **QUESTIONER** Then we have crusaders from Orion coming to this planet for mind control purposes. How do they do this?

RA As all, they follow the Law of One observing free will. Contact is made with those who call. Those then upon the planetary sphere act much as do you to disseminate the attitudes and philosophy of their particular understanding of the Law of One, which is service to self. These become the elite. Through these, the attempt begins to create a condition whereby the remainder of the planetary entities are enslaved by their own free will.

11.19 **QUESTIONER** Can you name any of the recipients of the crusaders—that is, any names that may be known on the planet today?

RA I am Ra. I am desirous of being in non-violation of the Free Will Distortion. To name those involved in the future of your space/time is to infringe; thus, we withhold this information. We request your contemplation of the fruits of the actions of those entities whom you may observe enjoying the distortion towards power. In this way, you may discern for yourself this information. We shall not interfere with the, shall we say, planetary game. It is not central to the harvest.

11.20 QUESTIONER How do the crusaders pass on their concepts to the incarnate individuals on Earth?

RA I am Ra. There are two main ways, just as there are two main ways of, shall we say, polarizing towards service to others. There are those mind/body/spirit complexes upon your plane who do exercises and perform disciplines in order to seek contact with sources of information and power leading to the opening of the gate to intelligent infinity.

There are others whose vibratory complex is such that this gateway is opened and contact with total service to self, with its primal distortion of manipulation of others, is then afforded with little or no difficulty, no training, and no control.

11.21 QUESTIONER What type of information is passed on from the crusaders to these people?

RA I am Ra. The Orion group passes on information concerning the Law of One with the orientation of service to self. The information can become technical just as some in the Confederation, in attempts to aid this planet in service to others, have provided what you would call technical information. The technology provided by this group is in the form of various means of control or manipulation of others to serve the self.

11.22 QUESTIONER Do you mean, then, that some scientists receive technical information, shall we say, telepathically that comes out then as usable gadgetry?

RA I am Ra. That is correct. However, very positively, as you would call this distortion, oriented so-called scientists have received information intended to unlock peaceful means of progress which redounded unto the last echoes of potential destruction due to further reception of other scientists of a negative orientation-distortion.

11.23 QUESTIONER Is this how we learned of nuclear energy? Was it mixed, both positive and negative orientation?

RA I am Ra. This is correct. The entities responsible for the gathering of the scientists were of a mixed orientation. The scientists were overwhelmingly positive in their orientation. The scientists who followed their work were of mixed orientation including one extremely negative entity, as you would term it.

11.24 **QUESTIONER** Is this extremely negative entity still incarnate on Earth?

RA I am Ra. This is correct.

11.25 **QUESTIONER** Then I assume you can't name him and would ask you where Nikola Tesla got his information?

RA I am Ra. The one known as Nikola received information from Confederation sources desirous of aiding this extremely, shall we say, angelically positive entity in bettering the existence of its fellow mind/body/spirit complexes. It is unfortunate, shall we say, that like many wanderers, the vibratory distortions of third-density illusion caused this entity to become extremely distorted in its perceptions of its fellow mind/body/spirit complexes so that its mission was hindered and, in the result, perverted from its purposes.

11.26 **QUESTIONER** How was Tesla's work supposed to benefit man on Earth, and what were its purposes?

RA I am Ra. The most desired purpose of the mind/body/spirit complex, Nikola, was the freeing of all planetary entities from darkness. Thus, it attempted to give to the planet the infinite energy of the planetary sphere for use in lighting and power.

11.27 **QUESTIONER** By freeing the planetary entities from darkness, precisely what do you mean?

RA I am Ra. [*Ra's reply was not able to be transcribed due to tape recorder malfunction. Following is the gist of their response.*] We intended to speak of freeing those of your planet from literal darkness.

11.28 **QUESTIONER** Would this freeing from darkness be commensurate with the Law of One, or does this have any real product?

RA I am Ra. The product of such a freeing would create two experiences.

Firstly, the experience of no need to find the necessary emolument for payment, in your money, for energy.

Secondly, the leisure afforded, thereby exemplifying the possibility and enhancing the probability of the freedom to then search the self for the beginning of seeking the Law of One.

Few there are working physically from daybreak to darkness, as you name them, upon your plane who can contemplate the Law of One in a conscious fashion.

11.29 **QUESTIONER** What about the Industrial Revolution in general? Was this planned in any way?

RA I am Ra. This will be the final question of this session.

That is correct. Wanderers incarnated in several waves, as you may call them, in order to bring into existence the gradual freeing from the demands of the diurnal cycles and lack of freedom of leisure.

11.30 **QUESTIONER** Well, that was the last question, so I will, as usual, ask if there's anything we can do to make the instrument more comfortable?

RA I am Ra. You are doing well. The most important thing is to carefully align the symbols. The adjustment made this particular time/space present will aid this instrument's physical complex in the distortion towards comfort.

May we ask if you have any short questions which we may resolve before closing the session?

11.31 **QUESTIONER** I don't know if this is a short question or not, so we can save it till next time, but my only question is why the crusaders from Orion do this. What is their ultimate objective? This is probably too long to answer.

RA I am Ra. This is not too long to answer. To serve the self is to serve all. The service of the self, when seen in this perspective, requires an ever-expanding use of the energies of others for manipulation to the benefit of the self with distortion towards power.

If there are further queries to more fully explicate this subject, we shall be with you again.

11.32 **QUESTIONER** Just was one thing I forgot. Is it possible to do another session late today?

RA I am Ra. It is well.

11.33 **QUESTIONER** Thank you.

RA I am Ra. I leave you in the love and the light of the One Infinite Creator. Go forth, then, rejoicing in the power and the peace of the One Creator. Adonai.

12.0   RA   I am Ra. I greet you in the love and the light of the Infinite Creator. I communicate now.

12.1   QUESTIONER   I got a call from Henry Puharich this afternoon. He will be here next month. I want to ask you if it is possible for him to join in our circle and ask questions. And also if Michel D'Obrenovic, who's also known as George Hunt Williamson, happens to come here, would it be all right for him to be in the circle?

RA   I am Ra. These entities, at present, are not properly attuned for the particular work due to vibrational distortions which, in turn, are due to a recent lack of time/space which you call busy-ness. It would be requested that the entities spend a brief time/space in each diurnal cycle of your planet in contemplation. At a future time/space in your continuum, you are requested to ask again.

This group is highly balanced to this instrument's vibratory distortions due to, firstly, contact with the instrument on a day-to-day basis. Secondly, due to contact with the instrument through meditation periods. Thirdly, through a personal mind/body/spirit-complex distortion towards contemplation which in sum causes this group to be effective.

12.2   QUESTIONER   Thank you. Continuing with the previous session, you mentioned that the Orion crusaders came here in chariots. Could you describe a chariot?

RA   I am Ra. The term chariot is a term used in warfare among your peoples. That is its significance. The shape of the Orion craft is one of the following: firstly, the elongated, ovoid shape which is of a darker nature than silver but which has a metallic appearance if seen in the light. In the absence of light, it appears to be red or fiery in some manner.

Other craft include disc-shaped objects of a small nature approximately twelve feet in your measurement in diameter, the box-like shape approximately forty feet to a side in your measurement. Other craft can take on a desired shape through the use of thought control mechanisms. There are various civilization complexes which work within this group. Some are more able to use intelligent infinity than others. The information is very seldom shared; therefore, the chariots vary greatly in shape and appearance.

12.3 **QUESTIONER** Is there any effort by the Confederation to stop the Orion chariots from arriving here?

RA I am Ra. Every effort is made to quarantine this planet. However, the network of Guardians, much like any other pattern of patrols on whatever level, does not hinder each and every entity from penetrating quarantine, for if request is made in light/love, the Law of One will be met with acquiescence. If the request is not made due to the slipping through the net, then there is penetration of this net.

12.4 **QUESTIONER** Who makes this request?

RA I am Ra. Your query is unclear. Please restate.

12.5 **QUESTIONER** I didn't quite understand. How does the Confederation stop the Orion chariot from coming through the quarantine? What actions do . . .

RA I am Ra. There is contact at the level of light-form, or light-body being, depending upon the vibratory level of the Guardian. These Guardians sweep reaches of your earth's energy fields attempting to be aware of any entities approaching. An entity which is approaching is hailed in the name of the One Creator. Any entity thus hailed is bathed in love/light and will of free will obey the quarantine due to the power of the Law of One.

12.6 **QUESTIONER** What would happen to the entity if he did not obey the quarantine after being hailed?

RA I am Ra. To not obey quarantine after being hailed on the level of which we speak would be equivalent to your not stopping upon walking into a solid brick wall.

12.7 **QUESTIONER** What would happen to the entity then if he did this? What'd happen to his chariot?

RA I am Ra. The Creator is one being. The vibratory level of those able to reach the quarantine boundaries is such that, upon seeing the love/light net, it is impossible to break this Law. Therefore, nothing happens. No attempt is made. There is no confrontation.

The only beings who are able to penetrate the quarantine are those who discover windows or distortions in the space/time continua surrounding your planet's energy fields. Through these windows they come. These windows are rare and unpredictable.

12.8 **QUESTIONER** Does this account for what we call the "UFO Flaps" where a large number of UFOs show up like in 1973?

RA I am Ra. This is correct.

12.9 **QUESTIONER** Well then, are most of the UFOs which are seen in our skies from the Orion group?

RA I am Ra. Many of those seen in your skies are of the Orion group. They send out messages. Some are received by those who are oriented towards service to others. These messages then are altered to be acceptable to those entities while warning of difficulties ahead. This is the most that self-serving entities can do when faced with those whose wish is to serve others. The contacts which the [Orion] group finds most helpful to their cause are those contacts made with entities whose orientation is towards service to self.

There are many thought-form entities in your skies which are of a positive nature and are the projections of the Confederation. Other sightings are due to the inadvertent visualization by your peoples' optical mechanisms of your own government's weaponry.

12.10 **QUESTIONER** Which group was it that contacted Henry Puharich in Israel, right around 1972?

RA I am Ra. We must refrain from answering this query due to the possibility/probability that the one you call Henry will read this answer. This would cause distortions in his future. It is necessary that each being use free and complete discernment from within the all-self which is at the heart of the mind/body/spirit complex.

12.11 **QUESTIONER** Does that also apply to answering who was contacting the group that I originally was in, in 1962?

RA I am Ra. This query may be answered. The group contacted was the Confederation.

12.12 **QUESTIONER** Did they have any of their craft in our area at that time?

RA I am Ra. There was no craft. There was a thought-form.

12.13 **QUESTIONER** You mentioned the Orion crusaders, when they do get through the net, give both technical and non-technical information. We know what you mean by technical information, but what type of non-technical information do they give to those they contact? Am I right in assuming that this is all done by telepathic communication?

RA I am Ra. This is correct. Through telepathy, the philosophy of the Law of One with the distortion of service to self is promulgated. In advanced groups, there are rituals and exercises given, and these have been written down just as the service-to-others oriented entities have written down the promulgated philosophy of their teachers. The philosophy concerns the service of manipulating others that they may experience service towards the other-self, thus through this experience becoming able to appreciate service to self. These entities thus would become oriented towards service to self and in turn manipulate yet others so that they, in turn, might experience the service towards the other-self.

12.14 **QUESTIONER** Would this be the origin of what we call black magic?

RA I am Ra. This is correct in one sense, incorrect in another. The Orion group has aided the so-called negatively oriented among your mind/body/spirit complexes. These same entities would be concerning themselves with service to self in any case, and there are many upon your so-called inner planes which are negatively oriented and thus available as inner teachers, or guides, and so-called possessors of certain souls who seek this distortion of service to self.

12.15 **QUESTIONER** Is it possible for an entity here on Earth to be so confused as to call both the Confederation and the Orion group in an alternating way, one, then the other, [*inaudible*] back to [*inaudible*]?

RA I am Ra. It is entirely possible for the untuned channel, as you call that service, to receive both positive and negative communications. If the entity at the base of its confusion is oriented towards service to others, the entity will begin to receive messages of doom. If the entity at the base of the complex of beingness is oriented towards service to self, the crusaders, who in this case do not find it necessary to lie, will simply begin to give the philosophy they are here to give.

Many of your so-called contacts among your people have been confused and self-destructive because the channels were oriented towards service to others, but in the desire for proof were open to the lying information of the crusaders who then were able to neutralize the effectiveness of the channel.

12.16 **QUESTIONER** Are most of these crusaders fourth-density?

RA I am Ra. There is a majority of fourth-density. That is correct.

12.17 **QUESTIONER** Does an individual in the fourth density normally appear, or are they normally invisible to us?

RA I am Ra. The use of the word "normal" is one which befuddles the meaning of the question. Let us rephrase for clarity. The fourth density is, by choice, not visible to third density. It is possible for fourth density to be visible. However, it is not the choice of the fourth-density entity to be visible due to the necessity for concentration upon a rather difficult vibrational complex which is the third density you experience.

12.18 **QUESTIONER** Are there any Confederation or Orion individuals living on Earth visible to us and important in our society at this time? Walking among us?

RA I am Ra. There are no entities of either group walking among you at this time. However, the crusaders of Orion use two types of entities to do their bidding, shall we say. The first type is a thought-form; the second, a kind of robot.

12.19 **QUESTIONER** Could you describe the robot?

RA I am Ra. The robot may look like any other being. It is a construct.

12.20 **QUESTIONER** Is the robot what is normally called "Men in Black?"

RA I am Ra. This is incorrect.

12.21 **QUESTIONER** Who are the Men in Black?

RA I am Ra. The Men in Black are a thought-form type of entity which have some beingness to their make-up. They have certain physical characteristics given them. However, their true vibrational nature is without third-density vibrational characteristics, and therefore they are able to materialize and dematerialize when necessary.

12.22 **QUESTIONER** Are all of these Men in Black then used by the Orion crusaders?

RA I am Ra. This is correct.

12.23 **QUESTIONER** If one were to visit me, and I grabbed him and locked him in a closet, could I keep him, or would he disappear?

RA I am Ra. It depends upon which type of entity you grab. You are perhaps able to perceive a construct. The construct might be kept for a brief period, although these constructs also have an ability to disappear. The programming on these constructs, however, makes it more difficult to remotely control them. You would not be able to grapple with a thought-form entity of the Men in Black, as you call it, type.

12.24 **QUESTIONER** Would this be against the Law of One, and I would be making a mistake by grabbing these entities?

RA I am Ra. There are no mistakes under the Law of One.

12.25 **QUESTIONER** What I'm saying is, would I be polarizing more toward self-service or toward service for others when I did this act of locking up the thought-form or construct?

RA I am Ra. You may consider that question for yourself. We interpret the Law of One, but not to the extent of advice.

12.26 **QUESTIONER** Thank you. Well, you spoke of wanderers. Who are wanderers? Where do they come from?

RA I am Ra. Imagine, if you will, the sands of your shores. As countless as the grains of sand are the sources of intelligent infinity.

When a social memory complex has achieved its complete understanding of its desire, it may conclude that its desire is service to others with the distortion towards reaching their hand, figuratively, to any entities who call for aid. These entities, whom you may call the Brothers and Sisters of Sorrow, move towards this calling of sorrow. These entities are from all reaches of the infinite creation and are bound together by the desire to serve in this distortion.

12.27 **QUESTIONER** How many of them are incarnate on Earth now?

RA I am Ra. The number is approximate due to an heavy influx of those birthed at this time due to an intensive need to lighten the planetary vibration and thus aid in harvest. The number approaches sixty-five million.

12.28 **QUESTIONER** Are most of these from the fourth density? What density do they come from?

RA I am Ra. Few there are of fourth density. The largest number of wanderers, as you call them, are of the sixth density. The desire to serve must be distorted towards a great deal of purity of mind and what you may call foolhardiness or bravery, depending upon your distortion complex judgment. The challenge/danger of the wanderer is that it will forget its mission, become karmically involved, and thus be swept into the maelstrom from which it had incarnated to aid the destruction.[1]

12.29 **QUESTIONER** What could one of these entities do to become karmically involved? Could you give us an example?

RA I am Ra. An entity which acts in a consciously unloving manner in action with other beings can become karmically involved.

12.30 **QUESTIONER** I just had a thought. Do any of these wanderers have physical ailments in this earth situation?

RA I am Ra. Due to the extreme variance between the vibratory distortions of third density and those of the more dense densities, if you will, wanderers have, as a general rule, some form of handicap, difficulty, or feeling of alienation which is severe. The most common of these difficulties are alienation, the reaction against the planetary vibration by personality disorders, as you would call them, and body complex ailments indicating difficulty in adjustment to the planetary vibrations such as allergies, as you would call them.

12.31 **QUESTIONER** Is there a best way for these entities to heal themselves of their physical ailments?

---

[1] This final sentence seems to have been confused in transmission. It's possible Ra intended to say something similar to: "The challenge/danger of the wanderer is that it will forget its mission, become karmically involved, and thus be swept into the maelstrom [into] which it had incarnated [in order] to [prevent] the destruction."

RA I am Ra. This will be the last complete question of this time/space.

The self-healing distortion is effected through realization of the intelligent infinity resting within. This is blocked in some way in those who are not perfectly balanced in bodily complexes. The blockage varies from entity to entity. It requires the conscious awareness of the spiritual nature of reality, if you will, and the corresponding pourings of this reality into the individual mind/body/spirit complex for healing to take place.

We will use this instrument as example. The portions of its ailment, as you call this distortion complex, that can be perfected in balance are due primarily to a blockage of the indigo-ray, or pineal, energy center. This center receives the intelligent energy from all sources lawful within the One Creation; that is, lawful in this third-density distortion or illusion. If there is no blockage, these energies pour or stream down into the mind/body/spirit complex, perfecting, moment by moment, the individual's body complex.

This instrument also experiences some distortion of the green-ray energy center which you may call the heart center. It is overly open due to an intensive desire-distortion on the part of this mind/body/spirit complex towards service to others, or as you may call it, universal love. This entity, therefore, spends itself without regard to its reserves of mind/body/spirit-complex distortion in regard to what you call strength or energy. This distortion is primarily due to the blockage of the indigo ray, as we have said before. The misapprehension-distortion of the instrument responsible for this blockage is the basic orientation towards a belief in unworthiness. The unworthiness-distortion blocks the free flow of intelligent energy.

The seventh, or violet, ray is unimpaired, this being not only an energy receptor but a sum total of the vibratory level of the individual. The other energy centers are also quite clear. The solution to healing in this case is action that puts into practice the peaceful understanding, in humility-distortion, that the entity is one with the Creator, therefore perfected and not separate. In each case of what you would call ill health, one or more of these energy centers is blocked. The intelligence of the mind/body/spirit complex needs, then, to be alerted either by the self as healer or by the catalyst of another healer, as we have said before.

Is there a short question before we close this session?

12.32 **QUESTIONER** Is it possible for you to tell us if any of the three of us are and have been wanderers?

RA I am Ra. In scanning each of the mind/body/spirit complexes present, we find an already complete assurance of this occurrence and, therefore, find no harm in recapitulating this occurrence. Each of those present are wanderers pursuing a mission, if you will.

12.33 **QUESTIONER** Thank you. Is there anything that we can do to make the instrument more comfortable?

RA I am Ra. We ask you to realign the object upon which the symbols sit. It is not a significant distortion for one session only, but you will find upon measuring the entire assemblage that the resting place is one point four degrees [1.4°] from the correct alignment, the resting place an additional one-half degree [0.5°] away from proper orientation. Do not concern yourselves overly with this in the space/time nexus present, but do not allow these distortions to remain over a long period or the contact will be gradually impaired.

I am Ra. I leave you in the love and in the light of the One Infinite Creator. Go forth, rejoicing in the power and the peace of the One Creator. Adonai.

SESSION 13

JANUARY 29, 1981

13.0   **RA** I am Ra. I greet you in the love and the light of the Infinite Creator. I communicate now.

13.1   **QUESTIONER** First thing I would like to do is apologize for the stupid questions that I've asked while searching for what we should do. I consider what we are doing a great honor and privilege to be also humble messengers of the Law of One, and at this time believe that the way to prepare this book is to start at the beginning of creation following the evolution of man, and the evolution of man on Earth, to the best of my [*inaudible*], at all times investigating how the Law of One was used [*inaudible*]. I think also that . . . that I need to finish the book. . . let the material that we have already carry the end of the book. [*inaudible*]

I would also suggest the title of the book, *The Law of One*. I'd like to state as the author, Ra. Would you agree to this?

RA I am Ra. Your query is unclear. Would you please state as separate queries each area of agreement?

13.2   **QUESTIONER** First, I'd like to start at the beginning of creation, as far back as we can go, and follow the development of man to the present time. Is this agreeable?

RA I am Ra. This is completely your discernment/understanding/ decision.

13.3   **QUESTIONER** Secondly, I would like to title the book *The Law of One*, by Ra. Is this agreeable?[1]

RA I am Ra. The title of the book is acceptable. The authorship by vibratory sound complex Ra is, in our distortion of understanding, incomplete. We are messengers.

---

[1] The original transcripts from the cassette recordings were published in four books under the title, *The Law of One*. (A fifth book containing fragments omitted from Books I–IV, along with accompanying commentary from Carla and Jim, was published years later in 1998.) See "The Relistening Report" at the end of this book for information about how the new transcripts were produced and consequently this book, *The Ra Contact*, published.

13.4 **QUESTIONER** Can you state who then should author the book?

RA I can only request that if your discernment/understanding suggests the use of this vibratory sound complex, Ra, the phrase "An humble messenger of the Law of One" be appended.

13.5 **QUESTIONER** Thank you. Can you tell me of the earliest, first known thing in the creation?

RA I am Ra. The first known thing in the creation is infinity. The infinity is creation.

13.6 **QUESTIONER** From this infinity then must have come what we experience as creation. What was the next step or the next evolvement?

RA I am Ra. Infinity became aware. This was the next step.

13.7 **QUESTIONER** After this, what happened?

RA Awareness led to the focus of infinity into infinite energy. You have called this by various vibrational sound complexes, the most common to your ears being "Logos" or "Love." The Creator is the focusing of infinity as an aware or conscious principle called by us, as closely as we can create understanding/learning in your language, intelligent infinity.

13.8 **QUESTIONER** Can you state the next step?

RA The next step is still, at this space/time nexus in your illusion, achieving its progression as you may see it in your illusion. The next step is an infinite reaction to the Creative Principle following the Law of One in one of its primal distortions, freedom of will. Thus many, many dimensions, infinite in number, are possible.

The energy moves from the intelligent infinity due, first, to the outpouring of randomized creative force, this then creating patterns which, in holographic style, appear as the entire creation no matter which direction or energy is explored. These patterns of energy begin then to regularize their own local, shall we say, rhythms and fields of energy, thus creating dimensions and universes.

13.9 **QUESTIONER** Then can you tell me how the galaxy and this planetary system were formed?

RA I am Ra. You must imagine a great leap of thought in this query, for at the last query the physical, as you call it, universes were not yet born.

The energies moved in increasingly intelligent patterns until the individualization of various energies emanating from the Creative Principle of intelligent infinity became such as to be co-Creators. Thus the so-called physical matter began. The concept of Light is instrumental in grasping this great leap of thought, as this vibrational distortion of infinity is the building block of that which is known as matter, the Light being intelligent and full of energy, thus being the first distortion of intelligent infinity which was called by the Creative Principle.

This Light of Love was made to have in its occurrences of being certain characteristics, among them the infinite whole paradoxically described by the straight line, as you would call it. This paradox is responsible for the shape of the various physical illusion entities you call solar systems, galaxies, and planets, all revolving and tending towards the lenticular.

13.10 **QUESTIONER** I think I made an error in asking that question, getting ahead of the process that you were describing. Would it be helpful to fill in that great leap that I mistakenly made?

RA I am Ra. I attempted to bridge the gap. However, you may question me in any manner you deem appropriate.

13.11 **QUESTIONER** Could you tell me . . . taking the question previous to the one that I asked about galaxy and planets, would you tell me the next step that occurred after that step?

RA I am Ra. The steps, as you call them, are, at the point of question, simultaneous and infinite.

13.12 **QUESTIONER** Could you tell me how intelligent infinity became, shall we say—I'm having difficulty with some of the language—how intelligent infinity became individualized from itself?

RA I am Ra. This is an appropriate question.

The intelligent infinity discerned a concept. This concept was discerned due to freedom of will of awareness. This concept was finity. This was the first and primal paradox or distortion of the Law of One. Thus the one intelligent infinity invested itself in an exploration of many-ness. Due to the infinite possibilities of intelligent infinity, there is no ending to many-ness. The exploration, thus, is free to continue infinitely in an eternal present.

13.13 **QUESTIONER** Was the galaxy that we are in created by the infinite intelligence, or was it created by a portion of the individualized infinite intelligence?

RA I am Ra. The galaxy, and all other things of material of which you are aware, are products of individualized portions of intelligent infinity. As each exploration began, it, in turn, found its focus and became co-Creator. Using intelligent infinity, each portion created an universe, and—allowing the rhythms of free choice to flow, playing with the infinite spectrum of possibilities—each individualized portion channeled the love/light into what you might call intelligent energy, thus creating the so-called natural laws of any particular universe.

Each universe, in turn, individualized to a focus, becoming, in turn, co-Creator, and allowing further diversity, thus creating further intelligent energies, regularizing or causing natural laws to appear in the vibrational patterns of what you would call a solar system. Thus, each solar system has its own, shall we say, local coordinate system of illusory natural laws.

It shall be understood that any portion, no matter how small, of any density or illusory pattern contains, as in an holographic picture, the One Creator which is infinity. Thus all begins and ends in mystery.

13.14 **QUESTIONER** Could you tell me how the individualized portion of intelligent infinity created our galaxy [*inaudible*] that the same portion created our planetary system and, if so, how this came about?

RA I am Ra. We may have misperceived your query. We were under the distortion/impression that we had responded to this particular query. Would you restate the query?

13.15 **QUESTIONER** Primarily, then, how the, shall we say, the planetary system that we are in now evolved—was it all created at once, or was there first our sun created and this [*inaudible*] was created?

RA I am Ra. The process is from the larger, in your illusion, to the smaller. Thus the co-Creator, individualizing the galaxy, created energy patterns which then focused in multitudinous focuses of further conscious awareness of intelligent infinity. Thus, the solar system of which you experience inhabitation is of its own patterns, rhythms, and so-called natural laws which are unique to itself. However, the progression is from the galaxy spiraling energy, to the solar spiraling energy, to the planetary spiraling energy, to the experiential circumstances of spiraling energy which begin the first density of awareness, or consciousness, of planetary entities.

13.16 **QUESTIONER** Could you tell me about this first density of planetary entities?

RA I am Ra. Each step recapitulates intelligent infinity in its discovery of awareness. In a planetary environment, all begins in what you would call chaos, energy undirected and random in its infinity. Slowly, in your terms of understanding, there forms a focus of self-awareness. Thus the Logos moves. Light comes to form the darkness according to the co-Creator's patterns and vibratory rhythms, so constructing a certain type of experience.

This begins with first density which is the density of consciousness, the mineral and water life upon the planet learning from fire and wind the awareness of being. This is the first density.

13.17 **QUESTIONER** Does this first density then progress to greater awareness?

RA The spiraling energy, which is the characteristic of what you call light, moves in straight-line spiral, thus giving spirals an inevitable vector upwards to a more comprehensive beingness with regards to intelligent infinity. Thus, first dimensional beingness strives towards the second-density lessons of a type of awareness which includes growth rather than dissolution or random change.

13.18 **QUESTIONER** Could you define what you mean by growth?

RA I am Ra. Picture, if you will, the difference between first-vibrational mineral or water life and the lower second-density beings which begin to move about within and upon its being. This movement is the characteristic of second density, the striving towards light and growth.

13.19 **QUESTIONER** By striving toward light, what do you mean?

RA I am Ra. A very simplistic example of second-density growth striving towards light is that of the leaf striving towards the source of light.

13.20 **QUESTIONER** Is there any physical difference between first and second density? For instance, if I could see a second-density planet and a first-density planet side by side, in my present condition, could I see both of them? Would they be both visible?

RA I am Ra. This is correct. All of the octave of your densities would be clearly visible were not the fourth through the seventh freely choosing not to be visible.

13.21 QUESTIONER Then how does the second density progress to the third?

RA I am Ra. The second density strives towards the third density, which is the density of self-consciousness, or self-awareness. The striving takes place through the higher second-density forms who are invested by third-density beings with an identity to the extent that they become self-aware mind/body complexes, thus becoming mind/body/spirit complexes and entering third density, the first density of consciousness of spirit.

13.22 QUESTIONER What is the density level of our planet Earth at this time?

RA I am Ra. The sphere upon which you dwell is third density in its beingness of mind/body/spirit complexes. It is now in a space/time continuum, fourth density. This is causing a somewhat difficult harvest.

13.23 QUESTIONER How does a third-density planet become a fourth-density?

RA I am Ra. This will be the last full question.

The fourth density is, as we have said, as regularized in its approach as the striking of a clock upon the hour. The space/time of your solar system has enabled this planetary sphere to spiral into space/time of a different vibrational configuration. This causes the planetary sphere to be able to be molded by these new distortions. However, the thought-forms of your people during this transition period are such that the mind/body/spirit complexes of both individual and societies are scattered throughout the spectrum instead of becoming able to grasp the needle, shall we say, and point the compass in one direction.

Thus, the entry into the vibration of love, sometimes called by your people the vibration of understanding, is not effective with the present societal complex. Thus, the harvest shall be such that many will repeat the third-density cycle. The energies of your wanderers, your teachers, and your adepts at this time are all bent upon increasing the harvest. However, there are few to harvest.

13.24 **QUESTIONER** I would like to apologize for asking sometimes wrong or inappropriate questions. It's difficult sometimes to ask precisely the right question. I don't wish to go over any ground that we've already covered. I notice this period is slightly shorter than previous periods. Is there a reason for this?

RA I am Ra. This instrument's vital energy is somewhat low.

13.25 **QUESTIONER** I am assuming from this that it would be a good idea not to have another session today. Is this correct?

RA I am Ra. It is well to have a session later if it is acceptable that we monitor this instrument and cease using it when it becomes low in the material which we take from it. We do not wish to deplete this instrument.

13.26 **QUESTIONER** This is always acceptable in any session. I will ask my final question. Is there anything that we can do to make the instrument more comfortable or facilitate these communications?

RA I am Ra. It is well. Each is most conscientious. Continue in the same. Is there any other short query?

13.27 **QUESTIONER** Tom Flaherty will be here this evening and will be helping in the evening session. Is this all right?

RA I am Ra. This is correct.

I am Ra. I leave you in the love and the light of the One Infinite Creator. Go forth, therefore, rejoicing in the power and the peace of the One Creator. Adonai.

SESSION 14

14.0   **RA** I am Ra. I greet you in the love and the light of the Infinite Creator. We communicate now.

14.1   **QUESTIONER** Going back over this morning's work, [*inaudible*]. You said the second density strives towards the third density, which is the density of self-consciousness, or self-awareness. The striving takes place through higher second-density forms invested by third-density beings. Could you explain what you mean by this?

RA I am Ra. Much as you would put on a vestment, so do your third-density beings invest or clothe some second-density beings with self-awareness. This is often done through the opportunity of what you call pets. It has also been done by various other means of investiture. These include many so-called religious practice complexes which personify and send love to various natural second-density beings in their group form.

14.2   **QUESTIONER** When this earth was second-density, how did the second-density beings on this earth become so invested?

RA There was not this type of investment as spoken but the simple third-density investment which is the line of spiraling light calling distortion upward from density to density. The process takes longer when there is no investment made by incarnate third-density beings.

14.3   **QUESTIONER** Then what was the second-density form—what did it look like—that became earth-man in the third density? What did he look like in the second density?

RA I am Ra. The difference between second- and third-density bodily forms would in many cases have been more like one to the other. In the case of your planetary sphere the process was interrupted by those who incarnated here from the planetary sphere you call Mars. They were adjusted by genetic changing and, therefore, there was some difference which was of a very noticeable variety rather than the gradual raising of the bipedal forms upon your second-density level to third-density level. This has nothing to do with the so-called placement of the soul. This has only to do with the circumstances of the influx of those from that culture.

14.4 **QUESTIONER** I understand from previous material that this occurred 75,000 years ago. Then it was our third-density process of evolution began. Can you tell me the history, hitting only the points of development, shall I say, that occurred within this 75,000 years, any particular times or points where the attempts were made to increase the development of this third density?

RA I am Ra. The first attempt to aid your peoples was at the time seven five oh oh oh [75,000]. This attempt, seventy-five thousand [75,000] of your years ago, has been previously described by us.[1]

The next attempt was approximately five eight oh oh oh, fifty-eight thousand [58,000] of your years ago, continuing for a long period in your measurement, with those of Mu, as you call this race, or mind/body/spirit social complex.

The next attempt was long in coming and occurred approximately thirteen thousand [13,000] of your years ago when some intelligent information was offered to those of Atlantis, this being of the same type of healing and crystal working of which we have spoken previously.[2]

The next attempt was one one oh oh oh, eleven thousand [11,000], of your years ago. These are approximations as we are not totally able to process your space/time continuum measurement system. This was in what you call Egypt, and of this we have also spoken.[3]

The same beings which came with us returned approximately three five oh oh [3,500] years later in order to attempt to aid the South American mind/body/spirit social complex once again. However, the pyramids of those so-called cities were not to be used in the appropriate fashion. Therefore, this was not pursued further.

There was a landing approximately three oh oh oh, three thousand [3,000], of your years ago also in your South America, as you call it. There were a few attempts to aid your peoples approximately two three oh oh [2,300] years ago, this in the area of Egypt.[4] The remaining part of

---

[1] Previously described in 9.6–12.

[2] Spoken previously in 2.2–3.

[3] Also spoken in 2.2.

[4] This has been corrected by Ra to 3,300 years ago in session 17.

the cycle, we have never been gone from your fifth dimension and have been working in this last minor cycle to prepare for harvest.

14.5 **QUESTIONER** Was the Egyptian visit of 11,000 years ago the only one where you actually walked the earth?

RA I am Ra. I understand your question distorted in the direction of selves rather than other-selves. We of the vibratory sound complex, Ra, have walked among you only at that time.

14.6 **QUESTIONER** I understood you to say in an earlier session that pyramids were built to ring the earth. How many pyramids were built?

RA I am Ra. There are six balancing pyramids and five two, fifty-two [52] others built for additional healing and initiatory work among your mind/body/spirit social complexes.

14.7 **QUESTIONER** What is a balancing pyramid?

RA I am Ra. Imagine, if you will, the many force fields of the earth in their geometrically precise web. Energies stream into the earth planes, as you would call them, from magnetically determined points. Due to growing thought-form distortions in understanding of the Law of One, the planet itself was seen to have the potential for imbalance. The balancing pyramidal structures were charged with crystals which drew the appropriate balance from the energy forces streaming into the various geometrical centers of electromagnetic energy which surround and shape the planetary sphere.

14.8 **QUESTIONER** Let me make a synopsis and you tell me if I am correct. All of these visits for the last 75,000 years were for the purpose of giving to the people of Earth an understanding of the Law of One, and this way allow them to progress upward through the fourth, fifth, sixth densities. This was to be a service to Earth. The pyramids were used also in giving the Law of One in their own way. The balancing pyramids, I'm not quite sure of. Am I right so far?

RA I am Ra. You are correct to the limits of the precision allowed by language.

14.9 **QUESTIONER** Did the balancing pyramid cause the earth from changing its axis?

RA I am Ra. This query is not clear. Please restate.

14.10 **QUESTIONER** Does the balancing refer to balancing of the individual who is initiated in the pyramid, or does it refer to the physical balancing of the earth on its axis in space?

RA I am Ra. The balancing pyramidal structures could [be] and were used for individual initiation. However, the use of these pyramids was also designed for the balancing of the planetary energy web.

The other pyramids are not placed properly for earth healing but for healing of mind/body/spirit complexes. It came to our attention that your density was distorted towards, what is called by our distortion-understanding of third density, a premature aging process. We were attempting to aid in giving the mind/body/spirit complexes of third density on your planetary sphere more of a time/space continuum in one incarnation pattern in order to have a fuller opportunity to learn/teach the Laws, or Ways, of the primal distortion of the Law of One which is Love.

14.11 **QUESTIONER** I will make this statement. You can tell me if I am correct. The way I understand it, the balancing pyramids were to do what we call increase the life span of entities here so that they would gain more wisdom of the Law of One while in the physical at one time. Is this correct?

RA I am Ra. This is correct. However, the pyramids not called by us by the vibrational sound complex, balancing pyramids, were more numerous and were used exclusively for the above purpose and the teach/learning of healers to charge and enable these processes.

14.12 **QUESTIONER** George Van Tassel built a machine in our western desert called an "Integratron." Will this machine work for that purpose of increasing the life span?

RA I am Ra. The machine is incomplete and will not function for the above-mentioned purpose.

14.13 **QUESTIONER** Who gave George the information on how to build it?

RA I am Ra. There were two contacts which gave the entity with vibratory sound complex, George, this information. One was of the

Confederation. The second was of the Orion group. The Confederation was caused to find the distortion towards non-contact due to the alteration of the vibrational mind complex patterns of the one called George. Thus, the Orion group used this instrument; however, this instrument, though confused, was a mind/body/spirit complex devoted at the heart to service to others, so the, shall we say, worst that could be done was to discredit this source.

14.14 **QUESTIONER** Would there be any value to the people of this planet now, at this time, to complete this machine?

RA I am Ra. The harvest is now. There is not at this time any reason to include efforts along these distortions towards longevity, but rather to encourage distortions toward seeking the heart of self, for this which resides clearly in the violet-ray energy field will determine the harvesting of each mind/body/spirit complex.

14.15 **QUESTIONER** Going back to the start of this 75,000-year period, there was the harvesting 25,000 years after the start, which would make it 50,000 years ago, I would assume. Can you tell me how many were harvested from our planet at that time?

RA I am Ra. The harvest was none.

14.16 **QUESTIONER** There was no harvest? What about 25,000 years ago? Was there a harvest then?

RA I am Ra. A harvesting began taking place in the latter portion, as you measure time/space, of the second cycle, with individuals finding the gateway to intelligent infinity. The harvest of that time, though extremely small, were those entities of extreme distortion towards service to the entities which now were to repeat the major cycle. These entities, therefore, remained in third density although they could, at any moment/present nexus, leave this density through use of intelligent infinity.

14.17 **QUESTIONER** Then the harvest 25,000 years ago, the entities who could have been harvested to the fourth density remained here in service to this planetary population. Is this correct?

RA I am Ra. This is correct. Thus, there was no harvest, but there were harvestable entities who shall choose the manner of their entrance into fourth dimension.

14.18 **QUESTIONER** Then for the last 2,300 years[5] you have been actively working to create as large a harvest as possible at the end of the total 75,000-year cycle. Can you state with respect to the Law of One why you do this, just as a statement of your reasons for this?

RA I am Ra. I speak for the social memory complex termed Ra. We came among you to aid you. Our efforts in service were perverted. Our desire then is to eliminate, as far as possible, the distortions caused by those misreading our information and guidance.

The general cause of service such as the Confederation offers is that of the primal distortion of the Law of One, which is service. The One Being of the creation is like unto a body, if you will accept this third-density analogy. Would we ignore a pain in the leg? A bruise upon the skin? A cut which is festering? No. There is no ignoring a call. We, the entities of sorrow, choose as our service the attempt to heal the sorrow which we are calling analogous to the pains of a physical body complex distortion.

14.19 **QUESTIONER** At what density level is Ra?

RA I am Ra. I am sixth density with a strong seeking towards seventh density. The harvest for us will be in only approximately two and one-half million of your years, and it is our desire to be ready for harvest as it approaches in our space/time continuum.

14.20 **QUESTIONER** And you ready yourselves for harvest through the best service you can provide. Is this correct?

RA This is correct. We offer the Law of One, the solving of paradoxes, the balancing of love/light and light/love.

14.21 **QUESTIONER** How long is one of your cycles?

RA I am Ra. One of our cycles computes to seven five oh, oh oh oh, oh oh oh [750,000,000], seven five million [75,000,000] of your years.[6]

---

5 This has been corrected by Ra to 3,300 years ago in session 17.

6 When Ra first recites the digits for this number they indicate 750 million, but then they state the number as 75 million. Don seeks clarification in the next question.

14.22 **QUESTIONER** 75 million?

RA That is correct.

14.23 **QUESTIONER** In your service in giving the Law of One, do you work with any planets other than the Earth at this time, or just Earth?

RA I am Ra. We work only with this planetary sphere at this time.

14.24 **QUESTIONER** You stated that you were called by 352,000 Earth entities. Does this mean that this number is the number who will understand and accept the Law of One? Am I correct?

RA I am Ra. We cannot estimate the correctness of your statement, for those who call are not in every case able to understand the answer to their calling. Moreover, those who were not calling previously may, with great trauma, discover the answers to the call nearly simultaneously with their late call. There is no time/space in call. Therefore, we cannot estimate the number of your mind/body/spirit complexes which will, in your space/time-continuum distortion, hear and understand.

14.25 **QUESTIONER** How do you perform your normal service? How have you normally given the Law of One over the last 2,300 years?[7] How have you normally given this to Earth people?

RA I am Ra. We have used channels such as this one, but in most cases the channels feel inspired by dreams and visions without being aware, consciously, of our identity or existence. This particular group has been accentuatedly trained to recognize such contact. This makes this group able to be aware of a focal, or vibrational, source of information.

14.26 **QUESTIONER** When you contact the entities in their dreams and otherwise, these entities, I assume, have to be first seeking in the direction of the Law of One. Is this correct?

RA I am Ra. This is correct. For example, the entities of the nation of Egypt were in a state of pantheism, as you may call the distortion towards separate worship of various portions of the Creator. We were able to contact one whose orientation was towards the One.

---

[7] This has been corrected by Ra to 3,300 years ago in session 17.

14.27 **QUESTIONER** The trauma—I'll just call it that—I assume this will, as the cycle ends, have some inconvenience [*inaudible*]. There will be some entities who start seeking or get catalicized, you might say, into seeking because of the trauma and will then maybe hear your words through possibly telepathy or written material such as we will publish as this book.

RA I am Ra. You are correct except in understanding that the inconveniences have begun.

14.28 **QUESTIONER** Can you tell me who was responsible for transmitting the book *Oahspe*?

RA I am Ra. This was transmitted by one of Confederation social memory complex status whose idea, as offered to the Council, was to use some of the known physical history of the so-called religions, or religious distortions, of your cycle in order to veil and partially unveil aspects or primal distortions of the Law of One. All names can be taken to be created for their vibrational characteristics. The information buried within has to do with a deeper understanding of love and light and the attempts of infinite intelligence through many messengers to teach/learn those entities of your sphere.

14.29 **QUESTIONER** Have there been any other books that you can name that are available for this purpose that have been given by the Confederation?

RA I am Ra. We cannot share this information, for it would distort your discernment patterns in your future. You may ask about a particular volume.

14.30 **QUESTIONER** *The Urantia Book*, which I haven't read. Who gave that?

RA I am Ra. This was given by a series of discarnate entities of your own Earth planes, the so-called inner planes. This material is not passed by the Council.

14.31 **QUESTIONER** The Edgar Cayce material. Who spoke through Edgar Cayce?

RA I am Ra. No entity spoke through Edgar Cayce.

14.32 **QUESTIONER** Where did the information come from that Edgar Cayce channeled?

RA I am Ra. We have explained before that the intelligent infinity is brought into intelligent energy from eighth density, or the octave.[8] The one, vibratory sound complex called Edgar, used this gateway to view the present, which is not the continuum you experience but the potential social memory complex of this planetary sphere. The term your peoples have used for this is the "Akashic Record" or the "Hall of Records." This is the last question which you may now ask.

14.33 **QUESTIONER** Is there anything that we can do to make the instrument more comfortable or help during the transmission?

RA I am Ra. We only reiterate the importance of alignment. This instrument is placed point two degrees [0.2°] away from the direction of the resting place, which is correct. This may be "eyed," shall we say, by sight and the instrument reminded. You are being conscientious. Is there any brief question we may answer before this session is closed?

14.34 **QUESTIONER** Can you tell me if we are accomplishing our effort reasonably well?

RA I am Ra. The Law is One. There are no mistakes.

I am Ra. I leave this instrument in the love and the light of the One Infinite Creator. Go forth, therefore, rejoicing in the power and the peace of the One Creator. Adonai.

---

[8] Explained before in 4.2, 5.1, 6.1, 11.8, and 11.20.

15.0 RA I am Ra. I greet you in the love and the light of the Infinite Creator. I communicate now.

15.1 QUESTIONER I would like to apologize for my past and any future stupid questions due to the fact that I am searching for the proper entry into investigating the Law of One. We will be eliminating the stupid ones from the book.[1]

I would like to ask if the use of the instrument is a function of the time we use the instrument, or the amount of information, or the number of words the instrument gives? In other words, do I have to hurry and ask the questions, or can I take my time to ask the questions?

RA I am Ra. There are two portions to your query. Firstly, this instrument's reserve of vital energy, which is a product of body, mind, and spirit distortions in the various complexes, is the key to the length of time which we may expend using this instrument. We searched your group when we contacted you, for each in your group possesses significantly more vital energy of the body complex. However, this instrument was tuned most appropriately by the mind/body/spirit-complex distortions of its beingness in this illusion. Therefore, we remained with this instrument.

Secondly, we communicate at a set rate which is dependent upon our careful manipulation of this instrument. We cannot be more, as you would say, quick. Therefore, you may ask questions speedily, but the answers we have to offer are at a set pace given.

15.2 QUESTIONER This isn't exactly what I meant. If it takes me, say, forty-five minutes to ask my questions, does that give the instrument only fifteen minutes to answer rather than an hour, or would we run over an hour and the instrument could answer for more?

RA I am Ra. The energy required for this contact is entered into this instrument by a function of time. Therefore, the time is the factor, as we understand your query.

---

[1] The missing questions and answers have been restored.

15.3 **QUESTIONER** Then I should ask my questions rapidly so that I do not reduce the time. Is this correct?

RA I am Ra. You shall do as you deem fit. However, we may suggest that to obtain the answers you require may mean that you invest some of what you experience as time. Although you lose the answer-time, you gain thereby in the specificity of the answer, as many times in the past we have needed clarification of hastily phrased questions.

15.4 **QUESTIONER** Thank you. The first question is: Why does rapid aging occur on this planet?

RA I am Ra. Rapid aging occurs upon this third-density planet due to an ongoing imbalance of receptor web complex in the etheric portion of the energy field of this planet. The thought-form distortions of your peoples have caused the energy streamings to enter the planetary magnetic atmosphere—if you would so term this web of energy patterns—in such a way that the proper streamings are not correctly imbued with balanced vibratory light/love from the, shall we say, cosmic level of this octave of existence.

15.5 **QUESTIONER** Do I assume correctly in assuming that one of your attempts in service to this planet was to help the population of this planet more fully understand and practice the Law of One so that this aging, rapid aging could be changed to normal aging?

RA I am Ra. You assume correctly to a great degree.

15.6 **QUESTIONER** Then it would be very beneficial for the people of this planet, in practicing the Law of One, to learn ways of service. Am I correct?

RA I am Ra. You are correct. If you will observe those oriented through a lifetime-experiential-distortion complex from near the beginning of that experience, you will observe a relatively youthful, as you would call it, appearance.

15.7 **QUESTIONER** What is the greatest service that our population on this planet could perform individually?

RA I am Ra. There is but one service. The Law is One. The offering of self to Creator is the greatest service—the unity, the fountainhead. The entity who seeks the One Creator is with infinite intelligence. From this seeking, from this offering, a great multiplicity of opportunities will evolve depending upon the mind/body/spirit complex's distortions with regard to the various illusory aspects, or energy centers, of the various complexes of your illusion.

Thus, some become healers, some workers, some teachers, and so forth.

15.8 **QUESTIONER** If an entity were perfectly balanced on this planet with respect to the Law of One, would he undergo the aging process?

RA I am Ra. A perfectly balanced entity would become tired rather than visibly aged. The lessons being learned, the entity would depart. However, this is appropriate and is a form of aging which your peoples do not experience. The understanding comes slowly, the body complex decomposing more rapidly.

15.9 **QUESTIONER** Can you tell me a little bit about the definition of the word "balancing" as we are using it?

RA I am Ra. Picture, if you will, the One Infinite. You have no picture. Thus, the process begins. Love creating Light, becoming love/light, streams into the planetary sphere according to the electromagnetic web of points, or nexi, of entrance. These streamings are then available to the individual who, like the planet, is a web of electromagnetic energy fields with points, or nexi, of entrance.

In a balanced individual each energy center is balanced and functioning brightly and fully. The blockages of your planetary sphere cause some distortion of intelligent energy. The blockages of the mind/body/spirit complex further distort, or unbalance, this energy. There is one energy. It may be understood as love/light, or light/love, or intelligent energy.

15.10 **QUESTIONER** Am I correct in assuming that one of the blockages of a mind/body/spirit complex might be due to an unbalance of, shall we say, ego, and this could be balanced using, say, a worthiness/unworthiness balance?

RA I am Ra. This is incorrect.

15.11 **QUESTIONER** Can you tell me how you balance the ego?

RA I am Ra. We cannot work with this concept as it is misapplied, and understanding cannot come from it.

15.12 **QUESTIONER** How does an individual go about balancing himself? What is the first step?

RA I am Ra. The steps are only one; that is, an understanding of the energy centers which make up the mind/body/spirit complex. This understanding may be briefly summarized as follows.

The first balancing is of the Malkuth, or Earth, vibratory energy complex, called the red-ray complex. An understanding and acceptance of this energy is fundamental.

The next energy complex which may be blocked is the emotional, or personal, complex also known as the orange-ray complex. This blockage will often demonstrate itself as personal eccentricities or distortions with regard to self-conscious understanding, or acceptance, of self.

The third blockage resembles most closely that which you have called ego. It is the yellow-ray, or solar plexus, center. Blockages in this center will often manifest as distortions towards power manipulation and other social behaviors concerning those close and those associated with the mind/body/spirit complex.

Those with blockages in these first three energy centers, or nexi, will have continuing difficulties in ability to further their seeking of the Law of One.

The center of heart, or green ray, is the center from which third-density beings may springboard, shall we say, towards infinite intelligence. Blockages in this area may manifest as difficulties in expressing what you may call universal love, or compassion.

The blue-ray center of energy streaming is the center which, for the first time, is outgoing as well as inpouring. Those blocked in this area may have difficulty in grasping the spirit/mind complexes of its own entity, and further difficulty in expressing such understandings of self. Entities blocked in this area may have difficulties in accepting communication from other mind/body/spirit complexes.

The next center is the pineal, or indigo-ray, center. Those blocked in this center may experience a lessening of the influx of intelligent energy due to manifestations which appear as unworthiness. This is that of which you spoke. As you can see, this is but one of many distortions due to the several points of energy influx into the mind/body/spirit complex.

The indigo-ray balancing is quite central to the type of work which revolves about the spirit complex (which has its influx then into the transformation, or transmutation, of third density to fourth density), it being the energy center receiving the least distorted outpourings of love/light from intelligent energy and having also the potential for the key to the gateway of intelligent infinity.

The remaining center of energy influx is simply the total expression of the entity's vibratory complex of mind, body, and spirit. It is as it will be. "Balanced" or "imbalanced" has no meaning at this energy level, for it gives and takes in its own balance. Whatever the distortion may be, it cannot be manipulated as can the others and, therefore, has no particular importance in viewing the balancing of an entity.

15.13 QUESTIONER You previously gave us some information about what we should do in balancing.[2] Is there any information that we can publish now about any particular exercises or methods of balancing these centers?

RA I am Ra. The exercises given for publication, seen in comparison with the material now given, are, in total, a good beginning. It is important to allow each seeker to enlighten itself rather than for any messenger to attempt in language to teach/learn for the entity, thus being teach/learner and learn/teacher. This is not in balance with your third density. We learn from you. We teach to you. Thus, we teach/learn. If we learned for you, this would cause imbalance in the direction of the distortion of free will.

There are other items of information allowable. However, you have not yet reached these items in your lines of questioning, and it is our belief/feeling complex that the questioner shall shape this material in such a way that your mind/body/spirit complexes shall have entry to it. Thus, we answer your queries as they arise in your mind complex.

15.14 QUESTIONER Yesterday you stated, "The harvest is now. There is not at this time any reason to include efforts upon these distortions toward longevity, but rather to encourage distortions towards the heart of self. For this which resides clearly in the violet-ray energy field will determine the harvest of each mind/body/spirit complex." Could you tell us how to seek, or the best way to seek, the heart of self?

---

2 Previously given in 5.2 and 15.12.

RA I am Ra. We have given you this information in several wordings.[3] However, we can only say the material for your understanding is the self: the mind/body/spirit complex. You have been given information upon healing, as you call this distortion.[4] This information may be seen in a more general context as ways to understand the self.

The understanding, experiencing, accepting, and merging of self with self and with other-self and, finally, with the Creator, is the path to the heart of self. In each infinitesimal part of your self resides the One in all of Its power. Therefore, we can only encourage these lines of contemplation, always stating the prerequisite of meditation, contemplation, or prayer as a means of subjectively/objectively using or combining various understandings to enhance the seeking process. Without such a method of reversing the analytical process, one could not integrate into unity the many understandings gained in such seeking.

15.15 **QUESTIONER** I don't mean to ask the same question twice, but there are some areas I consider so important that greater understanding may be obtained by possible restatement in other words. I thank you very much for your patience.

Yesterday, you also mentioned that when there was no harvest at the end of the last 25,000-year period: "There were harvestable entities who shall choose the manner of their entrance into the fourth density." Can you tell me what you mean by how "they will choose the manner of their entrance into the fourth density"?

RA I am Ra. These shepherds, or, as some have called them, the "Elder Race," shall choose the time/space of their leaving. They are unlikely to leave until their other-selves are harvestable also.

15.16 **QUESTIONER** What do you mean by their other-selves being harvestable?

RA I am Ra. The other-selves with whom these beings are concerned are those which did not attain harvest during the second major cycle.

15.17 **QUESTIONER** Could you tell me just a small amount of the history of what you call the Elder Race?

---

[3] Including 10.14 and 15.12.

[4] In 4.17 and 5.2.

RA I am Ra. The question is unclear. Please restate.

15.18 **QUESTIONER** I ask this question because I've heard about the Elder Race before in a book, *Road in the Sky*, by George Hunt Williamson, and I was wondering if this Elder Race was the same that he talked about?

RA I am Ra. The question now resolves itself, for we have spoken previously[5] of the manner of decision-making which caused these entities to remain here upon the closing of the second major cycle of your current master cycle.

There are some distortions in the descriptions of the one known as Michel[6]; however, these distortions have primarily to do with the fact that these entities are not a social memory complex, but rather a group of mind/body/spirit complexes dedicated to service. These entities work together, but are not completely unified; thus, they do not completely see each the other's thoughts, feelings, and motives. However, their desire to serve is the fourth-dimensional type of desire, thus melding them into what you may call a brotherhood.

15.19 **QUESTIONER** Why do you call them the Elder Race?

RA I am Ra. We called them thusly to acquaint you, the questioner, with their identity as is understood by your mind complex-distortion.

15.20 **QUESTIONER** Are there any wanderers with these Elder Race, or not?

RA I am Ra. These are planetary entities harvested—wanderers only in the sense that they chose, in fourth-density love, to immediately reincarnate in third density rather than proceeding towards fourth density. This causes them to be wanderers of a type, wanderers who have never left the earth plane because of their free will rather than because of their vibrational level.

15.21 **QUESTIONER** Well, in yesterday's material you stated, "We offer the Law of One, the solving of paradoxes." You also mentioned earlier that the first paradox, or the first distortion I meant, was the distortion of Free Will.

---

5   Spoken previously in 14.16–17 and 15.15.

6   Michel D'Obrenovic, also known as George Hunt Williamson.

Could you tell me if there's a sequence? Is there a first, second, third, fourth distortion of the Law of One?

RA I am Ra. Only up to a very short point. After this point, the many-ness of distortions are equal one to another. The First Distortion, Free Will, finds focus. This is the Second Distortion known to you as Logos, the Creative Principle, or Love. This intelligent energy thus creates a distortion known as Light.

From these three distortions come many, many hierarchies of distortions, each having its own paradoxes to be synthesized, no one being more important than another.

15.22 **QUESTIONER** You also said that you offered the Law of One, which is the balancing of love/light and light/love. Is there any difference between love/light and light/love?

RA I am Ra. This will be the final question of this time/space. There is the same difference between love/light and light/love as there is between teach/learning and learn/teaching. Love/light is the enabler, the power, the energy giver. Light/love is the manifestation which occurs when Light has been impressed with Love.

15.23 **QUESTIONER** Is there anything that we can do to make the instrument more comfortable? And can we have another session today?

RA I am Ra. This instrument requires a certain amount of manipulation of the physical, or body, complex due to a stiffness. Other than this, all is well, the energies being balanced. There is a slight distortion in the mental energy of this instrument due to concern for a loved one, as you call it. This is only slightly lowering the vital energies of the instrument. Given a manipulation, this instrument will be well for another working.

15.24 **QUESTIONER** By manipulation, do you mean she should go for a walk, or we should rub her back?

RA I am Ra. We meant the latter. The understanding must be added that this manipulation be done by one in harmony with the entity. Are there any short queries before we leave this instrument?

15.25 **QUESTIONER** Is it possible for you to tell us anything about what—since we are wanderers—anything about our previous density? Which density we came from?

RA I scan each and find it acceptable to share this information. The wanderers in this working are of two densities: one the density of five, that is, of light; one the density of love/light, or unity. To express the identity of which came from which density we observe to be an infringement upon the free will of each. Therefore, we state simply the two densities, both of which are harmoniously oriented towards work together.

I am Ra. I leave you in the love and the light of the Infinite Creator. Go forth, then, rejoicing in the power and the peace of the One Infinite Creator. Adonai.

SESSION 16

16.0 **RA** I am Ra. I greet you in the love and the light of the Infinite Creator. We communicate now.

16.1 **QUESTIONER** I would like to ask, considering the Free Will Distortion of the Law of One, how can the Guardians quarantine the earth? Is this quarantine within the Free Will Distortion?

RA I am Ra. The Guardians guard the free-will distortion of the mind/body/spirit complexes of third density on this planetary sphere. The events which require activation of quarantine were interfering with the free-will distortion of mind/body/spirit complexes.

16.2 **QUESTIONER** I may be wrong, but it seems to me that it would be the free will of, say, the Orion group to interfere. How is this balanced against the other concept you just gave?

RA I am Ra. The balancing is from dimension to dimension. The attempts of the so-called Crusaders to interfere with free will are acceptable upon the dimension of their understanding. However, the mind/body/spirit complexes of this dimension you call third form a dimension of free will which is not able to, shall we say, recognize in full the distortions towards manipulation.

Thus, in order to balance the dimensional variances in vibration, a quarantine was set up; this being a balancing situation whereby the free will of the Orion group is not stopped but given a challenge. Meanwhile, the third-density group is not hindered from free choice.

16.3 **QUESTIONER** Could these windows that occur let the Orion group come through once in a while? Does this have anything to do with this free-will distortion?

RA I am Ra. This is correct.

16.4 **QUESTIONER** Could you tell me how that works?

RA I am Ra. The closest analogy would be a random number generator, within certain limits.

16.5 **QUESTIONER** What is the source of this random number generator? Is it created by the Guardians to balance their guarding? Or is it a source other than the Guardians?

RA I am Ra. All sources are one. However, we understand your query. The window phenomenon is an other-self phenomenon from the Guardians. It operates from the dimensions beyond space/time in what you may call the area of intelligent energy. Like your cycles, such balancing, such rhythms are as a clock striking. In the case of the windows, no entities have the clock. Therefore, it seems random. It is not random in the dimension which produces this balance. That is why we stated the analogy was within certain limits.

16.6 **QUESTIONER** Then this window balancing prevents the Guardians from reducing their positive polarization by totally eliminating the Orion contact through shielding. Is this correct?

RA I am Ra. This is partially correct. In effect, the balancing allows an equal amount of positive and negative influx, this balanced by the mind/body/spirit distortions of the social complex. Thus in your particular planetary sphere, less negative, as you would call it, information, or stimulus, is necessary than positive due to the somewhat negative orientation of your social complex-distortion.

16.7 **QUESTIONER** In this way, total free will is balanced so that the individual may have an equal opportunity to choose service to others or service to self. Is this correct?

RA I am Ra. This is correct.

16.8 **QUESTIONER** This is a profound revelation, I believe, in the Law of Free Will. Thank you.

This is a minor question further to make an example of this principle, but if the Confederation landed on Earth, they would be taken as gods, breaking the Law of Free Will and thus reducing their polarization towards service to all. I assume that the same thing would happen if the Orion group landed. How would this affect their polarization towards service to self if they were able to land and became known as gods?

RA I am Ra. In the event of mass landing of the Orion group, the effect of polarization would be strongly towards an increase in the service to self, precisely the opposite of the former opportunity which you mentioned.

16.9   **QUESTIONER** If the Orion group was able to land, would this increase their polarization? What I am trying to get at is, is it better for them to work behind the scenes and get recruits, shall we say, from our planet, the person on our planet going towards service to self strictly on his own using his free will, or is it just as good for the Orion group to land upon our planet and demonstrate remarkable powers and get people like that?

RA I am Ra. The first instance is, in the long run, shall we put it, more salubrious for the Orion group in that it does not infringe upon the Law of One by landing, and thus does its work through those of this planet.[1]

In the second circumstance, a mass landing would create a loss of polarization due to the infringement upon the free will of the planet. However, it would be a gamble. If the planet then were conquered and became part of the Empire, the free will would then be re-established. This is restrained in action due to the desire of the Orion group to progress towards the One Creator. This desire to progress inhibits the group from breaking the Law of Confusion.

16.10   **QUESTIONER** You mentioned the word "Empire" in relation to the Orion group. I have thought for some time that the movie *Star Wars* was somehow an allegory, in part, for what is actually happening. Is this correct?

RA I am Ra. This is correct in the same way that a simple children's story is an allegory for physical/philosophical/social complex distortion-understanding.

16.11   **QUESTIONER** Is there a harvest of entities oriented towards service to self like there is a harvest here of entities oriented towards service to others?

RA I am Ra. There is one harvest. Those able to enter fourth density through vibrational complex levels may choose the manner of their further seeking of the One Creator.

16.12   **QUESTIONER** Then as we enter the fourth density there will be a split, shall we say, and part of the individuals who go into the fourth density will go

---

[1] In this context, *salubrious* may be defined as "conducive or favorable to health or well-being."

to planets, or places, where there is service to others, and the other part will go into places where there is service to self. Is this correct?

RA I am Ra. This is correct.

16.13 **QUESTIONER** Well, the Confederation established its quarantine, I understand, seventy-five thousand years ago. Has the Orion group been attempting to contact any part of this planet prior to that? Or did they . . . how long have they been attempting to contact this planet?

RA I am Ra. Approximately four five thousand [45,000] years ago an attempt was made. It was not successful. Approximately two six oh oh, two thousand six hundred [2,600], years ago the group sent an entity of social memory complex to this planetary sphere. This effort met with some success but was in the space/time continuum lessened in impact. Since approximately two three oh oh, two thousand three hundred [2,300], years ago, in your measurement, this group has constantly been working upon the harvest just as the Confederation.[2]

16.14 **QUESTIONER** Can you name the entity that they sent here twenty-six hundred years ago . . . two thousand six hundred years ago?[3]

RA I am Ra. This entity named by your peoples, Yahweh.

16.15 **QUESTIONER** Can you tell me the origin of the Ten Commandments?

RA I am Ra. The origin of these commandments follows the law of negative entities impressing information upon positively oriented mind/body/spirit complexes. The information attempted to copy, or ape, positivity while retaining negative characteristics.

16.16 **QUESTIONER** Was this done by the Orion group?

RA I am Ra. This is correct.

16.17 **QUESTIONER** What was their purpose in doing this?

RA I am Ra. The purpose of the Orion group, as mentioned before, is conquest and enslavement. This is done by finding and establishing an

---

[2] Ra corrected the last two dates in session 17. They should be 3,600 and 3,300 years ago, respectively.

[3] The correct time frame is 3,600 years. See Ra's statement opening session 17.

elite and causing others to serve the elite through various devices, such as the laws you mention and others given by this entity.

16.18 **QUESTIONER** Was the recipient of the laws, of the Ten Commandments, positively or negatively oriented?

RA The recipient was one of extreme positivity, thus accounting for some of the pseudo-positive characteristics of the information received. As with contacts which are not successful, this entity, vibratory complex Moishe, did not remain a credible influence among those who had first heard the philosophy of One, and this entity was removed from this third-density vibratory level in a lessened or saddened state, having lost what you may call the honor and faith with which he had begun the conceptualization of the Law of One and the freeing of those who were of his tribes, as they were called at that time/space.

16.19 **QUESTIONER** If this entity was positively oriented, how was the Orion group able to contact him?

RA I am Ra. This was an intensive, shall we say, battleground between positively oriented forces of Confederation origin and negatively oriented sources. The one called Moishe was open to impression and received the Law of One in its most simple form. However, the information became negatively oriented due to his people's pressure to do specific physical things in the third-density planes. This left the entity open for the type of information and philosophy of a self-service nature.

16.20 **QUESTIONER** It would be unlike an entity fully aware of the knowledge of the Law of One to ever say, "Thou shalt not." Is this correct?

RA I am Ra. This is correct.

16.21 **QUESTIONER** Can you give me some kind of history of your social memory complex and how you became aware of the Law of One?

RA I am Ra. The path of our learning is graven in the present moment. There is no history, as we understand your concept. Picture, if you will, a circle of being. We know the alpha and omega as infinite intelligence. The circle never ceases. It is present.

The densities we have traversed at various points in the circle correspond to the characteristics of cycles:

First, the cycle of awareness.

Second, the cycle of growth.

Third, the cycle of self-awareness.

Fourth, the cycle of love or understanding.

Fifth, the cycle of light or wisdom.

Sixth, the cycle of light/love, love/light, or unity.

Seventh, the gateway cycle.

Eighth, the octave which moves into a mystery we do not plumb.

16.22   **QUESTIONER** Thank you very much. In previous material, before we communicated with you, it was stated by the Confederation that there is actually no past or future—all is present. Would this be a good analogy?

RA I am Ra. There is past, present, and future in third density. In an overview such as an entity may have, removed from the space/time continuum, it may be seen that in the cycle of completion there exists only the present. We, ourselves, seek to learn this understanding. At the seventh level, or dimension, we shall, if our humble efforts are sufficient, become one with all, thus having no memory, no identity, no past or future, but existing in the all.

16.23   **QUESTIONER** Does this mean that you would have awareness of all that is?

RA I am Ra. This is partially correct. It is our understanding that it would not be our awareness but simply awareness of the Creator. In the Creator is all that there is. Therefore, this knowledge would be available.

16.24   **QUESTIONER** I was wondering how many inhabited planets there are in our galaxy and if they all reach higher density by the Law of One, or if there is any other way. It doesn't seem to me that there would be any other way to reach higher density. Is this correct?

RA I am Ra. Please restate your query.

16.25   **QUESTIONER** How many inhabited planets are there in our galaxy?

RA I am Ra. We are assuming that you intend all dimensions of consciousness, or densities of awareness, in this question. Approximately one-fifth of all planetary entities contain awareness of one or more densities. Some planetary spheres are hospitable only for certain densities.

Your planetary sphere, for instance, is at this time hospitable to levels, or densities, one, two, three, and four.

16.26 **QUESTIONER** Well, roughly how many total planets in this galaxy of stars that we're in have aware life regardless of density?

RA I am Ra. Approximately six seven, oh oh oh, oh oh oh [67,000,000].

16.27 **QUESTIONER** Can you tell me what percentage of those are third, fourth, fifth, sixth density, etc.? Roughly, very roughly.

RA I am Ra. A percentage seventeen for first density, a percentage twenty for second density, a percentage twenty-seven for third density, a percentage sixteen for fourth density, a percentage six for fifth density. The other information must be withheld. The free will of your future is not making this available.

We shall speak on one item. There is a fairly large percentage, approximately thirty-five percent of the intelligent planets, which do not fit in the percentiles. These mysteries are of sixth and seventh density and are not available for our speaking.

16.28 **QUESTIONER** Well, this first five densities—have all of them progressed from third density by knowledge and application of the Law of One?

RA I am Ra. This is correct.

16.29 **QUESTIONER** Then the only way for a planet to get out of the situation that we are in—or the only way for the population—is to become aware of, and start practicing, the Law of One. Is this correct?

RA This is correct.

16.30 **QUESTIONER** Can you tell me what percentage of third-, fourth-, and fifth-density planets which you have spoken of here are negatively polarized, polarized towards service for self?

RA I am Ra. This is not a query to which we may speak given the Law of Confusion. We may say only that the negatively, or self-service, oriented planetary spheres are much fewer. To give you exact numbers would not be appropriate.

16.31 **QUESTIONER** I would like to make an analogy about why there are fewer negatively oriented and ask you if the analogy is good.

In a positively oriented society with service to others, it would be simple to move a large boulder by getting everyone to help move it. In a society oriented towards service to self, it would be much more difficult to get everyone to work on the boulder for the good of all; therefore, it is much easier to get things done to create the service-to-other principle and to grow in positively oriented communities than it is in negative. Is this correct? [*Inaudible*]

RA I am Ra. This is correct.

16.32 **QUESTIONER** Thank you very much. Can you tell me how the Confederation of Planets was formed and why?

RA I am Ra. The desire to serve begins—in the dimension of love, or understanding—to be an overwhelming goal of the social memory complex. Thus, those percentiles of planetary entities, plus approximately four percent more of whose identity we cannot speak, found themselves long, long ago in your time seeking the same thing: service to others.

The relationship between these entities as they entered an understanding of other beings, other planetary entities, and other concepts of service was to share and continue together these commonly held goals of service. Thus, each voluntarily placed the social memory complex data in what you may consider a central thought complex available to all. This then created a structure whereby each entity could work in its own service while calling upon any other understandings needed to enhance the service. This is the cause of the formation and the manner of the working of the Confederation.

16.33 **QUESTIONER** With such a large number of planets in this galaxy, I was wondering if... you say there are approximately five hundred Confederation planets. That seems to me to be a relatively small percentage of the total number of fourth- and fifth-density planets around. Is there any reason for this relatively small percentage in this Confederation?

RA I am Ra. There are many Confederations. This Confederation works with the planetary spheres of seven of your galaxies, if you will, and is responsible for the callings of the densities of these galaxies.

16.34 **QUESTIONER** Would you define the word galaxy as you just used it?

RA We use that term in this sense as you would use star systems.

16.35 QUESTIONER I'm a little bit confused as to how many total planets then, roughly, does the Confederation that you are in serve?

RA I am Ra. I see the confusion. We have difficulty with your language.

The galaxy term must be split. We call galaxy that vibrational complex that is local. Thus, your sun is what we would call the center of a galaxy. We see you have another meaning for this term.

16.36 QUESTIONER Yes. In our science, the term galaxy refers to the lenticular star system that contains millions and millions of stars, and this had occurred earlier in our communications, this area of confusion. I'm glad to get it cleared up.

Now, using the term galaxy in the sense that I just gave you, of the lenticular star system that contains millions of stars, do you know of the evolution in other galaxies besides this one?

RA I am Ra. We are aware of life in infinite capacity. You are correct in this assumption.

16.37 QUESTIONER Can you tell me if the progression of life in the other galaxies is similar to progression in this one?

RA I am Ra. The progression is somewhat close to the same, asymptotically approaching congruency throughout infinity.[4] The free choosing of what you call galactic systems causes variations of an extremely minor nature from one of your galaxies to another.

16.38 QUESTIONER And then the Law of One is truly universal in creating the progression toward the eighth density, or octave, in all galaxies. Is this correct?

RA I am Ra. This is correct. There are infinite forms, infinite understandings, but the progression is one.

16.39 QUESTIONER I am assuming it is not necessary for an individual to understand the Law of One to go from third to fourth density. Is this correct?

---

4 In this context, *asymptotically* may be defined as "infinitely approaching a given value."

RA I am Ra. It is absolutely necessary that an entity consciously realize it does not understand in order for it to be harvestable. Understanding is not of this density.

16.40 **QUESTIONER** That is a very important point. I used the wrong word. What I meant to say was I believe that it was not necessary for an entity to be consciously aware of the Law of One to go from third to fourth density.

RA I am Ra. This is correct.

16.41 **QUESTIONER** At what point in densities is it necessary for an entity to be consciously aware of the Law of One to progress?

RA I am Ra. The fifth-density harvest is of those whose vibratory distortions consciously accept the honor/duty of the Law of One. This responsibility/honor is the foundation of this vibration.

16.42 **QUESTIONER** Can you tell me a little more about this honor/responsibility concept?

RA I am Ra. Each responsibility is an honor; each honor, a responsibility.

16.43 **QUESTIONER** I want to ask a rather questionable question. I may not put it in the book. I was wondering if cattle mutilations that we now experience across the country and elsewhere could be explained by you.

RA I am Ra. The greater part of your so-called mutilations take place according to the ways of your second-density beings which feed upon carrion. A portion of these so-called mutilations are those which are of what you may call multi-dimensional type: a thought-form construct using various parts in order to have life and being in third density.

16.44 **QUESTIONER** Where do these thought-forms come from?

RA I am Ra. This is a very ambiguous question. However, we will attempt to answer. Firstly, they come from the Creator. Secondly, they come from what you may call lower astral, inner plane thought. Thirdly, in construct visualization complex they reside in part beneath the crust of your planet.

16.45 **QUESTIONER** Are these one form in particular?

RA I am Ra. These entities may take any thought-form associated with an emotion of fear or terror.

16.46 **QUESTIONER** Are these thought-forms able to attack only cattle, or can they also attack human beings?

RA I am Ra. These thought-forms cannot attack third-density beings.

16.47 **QUESTIONER** Thank you. Can you tell me of the silver flecks that we have found sometimes on our faces or elsewhere?

RA I am Ra. These of which you speak are a materialization of a subjectively oriented signpost indicating to one mind/body/spirit complex, and no other, a meaning of subjective nature.

16.48 **QUESTIONER** Who creates the silver flecks? Are they real?

RA I am Ra. Picture, if you will, the increasing potential for learn/teaching. At some point a sign will be given to indicate the appropriateness or importance of that learn/teaching. The entity itself, in cooperation with the inner planes, creates whatever signpost is most understandable or noticeable to it.

16.49 **QUESTIONER** You're saying that we ourselves then create these?

RA I am Ra. Entities consciously do not create these. The roots of mind complex, having touched in understanding, intelligent infinity, create them.

16.50 **QUESTIONER** Thank you. Is it possible for you to give a small description of the conditions in fourth density?

RA I am Ra. We ask you to consider, as we speak, that there are no words for positively describing fourth density. We can only explain what is not and approximate what is. Beyond fourth density our ability grows more limited still until we become without words.

That which fourth density is not: it is not of words, unless chosen. It is not of heavy chemical vehicles for body complex activities. It is not of disharmony within self. It is not of disharmony within peoples. It is not within limits of possibility to cause disharmony in any way.

Approximations of positive statements: it is a plane of a type of bipedal vehicle which is much denser and more full of life. It is a plane wherein one is aware of the thoughts of other-selves. It is a plane where one is aware of the vibrations of other-selves. It is a plane of compassion and understanding of the sorrows of third density. It is a plane striving towards wisdom or light. It is a plane wherein individual differences are pronounced, although automatically harmonized by group consensus.

16.51   **QUESTIONER** Could you define the word density as we have been using it to give us a little greater idea of the concept of this term when used by you?

RA I am Ra. The term density is a, what you would call, mathematical one. The closest analogy is that of music, whereby after seven notes on your western type of scale, if you will, the eighth note begins a new octave. Within your great octave of existence which we share with you, there are seven octaves or densities. Within each density there are seven sub-densities. Within each sub-density, seven sub-sub-densities, and so on infinitely.

16.52   **QUESTIONER** I notice that the time we have used has gone slightly over an hour. I would prefer to continue, but I want to ask at this time as to the condition of the instrument.

RA I am Ra. This instrument is in balance. It is well to continue if you desire.

16.53   **QUESTIONER** All right. Continuing with what we were just talking about, namely densities: I understand then that each density has seven sub-densities, which again have seven sub-densities, which again have seven sub-densities. This expands at an extremely large rate as things are increased in powers of seven. Does this mean that in any density level anything that you can think of is happening? And many things that you never thought of are happening . . . are there . . . everything is happening . . . this is confusing . . .

RA I am Ra. From your confusion we select the concept with which you struggle, that being infinite opportunity. You may consider any possibility/probability complex as having an existence.

16.54   **QUESTIONER** Does what we do when we think of possibilities that can occur—say daydreaming—do these become real in these densities?

RA I am Ra. This depends upon the nature of the daydream. This is a large subject. Perhaps the simplest thing we can say is if the daydream, as you call it, is one which attracts to self, this then becomes reality to self. If it is contemplative general daydream, this may enter the infinity of possibility/probability complexes and occur elsewhere, having no particular attachment to the energy fields of the creator.

16.55 **QUESTIONER** To make this a little more clear, if I were to daydream strongly about building a ship, would this occur in one of these other densities?

RA I am Ra. This would, would have, or shall occur.

16.56 **QUESTIONER** And then if, say, an entity daydreams strongly about battling, let us say, another entity, would this occur?

RA I am Ra. In this case the entity's fantasy concerns the self and other-self; this binds the thought-form to the possibility/probability complex connected with the self which is the creator of this thought-form. This then would increase the possibility/probability of bringing this into third-density occurrence.

16.57 **QUESTIONER** Does the Orion group use this principle to create conditions brought about to suit their purpose?

RA I am Ra. We will answer more specifically than the question. The Orion group uses daydreams of hostile or other negative vibratory natures to feed back, or strengthen, these thought-forms.

16.58 **QUESTIONER** Do they ever use any, shall I say, gratifications of the physical body to amplify such daydreams?

RA I am Ra. They are able to do this only when there is a strong ability on the part of the receiving mind/body/spirit complex towards the perception of thought-forms. This could be termed an unusual characteristic but has indeed been a method used by Orion entities.

16.59 **QUESTIONER** The many wanderers coming to this planet now and in the recent past—are they subject to Orion thoughts?

RA I am Ra. As we have said before, wanderers become completely the creature of third density in mind/body complex. There is just as much chance of such influence to a wanderer entity as to a mind/body/spirit complex of this planetary sphere. The only difference occurs in the spirit complex which, if it wishes, has an armor of light, if you will, which enables it to recognize more clearly that which is not as it would appropriately be desired by the mind/body/spirit complex. This is not more than a bias and cannot be called an understanding.

Furthermore, the wanderer is, in its own mind/body/spirit complex, less distorted towards the, shall we say, deviousness of third-density positive/negative confusions. Thus, it often does not recognize, as easily as a more negative individual, the negative nature of thoughts or beings.

16.60 **QUESTIONER** Would then the wanderers, as they incarnate here, be high-priority targets, shall we say, of the Orion group?

RA I am Ra. This is correct.

16.61 **QUESTIONER** And if a wanderer were to be successfully infringed upon, shall I say, by the Orion group, what would happen to this wanderer at the harvest?

RA I am Ra. If the wanderer entity demonstrated, through action, a negative orientation towards other-selves it would be, as we have said before, caught into the planetary vibration and, when harvested, possibly repeat again the master cycle of third density as a planetary entity. This shall be the last full question of this session.

Is there a short question we may answer before we close the session?

16.62 **QUESTIONER** Only just to know if the instrument can be any more comfortable?

RA I am Ra. This instrument is as comfortable as it is possible for you to make it given the weakness distortions of its body complex. You are conscientious.

I am Ra. I leave you in the love and the light of the One Infinite Creator. Go forth, then, rejoicing in the power and the peace of the One Creator. Adonai.

SESSION 17

FEBRUARY 3, 1981

17.0 **RA** I am Ra. I greet you in the love and the light of the Infinite Creator.

Before we communicate by answer, we shall correct an error which we have discovered in the transmission of our information to you. We have difficulty dealing with your time/space. There may again be errors of this type. Feel free to question us that we may recalculate in your time/space measurements.

The error we have discovered concerns one of the arrivals of both the Orion group into your planetary sphere of influence and the corresponding arrival of emissaries of the Confederation. We gave dates of two six oh oh [2,600] years for the Orion entry, two three oh oh [2,300] for Confederation entry. This is incorrect. The recalculation indicates numbers three six oh oh [3,600] for Orion entry, three three oh oh [3,300] for Confederation entry.[1]

We communicate now.

17.1 **QUESTIONER** Thank you very much. I wish to say again . . . consider it an honor, great honor, and also a privilege, as my [*inaudible*]. And I would like to reiterate that my questions may sometimes go a little off because I keep going on something that I had already started to work into the applications of the Law of One to better understand primarily the free-will principle and further distortions that we discover.

I got three questions just now in meditation. I'll ask them first before we continue.

First, we are now in the fourth density. Will the effects of the fourth density increase in the next thirty years? Will we see more changes in our environment and our effect upon our environment?

RA I am Ra. The fourth density is a vibrational spectrum. Your time/space continuum has spiraled your planetary sphere and your, what we would call galaxy, what you call star, into this vibration. This will

---

[1] Footnotes have been added to 14.18, 14.25, and 16.13–14 indicating the correct timeframes.

cause the planetary sphere itself to electromagnetically realign its vortices of reception of the instreaming of cosmic forces expressing themselves as vibrational webs so that the earth will thus be fourth-density magnetized, as you might call it.

This is going to occur with some inconvenience, as we have said before, due to the energies of the thought-forms of your peoples which disturb the orderly constructs of energy patterns within your earth spirals of energy, which increases entropy and unusable heat. This will cause your planetary sphere to have some ruptures in its outer garment while making itself appropriately magnetized for fourth density. This is the planetary adjustment.

You will find a sharp increase in the number of people, as you call mind/body/spirit complexes, whose vibrational potentials include the potential for fourth-vibrational distortions. Thus there will seem to be, shall we say, a new breed. These are those incarnating for fourth-density work.

There will also be a sharp increase in the short run of negatively oriented, or polarized, mind/body/spirit complexes and social complexes due to the polarizing conditions of the sharp delineation between fourth-density characteristics and third-density self-service orientation.

Those who remain in fourth density upon this plane will be of the so-called positive orientation. Many will come from elsewhere, for it would appear that with all of the best efforts of the Confederation, which includes those from your peoples' inner planes, inner civilizations, and those from other dimensions, the harvest will still be much less than that which this planetary sphere is capable of comfortably supporting in service.

17.2   **QUESTIONER** Is it possible to help an entity to reach fourth-density level in these last days?

RA I am Ra. It is impossible to help another being directly. It is only possible to make catalyst available in whatever form, the most important being the radiation of realization of oneness with the Creator from the self, less important being information such as we share with you.

We, ourselves, do not feel an urgency for this information to be widely disseminated. It is enough that we have made it available to three, four, or five. This is extremely ample reward, for if one of these obtains fourth-density understanding due to this catalyst then we shall have fulfilled the Law of One in the distortion of service.

We encourage a dispassionate attempt to share information without concern for numbers or quick growth among others. That you attempt to make this information available is, in your term, your service. The attempt, if it reaches one, reaches all.

We cannot offer shortcuts to enlightenment. Enlightenment is of the moment, is an opening to intelligent infinity. It can only be accomplished by the self, for the self. Another self cannot teach/learn enlightenment, but only teach/learn information, inspiration, or a sharing of love, of mystery, of the unknown that makes the other-self reach out and begin the seeking process that ends in a moment. But who can know when an entity will open the gate to the present?

17.3 **QUESTIONER** In meditation a few nights ago I had the impression of a question about a crater in Russia. I believe it was in Tunguska. Can you tell me what caused the crater?

RA I am Ra. The destruction of a fission reactor caused this crater.

17.4 **QUESTIONER** Whose reactor?

RA I am Ra. This was what you may call a "drone" sent by Confederation which malfunctioned. It was moved to an area where its destruction would not cause infringement upon the will of mind/body/spirit complexes. It was then detonated.

17.5 **QUESTIONER** What was its purpose in coming here?

RA It was a drone designed to listen to the various signals of your peoples. You were, at that time, beginning work in a more technical sphere. We were interested in determining the extent and the rapidity of your advances. This drone was powered by a simple fission motor, or engine, as you would call it. It was not that type which you now know, but was very small. However, it has the same destructive effect upon third-density molecular structures. Thus as it malfunctioned, we felt it was best to pick a place for its destruction rather than attempt to retrieve it, for the possibility/probability modes of this maneuver looked very, very minute.

17.6 **QUESTIONER** Was its danger both blast and radiation?

RA I am Ra. There is very little radiation, as you know of it, in this particular type of device. There is radiation which is localized, but the localization is such that it does not drift with the winds as does the emission of your somewhat primitive weapons.

17.7 **QUESTIONER** I believe that an analysis of the trees in that area has shown a low radiation level. Is this the reason for such a low radiation level in the trees?

RA I am Ra. This is correct. The amount of radiation is very localized. However, the energy which is released is powerful enough to cause difficulties.

17.8 **QUESTIONER** Then was the Confederation responsible for Earth receiving nuclear power?

RA I am Ra. It is a point which one cannot judge what is cause. The basic equation which preceded this work was an equation brought through by a wanderer dedicated to service to the planet. That this work should have become foundation for instruments of destruction was not intended and was not given.

17.9 **QUESTIONER** Can you tell me who that wanderer was that brought through the equation?

RA I am Ra. This information seems harmless as this entity is no longer of your planetary third density. This entity was named, sound vibration complex, Albert.

17.10 **QUESTIONER** Thank you. Can you tell me who, before incarnation into this density, was the one known as Jesus of Nazareth?

RA I am Ra. I have difficulty with this question as it is phrased. Can you discover another form for this query?

17.11 **QUESTIONER** Yes. What I meant to say was can you tell me if Jesus of Nazareth came from the Confederation before incarnation here?

RA I am Ra. The one known to you as Jesus of Nazareth did not have a name. This entity was a member of fifth[2] density of the highest level of that sub-octave. This entity was desirous of entering this planetary sphere

---

2   This should be fourth. Ra corrects the error in the next answer.

in order to share the love vibration in as pure a manner as possible. Thus, this entity received permission to perform this mission. This entity was then a wanderer of no name, of Confederation origins, of fifth density, representing the fifth-density understanding of the vibration of understanding or love.

17.12 **QUESTIONER** Did you say the fifth vibration was that of love? Fifth density was that of love?

RA I am Ra. I have made an error. The fourth-density being is that which we intended to say, the highest level of fourth density going into the fifth. This entity could have gone on to the fifth but chose instead to return to third for this particular mission. This entity was of the highest sub-octave of the vibration of love. This is fourth density.

17.13 **QUESTIONER** When I am communicating with you as Ra, are you at times an individualized entity, or am I speaking to the entire complex?

RA I am Ra. You speak with Ra. There is no separation. You would call it a social memory complex thus indicating many-ness. To our understanding, you are speaking to an individualized portion of consciousness.

17.14 **QUESTIONER** Do I always speak to the same individualized portion of consciousness in each of the sessions?

RA I am Ra. You speak to the same entity through a channel or instrument. This instrument is at times lower in vital energy. This will sometimes hamper our proceedings. However, this instrument has a great deal of faithfulness to the task and gives whatever it has to this task. Therefore, we may continue even when energy is low. This is why we usually speak to the ending of the session due to our estimation of the instrument's levels of vital energy.

17.15 **QUESTIONER** I would like to make a point clear now that I am sure of myself. People of this planet, following any religion or no religion at all, or having no intellectual knowledge of the Law of One or of anything at all, can still be harvested into the fourth density if they are of that vibration. Is this not correct?

RA I am Ra. This is correct. However, you will find few who are harvestable whose radiance does not cause others to be aware of their, what you may call, spirituality, the quality of the mind/body/spirit-complex distortion. Thus, it is not particularly probable that an entity would be completely unknown to his immediate acquaintances as an unusually radiant personality, even were this individual not caught up in any of the distortions of your so-called religious systems.

17.16   **QUESTIONER** When Jesus of Nazareth incarnated, was there an attempt by the Orion group to discredit him in some way?

RA I am Ra. This is correct.

17.17   **QUESTIONER** Can you tell me what the Orion group did in order to try to cause his downfall?

RA I am Ra. We may describe in general what occurred. The technique was that of building upon other negatively oriented information. This information had been given by the one whom your peoples called Yahweh. This information involved many strictures upon behavior and promised power of the third-density, service-to-self nature. These two types of distortions were impressed upon those already oriented to think these thought-forms.

This eventually led to many challenges of the entity known as Jesus. It eventually led to one, sound vibration complex Judas, as you call this entity, who believed that it was doing the appropriate thing in bringing about, or forcing upon the one you call Jesus, the necessity for bringing in the third-density planetary-power distortion of third-density rule over others.

This entity, Judas, felt that, if pushed into a corner, the entity you call Jesus would then be able to see the wisdom of using the power of intelligent infinity in order to rule others. The one you call Judas was mistaken in this estimation of the reaction of the entity, Jesus, whose teach/learning was not oriented towards this distortion. This resulted in the destruction of the bodily complex of the one known as Jesus to you.

17.18   **QUESTIONER** Then if the entity Jesus was fourth density, and there are wanderers on the planet today who came from fifth and sixth density, what was it that Jesus did that enabled him to be such a good healer, and could these fifth- and sixth-density beings here today do the same?

RA I am Ra. Those who heal may be of any density which has the consciousness of the spirit. This includes third, fourth, fifth, sixth, and seventh. The third density can be one in which healing takes place just as the others. However, there is more illusory material to understand, to balance, to accept, and to move forward from.

The gate to intelligent infinity can only be opened when an understanding of the instreamings of intelligent energy are opened unto the healer. These are the so-called Natural Laws of your local space/time continuum and its web of electromagnetic sources, or nexi, of instreaming energy.

Know then, first, the mind and the body. Then as the spirit is integrated and synthesized, those are harmonized into a mind/body/spirit complex which can move among the dimensions and which can open the gateway to intelligent infinity, thus healing self by light and sharing that light with others.

True healing is simply the radiance of the self causing an environment in which a catalyst may occur which initiates the recognition of self, by self, of the self-healing properties of the self.

17.19 **QUESTIONER** How did Jesus learn this during his incarnation?

RA I am Ra. This entity learned the ability by a natural kind of remembering at a very young age. Unfortunately, this entity first discovered his ability to penetrate intelligent infinity by becoming the distortion you call "angry" at a playmate. This entity was touched by the entity, known as Jesus to you, and was fatally wounded.

Thus the one known as Jesus became aware that there dwelt in him a terrible potential. This entity determined to discover how to use this energy for the good, not for the negative. This entity was extremely positively polarized and remembered more than most wanderers do.

17.20 **QUESTIONER** How did this aggressive action against a playmate affect Jesus in his spiritual growth? Where did he go after his physical death?

RA I am Ra. The entity you call Jesus was galvanized by this experience and began a lifetime of seeking and searching. This entity studied first day and night in its own religious constructs, which you call Judaism, and was learned enough to be a rabbi, as you call the teach/learners of this particular rhythm or distortion of understanding, at a very young age.

At the age of approximately thirteen and one-half of your years, this entity left the dwelling place of its earthly family, as you would call it, and walked into many other places seeking further information. This went on sporadically until the entity was approximately twenty-five, at which time it returned to its family dwelling and learned and practiced the art of its earthly father.

When the entity had become able to integrate or synthesize all experiences, the entity began to speak to other-selves and teach/learn what it had felt during the preceding years to be of an worthwhile nature.

The entity was absolved karmically of the destruction of an other-self when it was in its last portion of lifetime and spoke upon what you would call a cross saying, "Father, forgive them, for they know not what they do." In forgiveness lies the stoppage of the wheel of action, or what you call karma.

17.21 **QUESTIONER** Then in which density does the entity known as Jesus now reside?

RA I am Ra. This information is harmless though unimportant. This entity studies now the lessons of the wisdom vibration, the fifth density, also called the light vibration.

17.22 **QUESTIONER** In our culture there is a great saying that he will return. Can you tell me if this is planned?

RA I am Ra. I will attempt to sort out this question. It is difficult. This entity became aware that it was not an entity of itself but operated as a messenger of the One Creator, whom this entity saw as Love. This entity was aware that this cycle was in its last portion and spoke to the effect that those of its consciousness would return at the harvest.

The particular mind/body/spirit complex you call Jesus is, as what you would call an entity, not to return except as a member of the Confederation occasionally speaking through a channel. However, there are others of the identical congruency of consciousness that will welcome those to the fourth density. This is the meaning of the returning.

17.23 **QUESTIONER** You spoke of the alleviation of karma being forgiveness. Are . . . I'm having a hard time phrasing this question. I think I'll have to come back to it. I'll ask this other question.

Can you tell me why the earth will be fourth-density positive instead of fourth-density negative after the cycle is complete, since it seems that there is a greater negative population?

RA I am Ra. The earth seems to be negative. That is due to the quiet, shall we say, horror which is the common distortion which those good, or positively oriented, entities have towards the occurrences which are of your space/time present. However, those oriented and harvestable in the ways of service to others greatly outnumber those whose orientation towards service to self has become that of harvestable quality.

17.24 **QUESTIONER** In other words, there will be fewer negative entities being harvested into fourth density than there will be positive. Is this correct?

RA I am Ra. This is correct. The great majority of your peoples will repeat third density.

17.25 **QUESTIONER** How did Taras Bulba, Genghis Khan, and Rasputin get harvested prior to the harvest?

RA I am Ra. It is the right/privilege/duty of those opening consciously the gate to intelligent infinity to choose the manner of their leaving of the density. Those of negative orientation who so achieve this right/duty most often choose to move forward in their learn/teaching of service to self.

17.26 **QUESTIONER** Is this the reason for what we call spontaneous combustion?

RA I am Ra. This is not correct.

17.27 **QUESTIONER** Can you tell me what causes that phenomenon?

RA I am Ra. Picture, if you will, a forest. One tree is struck by lightning. It burns. Lightning does not strike elsewhere. Elsewhere does not burn. There are random occurrences which do not have to do with the entity but with the window phenomenon of which we spoke.

17.28 **QUESTIONER** Are these particular entities all uniquely the same, or are they just random entities?

RA I am Ra. The latter is correct.

17.29 **QUESTIONER** Am I to understand that the harvest will occur in the year 2011, or will it be spread?

RA I am Ra. This is an approximation. We have stated we have difficulty with your time/space. This is an appropriate probable/possible time/space nexus for harvest. Those who are not in incarnation at this time will be included in the harvest.

17.30 **QUESTIONER** Well, if an entity wants to learn ways of it, wants to be of service to others rather than service to self while he is in this third density, are there best ways of being of service to others, or is any way just as good as any other way?

RA I am Ra. The best way to be of service to others has been explicitly covered in previous material.[3] We will iterate briefly.

The best way of service to others is the constant attempt to seek to share the love of the Creator as it is known to the inner self. This involves self-knowledge and the ability to open the self to the other-self without hesitation. This involves, shall we say, radiating that which is the essence, or the heart, of the mind/body/spirit complex.

Speaking to the intention of your question, the best way for each seeker in third density to be of service to others is unique to that mind/body/spirit complex. This means that the mind/body/spirit complex must then seek within itself the intelligence of its own discernment as to the way it may best serve other-selves. This will be different for each. There is no best. There is no generalization. Nothing is known.

17.31 **QUESTIONER** Thank you very much. I don't wish to take up extra time by asking questions over again. Some are so important I try to ask some similar questions in different ways to expand on the answer. Seems to be [*inaudible*] what we're getting at, maybe not.

In the book *Oahspe* it states that if an individual is more than fifty percent for others—that is, goes over the 50% service to others and is less than fifty percent for service to self—then he is harvestable. Is this a correct statement?

RA I am Ra. This is correct if the harvesting is to be for the positive fourth-dimensional level.

---

3 This has been discussed in various places, most explicitly and poignantly in 15.7.

17.32 **QUESTIONER** What must be the entity's percentage, shall we say, if he is to be harvested for the negative?

RA I am Ra. The entity who wishes to pursue the path of service to self must attain a grade of five—that is five percent service to others, ninety-five percent service to self. It must approach totality. The negative path is quite difficult to attain harvestability upon and requires great dedication.

17.33 **QUESTIONER** Why is the negative path so much more difficult a path to attain harvestability upon than the positive?

RA I am Ra. This is due to a distortion of the Law of One which indicates that the gateway to intelligent infinity be a gateway at the end of a strait and narrow path,[4] as you may call it. To attain fifty-one percent dedication to the welfare of other-selves is as difficult as attaining a grade of five percent dedication to other-selves. The, shall we say, sinkhole of indifference is between those two.

17.34 **QUESTIONER** Well, then if an entity is harvested into fourth density with a grade, let's say, of fifty-one percent for others, forty-nine percent for self, what level of the fourth density would he go into? I'm assuming there are different levels of the fourth density.

RA I am Ra. This is correct. Each enters the sub-density which vibrates in accordance with the entity's understanding.

17.35 **QUESTIONER** How many levels do we have here in the third density at this time?

RA I am Ra. The third density has an infinite number of levels.

17.36 **QUESTIONER** I've heard that there are seven astral and seven devachanic primary levels. Is this correct?

RA I am Ra. You speak of some of the more large distinctions in levels in your inner planes. That is correct.

17.37 **QUESTIONER** Well, who inhabit the astral, and who inhabit the devachanic planes?

---

4 "Strait" is used instead of "straight" because it is a better contextual fit and because of Ra's love of archaic and poetic language.

RA I am Ra. Entities inhabit the various planes due to their vibrational nature. The astral plane varies from thought-forms in the lower extremities to enlightened beings who become dedicated to teach/learning in the higher astral planes.

In the devachanic planes, as you call them, are those whose vibrations are even more close to the primal distortions of love/light.

Beyond these planes there are others.

17.38 **QUESTIONER** Well, does each . . . does . . . this is difficult. Our physical plane—are there seven sub-planes to what we call our physical plane here?

RA I am Ra. You are correct. This is difficult to understand.

There are an infinite number of planes. In your particular space/time-continuum distortion there are seven sub-planes of mind/body/spirit complexes. You will discover the vibrational nature of these seven planes as you pass through your experiential distortions, meeting other-selves of the various levels which correspond to the energy influx centers of the physical vehicle.

The invisible, or inner, third-density planes are inhabited by those who are not of body complex natures such as yours; that is, they do not collect about their spirit/mind complexes a chemical body. Nevertheless, these entities are divided in what you may call an artificial dream within a dream into various levels. In the upper levels desire to communicate knowledge back down to the outer planes of existence becomes less, due to the intensive learn/teaching which occurs upon these levels.

17.39 **QUESTIONER** Then is it necessary to penetrate one plane at a time as we move from what we call third-density physical through these planes?

RA I am Ra. It has been our experience that some penetrate several planes at one time. Others penetrate them slowly. Some in eagerness attempt to penetrate the higher planes before penetrating the energies of the so-called lower, or more fundamental, planes. This causes energy imbalance.

You will find ill health, as you call this distortion, to frequently be the result of a subtle mismatch of energies in which some of the higher energy levels are being activated by the conscious attempts of the entity while the entity has not penetrated the lower energy centers, or sub-densities, of this density.

17.40 **QUESTIONER** Is there a best way to meditate?

RA I am Ra. No.

17.41 **QUESTIONER** At this time, near the end of the cycle, how are reincarnations into the physical allocated, shall I say, on this planet? In our own [*inaudible*].

RA I am Ra. Entities wishing to obtain critically needed experience in order to become harvestable are incarnated with priority over those who will, without too much probable/possible doubt, need to re-experience this density.

17.42 **QUESTIONER** How long has this been going on, this type of allocation?

RA I am Ra. This has been going on since the first individual entity became conscious of its need to learn the lessons of this density. This was the beginning of what you may call a seniority by vibration.

17.43 **QUESTIONER** Can you explain what you mean by a seniority by vibration?

RA I am Ra. This will be the final question of this session of working.

The seniority by vibration is the preferential treatment, shall we say, which follows the ways of the Law of One which encourages harvestable individuals. Each individual becoming aware of the time of harvest and the need, on a self-level, to bend mind, body, and spirit towards the learn/teaching of these lessons, is given priority in order that this entity may have the best possible chance, shall we say, of succeeding in this attempt.

May we ask at this time if there are any questions?

17.44 **QUESTIONER** My only question: is there anything we can do to make the instrument [*inaudible*]?

RA I am Ra. This instrument is not wearing the appropriate apparel for this work. As inpourings occur in the regions of the, what you may call, seventh chakra, as you speak of these energy centers, filtering through the sixth and so forth, the entity's other, or base, chakras become somewhat de-energized. Thus, this entity should be more careful in its selection of warm apparel for the part of the body complex you call the feet.

May we answer any other brief questions?

17.45 **QUESTIONER** Just—we want to put heavier clothing on the feet. Is this correct?

RA I am Ra. This is correct.

I will leave this instrument now. I leave you in the love and the light of the One Infinite Creator. Adonai.

18.0   **RA** I am Ra. I greet you in the love and the light of the Infinite Creator. We communicate now.

18.1   **QUESTIONER** I was thinking last night that if I were in the place of Ra at this time, the first distortion of the Law of One might cause me to mix some erroneous data with the true information that I was transmitting to this group. Do you do this?

RA I am Ra. We do not intentionally do this. However, there will be confusion. The errors which have occurred have occurred due to the occasional variation in the vibrational complex of this instrument due to its ingestion of a chemical substance. It is not our intent in this particular project to create erroneous information but to express in the confining ambiance of your language system the feeling of the infinite mystery of the One Creation in its infinite and intelligent unity.

18.2   **QUESTIONER** Can you tell me what the chemical substance is that was ingested? Causes poor contact?

RA I am Ra. This is not a clear query. Could you please restate?

18.3   **QUESTIONER** You just stated that you had some problems with the instrument because of the ingestion, by the instrument, of some chemical substance. Can you tell me what the substance was?

RA I am Ra. The substance of which we speak is called vibratory sound complex LSD. It does not give poor contact if it is used in conjunction with the contact. The difficulty of this particular substance is that there is, shall we say, a very dramatic drop-off of the effect of this substance. In each case this instrument began the session with the distortion towards extreme vital energy which this substance produces.

However, this entity was, during the session, at the point where this substance no longer was in sufficient strength to amplify the entity's abilities to express vital energy. Thus, first the phenomenon of, shall we say, a spotty contact, and then, as the instrument relies again upon its own vibrational complexes of vital energy, the vital energy being in this case very low, it became necessary to abruptly cut off communication in order to preserve and nurture the instrument. This particular chemical substance is both helpful and unhelpful in these contacts for the causes given.

18.4 **QUESTIONER** Are there any foods that are helpful or harmful that the instrument might eat?

RA I am Ra. This instrument has body-complex distortion towards ill health in the distortion direction corrected best by ingestion of the foodstuffs of your grains and your vegetables, as you call them. However, this is extremely unimportant when regarded as an aid with equality to other aids such as attitude which this instrument has in abundance. It, however, aids the vital energies of this instrument, with less distortion towards ill health, to ingest foodstuffs in the above manner with occasional ingestion of what you call your meats, due to the instrument's need to lessen the distortion towards low vital energy.

18.5 **QUESTIONER** Thank you. I have a question here from Jim that I will read verbatim:

"Much of the mystic tradition of seeking on Earth holds that belief that the individual self must be erased or obliterated and the material world ignored for an entity to reach 'nirvana,' as it's called, or enlightenment. What is the proper role of the individual self and its worldly activities in aiding an entity to grow more into the Law of One?"

RA I am Ra. The proper role of the entity is, in this density, to experience all things desired, to then analyze, understand, and accept these experiences, distilling from them the love/light within them. Nothing shall be overcome. That which is not needed falls away.

The orientation develops due to analysis of desire. These desires become more and more distorted towards conscious application of love/light as the entity furnishes itself with distilled experience.

We have found it to be inappropriate in the extreme to encourage the overcoming of any desires, except to suggest the imagination rather than the carrying out in the physical plane, as you call it, of those desires not consonant with the Law of One—this preserving the primal distortion of Free Will.

The reason it is unwise to overcome is that overcoming is an unbalanced action creating difficulties in balancing in the time/space continuum. Overcoming thus creates the further environment for holding onto that which apparently has been overcome.

All things are acceptable in the proper time for each entity, and in experiencing, in understanding, in accepting, in then sharing with other-selves, the appropriate description shall be moving away from distortions of one kind to distortions of another which may be more consonant with the Law of One.

It is, shall we say, a shortcut to simply ignore or overcome any desire. It must instead be understood and accepted. This takes patience and experience which can be analyzed with care, with compassion for self and for other-self.

18.6   **QUESTIONER** Basically, I would say that to infringe on the free will of another self, or another entity, would be the basic thing never to do under the Law of One. Can you state any other breaking of the Law of One than this basic rule?

RA I am Ra. As one proceeds from the primal distortion of Free Will, one proceeds to the understanding of the focal points of intelligent energy which have created the intelligences or the ways of a particular mind/body/spirit complex in its environment, both what you would call natural and what you would call man-made.

Thus, the distortions to be avoided are those which do not take into consideration the distortions of the focus of energy of love/light, or shall we say, the Logos of this particular sphere, or density. These include the lack of understanding of the needs of the natural environment, the needs of other-selves' mind/body/spirit complexes. These are many due to the various distortions of man-made complexes in which the intelligence and awareness of entities themselves have chosen a way of using the energies available.

Thus, what would be an improper distortion with one entity is proper with another. We can suggest an attempt to become aware of the other-self as self and thus do that action which is needed by other-self, understanding from the other-self's intelligence and awareness. In many cases this does not involve the breaking of the distortion of Free Will into a distortion, or fragmentation, called infringement. However, it is a delicate matter to be of service, and compassion, sensitivity, and an ability to empathize are helpful in avoiding the distortions of man-made intelligence and awareness.

The area, or arena, called the societal complex is an arena in which there are no particular needs for care, for it is the prerogative honor/duty of those in the particular planetary sphere to act according to its free will for the attempted aid of the social complex.

Thus, you have two simple directives: awareness of the intelligent energy expressed in nature; awareness of the intelligent energy expressed in self to be shared, when it seems appropriate, by the entity with the social complex. And you have one infinitely subtle and various set of distortions of which you may be aware; that is, distortions with respect to self and other-selves not concerning free will but concerning harmonious relationships and service to others as other-selves would most benefit.

18.7 **QUESTIONER** As an entity in this density grows from childhood, he becomes more aware of his responsibilities. Is there an age below which an entity is not responsible for his actions, or is he responsible from the time of birth?

RA I am Ra. An entity incarnating upon the earth plane becomes conscious of self at a varying point in its time/space progress through the continuum. This may have a median, shall we say, of approximately fifteen of your months. Some entities become conscious of self at a period closer to incarnation, some at a period farther from this event. In all cases responsibility then becomes retroactive from that point backwards in the continuum so that distortions are to be understood by the entity and dissolved as the entity learns.

18.8 **QUESTIONER** Then an entity, say, four years old would be totally responsible for any actions that were against or inharmonious with the Law of One. Is this correct?

RA I am Ra. This is correct. It may be noted that it has been arranged by your social complex structures that the newer entities to incarnation are to be provided with guides of a physical mind/body/spirit complex, thus being able to learn quickly what is consonant with the Law of One.

18.9 **QUESTIONER** Who are these guides?

RA I am Ra. These guides are what you call parents, teachers, and friends.

18.10 **QUESTIONER** I see. The entity Aleister Crowley wrote, "Do what thou wilt is the whole of the law." He was obviously in understanding, to some extent, of the Law of One. Where is this entity now?

RA I am Ra. This entity is within your inner planes. This entity is in an healing process.

18.11 **QUESTIONER** Did this entity, then, even though he intellectually understood the Law of One, misuse it and therefore have to go through this healing process?

RA I am Ra. This entity became, may we use the vibration sound complex, overstimulated with the true nature of things. This overstimulation resulted in behavior that was beyond the conscious control of the entity. The entity thus—in many attempts to go through the process of balancing, as we have described the various energy centers beginning with the red ray and moving upwards—became somewhat overly impressed, or caught up, in this process and became alienated from other-selves.

This entity was positive. However, its journey was difficult due to the inability to use, synthesize, and harmonize the understandings of the desires of self so that it might have shared, in full compassion, with other-selves. This entity thus became very unhealthy, as you may call it, in a spiritual complex manner, and it is necessary for those with this type of distortion towards inner pain to be nurtured in the inner planes until such an entity is capable of viewing the experiences again with the lack of distortion towards pain.

18.12 **QUESTIONER** You stated yesterday that forgiveness is the eradicator of karma. I am assuming that balanced forgiveness for the full eradication of karma would require forgiveness not only of other-selves, but forgiveness of self. Am I correct?

RA I am Ra. You are correct. We will briefly expand upon this understanding in order to clarify.

Forgiveness of other-self is forgiveness of self. An understanding of this insists upon full forgiveness upon the conscious level of self and other-self, for they are one. A full forgiveness is thus impossible without the inclusion of self.

18.13 **QUESTIONER** Thank you. A most important point to my way of thinking.

You mentioned that there were a number of Confederations. Do all serve the Infinite Creator in basically the same way, or do some specialize in some particular types of service?

RA I am Ra. All serve the One Creator. There is nothing else to serve, for the Creator is all that there is. It is impossible not to serve the Creator. There are simply various distortions of this service.

As in the Confederation which works with your peoples, each Confederation is a group of specialized individual social memory complexes, each doing that which it expresses to bring into manifestation.

18.14 **QUESTIONER** Can you tell me how Yahweh communicated to Earth's people?

RA I am Ra. This is a somewhat complex question.

The first communication was what you would call genetic. The second communication was the walking among your peoples to produce further genetic changes in consciousness. The third was a series of dialogues with chosen channels.

18.15 **QUESTIONER** Can you tell me what these genetic changes were and how they were brought about?

RA I am Ra. Some of these genetic changes were in a form similar to what you call the cloning process. Thus, entities incarnated in the image of the Yahweh entities. The second was a contact of the nature you know as sexual, changing the mind/body/spirit complex through the natural means of the patterns of reproduction devised by the intelligent energy of your physical complex.

18.16 **QUESTIONER** Can you tell me specifically what they did in this case?

RA I am Ra. We have answered this question. Please restate for further information.

18.17 **QUESTIONER** Can you tell me the difference between the . . . the sexual programming, let us say, prior to Yahweh's intervention and after intervention?

RA I am Ra. This is a question which we can only answer by stating that intervention by genetic means is the same no matter what the source of this change.

18.18 **QUESTIONER** Can you tell me Yahweh's purpose in making the genetic sexual changes?

RA I am Ra. The purpose, seven five oh oh oh [75,000] years ago, as you measure time, [of] the changes subsequent to that time were of one purpose only: that to express in the mind/body complex those characteristics which would lead to further and more speedy development of the spiritual complex.

18.19 **QUESTIONER** How did these characteristics go about leading to the more spiritual development?

RA I am Ra. The characteristics which were encouraged included sensitivity of all the physical senses to sharpen the experiences and the strengthening of the mind complex in order to promote the ability to analyze these experiences.

18.20 **QUESTIONER** When did Yahweh act to perform the genetic changes that Yahweh performed?

RA I am Ra. The Yahweh group worked with those of the planet you call Mars seven five, seventy-five thousand [75,000] years ago in what you would call the cloning process. There are differences, but they lie in the future of your time/space continuum, and we cannot break the free will Law of Confusion.

The two six oh oh [2,600], approximately, time was the second time—we correct ourselves—three six oh oh [3,600], approximately the time of attempts by those of the Orion group during this cultural complex. This was a series of encounters in which the ones called Anak were impregnated with the new genetic coding by your physical complex means so that the organisms would be larger and stronger.

18.21 **QUESTIONER** Why did they want larger and stronger organisms?

RA The ones of Yahweh were attempting to create an understanding of the Law of One by creating mind/body complexes capable of grasping the Law of One. The experiment was a decided failure from the view of the desired distortions due to the fact that rather than assimilating the Law of One, it was a great temptation to consider the so-called social complex, or sub-complex, as elite or different, and better, than other-selves, this one of the techniques of service to self.

18.22 **QUESTIONER** Then the Orion group . . . I'm not quite sure that I understand this. Do you mean that the Orion group produced this larger body complex to create an elite so that the Law of One could be applied in what we call the negative sense?

RA I am Ra. This is incorrect. The entities of Yahweh were responsible for this procedure in isolated cases as experiments in combating the Orion group.

However, the Orion group were able to use this distortion of mind/body complex to inculcate the thoughts of the elite rather than concentrations upon the learning/teaching of oneness.

18.23 **QUESTIONER** Well, was Yahweh then of the Confederation?

RA I am Ra. Yahweh was of the Confederation but was mistaken in its attempts to aid.

18.24 **QUESTIONER** Then Yahweh's communications did not help or did not create what Yahweh wished for them to create. Is this correct?

RA I am Ra. The results of this interaction were quite mixed. Where the entities were of a vibrational sum characteristic which embraced oneness, the manipulations of Yahweh were very useful. Wherein the entities of free will had chosen a less positively oriented configuration of sum total vibratory complex, those of the Orion group were able, for the first time, to make serious inroads upon the consciousness of the planetary complex.

18.25 **QUESTIONER** Can you tell me specifically what allowed the most serious of these inroads to be made by the Orion group?

RA I am Ra. This will be the final full question.

Specifically, those who are strong, intelligent, etc., have a temptation to feel different from those who are less intelligent and less strong. This is a distorted perception of oneness with other-selves. It allowed the Orion group to form the concept of the holy war, as you may call it. This is a seriously distorted perception. There were many of these wars of a destructive nature.

18.26 **QUESTIONER** Thank you very much. I believe that to be a very important point in understanding the total workings of the Law of One. It'll be helpful. As you probably know, I must work for the next three days, so we will possibly have another session tonight if you think it is possible. And the next session after that would not be until four days from now. Do you believe another session tonight is possible?

RA I am Ra. This instrument is somewhat weak. This is a distortion caused by lack of vital energy. Thus, nurturing the instrument in physical balancing will allow another session. Do you understand?

18.27 **QUESTIONER** Not completely. What specifically shall we do for physical balancing?

RA I am Ra. One: take care with the foodstuffs. Two: manipulate the physical complex to alleviate the distortion towards physical complex pain. Three: encourage a certain amount of what you would call your exercise. The final injunction: to take special care with the alignments this second session so that the entity may gain as much aid as possible from the various symbols. We suggest you check these symbols most carefully. This entity is slightly misplaced from the proper configuration. Not important at this time. More important when a second session is to be scheduled.

I am Ra. I leave you in the love and the light of the One Infinite Creator. Go forth, therefore, rejoicing in the power and the peace of the One Creator. Adonai.

19.0 **RA** I am Ra. I greet you in the love and the light of the Infinite Creator. We communicate now.

19.1 **QUESTIONER** I have been thinking over the scope of this book and will read this that I have thought. We are concerned in this communication with the evolution of mind, body, and spirit. I would like to fully investigate through questioning the mechanism of evolution in order to allow those interested individuals to participate in their own evolution. It seems to me that a good place to start would be the transition from the second to third density, then to investigate, in detail, the evolution of third-density entities of Earth, paying particular attention to the mechanisms which help or hinder that evolution. This is my intent for direction of this working session. I hope that this is a correct direction.

What I would like to know first is: do all entities make a transition from second to third density, or are there some other entities who have never gone through this transition?

RA I am Ra. Your question presumes the space/time continuum understandings of the intelligent energy which animates your illusion. Within the context of this illusion we may say that there are some which do not transfer from one particular density to another, for the continuum is finite.

In the understanding which we have of the universe, or creation, as one infinite being—its heart beating as alive in its own intelligent energy—it merely is one beat of the heart of this intelligence from creation to creation. In this context each and every entity of consciousness has/is/will experienced/experiencing/experience each and every density.

19.2 **QUESTIONER** Let's take the point at which an individualized entity of second density is ready for transition to third. Is this second-density being what we would call animal?

RA I am Ra. There are three types of second-density entities which become, shall we say, enspirited. The first is the animal. This is the most predominant. The second is the vegetable, most especially that which you call sound vibration complex "tree." These entities are capable of giving and receiving enough love to become individualized. The third category is mineral. Occasionally a certain location—place, as you may call it— becomes energized to individuality through the love it receives and gives in relationship to a third-density entity which is in relationship to it. This is the least common transition.

19.3 **QUESTIONER** When this transition from second to third density takes place, how does the entity, whether it be animal, tree, or mineral, become enspirited?

RA I am Ra. Entities do not become enspirited. They become aware of the intelligent energy within each portion, cell, or atom, as you may call it, of its beingness.

This awareness is that which is awareness of that already given. From the infinite come all densities. The self-awareness comes from within—given the catalyst of certain experiences—understanding, as we may call this particular energy, the upward spiraling of the cell, or atom, or consciousness.

You may then see that there is an inevitable pull towards the, what you may call, eventual realization of self.

19.4 **QUESTIONER** Then after the transition into the third density, am I correct in assuming that these entities would then be in— We'll take Earth as an example. Would the entities, then, look like us? They would be in human form? Is this correct?

RA I am Ra. This is correct, taking your planetary sphere as an example.

19.5 **QUESTIONER** When the first second-density entities became third on this planet, was this with the help of the transfer of beings from Mars, or were there second-density entities that evolved into third density with no outside influence?

RA I am Ra. There were some second-density entities which made the graduation into third density with no outside stimulus but only the efficient use of experience.

Others of your planetary second density joined the third-density cycle due to harvesting efforts by the same sort of sending of vibratory aid as those of the Confederation send you now. This communication was, however, telepathic, rather than telepathic/vocal or telepathic/written, due to the nature of second-density beings.

19.6   **QUESTIONER** Who sent the aid to the second-density beings?

RA I am Ra. We call ourselves the Confederation of Planets in the Service of the Infinite Creator. This is a simplification in order to ease the difficulty of understanding among your people. We hesitate to use the term, sound vibration, "understanding," but it is closest to our meaning.

19.7   **QUESTIONER** Then the Confederation also aided in second density to third density transition. Is this correct?

RA I am Ra. We must qualify correctness of this query. A portion of the Confederation which is not working with third density but finds its aid best used in other harvests—that is, the second-density harvest—is responsible for aid in these harvests.

The Confederation, as we have stated previously in these sessions, is composed of many of those in other densities, in your own density, within your planetary sphere, and within the inner, or angelic, realms. Each of those entities developing a mind/body/spirit complex, and then developing a social memory complex, and then dedicating this social memory complex to the singular service to the One Creator, may join the Confederation.

19.8   **QUESTIONER** Well, did this second density to third density transition take place then 75,000 years ago? Approximate?

RA I am Ra. This is correct.

19.9   **QUESTIONER** Where did the second-density beings get physical vehicles of third-density type to incarnate into?

RA I am Ra. There were among those upon this second-density plane those forms which, when exposed to third-density vibrations, became the third-density, as you would call sound vibration, human, entities.

That is, there was loss of the body hair, as you call it; the clothing of the body to protect it; the changing of the structure of the neck, jaw, and forehead in order to allow the easier vocalization; and the larger cranial development characteristic of third-density needs. This was a normal transfiguration.

19.10 **QUESTIONER** Over approximately how long a period of time does . . . was this transfiguration? It must have been very short.

RA I am Ra. The assumption is correct, in our terms at least—within a generation and one-half, as you know these things. Those who had been harvested of this planet were able to use the newly created physical complex of chemical elements suitable for third-density lessons.

19.11 **QUESTIONER** Can you tell me how this new bodily complex was suited to third-density lessons and what those lessons were?

RA I am Ra. There is one necessity for third density. That necessity is self-awareness, or self-consciousness. In order to be capable of such, this chemical complex of body must be capable of the abstract thought. Thus, the fundamental necessity is the combination of rational and intuitive thinking. This was transitory in the second-density forms, operating largely upon intuition, which proved through practice to yield results.

The third-density mind was capable of processing information in such a way as to think abstractly and in what could be termed "useless" ways, in the sense of survival. This is the primary requisite.

There are other important ingredients: the necessity for a weaker physical vehicle to encourage the use of the mind, the development of the already present awareness of the social complex. These also being necessary: the further development of physical dexterity in the sense of the hand, as you call this portion of your body complex.

19.12 **QUESTIONER** This seems to be a carefully planned, or engineered, stage of development. Can you tell me anything of the origin of this plan for the development?

RA I am Ra. We go back to previous information.[1] Consider and remember the discussion of the Logos. With the primal distortion of free will, each galaxy developed its own Logos. This Logos has complete free will in determining the paths of intelligent energy which promote the lessons of each of the densities, given the conditions of the planetary spheres and the sun bodies.

19.13 **QUESTIONER** I will make a statement with respect to my understanding, then, and ask if I am correct. There is a, what I would call, a physical

---

[1] Previous information from 13.7–16 and 18.6.

catalyst operating at all times upon the entities in third density. I assume this operated approximately the same way in second density. It's a catalyst that acts through what we call pain and emotion.

Is the primary reason for the weakening of the physical body and the elimination of body hair, etc., so that this catalyst would act more strongly upon the mind and therefore create the evolutionary process?

RA I am Ra. This is not entirely correct, although closely associated with the distortions of our understanding.

Consider, if you will, the tree for instance. It is self-sufficient. Consider, if you will, the third-density entity. It is self-sufficient only through difficulty and deprivation. It is difficult to learn alone, for there is a built-in handicap, at once the great virtue and the great handicap of third density. That is the rational/intuitive mind.

Thus, the weakening of the physical vehicle, as you call it, was designed to distort entities towards a predisposition to deal with each other. Thus, the lessons which approach a knowing of love can be begun.

This catalyst then is shared between peoples as an important part of each self's development as well as the experiences of the self in solitude and the synthesis of all experience through meditation. The quickest way to learn is to deal with other-selves. This is a much greater catalyst than dealing with the self. Dealing with the self without other-selves is akin to living without what you would call mirrors. Thus, the self cannot see the fruits of its beingness. Thus, each may aid each by reflection. This is also a primary reason for the weakening of the physical vehicle, as you call the physical complex.

19.14 QUESTIONER Then we have second-density beings who have, primarily, motivation towards service to self and possibly a little bit of service to others with respect to their immediate families, going into third density and carrying this bias with them but being in a position now where this bias will slowly be modified to one which is aimed toward a social complex, and then ultimately toward union with the all. Am I correct?

RA I am Ra. You are correct.

19.15 QUESTIONER Then the newest third-density beings who've just made the transition from second are still strongly biased towards self-service. There must be many other mechanisms to create an awareness of the possibility of service to others.

I am wondering, first—two things. I'm wondering about the mechanism, and I am wondering when the split takes place, where the entity is able to continue on the road towards service to self that will eventually take him to fourth or fifth density.

I would assume that an entity can continue . . . can start, say, in second density with service totally to self and continue right on through and just stay on what we would call the path of service to self and never ever be pulled over. Is this correct?

RA I am Ra. This is incorrect. The second-density concept of serving self includes the serving of those associated with tribe or pack. This is not seen in second density as separation of self and other-self. All is seen as self since in some forms of second-density entities, if the tribe or pack becomes weakened, so does the entity within the tribe or pack.

The new or initial third-density entity has this innocent, shall we say, bias or distortion towards viewing those in the family, the society, as you would call, perhaps, country, as self. Thus, though a distortion not helpful for progress in third density, it is without polarity.

The break becomes apparent when the entity perceives other-selves as other-selves and consciously determines to manipulate other-selves for the benefit of the self. This is the beginning of the road of which you speak.

19.16 QUESTIONER Then, through free will, sometime in the third-density experience, the path splits, and an entity consciously . . . probably does not consciously choose. Does an entity consciously choose this path at the initial splitting point?

RA I am Ra. We speak in generalities, which is dangerous for always inaccurate. However, we realize you look for the overview, so we will eliminate anomalies and speak of majorities.

The majority of third-density beings is far along the chosen path before realization of that path is conscious.

19.17 QUESTIONER Can you tell me what bias creates their momentum toward the chosen path of service to self?

RA I am Ra. We can speak only in metaphor. Some love the light. Some love the darkness. It is a matter of the unique and infinitely various Creator choosing and playing among its experiences as a child upon a picnic. Some enjoy the picnic and find the sun beautiful, the food delicious, the games refreshing, and glow with the joy of creation. Some find the night delicious, their picnic being pain, difficulty, sufferings of others, and the examination of the perversities of nature. These enjoy a different picnic.

All these experiences are available. It is free will of each entity which chooses the form of play, the form of pleasure.

19.18   **QUESTIONER** I assume that an entity on either path can decide to choose paths at any time and possibly retrace steps, the path-changing being more difficult the farther along is gone. Is this correct?

RA I am Ra. This is incorrect. The further an entity has, what you would call, polarized, the more easily this entity may change polarity, for the more power and awareness the entity will have.

Those truly helpless are those who have not consciously chosen but who repeat patterns without knowledge of the repetition or the meaning of the pattern.

19.19   **QUESTIONER** I believe we have a very, very important point here. It then seems that there is an extreme potential in this polarization the same as there is in— To make an analogy, using electricity: we have a positive and negative pole. The more you build the charge on either of these, the greater the potential difference and the greater the ability to do work, as we call it, in the physical.

This would seem to me to be the exact analogy that we have in consciousness here. Is this correct?

RA I am Ra. This is precisely correct.

19.20   **QUESTIONER** Well, this would seem then that there is a relationship then between what we perceive as physical phenomena, say the electrical phenomena, and the phenomena of consciousness, and that they, having stemmed from the One Creator, are practically identical but have slightly different actions as we [*inaudible*]. Is this correct?

RA I am Ra. Again we oversimplify to answer your query.

The physical complex alone is created of many, many energy, or electromagnetic, fields interacting due to intelligent energy. The mental configurations, or distortions, of each complex further adding fields of electromagnetic energy and distorting the physical complex patterns of energy. The spiritual aspect serving as a further complexity of fields which is of itself perfect, but which can be realized in many distorted and unintegrated ways by the mind and body complexes of energy fields.

Thus, instead of one, shall we say, magnet with one polarity, you have in the body/mind/spirit complex one basic polarity expressed in what you would call violet-ray energy (the sum of the energy fields), but which is affected by thoughts of all kinds generated by the mind complex; by distortions of the body complex; and by the numerous relationships between the microcosm (which is the entity) and the macrocosm in many forms—which you may represent by viewing the stars, as you call them, each with a contributing energy ray which enters the electromagnetic web of the entity due to its individual distortions.

19.21   **QUESTIONER** Is this then the root of what we call astrology?

RA I am Ra. This will be the last full question of this session.

The root of astrology, as you speak it, is one way of perceiving the primal distortions which may be predicted along probability/possibility lines given the, shall we say, cosmic orientations and configurations at the time of the entrance into the physical/mental complex of the spirit and at the time of the physical/mental/spiritual complex into the illusion.

This then has the possibility of suggesting basic areas of distortion. There is no more than this. The part astrology plays is likened unto that of one root among many.

19.22   **QUESTIONER** I just have two little questions here at the end. The instrument wanted me to ask if there was any other substances, foods, etc., that she should not eat or drink, or anything she should not do because she does not wish to have poor contact for any reason.

RA I am Ra. There is no activity which this instrument engages in which affects its abilities negatively. There is one activity which affects its abilities positively. This is the sexual activity, as you would call it.

There are substances ingested which do not aid the individual in the service it has chosen, this being that which you would call the marijuana.

This is due to the distortion towards chemical lapses within the mind complex causing lack of synaptic continuity. This is a chemical reaction of short duration. This instrument, however, has not used this particular substance at any time while performing this service.

We believe we have covered the use of such chemical agents as LSD, this being positive to a certain extent due to the energizing, or speeding up, of the vital forces. However, it is not recommended for this instrument due to the toll it takes upon the vital energies once the substance wears off, this being true of any speeding-up chemical.

19.23 **QUESTIONER** The only other question I have, is there anything that we can do to make the instrument more comfortable? And, is it . . . wanted to ask about another session, but I guess it's too late today. I didn't realize.

RA I am Ra. This instrument is well aligned. You are being very conscientious. We request you take more care in being assured that this instrument is wearing footwear of what you would call sound vibratory complex "shoes."

I am Ra. I leave you in the love and the light of the One Infinite Creator. Go forth, therefore, rejoicing in the power and the peace of the One Creator. Adonai.

20.0   **RA** I am Ra. I greet you in the love and the light of the Infinite Creator. I communicate now.

20.1   **QUESTIONER** I was thinking the best way to do the book is to continue working on the history of evolution and its mechanism until we completely make it through the third density and what will occur into the first part of the fourth density, so that the mechanisms of developing the mind/body/spirit complex will be brought out. If I get stymied some place in one of these sessions as to what questions to ask and where—not to waste time—I may ask some questions that I will use later in the book, but we'll try to always continue along these lines.

First question, to go back just a little bit, is what happened to the second-density entities who were on this planet who were unharvestable? I assume there were some that didn't make the harvest into the third density. Can you tell me this?

RA I am Ra. The second density is able to repeat, during third density, a portion of its cycle.

20.2   **QUESTIONER** Then the second-density entities that did not get harvested at the beginning of this 75,000-year period—some are still in second density on this planet. Were any of these who remained in second density harvested into third density in the past 75,000 years?

RA I am Ra. This has been increasingly true.

20.3   **QUESTIONER** So more and more second-density entities are making it into third density. Can you give me an example of a second-density entity coming into third density, say, in the recent past?

RA I am Ra. Perhaps the most common occurrence of second-density graduation during third-density cycle is the so-called pet: the animal which is exposed to the individualizing influences of the bond between animal and third-density entity. This individuation causes a sharp rise in the potential of the second-density entity so that, upon the cessation of physical complex, the mind/body complex does not return unto the undifferentiated consciousness of that species, if you will.

20.4 **QUESTIONER** Then can you give me an example of an entity in third density that was just previously a second-density entity? What type of entity do they become here?

RA I am Ra. As a second-density entity returns as third-density for the beginning of this process of learning, the entity is equipped with the lowest, if you will so call these vibrational distortions, forms of third-density consciousness; that is, equipped with self-consciousness.

20.5 **QUESTIONER** This would be a human in our form, then, who would be beginning the understandings of third density. Is this correct?

RA I am Ra. This is correct.

20.6 **QUESTIONER** Speaking of the rapid change that occurred in the physical vehicle, the change from second to third density: this, you said, occurred in approximately a generation and a half. Body hair was lost and there were structural changes.

I am aware of the physics of Dewey B. Larson, who states that all is motion, or vibration. Am I correct in assuming that the basic vibration, which makes up the physical world as we experience it, changes, thus creating a different set of parameters, shall I say, in this short period of time between density changes, allowing for the new type of vehicle? Am I correct?

RA I am Ra. This is correct.

20.7 **QUESTIONER** Just as a sideline, a side question here: Is the physics of Dewey Larson correct?

RA I am Ra. The physics of sound vibrational complex, Dewey, is a correct system as far as it is able to go. There are those things which are not included in this system. However, those coming after this particular entity, using the basic concepts of vibration and the study of vibrational distortions, will begin to understand that which you know of as gravity and those things you consider as "n" dimensions. These things are necessary to be included in a more universal, shall we say, physical theory.

20.8 **QUESTIONER** Was this entity, Dewey, then . . . did he bring this material through in his incarnation for use primarily in fourth density?

RA I am Ra. This is correct.

20.9 **QUESTIONER** Thank you. Yesterday we were speaking of the split that takes place in third density when an entity, either consciously or because of bias, chooses the path of service to others or service to self. The philosophical question of why such a split even exists came up. It is my impression that as it is in electricity, if we have no polarity in electricity, we have no electricity; we have no action; we have no— Therefore, I am assuming that in consciousness, without such polarity, there would be no action or experience. Is this correct?

RA This is correct. You may use the general term "work."

20.10 **QUESTIONER** Then the concept of service to self or service to others is mandatory if we wish to have work, whether it be work in consciousness or work in the mechanical, or Newtonian concept in the physical. Is this correct?

RA I am Ra. This is correct with one addendum. The coil, as you may understand this term, is wound, is potential, is ready. The thing that is missing without polarizing is the charge.

20.11 **QUESTIONER** Then the charge is provided by individualized consciousness. Is this correct?

RA I am Ra. The charge is provided by the individualized entity using the inpourings and instreamings of energy by the choices of free will.

20.12 **QUESTIONER** Thank you. As soon as the third density started 75,000 years ago and we have incarnate third-density entities, what was the average human life span at that time?

RA I am Ra. At the beginning of this particular portion of your space/time continuum the average lifetime was approximately nine hundred of your years.

20.13 **QUESTIONER** Did the average life span grow longer or shorter as we progress on into third-density experience?

RA I am Ra. There is a particular use for this span of life in this density, and given the harmonious development of the learning/teachings of this density, the life span of the physical complex would remain the same throughout the cycle. However, your particular planetary sphere developed vibrations by the second major cycle which shortened the life span dramatically.

20.14 **QUESTIONER** Assuming a major cycle is 25,000 years, at the end of the first 25,000-year cycle, how long was the life span?

RA The life span at the end of the first cycle which you call major was approximately seven hundred of your years.

20.15 **QUESTIONER** Then in 25,000 years we lost two hundred years of life span. Is this correct?

RA I am Ra. This is correct.

20.16 **QUESTIONER** Can you tell me the reason for this shortening of life span?

RA I am Ra. The causes of this shortening are always an ineuphonious, or inharmonious, relational vibration between other-selves. In the first cycle this was not severe due to the dispersion of peoples, [but there was] the growing feeling-complex distortions towards separateness from other-selves.[1]

20.17 **QUESTIONER** I'm assuming at the start of one of these cycles there could have been either a positive polarization that would generally occur over the 25,000 years or a negative polarization. Is the reason for the negative polarization and the shortening of the cycle the influx of entities from Mars who had already polarized somewhat negatively?

RA I am Ra. This is incorrect. There was not a strong negative polarization due to this influx. The lessening of the life span was due primarily to the lack of the building up of positive orientation. When there is no progress, those conditions which grant progress are gradually lost. This is one of the difficulties of remaining unpolarized. The chances, shall we say, of progress become steadily less.

20.18 **QUESTIONER** The way I understand it, at the beginning of this 75,000-year cycle, then, we have a mixture of entities—those who have graduated from second density on Earth to become third-density and then a group of entities transferred from the planet Mars to incarnate into third density here. Is this correct?

---

[1] This sentence has been edited in an attempt to clarify what we believe to be Ra's intended meaning. The original sentence reads: "In the first cycle this was not severe, but due to the dispersion of peoples and the growing feeling-complex distortions towards separateness from other-selves."

RA I am Ra. This is correct.

20.19 **QUESTIONER** What— Continue.

RA You must remember that those transferred to this sphere were in the middle of their third density, so that this third density was an adaptation rather than a beginning.

20.20 **QUESTIONER** Thank you. What percentage of the entities, roughly, were . . . who were in third density here at that time were Martian, and what percentage were harvested out of Earth's second density?

RA I am Ra. There were perhaps one-half of the third-density population being entities from the Red Planet, Mars, as you call it; perhaps one-quarter from second density of your planetary sphere; approximately one-quarter from other sources, other planetary spheres whose entities chose this planetary sphere for third-density work.

20.21 **QUESTIONER** When they incarnated here did they mix? Did all three of these types mix together in societies or groups, or were they separated by group or society?

RA I am Ra. They remained largely unmixed.

20.22 **QUESTIONER** Then did this unmixing lend to a possibility of separation of group, then, or the possibility of warlike attitude between groups?

RA I am Ra. This is correct.

20.23 **QUESTIONER** Did this then help to reduce the life span?

RA I am Ra. This did reduce the life span, as you call it.

20.24 **QUESTIONER** Can you tell me why nine hundred years is the optimum life span?

RA I am Ra. The mind/body/spirit complex of third density has perhaps one hundred times as intensive a program of catalytic action from which to distill distortions and learn/teachings than any other of the densities. Thus the learn/teachings are most confusing to the mind/body/spirit complex which is, shall we say, inundated by the ocean of experience.

During the first, shall we say, perhaps 150 to 200 of your years, as you measure time, a mind/body/spirit complex is going through the process of a spiritual childhood, the mind and the body not enough in a disciplined configuration to lend clarity to the spiritual influxes. Thus, the remaining time span is given to optimize the understandings which result from experience itself.

20.25 **QUESTIONER** Then at present it would seem that our life span is much too short for those who are new to third-density lessons. Is this correct?

RA I am Ra. This is correct. Those entities which have, in some way, learned/taught themselves the appropriate distortions for rapid growth can now work within the confines of the shorter life span. However, the greater preponderance of your entities find themselves in what may be considered a perpetual childhood.

20.26 **QUESTIONER** Thank you. Now, back in the first 25,000-year period, or major cycle, what type of aid was given by the Confederation to the entities who were in this 25,000-year period so that they could have the opportunity to grow?

RA I am Ra. The Confederation members which dwell in inner-plane existence within the planetary complex of vibratory densities worked with these entities. There was also the aid of one of the Confederation which worked with those of Mars in making the transition.

For the most part the participation was limited, as it was appropriate to allow the full travel of the workings of the confusion mechanism to operate in order for the planetary entities to develop that which they wished in, shall we say, freedom within their own thinking.

It is often the case that a third-density planetary cycle will take place in such a way that there need be no outside, shall we say, or other-self aid in the form of information. Rather, the entities themselves are able to work themselves towards the appropriate polarizations and goals of third-density learn/teachings.

20.27 **QUESTIONER** I will make this assumption, then: if maximum efficiency had been achieved in this 25,000-year period the entities would have polarized either toward service toward self or service to others, one or the other. This would have then made them harvestable at the end of that 25,000-year period to either service-to-self or service-to-others type of fourth density, in which case they would have had to move to another planet because this one would have been in third density for fifty more thousand years. Is this correct?

RA I am Ra. Let us untangle your assumption which is complex and correct in part.

The original desire is that entities seek and become one. If entities can do this in a moment, they may go forward in a moment; and thus were this to occur in a major cycle, indeed the third-density planet would be vacated at the end of that cycle.

It is, however, more toward the median, or mean, shall we say, of third-density developments throughout the one infinite universe that there be a small harvest after the first cycle; the remainder having significantly polarized, the second cycle having a much larger harvest; the remainder being even more significantly polarized, the third cycle culminating the process and the harvest being completed.

20.28 **QUESTIONER** Very good. Then was the Confederation, shall we say, watching to see, and expecting to see, a harvest at the end of the 25,000-year period in which a percentage would be harvestable fourth-density positive and a percentage harvestable fourth-density negative?

RA I am Ra. This is correct. You may see our role in the first major cycle as that of the gardener who, knowing the season, is content to wait for the spring. When the springtime does not occur, the seeds do not sprout; then it is that the gardener must work in the garden.

20.29 **QUESTIONER** Am I to understand, then, there was neither harvestable entities of positive or negative polarity at the end of that 25,000 years?

RA I am Ra. This is correct. Those whom you call the Orion group made one attempt to offer information to those of third density during that cycle. However, the information did not fall upon the ears of any who were concerned to follow this path to polarity.

20.30 **QUESTIONER** What technique did the Orion group use to give this information?

RA I am Ra. The technique used was of two kinds:

One, the thought transfer, or what you may call telepathy.

Two, the arrangement of certain stones in order to suggest strong influences of power, this being those of statues and of rock formations in your Pacific areas, as you now call them, and to an extent in your Central American regions, as you now understand them.

20.31   **QUESTIONER** Are you speaking in part of the stone heads of Easter Island?

RA I am Ra. This is correct.

20.32   **QUESTIONER** How would such stone heads influence a people to take the path of service to self?

RA I am Ra. Picture, if you will, the entities living in such a way that their mind/body/spirit complexes are at what seems to be the mercy of forces which they cannot control. Given a charged entity, such as a statue or a rock formation charged with nothing but power, it is possible for the free will of those viewing this particular structure or formation to ascribe to this power, power over those things which cannot be controlled. This, then, has the potential for the further distortion to power over other-selves.

20.33   **QUESTIONER** How were these stone heads constructed?

RA I am Ra. These were constructed by thought after a scanning of the deep mind, the trunk of mind tree, looking at the images most likely to cause the experience of awe in the viewer.

20.34   **QUESTIONER** Well, then, did Orion entities do this themselves? Did they land in physical, or did they do it from mental planes, or did they use one of the incarnate entities to construct these by thought?

RA I am Ra. Nearly all of these structures and formations were constructed at a distance by thought. A very few were created in later times in imitation of original constructs by entities upon your Earth plane/density.

20.35   **QUESTIONER** What density Orion entity did the creation of these heads?

RA I am Ra. The fourth density, the density of love, or understanding, was the density of the particular entity which offered this possibility to those of your first major cycle.

20.36   **QUESTIONER** You use the same nomenclature for fourth-density negative as for fourth-density positive. Both are called the dimension of love or understanding. Is this correct?

RA I am Ra. This is correct. Love and understanding, whether it be of self or of self towards other-self, is one.

20.37 **QUESTIONER** Now, what was the approximate date in years past of the construction of these heads?

RA I am Ra. This approximately was six zero, sixty thousand [60,000], of your years in the past time/space of your continuum.

20.38 **QUESTIONER** What structures were built in South America?

RA I am Ra. In this location were fashioned some characteristic statues, some formations of what you call rock and some formations involving rock and earth.

20.39 **QUESTIONER** Were the lines at Nazca included in this?

RA I am Ra. This is correct.

20.40 **QUESTIONER** Since this can only be seen from an altitude, of what benefit was this?

RA I am Ra. The formations were of benefit because charged with energy of power.

20.41 **QUESTIONER** I'm a little confused. These lines at Nazca are hardly understandable for an entity walking on the surface. He cannot see anything but a disruption of the surface. However, if you go up to a high altitude you can see the patterns. How was it of benefit to the entities walking on the surface?

RA I am Ra. At the remove of the amount of time/space which is now your present it is difficult to perceive that at the time/space sixty thousand [60,000] years ago the earth was formed in such a way as to be visibly arranged in powerful structural designs, from the vantage point of distant hills.

20.42 **QUESTIONER** In other words at that time there were hills overlooking these lines?

RA I am Ra. This will be the final full question of this session.

The entire smoothness, as you see this area now, was built up in many places in hills. The time/space continuum has proceeded with wind and weather, as you would say, to erode to a great extent both the somewhat formidable structures of earth designed at that time and the nature of the surrounding countryside.

20.43 **QUESTIONER** I think I understand then. Then these lines are just the faint traces of what used to be there?

RA I am Ra. This is correct.

20.44 **QUESTIONER** Thank you. We need to know whether or not it is possible to continue with another session later today, and if there is anything we can do to make the instrument more comfortable?

RA I am Ra. It is possible. We ask that you observe carefully the alignment of the instrument. Otherwise, you are conscientious.

Is there any short query before we close?

20.45 **QUESTIONER** I intend in the next session to focus on the development of the positively oriented entities in the first 25,000 years. I know that you can't make suggestions. But this seems to me to be the— I hope that I am going in the right path in investigating the entire development and influences in the history of our third density. Can you give me any comment on this at all?

RA I am Ra. The choices are yours according to your discernment.

I am Ra. I leave you in the love and the light of the One Infinite Creator. Go forth, therefore, rejoicing in the power and the peace of the One Creator. Adonai.

SESSION 21

21.0 **RA** I am Ra. I greet you in the love and the light of the Infinite Creator. We communicate now.

21.1 **QUESTIONER** I have a couple of questions I don't want to forget to ask in this period. I'll ask them first.

The first question is: Would the future content of this book be affected in any way if the instrument reads the material we have already obtained?

RA I am Ra. The future, as you measure in time/space, communications which we offer through this instrument have no connection with the instrument's mind complex. This is due to two things:

First, the fidelity of the instrument in dedicating its will to the service of the Infinite Creator.

Secondly, the distortion/understanding of our social memory complex that the most efficient way to communicate material with as little distortion as possible, given the necessity of the use of sound vibration complexes, is to remove the conscious mind complex from the spirit/mind/body complex so that we may communicate without reference to any instrument orientation.

21.2 **QUESTIONER** A little appendage to this: Do you use your vocabulary or the instrument's vocabulary to communicate with us?

RA I am Ra. We use the vocabulary of the language with which you are familiar. This is not the instrument's vocabulary. However, this particular mind/body/spirit complex retains the use of a sufficiently large number of sound vibration complexes that the distinction is often without any importance.

21.3 **QUESTIONER** Andrija Puharich will be visiting later this month. Can he read the unpublished healing material?

RA I am Ra. The entity of whom you speak has a knowledge of this material in its conscious memory in somewhat altered form. Therefore, it is harmless to allow this entity to become acquainted with this material. However, we request the mind/body/spirit complex, Henry, be sufficiently prepared by means of meditation, contemplation, or prayer before entering these workings. At present, as we have said before, this mind/body/spirit complex is not of proper vibrational distortion.

21.4 **QUESTIONER** I had already determined to exclude him from these workings. I have only determined to let him read the material. The only other thing is that I have noticed that within the material as it exists now, there is a certain statement which will allow him to understand who I believe Spectra really was. It seems my duty to remove this from his knowledge to preserve the same free will that you attempted to preserve by not defining the origin of Spectra, his contact in Israel. Am I correct?

RA I am Ra. This is a matter for your discretion.

21.5 **QUESTIONER** That's what I thought you'd say.

Well, now we'll get back to the business at hand—of doing the book. I want, as we cover this early part of the 75,000-year cycle, I would . . . I would like to go back a little bit, quite some distance perhaps, before the 75,000 years occurred, and take one more look at the transfer of entities from Maldek to clear up this point. I'd like to check the time that you gave us, because we had some distortions in numbers back in the early part of this, and I'm afraid this might be distorted. These entities from Maldek were transferred how many years ago?

RA I am Ra. The entities of which you speak underwent several transitions, the first occurring five zero zero thousand [500,000] of your years, approximately, in your past, as you measure time. At this time, the entities were transformed into a knot. This continued for what you would call eons of your time. Those aiding them were repeatedly unable to reach them.

At a period approximately two zero zero thousand [200,000] years in your past, as you measure time, a Confederation entity was able to begin to relax this knot from which none had escaped during planetary annihilation. These entities then were transformed again into the inner, or time/space, dimensions and underwent a lengthy process of healing. When this was accomplished, these entities were then able to determine the appropriate movement, shall we say, in order to set up conditions for alleviation of the consequences of their actions.

At a time four six zero zero zero, forty-six thousand [46,000] of your years in your past, as you measure time, this being approximate, these entities chose incarnation within the planetary sphere.[1]

21.6 **QUESTIONER** I see. Then no incarnation occurred before this master 75,000-year cycle of Maldek entities. Correct?

RA I am Ra. This is correct in the sense of incarnation in third-density time/space.[2]

21.7 **QUESTIONER** Were there any of these entities then incarnated in second density before the 75,000-year cycle?

RA I am Ra. This is incorrect. These particular entities were incarnate in time/space third density, that is, the so-called inner planes, undergoing the process of healing and approaching realization of their action.

21.8 **QUESTIONER** I don't mean to be covering ground that we've already covered, but there're some points that we have trouble with fully understanding, and sometimes I have to ask the question a different way to fully understand it. Thank you.

So at the start of this 75,000-year cycle we know that the quarantine was set up. I am assuming then that the Guardians were aware of the infringements on free will that would occur if they didn't set this up at that time and therefore did it. This— Is this correct?

RA I am Ra. This is partially incorrect. The incorrectness is as follows: those entities whose third-density experience upon your Red Planet was brought to a close prematurely were aided genetically while being transferred to this third density. This, although done in a desire to aid, was seen as infringement upon free will. The light quarantine, which consists of the Guardians, or gardeners, as you may call them, which would have been in effect thus was intensified.

21.9 **QUESTIONER** Now, when the 75,000-year cycle started, the life span was approximately nine hundred years, average. What was the process and scheduling of . . . mechanism, shall I say, of reincarnation at that time,

---

[1] The dates given in this answer seem to conflict with those given in 10.1.

[2] Ra possibly intended to say space/time here.

and how did the time in between incarnations into third-density physical apply to the growth of the mind/body/spirit complex?

RA I am Ra. This query is more complex than most. We shall begin. The incarnation pattern of the beginning third-density mind/body/spirit complex begins in darkness, for you may think, or consider, of your density as one of, as you may say, a sleep and a forgetting. This is the only plane of forgetting. It is necessary for the third-density entity to forget so that the mechanisms of confusion, or free will, may operate upon the newly individuated consciousness complex.

Thus, the beginning entity is one in all innocence oriented towards animalistic behavior using other-selves only as extensions of self for the preservation of the all-self. The entity becomes slowly aware that it has needs, shall we say, that are not animalistic; that is, that are useless for survival. These needs include: the need for companionship, the need for laughter, the need for beauty, the need to know the universe about it. These are the beginning needs.

As the incarnations begin to accumulate, further needs are discovered: the need to trade, the need to love, the need to be loved, the need to elevate animalistic behaviors to a more universal perspective.

During the first portion of third-density cycles, incarnations are automatic and occur rapidly upon the cessation of energy complex of the physical vehicle. There is small need to review or to heal the experiences of the incarnation. As, what you would call, the energy centers begin to be activated to a higher extent, more of the content of experience during incarnation deals with the lessons of love.

Thus the time, as you may understand it, between incarnations is lengthened to give appropriate attention to the review and the healing of experiences of the previous incarnation. At some point in third density, the green-ray energy center becomes activated, and at that point incarnation ceases to be automatic.

21.10 **QUESTIONER** When incarnation ceases to become automatic I am assuming that the entity can decide when he needs to reincarnate for the benefit of his own learning. Does he also select his parents?

RA I am Ra. This is correct.

21.11 **QUESTIONER** At this time in our cycle, near the end, what percentage of the entities, approximately, incarnating are making their own choices?

RA I am Ra. The approximate percentage is five four, fifty-four [54] percent.

21.12 **QUESTIONER** Thank you. During this first 25,000-year cycle was there any industrial development at all? Was there any machinery available during this period to the people?

RA I am Ra. Using the term "machine" to the meaning which you ascribe, the answer is no. However, there were, shall we say, various implements of wood and rock which were used in order to obtain food and for use in aggression.

21.13 **QUESTIONER** At the end of this first 25,000-year cycle, then, was there any physical change that occurred rapidly like that which occurs at a 75,000-year cycle, or is this just an indexing time for a harvesting period?

RA I am Ra. There was no change except that which, according to intelligent energy, or what you may term physical evolution, suited physical complexes to their environment—this being of the color of the skin due to the area of the sphere upon which entities lived, the gradual growth of peoples due to improved intake of foodstuffs.

21.14 **QUESTIONER** Then we have a condition where at the end of the first 25,000-year period, I would say the— I am guessing that the Guardians discovered that there was no harvest of either positive or negatively oriented entities. Tell me then what happened? What action was taken, etc.?

RA I am Ra. There was no action taken except to remain aware of the possibility of a calling for help or understanding among the entities of this density. The Confederation is concerned with the preservation of the conditions conducive to learning. This, for the most part, revolves about the primal distortion of Free Will.

21.15 **QUESTIONER** Then the Confederation gardeners did nothing, I'm assuming, until some of the plants in their garden, shall I say, called them for help. Is this correct?

RA I am Ra. This is correct.

21.16 **QUESTIONER** When did the first call occur, and how did it occur?

RA The first calling was approximately four six thousand, forty-six thousand [46,000] of your years ago. This calling was of those of Maldek. These entities were aware of their need for rectifying the consequences of their action and were in some confusion in an incarnate state as to the circumstances of their incarnation: the unconscious being aware, the conscious being quite confused. This created a calling. The Confederation sent love and light to these entities.

21.17 **QUESTIONER** How did the Confederation send this love and light? Precisely what did they do?

RA I am Ra. There dwell within the Confederation planetary entities who, from their planetary spheres, do nothing but send love and light as pure streamings to those who call. This is not in the form of conceptual thought but of pure and undifferentiated love.

21.18 **QUESTIONER** Did the first distortion of the Law of One require then that equal time, shall I say, be given to the self-service oriented group?

RA I am Ra. In this case this was not necessary for some of your time due to the orientation of the entities.

21.19 **QUESTIONER** What was their orientation?

RA The orientation of these entities was such that the aid of the Confederation was not perceived.

21.20 **QUESTIONER** Since it was not perceived it was not necessary to balance this. Is that correct?

RA I am Ra. This is correct. What is necessary to balance is opportunity. When there is ignorance, there is no opportunity. When there exists a potential, then each opportunity shall be balanced, this balancing caused by not only the positive and negative orientations of those offering aid but also the orientation of those requesting aid.

21.21 **QUESTIONER** I see. I want to clear up a point here, then. When was the first contact by the Orion group? In years?

RA I am Ra. As we have said, the Orion group attempted contact approximately six zero thousand [60,000] of your years in the past, as you measure time.

21.22 **QUESTIONER** I'm sorry, I meant the first attempt in the second major cycle. I'm now working in the second 25,000 years. How many years ago was the Orion group's attempt in that cycle?

RA I am Ra. The Orion group next attempted in more fertile territory approximately three six zero zero [3,600] of your years in the past, as you measure time.

21.23 **QUESTIONER** In other words, there was no attempt 46,000 years ago by the Orion group to contact. Is that correct?

RA I am Ra. This is correct.

21.24 **QUESTIONER** As we progress into the second 25,000-year cycle, did— At this time, during this period, was this the period of Lemuria?

RA I am Ra. This is incorrect. However, those who escaped the destruction of Lemuria by natural catastrophe, and were thus of Lemurian background, continued their learn/teachings at locations ranging from your South America onward through the Americas, as you know them, and continuing over what was at that time a bridge which no longer exists. There were those in what you would call Russia . . . [*tape ends*]

21.25 **QUESTIONER** Just to quickly refresh my mind: how many years ago did Lemuria suffer its catastrophe?

RA I am Ra. This was approximately fifty thousand [50,000] of your years ago. The origins being approximately five three, fifty-three thousand [53,000] of your years ago, the damage being completed in that last small cycle of the first master cycle.

21.26 **QUESTIONER** Did you mean to say master or major cycle?

RA I am Ra. The appropriate sound vibration complex is major cycle.

21.27 **QUESTIONER** Thank you. Then did the ending of this first major cycle have something to do with the destruction of Lemuria, or did this destruction just happen to occur at the end of that cycle?

RA I am Ra. There is a confluence of energies at the ending of a major cycle. This encouraged what was already an inevitable adjustment in the movement of the surfaces of your planetary sphere.

21.28 **QUESTIONER** Thank you very much. I apologize for being so stupid in making my questions, but this has cleared up the point nicely for me. Thank you.

Then in the second 25,000-year major cycle was there any great civilization that developed?

RA I am Ra. In the sense of greatness of technology there were no great societies during this cycle. There was some advancement among those of Deneb who had chosen to incarnate as a body in what you would call China.

There were appropriately positive steps in activating the green-ray energy complex in many portions of your planetary sphere including the Americas, the continent which you call Africa, the island which you call Australia, and that which you know as India, as well as various scattered peoples.

None of these became what you would name great as the greatness of Lemuria or Atlantis is known to you due to the formation of strong social complexes and in the case of Atlantis, very great technological understandings.

However, in the South American area of your planetary sphere, as you know it, there grew to be a great vibratory distortion towards love. These entities were harvestable at the end of the second major cycle without ever having formed strong social or technological complexes.

This will be the final question in completion of this session. Is there a query we may answer quickly before we close, as this instrument is somewhat depleted?

21.29 **QUESTIONER** I just wanted to apologize for a bit of confusion on my part in carrying on to this second 25,000 years.

I would just like to ask if there is anything I could do to make the instrument more comfortable? We would hope to have a second session later today.

RA I am Ra. You may observe a slight misalignment between book, candle, and perpendicularity of censer. This is not significant, but as we have said, the cumulative effects upon this instrument are not well. You are conscientious. It is well to have a second session given the appropriate exercising and manipulation of this instrument's physical complex.

I am Ra. I leave you in the love and the light of the One Infinite Creator. Go forth, therefore, rejoicing in the power and the peace of the One Creator. Adonai.

Session 22

22.0 RA I am Ra. I greet you in the love and in the light of the Infinite Creator. I communicate now.

22.1 QUESTIONER The instrument would like to ask a couple of questions of you. I'll get them out of the way first. The instrument would like to know why she smells the incense at various times during the day in various places?

RA I am Ra. This instrument has spent a lifetime in dedication to service. This has brought this instrument to this nexus in space/time with the conscious and unconscious distortion towards service, with the further conscious distortion towards service by communication. Each time, as you would put it, that we perform this working our social-memory-complex-vibrational distortion meshes more firmly with this instrument's unconscious distortions towards service. Thus we are becoming a part of this instrument's vibratory complex and it a part of ours. This occurs upon the unconscious level, the level whereby the mind has gone down through to the roots of consciousness which you may call cosmic.

This instrument is not consciously aware of this slow changing of the meshing vibratory complex. However, as the dedication on both levels continues, and the workings continue, there are signals sent from the unconscious in a symbolic manner. Because this instrument is extremely keen in its sense of smell this association takes place unconsciously, and the thought-form of this odor is witnessed by the entity.

22.2 QUESTIONER Secondly, she would like to know why she feels more healthy now after she does these sessions. She's generally feeling more healthy as time goes on.

RA I am Ra. This is a function of the free will of the entity. This entity has, for many of your years, prayed a certain set of sound vibration complexes before opening to communication. Before the trance state was achieved this prayer remained within the conscious portion of the mind complex and, though helpful, was not as effective as the consequence of this prayer, as you would call this vibrational sound complex, which then goes directly into the unconscious level, thus more critically affecting the communication from the spiritual complex.

Also, this entity has begun, due to this working, to accept certain limitations which it placed upon itself in order to set the stage for services such as it now performs. This also is an aid to re-aligning the distortions of the physical complex with regard to pain.

22.3   **QUESTIONER** Thank you. I'll ask a couple of questions to clear up the end of the second cycle, the second major cycle. And then we'll go on to the third and last of the major cycles.

Can you tell me the life span, the average life span, at the end of the second major cycle?

RA I am Ra. By the end of the second major cycle the life span was as you know it, with certain variations among geographically isolated peoples more in harmony with intelligent energy and less bellicose.

22.4   **QUESTIONER** Can you tell me the length of that . . . average span, in years, at the end of the second major cycle?

RA I am Ra. The average is perhaps misleading. To be precise, many spent approximately thirty-five to forty of your years in one incarnation, with the possibility not considered abnormal of a life span approaching one hundred of your years.

22.5   **QUESTIONER** Then can you give me a— Can I assume, then, that this drastic drop from 700-year life span to one less than one hundred years in length during this second 25,000-year period was because of an intensification of a . . . of a condition of lack of service to others? Is this correct?

RA I am Ra. This is, in part, correct. By the end of the second cycle, the Law of Responsibility had begun to be effectuated by the increasing ability of entities to grasp those lessons which there are to be learned in this density. Thus, entities had discovered many ways to indicate a bellicose nature, not only as tribes or what you call nations, but in personal relationships, each with the other: the concept of barter having given way in many cases to the concept of money; also, the concept of ownership having won ascendancy over the concept of non-ownership on an individual or group basis.

Each entity, then, was offered many more subtle ways of demonstrating either service towards others or service to self, with the distortion of the manipulation of others. As each lesson was understood, those lessons of sharing, of giving, of receiving in free gratitude—each lesson could be rejected in practice.

Without demonstrating the fruits of such learn/teaching the life span became greatly reduced, for the ways of honor/duty were not being accepted.

22.6 **QUESTIONER** Would this shortened life span help the entity in any way in that he would have more times in between incarnations to review his mistakes, or would this shortened life span hinder him?

RA I am Ra. Both are correct. The shortening of the life span is a distortion of the Law of One which suggests that an entity not receive more experience in more intensity than it may bear. This is only in effect upon an individual level and does not hold sway over planetary or social complexes.

Thus the shortened life span is due to the necessity for removing an entity from the intensity of experience which ensues when wisdom and love are, having been rejected, reflected back into the consciousness of the Creator without being accepted as part of the self, this then causing the entity to have the need for healing and for much evaluation of the incarnation.

The incorrectness lies in the truth that, given appropriate circumstances, a much longer incarnation in your space/time continuum is very helpful for continuing this intensive work until conclusions have been reached through the catalytic process.

22.7 **QUESTIONER** You spoke of the South American group that was harvestable at the end of the second cycle. How long was their average life span at the end of the second cycle?

RA I am Ra. This isolated group had achieved life spans stretching upwards towards the nine-hundred-year [900-year] life span appropriate to this density.

22.8 **QUESTIONER** Then I'm assuming the planetary action that we're experiencing now, which shortens, it seems, all life spans here, was not strong enough at that time to affect them and shorten their life span regardless. Is this correct?

RA I am Ra. This is correct. It is well to remember that at that nexus in space/time great isolation was possible.

22.9 **QUESTIONER** About how many people populated the earth totally at that time; that is, incarnated in the physical at any one time?

RA I am Ra. I am assuming that you intend to query regarding the number of incarnate mind/body/spirit complexes at the end of the second major cycle, this number being approximately three four five, oh oh oh, three hundred forty-five thousand [345,000] entities.

22.10 **QUESTIONER** Approximately how many were harvestable out of the total number?

RA I am Ra. There were approximately one hundred fifty [150] entities harvestable.

22.11 **QUESTIONER** A very small number. Then as the next cycle started . . . are these the entities then that stayed to work on the planet?

RA I am Ra. These entities were visited by the Confederation and became desirous of remaining in order to aid the planetary consciousness. This is correct.

22.12 **QUESTIONER** What type of visit did the Confederation make to this group of 150 entities?

RA I am Ra. A light being appeared bearing that which may be called a shield of light. It spoke of the oneness and infinity of all creation and of those things which await those ready for harvest. It described in golden words the beauties of love as lived. It then allowed a telepathic linkage to progressively show those who were interested the plight of third density when seen as a planetary complex. It then left.

22.13 **QUESTIONER** And did all of these entities then decide to stay and help during the next 25,000-year cycle?

RA I am Ra. This is correct. As a group they stayed. There were those peripherally associated with this culture which did not stay. However, they were not able to be harvested either and so, beginning at the very highest, shall we say, of the sub-octaves of third density, repeated this density. Many of those who have been of a loving nature are not wanderers but those of this particular origin of second cycle.

22.14 **QUESTIONER** Are all of these entities still with us in this cycle?

RA I am Ra. The entities repeating the third-density major cycle have, in some few cases, been able to leave. These entities have chosen to join their brothers and sisters, as you would call these entities.

22.15 **QUESTIONER** Were any of these entities names that we know from our historical past? That have appeared as incarnated beings we find in our history?

RA I am Ra. The one known as sound vibration complex, Saint Augustine, is of such a nature. The one known as Saint Teresa of such a nature. The one known as Saint Francis of Assisi of such nature. These entities, being of monastic background, as you would call it, found incarnation in the same type of ambiance appropriate for further learning.

22.16 **QUESTIONER** Well, then as the cycle terminated 25,000 years ago, what was the reaction of the Confederation to the lack of harvest?

RA I am Ra. We became concerned.

22.17 **QUESTIONER** Was any action taken immediately, or did you wait for a call?

RA I am Ra. The Council of Saturn acted only in allowing the entry into third density of other mind/body/spirit complexes of third density, not wanderers, but those who sought further third-density experience. This was done randomly so that free will would not be violated, for there was not yet a call.

22.18 **QUESTIONER** Was the next action taken by the Confederation when a call occurred?

RA I am Ra. This is correct.

22.19 **QUESTIONER** Who, or what group, produced this call, and what action was taken by the Confederation?

RA The calling was that of Atlanteans. This calling was for what you would call understanding with the distortion towards helping other-selves. The action taken is that which you take part in at this time: the impression of information through channels, as you would call them.

22.20 **QUESTIONER** Was this first calling then at a time before Atlantis became technologically advanced?

RA I am Ra. This is basically correct.

22.21 **QUESTIONER** Then did the technological advancement of Atlantis come because of this call? I am assuming the call was answered to bring them the Law of One and the Law of Love as a distortion of the Law of One, but did they also then get technological information that caused them to grow into such a highly technological society?

RA I am Ra. Not at first. At about the same time as we first appeared in the skies over Egypt and continuing thereafter, other entities of the Confederation appeared unto Atlanteans who had reached a level of philosophical understanding, shall we misuse this word, which was consonant with communication to encourage and inspire studies in the mystery of unity.

However, requests being made for healing and other understandings, information was passed having to do with crystals and the building of pyramids as well as temples, as you would call them, which were associated with training.

22.22 **QUESTIONER** Was this training the same type of initiatory training that was done with the Egyptians?

RA I am Ra. This training was different in that the social complex was more, shall we say, sophisticated and less contradictory and barbarous in its ways of thinking. Therefore the temples were temples of learning rather than the attempt being made to totally separate and put upon a pedestal the healers.

22.23 **QUESTIONER** Then were there what we would call priests trained in these temples?

RA I am Ra. You would not call them priests in the sense of celibacy, of obedience, and of poverty. They were priests in the sense of those devoted to learning.

The difficulties became apparent as those trained in this learning began to attempt to use crystal powers for those things other than healing, as they were involved not only with learning but became involved with what you would call the governmental structure.

22.24 **QUESTIONER** Was all of their information given to them in the way you're giving our information now, through an instrument such as this instrument?

RA I am Ra. There were visitations from time to time but none of importance in the, shall we say, historical passage of events in your space/time continuum.

22.25 **QUESTIONER** Was it necessary for them to have a unified social complex for these visitations to occur? What conditions were . . . I'm saying, what conditions were necessary for these visitations to occur?

RA I am Ra. The conditions were two: the calling of a group of people whose square overcame the integrated resistance of those unwilling to search or learn; the second requirement, the relative naïveté of those members of the Confederation who felt that direct transfer of information would necessarily be as helpful for Atlanteans as it had been for the Confederation entity.

22.26 **QUESTIONER** I see then. What you're saying is these naïve Confederation entities had had the same thing happen to them in the past, so they were doing the same thing for the Atlantean entities. Is this correct?

RA I am Ra. This is correct. We remind you that we are one of the naïve members of that Confederation and are still attempting to recoup the damage for which we feel responsibility. It is our duty as well as honor to continue with your peoples, therefore, until all traces of the distortions of our teach/learnings have been embraced by their opposite distortions and balance achieved.

22.27 **QUESTIONER** I see. Then I will state the picture I have now of Atlantis, and you can tell me if I'm correct.

We have a condition where a large enough number of the entities of Atlantis had started at least going in the direction of the Law of One and living the Law of One for their call to be heard by the Confederation. This call was heard because, using the Law of One, it overrode the opposition of the Atlantean entities that were not calling. The Confederation then used channels such as we use now for communication and also made contact directly, but this turned out to be a mistake because it was perverted by some of the entities of Atlantis. Is this correct?

RA This is correct with one exception. There is only one law. That is the Law of One. Other so-called laws are distortions of this law, some of them primal and most important for progress to be understood. However, it is well that each so-called law, which we also call "way," be understood as a distortion rather than a law. There is no multiplicity to the Law of One.

This will be the final question in length of this working. Please ask it now.

22.28 QUESTIONER What was the—the only question I was going to ask, that I can think of was— Could you give me the average life span of the Atlantean population?

RA I am Ra. The average life span, as we have said, is misleading. The Atlanteans were, in the early part of their cultural experience, used to life spans from seventy [70] to one hundred forty [140] years, this being, of course, approximate. Due to increasing desire for power, the lifetime decreased rapidly in the later stages of this civilization, and thus the healing and rejuvenating information was requested.

Do you have any brief queries before we close?

22.29 QUESTIONER Is there any way that we can make the instrument more comfortable or anything that we can do for her?

RA I am Ra. The instrument is well. It is somewhat less easy to maintain clear contact during a time when some or one of the entities in the circle of working is or are not fully conscious. We request that entities in the circle be aware that their energy is helpful for increasing the vitality of this contact. We thank you for being conscientious in the asking.[1]

I am Ra. It is a great joy to leave you in the love and the light of the One Infinite Creator. Go forth, therefore, rejoicing in the power and the peace of the One Creator. Adonai.

---

[1] There was a visitor present for this session who laid down on the floor to meditate and subsequently fell asleep.

SESSION 23

23.0   **RA** I am Ra. I greet you in the love and the light of the Infinite Creator. We communicate now.

23.1   **QUESTIONER** You were speaking yesterday of the first contact made by the Confederation which occurred during our third major cycle. You stated that you appeared in the skies over Egypt at the same time, approximately, aid was first given to Atlantis. Can you tell me why you went to Egypt and your, shall we say, orientation of attitude and thinking when you first went to Egypt?

RA I am Ra. At the time of which you speak there were those who chose to worship the hawk-headed sun god which you know as vibrational sound complex, "Horus." This vibrational sound complex has taken other vibrational sound complexes, the object of worship being the sun disc represented in some distortion.

We were drawn to spend some time, as you would call it, scanning the peoples for a serious interest amounting to a seeking with which we might help without infringement. We found that at that time the social complex was quite self-contradictory in its so-called religious beliefs, and, therefore, there was not an appropriate calling for our vibration. Thus, at that time, which you know of as approximately eighteen thousand [18,000] of your years in your past, we departed without taking action.

23.2   **QUESTIONER** You stated yesterday that you appeared in the skies over Egypt at that time. Were the Egyptian entities able to see you in their skies?

RA I am Ra. This is correct.

23.3   **QUESTIONER** What did they see, and how did this affect their attitudes?

RA I am Ra. They saw what you would speak of as crystal-powered bell-shaped craft.

This did not affect them due to their firm conviction that many wondrous things occurred as a normal part of a world, as you would call it, in which many, many deities had powerful control over supernatural events.

23.4 **QUESTIONER** Did you have a reason for being visible to them rather than invisible?

RA I am Ra. This is correct.

23.5 **QUESTIONER** Can you tell me your reason for being visible to them?

RA I am Ra. We allowed visibility because it did not make any difference.

23.6 **QUESTIONER** I see. Then at this time you did not contact them. Can you tell me the same . . . answer the same questions I just asked with respect to your next attempt to contact the Egyptians?

RA I am Ra. The next attempt was prolonged. It occurred over a period of time. The nexus, or center, of our efforts was a decision upon our parts that there was a sufficient calling to attempt to walk among your peoples as brothers.

We laid this plan before the Council of Saturn, offering ourselves as service-oriented wanderers of the type which land directly upon the inner planes without incarnative processes. Thus we emerged, or materialized, in physical-chemical complexes representing as closely as possible our natures, this effort being to appear as brothers and spend a limited amount of time as teachers of the Law of One, for there was an ever-stronger interest in the sun body, and this vibrates in concordance with our particular distortions.

We discovered that for each word we could utter, there were thirty impressions we gave by our very being which confused those entities we had come to serve. After a short period we removed ourselves from these entities and spent much time attempting to understand how best to serve those to whom we had offered ourselves in love/light.

The ones who were in contact with that geographical entity which you know of as Atlantis had conceived of the potentials for healing by use of the pyramid-shape entities. In considering this and making adjustments for the differences in the distortion complexes of the two geographical cultures, as you would call them, we went before the Council again, offering this plan to the Council as an aid to the healing and the longevity of those in the area you know of as Egypt. In this way we hoped to facilitate the learning process as well as offering philosophy articulating the Law of One. Again the Council approved.

Approximately eleven thousand [11,000] of your years ago we entered, by thought-form, your—we correct this instrument. We sometimes have difficulty due to low vitality. Approximately eight five zero zero [8,500] years ago, having considered these concepts carefully, we returned, never having left in thought, to the thought-form areas of your vibrational planetary complex and considered for some of your years, as you measure time, how to appropriately build these structures.

The first, the Great Pyramid, was formed approximately six thousand [6,000] of your years ago. Then, in sequence, after this performing by thought of the building or architecture of the Great Pyramid, using the more, shall we say, local or earthly material rather than thought-form material to build other pyramidical structures. This continued for approximately fifteen hundred [1,500] of your years.

Meanwhile, the information concerning initiation and healing by crystal was being given. The one known as "Akhenaten" was able to perceive this information without significant distortion and, for a time, moved, shall we say, heaven and earth in order to invoke the Law of One and to order the priesthood of these structures in accordance with the distortions of initiation and true compassionate healing. This was not to be long-lasting.

At this entity's physical dissolution from your third-density physical plane, as we have said before, our teachings became quickly perverted, our structures returning once again to the use of the so-called "royal," or those with distortions towards power.

23.7 **QUESTIONER** When you spoke of pyramid healing, I am assuming that the primary healing was for the mind. Is this correct?

RA I am Ra. This is partially correct. The healing, if it is to be effectuated, must be a funneling without significant distortion of the instreamings through the spiritual complex into the tree of mind. There are parts of this mind which block energies flowing to the body complex. In each case, in each entity, the blockage may well differ.

First, however, it is necessary to activate the sense of the spiritual channel or shuttle. Then whether the blockage is from spiritual to mental, or from mental to physical, or whether it may simply be a random and purely physical trauma, healing may then be carried out.

23.8   **QUESTIONER** When you started building the pyramid at Giza using thought, were you at that time in contact with incarnate Egyptians, and did they observe this building?

RA I am Ra. At that time we were not in close contact with incarnate entities upon your plane. We were responding to a general calling of sufficient energy in that particular location to merit action. We sent thoughts to all who were seeking our information.

The appearance of the pyramid was a matter of tremendous surprise. However, it was carefully designed to coincide with the incarnation of one known as a great architect. This entity was later made into a deity, in part due to this occurrence.

23.9   **QUESTIONER** What name did they give this deity?

RA I am Ra. This deity had the sound vibration complex Imhotep.

23.10   **QUESTIONER** Thank you. Then as an overall success, what can you tell me about the relative success of the pyramid in any way at all? I understand that it was . . . the pyramids for the purpose were basically unsuccessful in that they didn't produce the rise in consciousness that you'd hoped for, but there must have been some success. Can you tell me of that?

RA I am Ra. We ask you to remember that we are of the Brothers and Sisters of Sorrow. When one has been rescued from that sorrow to a vision of the One Creator, then there is no concept of failure.

Our difficulty lay in the honor/responsibility of correcting the distortions of the Law of One which occurred during our attempts to aid these entities. The distortions are seen as responsibilities rather than failures; the few who were inspired to seek, our only reason for the attempt.

Thus, we would perhaps be in the position of paradox in that as one saw an illumination, we were what you call successful, and as others became more sorrowful and confused, we were failures. These are your terms. We persist in seeking to serve.

23.11   **QUESTIONER** You probably can't answer this question, but I will ask it now since we are in the area that I think this occurred in. I feel this somewhat of a duty of mine to ask this question because Henry Puharich will be visiting me later this month. Was this entity involved in any of these times of which you have just spoken?

RA I am Ra. You are quite correct in your assumption that we can speak in no way concerning the entity Henry. If you will consider this entity's distortions with regard to what you call "proof" you will understand/grasp our predicament.

23.12 **QUESTIONER** I had assumed before I asked the question that that would be the answer. I only asked it for his benefit because he would have wished for me to.

Can you tell me what happened to Akhenaten after his physical death?

RA I am Ra. This entity was then put through the series of healing and review of incarnational experience which is appropriate for third-density experience. This entity had been somewhat in the distortions of power ameliorated by the great devotion to the Law of One. This entity thus resolved to enter a series of incarnations in which it had no distortions towards power.

23.13 **QUESTIONER** Thank you. Can you tell me what the average life span was at the time of Akhenaten, for the Egyptians?

RA I am Ra. The average life span of these people was approximately thirty-five to fifty of your years. There was much, what you would call, disease of a physical complex nature.

23.14 **QUESTIONER** Can you tell me of the reasons for the disease? I think I already know, but I think it might be good for the book to state this at this time.

RA I am Ra. This is, as we have mentioned before, not particularly informative with regard to the Law of One. However, the land you know of as Egypt at that time was highly barbarous in its living conditions, as you would call them. The river which you call Nile was allowed to flood and to recede, thus providing the fertile grounds for the breeding of diseases which may be carried by insects. Also, the preparation of foodstuffs allowed diseases to form. Also, there was difficulty in many cases with sources of water, and water which was taken caused disease due to the organisms therein.

23.15 **QUESTIONER** I was really questioning more about the more basic cause of the disease rather than the mechanism of its transmission. I was going back to the root or thought which created the possibility of this disease. Could you shortly tell me if I am correct in assuming that the general reduction of thought over the long time on planet Earth with respect to an understanding of the Law of One created a condition in which this, what we call, disease could develop? Is this correct?

RA I am Ra. This is correct and perceptive. You, as questioner, begin now to penetrate the outer teachings.

The root cause in this particular society was not so much a bellicose action—although there were, shall we say, tendencies—but rather the formation of a money system and a very active trading and development of those tendencies towards greed and power; thus, the enslaving of entities by other entities and the misapprehension of the Creator within each entity.

23.16 **QUESTIONER** Thank you. Now, I understand, if I am correct, that a South American contact was also made. Can you tell me of the . . . approximately the same question I asked about your contact, with respect to the attitude or . . . about the contact, and its ramifications, and the plan for the contact, and why the people were contacted in South America?

RA I am Ra. This will be the final full question of this session. The entities who walked among those in your South American continent were called by a similar desire upon the part of the entities therein to learn of the manifestations of the sun. They worshiped this source of light and life.

Thus, these entities were visited by light beings not unlike ourselves. Instructions were given, and they were more accepted and less distorted than ours. The entities themselves began to construct a series of underground and hidden cities including pyramid structures.

These pyramids were somewhat at variance from the design that we had promulgated. However, the original ideas were the same with the addition of a desire, or intention, of creating places of meditation and rest, a feeling of the presence of the One Creator; these pyramids then being for all people, not only initiates and those to be healed.

They left this density when it was discovered that their plans were solidly in motion and, in fact, had been recorded. During the next approximately three thousand five hundred [3,500] years these plans became, though somewhat distorted, in a state of near-completion in many aspects.

Therefore, as is the case in all breakings of the quarantine, the entity who was helping the South American entities along the South American ways you call, in part, the Amazon River went before the Council of Saturn to request a second attempt to correct in person the distortions which had occurred in their plans. This having been granted, this entity, or social memory complex, returned, and the entity chosen as messenger came among the peoples once more to correct the errors.

Again, all was recorded, and the entity rejoined its social memory complex and left your skies.

As in our experience, the teachings were, for the most part, greatly and grossly perverted to the extent, in later times, of actual human sacrifice rather than healing of humans. Thus, this social memory complex is also given the honor/duty of remaining until those distortions are worked out of the distortion complexes of your peoples.

May we ask if there are any questions of a brief nature before we close?

23.17 **QUESTIONER** The only questions I have, is there anything we can do to make the instrument more comfortable, and since you stated that she seems to be low on energy, is it possible at all to have another session later today?

RA I am Ra. All is well with alignments. However, this instrument would benefit from rest from the trance state for this diurnal period.

23.18 **QUESTIONER** Thank you.

RA Is there any other brief question?

23.19 **QUESTIONER** This is a dumb question, but there was a movie called *Battle Beyond the Stars*. I don't know if you are familiar with it or not. I guess you are. It seemed to have what you're telling us included in the script. Is this correct? Do you know anything about it?

RA I am Ra. This particular creation of your entities had some distortions of the Law of One and its scenario upon your physical plane. This is correct.

I am Ra. I leave this instrument now. I leave each of you in the love and the light of the One Infinite Creator. Go forth, therefore, rejoicing in the power and the peace of the One Creator. Adonai.

24.0 **RA** I am Ra. I greet you in the love and in the light of the Infinite Creator. I communicate now.

24.1 **QUESTIONER** We are a little concerned about the physical condition of the instrument. She has a slight congestion. If you can tell me of the suitability of this session at all, I would appreciate it.

RA I am Ra. This instrument's vital energies of the physical complex are low. The session will be appropriately shortened.

24.2 **QUESTIONER** She requests that if it is possible for you to cause the instrument's vehicle to cough at intervals that would help her. Is this possible?

RA I am Ra. Please restate query, specifying interval.

24.3 **QUESTIONER** She requests that you cause the instrument to cough about at least after each communication. Is this possible?

RA I am Ra. This is possible. [*Cough.*]

24.4 **QUESTIONER** Thank you. The way I intend to continue with the book is to follow on through the last 25,000-year cycle that we're in now and possibly investigate a little of fourth-density conditions and thereby find many places that we can go back and delve further into the Law of One. The first material I expect to be not too deep with respect to the Law of One. I hope to get into greater philosophical areas of the Law of One in more advanced sessions so as to make the material progress so that it will be understandable. I hope that I'm following the right direction in this.

In the last session, you mentioned that during this last 25,000-year cycle the Atlanteans, Egyptians, and those in South America were contacted, and then the Confederation departed. I understand the Confederation did not come back for some time. Could you tell me of the reasons, and consequences, and attitudes with respect to the next contact with those here on planet Earth?

RA I am Ra. In the case of the Atlanteans, enlargements upon the information given resulted in those activities distorted towards bellicosity, which resulted in the final second Atlantean catastrophe one zero eight two one [10,821] of your years in the past, as you measure time.

Many, many were displaced due to societal actions both upon Atlantis and upon those areas of what you would call North African deserts to which some Atlanteans had gone after the first conflict. Earth changes continued due to these, what you would call, nuclear bombs and other crystal weapons, sinking the last great land masses approximately nine six zero zero [9,600] of your years ago.

In the Egyptian and the South American experiments results, though not as widely devastating, were as far from the original intention of the Confederation. It was clear to not only us but also to the Council and the Guardians that our methods were not appropriate for this particular sphere.

Our attitude, thus, was one of caution, observation, and continuing attempts to creatively discover methods whereby contact from our entities could be of service with the least distortion and, above all, with the least possibility of becoming perversions, or antitheses, of our intentions in sharing information.

24.5 **QUESTIONER** Could you have the instrument cough, please?

RA [*Cough.*]

24.6 **QUESTIONER** Thank you. Then I assume the Confederation stayed away from Earth for a period of time. What condition created the next contact the Confederation made?

RA I am Ra. In approximately three six zero zero [3,600] of your years in the past, as you measure time, there was an influx of those of the Orion group, as you call them. Due to the increasing negative influences upon thinking and acting distortions, they were able to begin working with those whose impression from olden times, as you may say, was that they were special and different.

An entity of the Confederation, many, many thousands of your years in the past, the one you may call Yahweh, had, by genetic cloning, set up these particular biases among these peoples who had come gradually to dwell in the vicinity of Egypt, as well as in many, many other places, by dispersion after the down-sinking of the land mass Mu. Here the Orion group found fertile soil in which to plant the seeds of negativity; these seeds, as always, being those of the elite, the different, those who manipulate or enslave others.

The one known as Yahweh felt a great responsibility to these entities. However, the Orion group had been able to impress upon the peoples the name Yahweh as the one responsible for this elitism. Yahweh then was able to take, what you would call, stock of its vibratory patterns and became, in effect, a more eloquently effective sound vibration complex.

In this complex the old Yahweh, now unnamed, but meaning "He comes," began to send positively oriented philosophy. This was approximately, in your past, of two—we correct this instrument—three three zero zero [3,300] years. Thus, the intense portion of what has become known as Armageddon was joined.

24.7   **QUESTIONER** Could you create another cough for us, please?

RA [*Cough.*]

24.8   **QUESTIONER** Thank you. I have a question about how the Orion group got in 3,600 years ago. How did they get through the quarantine? Was that a random window effect?

RA I am Ra. At that time this was not entirely so as there was a proper calling for this information. When there is a mixed calling, the window effect is much more put into motion by the ways of the densities.

The quarantine in this case was, shall we say, not patrolled so closely, due to the lack of strong polarity, the windows thus needing to be very weak in order for penetration. As your harvest approaches, those forces of what you would call light work according to their call. The ones of Orion have the working only according to their call. This calling is in actuality not nearly as great.

Thus, due to the Way of Empowering, or Squares, there is much resistance to penetration. Yet free will must be maintained, and those desiring negatively oriented information, as you would call it, must then be satisfied by those moving through by the window effect. [*Cough.*]

24.9   **QUESTIONER** Then Yahweh, in an attempt to correct what he saw as what I might call a mistake (I know you don't want to call it that), started 3,300 years ago with the positive philosophy. Were both the Orion and Yahweh philosophies impressed telepathically, or were there other techniques used?

RA I am Ra. There were two other techniques used: one by the entity no longer called Yahweh, who still felt that if it could raise up entities which were superior to the negative forces, that these superior entities could spread the Law of One. Thus this entity, Yod Heh Shin Vau Heh, came among your people in form according to incarnate being and mated in the normal reproductive manner of your physical complexes, thus birthing a generation of much larger beings, these beings called "Anak."[1]

The other method used to greater effect later in the scenario, as you would call it, was the thought-form such as we often use among your peoples to suggest the mysterious or the sublime. You may be familiar with some of these appearances.

24.10 **QUESTIONER** Could you state some of those after making the instrument cough, please?

RA [*Cough.*] I am Ra. This is information which you may discover. However, we will briefly point the way by indicating the so-called wheel within a wheel and the cherubim with sleepless eye.

24.11 **QUESTIONER** Very good. Did the Orion group use similar methods for their impression 3,600 years ago?

RA I am Ra. The group, or empire, had an emissary in your skies at that time.

24.12 **QUESTIONER** Can you describe that emissary?

RA This emissary was of your fiery nature, which was hidden by the nature of cloud in the day. This was to obliterate the questions of those seeing such a vehicle and to make it consonant with these entities' concept of what you may call the Creator.

24.13 **QUESTIONER** And then how was the impression or information passed on to the entities after they saw this fiery cloud?

---

1 The Anak, or Anakim, were a race of giants described in biblical texts.

RA I am Ra. By thought transfer and by the causing of fiery phenomena and other events to appear as being miraculous through the use of thought-forms.

24.14 **QUESTIONER** Then were there any prophets that we have now recorded that sprung from this era or soon after it?

RA I am Ra. Those of the empire were not successful in maintaining their presence for long after the approximate three zero zero zero [3,000] date in your history and were, perforce, left with the decision to physically leave the skies. The so-called prophets were often given mixed information, but the worst that the Orion group could do was to cause these prophets to speak of doom, as prophecy in those days was the occupation of those who love[d] their fellow beings and wish[ed] only to be of service to them and to the Creator.

24.15 **QUESTIONER** After making the instrument cough . . .

RA [*Cough.*]

24.16 **QUESTIONER** Could you tell me if you're saying the Orion group was successful in polluting, shall we say, some of the positively oriented prophets with messages of doom?

RA I am Ra. This is correct. Your next query shall be the last full query for this session.

24.17 **QUESTIONER** Could you tell me why the Orion group had to leave after—I believe, it figures to be a six-hundred-year period—why they had to vacate?

RA I am Ra. Although the impression that they had given to those who called them [was] that these entities were an elite group, that which you know as Diaspora occurred, causing much dispersion of these peoples so that they became an humbler and more honorable breed, less bellicose and more aware of the loving-kindness of the One Creator.

The creation about them tended towards being somewhat bellicose, somewhat oriented towards the enslavement of others, but they themselves, the target of the Orion group by means of their genetic superiority/weakness, became what you may call the underdogs, thereby letting the feelings of gratitude for their neighbors, their family, and their

One Creator begin to heal the feelings of elitism which led to the distortions of power over others which had caused their own bellicosity.

Any short queries may be asked now.

24.18 **QUESTIONER** There's one thing that's been bothering me a little bit which I was just reading about—

RA [*Cough.*]

24.19 **QUESTIONER** It's not too important, but I would really be interested to know if Dwight Eisenhower met with either the Confederation or the Orion group during the 1950s or that time?

RA I am Ra. The one of which you speak met with thought-forms which are indistinguishable from third density. This was a test. We, the Confederation, wished to see what would occur if this extremely positively oriented and simple, congenial person with no significant distortions towards power happened across peaceful information and the possibilities which might append therefrom.

We discovered that this entity did not feel that those under his care could deal with the concepts of other beings and other philosophies. Thus an agreement reached then allowed him to go his way, ourselves to do likewise; and a very quiet campaign, as we have heard you call it, be continued alerting your peoples to our presence gradually. Events have overtaken this plan.

[*Cough.*] Is there any short query before we close?

24.20 **QUESTIONER** The only other question that went with that is: was there a crashed spaceship, and are there small bodies now stored in our military installations?

RA I am Ra. We do not wish to infringe upon your future. Gave we you this information, we might be giving you more than you could appropriately deal with in the space/time nexus of your present somewhat muddled configuration of military and intelligence thought. Therefore, we shall withhold this information.

24.21 **QUESTIONER** OK. Sorry to bother you with these type of questions—

RA [*Cough.*]

24.22 **QUESTIONER** —but they were just bothering me. We will continue in our next session with the Law of One and keep that uppermost in the scope of the book, and try to get more deeply into the philosophy as we build a framework for reference to the philosophy. Thank you very much.

RA I—

24.23 **QUESTIONER** Oh, please, I'm almost ready. Is there anything that we can do to make the instrument more comfortable?

RA I am Ra. You are conscientious. Be careful only to adjust this instrument's upper appendages if its upper body is elevated.

I am Ra. All is well. It is our joy to speak with you. We leave in the love and the light of the One Infinite Creator. Go forth, therefore, rejoicing in the power and the peace of the One Creator. Adonai.

SESSION 25
FEBRUARY 16, 1981

25.0   **RA** I am Ra. I greet you in the love and the light of the Infinite Creator. We communicate now.

25.1   **QUESTIONER** . . . asking first what cause or complex of causes has led to the instrument's chest cold, as it is called?

RA I am Ra. This distortion towards illness was caused by the free will of the instrument in accepting a chemical substance which you call LSD. This was carefully planned by those entities which do not desire this instrument to remain viable. The substance has within it the facility of removing large stores of vital energy from the ingestor.

The first hope of the Orion entity which arranged this opportunity was that this instrument would become less polarized towards what you call the positive. Due to conscious efforts upon the part of this instrument, using the substance as a programmer for service to others and for thankfulness, this instrument was spared this distortion and there was no result satisfactory to the Orion group.

The second hope lay in the possible misuse of the most powerful means of transmission of energy between your peoples in the area of body-complex distortions. We have not previously spoken of the various types of energy blockages and transfers, positive and negative, that may take place due to participation in your sexual reproductive complex of actions. This entity, however, is a very strong entity with very little distortion from universal green-ray love energy. Thus this particular plan was not effected either, as the entity continued to give of itself in this context in an open, or green-ray, manner rather than attempting to receive,[1] or to manipulate, other-self.

The only remaining distortion available, since this entity would not detune and would not cease sharing love universally under this chemical substance, was simply to drain this entity of as much energy as possible. This entity has a strong distortion towards busyness which it has been attempting to overcome for some time, realizing it not to be the

---

[1]   Ra possibly intended to say "deceive."

appropriate attitude for this work. In this particular area the ingestion of this substance did indeed, shall we say, cause distortions away from viability due to the busyness and the lack of desire to rest; this instrument staying alert for much longer than appropriate. Thus much vital energy was lost, making this instrument unusually susceptible to infections such as it now experiences.

25.2 QUESTIONER The second question the instrument requested was: "How may I best revitalize myself, not only now, but in the future?"

RA I am Ra. This instrument is aware of the basic needs of its constitution, those being: meditation, acceptance of limitations, experiences of joy through association with others and with the beauty as of the singing; and the exercising with great contact, whenever possible, with the life forces of second density, especially those of trees; this entity also needing to be aware of the moderate but steady intake of foodstuffs, exercise being suggested at a fairly early portion of the day and at a later portion of the day before the resting.

25.3 QUESTIONER The third question that she requested to be asked was: "How may Don and Jim help to revitalize me?"

RA I am Ra. This is not an appropriate question for full answer. We can say only that these entities are most conscientious. We may add that due to this instrument's distortion towards imbalance in the space/time nexus, it would be well were this entity accompanied during exercise.

25.4 QUESTIONER Thank you. We shall now continue with the material from yesterday. You stated that about 3,000 years ago the Orion group left due to Diaspora. Was the Confederation then able to make any progress after the Orion group left?

RA I am Ra. For many of your centuries, both the Confederation and the Orion Confederation busied themselves with each other upon planes above your own, shall we say, planes in time/space whereby machinations were conceived and the armor of light girded on. Battles have been and are continuing to be fought upon these levels.

Upon the earth plane, energies had been set in motion which did not cause a great deal of call. There were isolated instances of callings, one such taking place beginning approximately two six zero zero [2,600] of your years in the past in what you would call Greece at this time, and resulting in writings and understandings of some facets of the Law of One. We especially note the one known as Thales and the one known as Heraclitus, those being of the philosopher career, as you may call it, teaching their students. We also point out the understandings of the one known as Pericles.

At this time there was a limited amount of visionary information which the Confederation was allowed to telepathically impress. However, for the most part during this time empires died and rose according to the attitudes and energies set in motion long ago, not resulting in strong polarization but rather in that mixture of the positive and the warlike, or negative, which has been characteristic of this final minor cycle of your beingness.

25.5   **QUESTIONER** You spoke of an Orion Confederation and a battle being fought between the Confederation and the Orion Confederation. Is it possible to convey any concept of how this battle is fought?

RA I am Ra. Picture, if you will, your mind. Picture it then in total unity with all other minds of your society. You are then single-minded, and that which is a weak electrical charge in your physical illusion is now an enormously powerful machine whereby thoughts may be projected as things.

In this endeavor the Orion group charges, or attacks, the Confederation arms with light. The result, a standoff, as you would call it, both energies being somewhat depleted by this and needing to regroup; the negative depleted through failure to manipulate, the positive depleted through failure to accept that which is given.

25.6   **QUESTIONER** Could you amplify the meaning of what you said by "failure to accept that which is given?"

RA I am Ra. At the level of time/space at which this takes place in the form of what you may call thought-war, the most accepting and loving energy would be to so love those who wished to manipulate that those entities were surrounded, engulfed, and transformed by positive energies.

This, however, being a battle of equals, the Confederation is aware that it cannot, on equal footing, allow itself to be manipulated in order to remain purely positive, for then, though pure, it would not be of any consequence, having been placed by the so-called powers of darkness under the heel, as you may say.

It is thus that those who deal with this thought-war must be defensive rather than accepting in order to preserve their usefulness in service to others. Thusly, they cannot accept fully what the Orion Confederation wishes to give, that being enslavement. Thusly, some polarity is lost due to this friction, and both sides, if you will, must then regroup.

It has not been fruitful for either side. The only consequence which has been helpful is a balancing of the energies available to this planet so that these energies have less necessity to be balanced in this space/time, thus lessening the chances of planetary annihilation.

25.7   **QUESTIONER** Very important point, I believe. Does a portion of the Confederation then engage in this thought battle? What percentage engages?

RA I am Ra. This is the most difficult work of the Confederation. Only four planetary entities at any one time are asked to partake in this conflict.

25.8   **QUESTIONER** What density are these four planetary entities?

RA I am Ra. These entities are of the density of love, numbering four.

25.9   **QUESTIONER** Then I am assuming this is the most effective density for this work. Would this density—an entity of this density—be more effective for this type of work than, say, an entity of density five or six?

RA I am Ra. The fourth density is the only density besides your own which, lacking the wisdom to refrain from battle, sees the necessity of the battle. Thus it is necessary that fourth-density social memory complexes be used.

25.10   **QUESTIONER** Am I correct in assuming, then, that fourth density on both sides of the . . . of both the Orion and the Confederation sides are in this battle, and that the densities fifth and sixth on the Orion side do not engage in this? Is this correct?

RA I am Ra. This will be the last full question as this entity's energies are low.

It is partially correct. Fifth- and sixth-density entities positive would not take part in this battle. Fifth-density negative would not take part in this battle. Thus, the fourth density of both orientations join in this conflict.

May we ask for a few short questions before we close?

25.11 **QUESTIONER** Well, I will first ask the answer at the end if there's anything we can do to make the instrument really comfortable. I'll only ask the questions that the instrument has—or answer the questions that the instrument has energy left to give, but I really would like to know of the orientation of fifth-density negative for not participating in this battle.

RA I am Ra. The fifth density is the density of light, or wisdom. The so-called negative service-to-self entity in this density is at an high level of awareness and wisdom and has ceased activity except by thought. The fifth-density negative is extraordinarily compacted and separated from all else.

25.12 **QUESTIONER** Thank you very much. We do not wish to deplete the instrument, so is there anything that we can do to make the instrument more comfortable?

RA I am Ra. You are very conscientious. As we requested previously, it would be well to observe the angles taken by the more upright posture of the entity. It is causing some nerve blockage in the portion of the body complex called the elbows.

I am Ra. I leave you in the love and in the light of the One Infinite Creator. Go forth, then, rejoicing in the power and the peace of the One Creator. Adonai.

SESSION 26

26.0   **RA** I am Ra. I greet you in the love and the light of the Infinite Creator. I communicate now.

26.1   **QUESTIONER** The first question is that, is any of the changing of what we've done here for the instrument going to affect communication of the instrument in any way? Have we set up here all right?

RA I am Ra. This is correct.

26.2   **QUESTIONER** And do you mean that everything is satisfactory for continued communication?

RA I am Ra. We meant that the changes affect this communication.

26.3   **QUESTIONER** Should we discontinue this communication because of these changes, or should we continue?

RA I am Ra. You may do as you wish. However, we would be unable to use this instrument at this space/time nexus without these modifications.

26.4   **QUESTIONER** Assuming that it is all right to continue, we're down to the last 3,000 years of this present cycle, and I was wondering if the Law of One in either written or spoken form has been made available within this past 3,000 years in any complete way such as we're doing now? Is it available in any other source?

RA I am Ra. There is no possibility of a complete source of information of the Law of One in this density. However, certain of your writings passed to you as your so-called holy works have portions of this law.

26.5   **QUESTIONER** Does the Bible as we know it have portions of this law in it?

RA I am Ra. This is correct.

26.6   **QUESTIONER** Can you tell me if the Old Testament has any of the Law of One?

RA I am Ra. This is correct.

26.7 **QUESTIONER** Which has more of the Law of One in it, the Old Testament or the New Testament?

RA I am Ra. Withdrawing from each of the collections of which you speak the portions having to do with the Law of One, the content is approximately equal. However, the so-called Old Testament has a larger amount of negatively influenced material, as you would call it.

26.8 **QUESTIONER** Can you tell me about what percentage is Orion-influenced in both the Old and the New Testaments?

RA We prefer that this be left to the discretion of those who seek the Law of One. We are not speaking in order to judge. Such statements would be construed by some of those who may read this material as judgmental. We can only suggest a careful reading and inward digestion of the contents. The understandings will become obvious.

26.9 **QUESTIONER** Thank you. Could you please make the instrument cough?

RA [*Cough.*]

26.10 **QUESTIONER** Thank you. Have you communicated with any of our population in the third-density incarnate state in recent times?

RA I am Ra. Please restate, specifying "recent times" and the pronoun, "you."

26.11 **QUESTIONER** Has Ra communicated with any of our population in this century, in the last, say, eighty years?

RA I am Ra. We have not.

26.12 **QUESTIONER** Has the Law of One been communicated within the past eighty years by any other source to an entity in our population?

RA I am Ra. The Ways of One have seldom been communicated, although there are rare instances in the previous eight zero [80] of your years, as you measure time.

There have been many communications from fourth density due to the drawing towards the harvest to fourth density. These are the Ways of Universal Love and Understanding. The other teachings are reserved for those whose depth of understanding, if you will excuse this misnomer, recommend and attract such further communication.

26.13 **QUESTIONER** Did the Confederation then step up its program of helping planet Earth sometimes, some time late in this last major cycle? It seems that they did from the previous data, especially with the Industrial Revolution. Can you tell me the attitudes and reasonings behind this step up? Is there any reason other than that they just wanted to produce more leisure time in the last, say, a hundred years of the cycle? Is this the total reason?

RA I am Ra. This is not the total reason. Approximately two zero zero [200] of your years in the past, as you measure time, there began to be a significant amount of entities who, by seniority, were incarnating for learn/teaching purposes rather than for the lesser of the learn/teachings of those less aware of the process. This was our signal to enable communication to take place.

The wanderers which came among you began to make themselves felt at approximately this time, firstly offering ideas or thoughts containing the distortion of Free Will. This was the prerequisite for further wanderers which had information of a more specific nature to offer. The thought must precede the action.

26.14 **QUESTIONER** Could you please make the instrument cough?

RA [*Cough.*]

26.15 **QUESTIONER** Wondering if the one, Abraham Lincoln, could have possibly been a wanderer?

RA I am Ra. This is incorrect. This entity was a normal, shall we say, Earth being which chose to leave the vehicle and allow an entity to use it on a permanent basis. This is relatively rare compared to the phenomenon of wanderers.

You would do better considering the incarnations of wanderers such as the one known as Thomas, the one known as Benjamin.

26.16 **QUESTIONER** I am assuming you mean Thomas Edison and Benjamin Franklin?

RA This is incorrect. We were intending to convey the sound vibration complex, Thomas Jefferson. The other, correct.

26.17 **QUESTIONER** Thank you. Can you tell me where the entity that used Lincoln—Abraham's—body, what density he came from and where?

RA I am Ra. This entity was fourth-vibration.

26.18 **QUESTIONER** I assume positive?

RA That is correct.

26.19 **QUESTIONER** Was his assassination in any way influenced by Orion or any other negative force?

RA I am Ra. This is correct.

26.20 **QUESTIONER** Thank you. In the recent past of the last thirty to forty years the UFO phenomena has become known to our population. What was the original reason for— I know there've been UFOs throughout history, but what was the original reason for the increase in what we call UFO activity say in the past forty years?

RA I am Ra. Information which Confederation sources had offered to your entity, Albert [Einstein], became perverted, and instruments of destruction began to be created, examples of this being the Manhattan Project and its product.

Information offered through wanderer, sound vibration, Nikola [Tesla], also being experimented with for potential destruction: example, your so-called Philadelphia Experiment.

Thus, we felt a strong need to involve our thought-forms in whatever way we of the Confederation could be of service in order to balance these distortions of information meant to aid your planetary sphere.

26.21 **QUESTIONER** Then what you did, I am assuming, then, is to create an air of mystery with the UFO phenomena, as we call it, and then by telepathy send many messages that could be either accepted or rejected under the . . . following, of course, the Law of One, so that the population would start thinking seriously about the consequences of what they were doing. Is this correct?

RA I am Ra. This is partially correct. There are other services we may perform. Firstly, the integration of souls or spirits, if you will, in the event of use of these nuclear devices in your space/time continuum. This the Confederation has already done.

26.22 **QUESTIONER** I don't fully understand what you mean by that. Could you expand a little bit?

RA I am Ra. The use of intelligent energy transforming matter into energy is of such a nature among these weapons that the transition from space/time third density to time/space third density, or what you may call your heaven worlds, is interrupted in many cases.

Therefore, we are offering ourselves as those who continue the integration of soul, or spirit complex, during transition from space/time to time/space.

26.23 **QUESTIONER** Could you please give me an example from, let us say, Hiroshima or Nagasaki of how this is done?

RA I am Ra. Those who were destroyed, not by radiation, but by the trauma of the energy release, found not only the body/mind/spirit complex made unviable, but also a disarrangement of that unique vibratory complex you have called the spirit complex, which we understand as a mind/body/spirit complex, to be completely disarranged without possibility of re-integration. This would be the loss to the Creator of part of the Creator, and thus we were given permission not to stop the events, but to ensure the survival of the, shall we say, disembodied mind/body/spirit complex. This we did in those events which you mention, losing no spirit, or portion, or holograph, or microcosm of the macrocosmic Infinite One.

26.24 **QUESTIONER** Could you please make the instrument cough, and then tell me just vaguely how you accomplished this?

RA [*Cough.*] I am Ra. This is accomplished through our understanding of dimensional fields of energy. The higher, or more dense, energy field will control the less dense.

26.25 **QUESTIONER** But then, in general then, you're saying that if we . . . you will allow Earth, the population of this planet, to have a nuclear war and many deaths from that war, but you will be able to create a condition where these deaths will be no more traumatic, shall I say, with respect to entrance to the heaven world, or astral world, or whatever we call it, than death by a bullet or normal means of dying of old age. Is this correct?

RA I am Ra. This is incorrect. It would be more traumatic. However, the entity would remain an entity.

26.26 **QUESTIONER** Can you tell me the condition of the entities who were, shall I say, killed in Nagasaki and Hiroshima. At this time, what is their condition?

RA I am Ra. They of this trauma have not yet fully begun the healing process. They are being helped as much as is possible.

26.27 **QUESTIONER** When the healing process is complete with these entities, will this experience of the death due to the nuclear bomb cause them to be, shall we say, regressed in their climb toward the fourth density?

RA I am Ra. Such actions as nuclear destruction affect the entire planet. There are no differences at this level of destruction, and the planet will need to be healed.

26.28 **QUESTIONER** I was thinking specifically if an entity was in Hiroshima or Nagasaki at that time and he was reaching harvestability at the end of our cycle, would this death by nuclear bomb possibly create such trauma that he would not be able to be harvestable at the end of the cycle? That was specifically my question.

RA I am Ra. This is incorrect. Once the healing has taken place the harvest may go forth unimpeded. However, the entire planet will undergo healing for this action, no distinction being made betwixt victim and aggressor, this due to damage done to the planet.

26.29 **QUESTIONER** Could you please make the instrument cough? And—

RA [*Cough.*]

26.30 **QUESTIONER** And then, can you describe the mechanism of the planetary healing?

RA I am Ra. Healing is a process of acceptance, forgiveness, and, if possible, restitution. The restitution not being available in time/space, there are many among your peoples now attempting restitution while in the physical.

26.31 **QUESTIONER** How do these people attempt this restitution in the physical?

RA I am Ra. These attempt feelings of love towards the planetary sphere, and comfort and healing of the scars, and the imbalances of these actions.

26.32 **QUESTIONER** Then as the UFO phenomena was made obvious to many of the population, many groups of people reported contact; many groups of people reported telepathic communication with UFO entities and many recorded the results of what they considered telepathic communication.

Was the Confederation, shall we say, oriented to impressing telepathic communication on groups that became interested in UFOs?

RA I am Ra. This is correct although some of our members have removed themselves from the time/space using thought-form projections into your space/time and have chosen, from time to time, with permission of the Council, to appear in your skies without landing.

26.33 **QUESTIONER** Then are all of the landings that have occurred—except for the landing when Eisenhower was contacted—are all of those landings of the Orion group or similar type groups?

RA I am Ra. Except for isolated instances of those of, shall we say, no affiliation, this is correct.

26.34 **QUESTIONER** Is it necessary in each case for the entity who is contacted in one of these landings to be calling the Orion group, or do some of these entities come in contact with the Orion group even though they are not calling that group?

RA I am Ra. You must plumb the depths of fourth-density negative understanding. This is difficult for you. Once having reached third-density space/time continuum through your so-called windows, these crusaders may plunder as they will, the results completely a function of the polarity of the, shall we say, witness, subject, or victim.

This is due to the sincere belief of fourth-density negative that to love self is to love all. Each other-self which is thus either taught or enslaved thus has a teacher which teaches love of self. Exposed to this teaching, it is intended that there be brought to fruition an harvest of fourth-density negative, or self-serving mind/body/spirit complexes.[1]

---

[1] At this point in the original publications Don inserted the text from 53.6–17. In so doing he hoped to give a more balanced picture of "close encounters" with both positive and negative UFOs. Don felt that readers may get an incomplete, even

26.35 **QUESTIONER** Could you make the instrument cough, please?

RA [*Cough.*]

26.36 **QUESTIONER** Then I am assuming all of the UFO groups who were getting telepathic contact from the Confederation were, shall we say, high-priority targets for the Orion crusaders, and I would assume that a large percentage of them were, shall we say, had their information polluted then.

Can you tell me, do you have any idea what percentage of these groups were heavily polluted by the Orion information, and if any of them were able to remain purely a Confederation channel?

RA I am Ra. To give you this information would be to infringe upon the free will, or confusion, of some living. We can only ask each group to consider the relative effect of philosophy and your so-called specific information. It is not the specificity of the information which attracts negative influences; it is the importance placed upon it.

This is why we iterate quite often, when asked for specific information, that it pales to insignificance, just as the grass withers and dies while the love and the light of the One Infinite Creator redounds to the very infinite realms of creation forever and ever, creating and creating itself in perpetuity.

Why, then, be concerned with the grass that blooms, withers, and dies in its season only to grow once again due to the infinite love and light of the One Creator? This is the message we bring. Each entity is only superficially that which blooms and dies. In the deeper sense, there is no end to beingness.

26.37 **QUESTIONER** Thank you very much. Could you please make the instrument cough?

RA [*Cough.*]

26.38 **QUESTIONER** As you have stated before, it is a strait and narrow path. There are many distractions.

I plan to create an introduction, shall I say, to the Law of One, traveling

---

distorted picture from session 26 without the complementary information gained in session 53.

through and hitting the high points of this 75,000 year cycle, possibly a few questions into the general future. After this introduction to the Law of One, as I call it, I would like to get directly to the main work, which is creating an understanding that can be disseminated to those who would ask for it—and only to those who would ask for it—for an understanding that can allow them to greatly accelerate their evolution. I am very appreciative and feel it a great honor and privilege to be doing this and hope that we can accomplish this next phase.

I have a question that the instrument has asked that I would like to ask for the instrument. She says, "You speak of various types of energy blockages and transfers, positive and negative, that may take place due to participation in our sexual reproductive complex of actions." She states, "Please explain these blockages and energy transfers with emphasis upon what an individual seeking to be in accordance with the Law of One may positively do in this area." Is it possible for you to answer this question?

RA I am Ra. It is partially possible, given the background we have laid. This is properly a more advanced question. Due to the specificity of the question we may give general answer.

The first energy transfer is red ray. It is a random transfer having to do only with your reproductive system.

The orange- and the yellow-ray attempts to have sexual intercourse create, firstly, a blockage if only one entity vibrates in this area, thus causing the entity vibrating sexually in this area to have a never-ending appetite for this activity. What these vibratory levels are seeking is green-ray activity. There is the possibility of orange- or yellow-ray energy transfer; this being polarizing towards the negative: one being seen as object rather than other-self, the other seeing itself as plunderer, or master, of the situation.

In third[2] ray there are two possibilities. Firstly, if both vibrate in third ray, there will be a mutually strengthening energy transfer. The negative or female, as you call it, drawing the energy from the roots of the beingness up through the energy centers, thus being physically revitalized; the positive, or male, polarity, as it is deemed in your illusion, finding in this energy transfer an inspiration which satisfies and feeds the spirit portion of the body/mind/spirit complex; thus both being polarized and releasing

---

2 This should be fourth or green. Don and Ra corrected the error in session 32.3–4.

the excess of that which each has in abundance by nature of intelligent energy, that is, negative/intuitive, positive/physical energies as you may call them—this energy transfer being blocked only if one or both entities have fear of possession, of being possessed, of desiring possession, or desiring being possessed.

The other green-ray possibility is that of one entity offering green-ray energy, the other not offering energy of the universal love energy, this resulting in a blockage of energy for the one not green ray, thus increasing frustration or appetite; the green-ray being polarizing slightly towards service to others.

The blue-ray energy transfer is somewhat rare among your people at this time but is of great aid due to energy transfers involved in becoming able to express the self without reservation or fear.

The indigo-ray transfer is extremely rare among your people. This is the sacramental portion of the body complex whereby contact may be made through the violet ray with intelligent infinity. No blockages may occur at these latter two levels due to the fact that if both entities are not ready for this energy, it is not visible, and neither transfer nor blockage may take place. It is as though the distributor were removed from a powerful engine.

This instrument was able, as an example of this working, to baffle the Orion group during [*tape blank*] experiences, as you call this substance, due to the fact that it effectively completely opened other-self to third-ray—we correct this instrument, it is growing low in vital energy—green-ray energy and partially open other-self to blue-ray interaction.[3]

May we ask if you have any queries before we close?

26.39 **QUESTIONER** If you would please make the instrument cough, I will ask one—two quick things.

RA [*Cough.*]

26.40 **QUESTIONER** The instrument asks, "How long do the debilitative effects that I am experiencing from the use of LSD last, and is there anything that we can do to make the instrument more comfortable?"

---

[3] Ra is referring to the instrument's experience described in 18.3 and elsewhere.

RA I am Ra. Firstly, the period of weakness of bodily complex is approximately three of your lunar cycles, the first ingestion causing approximately one of your lunar cycles; the second having a cumulative or doubling effect.

Secondly, this instrument is well. You are most conscientious.

I am Ra. I leave you, my friends, in the love and the light of the One Infinite Creator. Go forth, then, merry and glad and rejoicing in the power and the peace of the One Creator. Adonai.

Session 27

27.0   **RA** I am Ra. I greet you in the love and the light of the One Infinite Creator. I communicate now.

27.1   **QUESTIONER** This session I thought we would start Book II of *The Law of One*,[1] which will focus on what we consider to be the only important aspect of our being.

However, Jim has felt the obligation to ask two questions that were asked of him by Paul Shockley, and I will ask those two first, in case you are able to answer them before we really get started. First question is: Paul Shockley is presenting channeling—correction, Paul Shockley is presently channeling the same source which Edgar Cayce channeled, and Paul has received information that he took part in the design and construction of the Egyptian pyramids. Can you tell us what his role was in that effort?

RA I am Ra. This was in your space/time continuum two periods and two lifetimes. The first of a physical nature working with Confederation entities in what you know of as Atlantis, this approximately thirteen thousand [13,000] of your years ago. This memory, shall we say, being integrated into the unconscious of the mind/body/spirit complex of this entity due to its extreme desire to remember the service of healing and polarization possible by the mechanisms of the crystal and the charged healer.

The second experience being approximately one thousand [1,000] of your years later during which experience this entity prepared, in some part, the consciousness of the people of what you now call Egypt, that they were able to offer the calling that enabled those of our social memory complex to walk among your peoples. During this life experience this entity was of a priest and teaching nature and succeeded in remembering in semi-distorted form the learn/teachings of the Atlantean pyramidal experiences. Thus, this entity became a builder of the archetypal thought of the Law of One with distortion towards healing, which aided our people in bringing this through into a physical manifestation at what you would call a later period in your time measurement.

---

[1]   See footnote on 13.3 for information regarding the original books.

27.2 **QUESTIONER** The second question is: Paul has also received information that mentions that there were other beings aiding in the construction of the pyramids who were not fully materialized in the third density. They were materialized from the waist up to their heads, but were not materialized from the waist down to their feet. Did such entities exist in the construction of the pyramids, and who were they?

RA I am Ra. Consider, if you will, the intelligent infinity present in the absorption of livingness and beingness as it becomes codified into intelligent energy due to the thought impressions of those assisting the living stone into a new shape of beingness. The release and use of intelligent infinity for a brief period begins to absorb all the consecutive, or interlocking, dimensions, thus offering brief glimpses of those projecting to the material their thought. These beings thus beginning to materialize but not remaining visible. These beings were the thought-form, or third-density-visible, manifestation of our social memory complex as we offered contact from our intelligent infinity to the intelligent infinity of the stone.

27.3 **QUESTIONER** Thank you very much. I will now proceed with the process of starting the second book of *The Law of One*.[2] This, I will assume, will be a much more difficult task than the first book because we want to focus on things that are not transient, and as questioner I may have difficulty at times.

When I do have this difficulty, I may fall back on some partially transient questions simply because I will not be able to formulate what I really need to formulate, and I apologize for this. But I will try my best to stay on the track and eliminate things of no value from the book if they do occur during my questioning.[3]

The statement I will make to begin with I have written. It is: Most entities in this density focus their minds on some transient condition or activity with little regard to its value as a tool, or an aid, to their growth and understanding of the true, or undistorted, essence of the creation of which they are an integral part.

---

[2] See footnote on 13.3 for information regarding the original books.

[3] Any eliminated questions and answers have been restored.

We will attempt, by starting at the beginning of creation, to establish an overview of ourselves in the creation, thereby arriving at a more informed point of inspection of what we consider to be reality. It is hoped that this process will allow us to participate more effectively in the process of evolution.

I would like to start with definitions of words that we have been using that possibly we have not—and possibly cannot—totally understand, but since the first words that we use are intelligent infinity, I would like for you to define each of these words and give me the definition of their combination.

RA I am Ra. Your vibrations of mind complex indicate a query. However, your vibrational sound complex indicate a preference. Please restate.

27.4 **QUESTIONER** Would you define the word intelligent in the concept of intelligent infinity?

RA I am Ra. We shall address the entire spectrum of this question before defining as requested. Your language, using vibrational sound complexes, can be at best an approximation of that which is closer to an understanding, if you will, of the nature of conscious thought. Perceptions are not the same as sound vibration complexes, and the attempt to define will therefore be a frustrating one for you, although we are happy to aid you within the limits of your sound vibration complexes.

To define intelligent apart from infinity is difficult, for these two vibration complexes equal one concept. It is much like attempting to divide your sound vibration concept, faith, into two parts. We shall attempt to aid you, however.

27.5 **QUESTIONER** It is not necessary to divide it. The definition of intelligent infinity as one part is sufficient. Could you please now define intelligent infinity?

RA I am Ra. This is exponentially simpler and less confusing. There is unity. This unity is all that there is. This unity has a potential and kinetic. The potential is intelligent infinity. Tapping this potential will yield work. This work has been called by us, intelligent energy.

The nature of this work is dependent upon the particular distortion of Free Will which, in turn, is the nature of a particular intelligent energy, or kinetic focus, of the potential of unity, or that which is all.

27.6 **QUESTIONER** I'd like to expand a little on the concept of work. In Newtonian physics the concept of work is what we call a force which moves through space. It's the product of force and distance as we measure it. I'm assuming that the work of which you speak is a much broader term including possibly work in consciousness. Am I correct?

RA I am Ra. As we use this term it is universal in application. Intelligent infinity has a rhythm, or flow, as of a giant heart beginning with the Central Sun, as you would think or conceive of this; the presence of the flow inevitable as a tide of beingness without polarity, without finity; the vast and silent all beating outward, outward, focusing outward and inward until the focuses are complete. The intelligence or consciousness of foci have reached a state where their, shall we say, spiritual nature or mass calls them inward, inward, inward until all is coalesced. This is the rhythm of reality as you spoke.

27.7 **QUESTIONER** Now I think I have extracted an important point from this in that in intelligent infinity we have work without polarity, or a potential difference does not have to exist. Is this correct?

RA I am Ra. There is no difference, potential or kinetic, in unity. The basic rhythms of intelligent infinity are totally without distortion of any kind. The rhythms are clothed in mystery, for they are being itself. From this undistorted unity, however, appears a potential in relation to intelligent energy.

In this way you may observe the term to be somewhat two-sided: One use of the term, that being as the undistorted unity, being without any kinetic or potential side. The other application of this term, which we use undifferentiatedly for lack of other term, in the sense of the vast potential tapped into by foci or focuses of [intelligent] energy.[4]

27.8 **QUESTIONER** Now, I understand that the first distortion of intelligent infinity is the distortion of what we call Free Will. Can you give me a definition of this distortion?

---

[4] This statement has been edited to add clarity to what we believe to be Ra's intended meaning. The original statement reads: "The other application of this term, which we use undifferentiatedly for lack of other term, in the sense of the vast potential tapped into by foci or focuses of energy we call intelligent energy."

RA I am Ra. In this distortion of the Law of One it is recognized that the Creator will know Itself.

27.9 **QUESTIONER** Then am I correct then in assuming that the Creator will know Itself—the Creator then grants for this knowing the concept of freedom, total freedom of choice in the ways of knowing? Am I correct?

RA I am Ra. This is quite correct.

27.10 **QUESTIONER** This then being the first distortion of the Law of One, which I am assuming is the Law of Intelligent Infinity, from all other— correction, all other distortions which are the total experience of the creation spring from this. Is this correct?

RA I am Ra. This is both correct and incorrect. In your illusion all experience springs from the Law of Free Will, or the Way of Confusion. In another sense, which we are learning, the experiences are this distortion.

27.11 **QUESTIONER** I will have to think about that and ask questions on it in the next session, so I will go on to what you have given me as the Second Distortion which is the distortion of Love. Is this correct?

RA I am Ra. This is correct.

27.12 **QUESTIONER** I would like for you to define Love in the sense . . . in its sense as the Second Distortion.

RA I am Ra. This must be defined against the background of intelligent infinity, or unity, or the One Creator, with the primal distortion of Free Will. The term Love then may be seen as the focus, the choice of attack, the type of energy of an extremely, shall we say, high order which causes intelligent energy to be formed from the potential of intelligent infinity in just such and such a way. This then may be seen to be an object rather than an activity by some of your peoples, and the principle of this extremely strong energy focus being worshiped as the Creator instead of unity, or oneness, from which all Loves emanate.

27.13 **QUESTIONER** Is Love . . . is there a manifestation of Love that we could call vibration?

RA I am Ra. Again we reach semantic difficulties. The vibration, or density, of love, or understanding, is not a term used in the same sense as the Second Distortion, Love; the distortion Love being the great activator and primal co-Creator of various creations using intelligent infinity; the vibration love being that density in which those who have learned to do an activity called "loving" without significant distortion, then seek the Ways of Light or Wisdom.

Thus in vibratory sense love comes into light. In the sense of the activity of unity in its free will, love uses light and has the power to direct light in its distortions. Thus vibratory complexes recapitulate in reverse the creation in its unity, thus showing the rhythm, or flow, of the great heartbeat, if you will use this analogy.

27.14 **QUESTIONER** I will make a statement that I have extracted from the physics of Dewey Larson which may or may not be close to what we are trying to explain. Larson says that all is motion, which we can take as vibration; and that vibration, which is pure vibration and is not physical in any way, or in any form, or in any density, that vibration, by . . . first product of that vibration is what we call the photon, particle of light.

I was trying to make an analogy between this physical solution and the concept of love and light. Is this close to the concept of Love creating Light, or not?

RA I am Ra. You are correct.

27.15 **QUESTIONER** Then I will expand a bit more on this concept. We have the infinite vibration of Love which can occur, I am assuming, at varying frequencies, if this has a meaning in this. I would assume that it begins at one basic frequency.

Does this have any meaning? Am I making sense? Is this correct?

RA I am Ra. Each Love, as you term the prime movers, comes from one frequency, if you wish to use this term. This frequency is unity. We would perhaps liken it rather to a strength than a frequency, this strength being infinite, the finite qualities being chosen by the particular nature of this primal movement.

27.16 **QUESTIONER** Then this vibration which is, for lack of better understanding, which we would call pure motion; it is pure Love. It is. . . it is not . . . there is nothing that is yet condensed, shall we say, to form any type, or density, of illusion. This Love then creates, by this process of vibration, a photon, as we call it, which is the basic particle of light. This photon then, by added vibrations and rotations, further condenses into particles of the densities, the various densities that we experience. Is this correct?

RA I am Ra. This is correct.

27.17 **QUESTIONER** Now, this— Then light which forms the densities has what we call color, and this color is divided into seven categories of color. Can you tell me, is there a reason or an explanation for these categories of color? Can you tell me something about that?

RA I am Ra. This will be the last complete question of this session as this instrument is low on vital energy. We will answer briefly, and then you may question further in consequent sessions.

The nature of the vibratory patterns of your universe is dependent upon the configurations placed upon the original material, or Light, by the focus, or Love, using Its intelligent energy to create a certain pattern of illusions, or densities, in order to satisfy Its own intelligent estimate of a method of knowing Itself. Thus the colors, as you call them, are as strait, or narrow, or necessary as is possible to express, given the will of Love.

There is further information which we shall be happy to share by answering your questions. However, we do not wish to deplete this instrument. Is there a short query necessary before we leave?

27.18 **QUESTIONER** The only thing I need to know is, is there is anything we can do to make the instrument more comfortable or help her or the contact?

RA I am Ra. This instrument is slightly uncomfortable. Perhaps a simpler configuration of the body would be appropriate given the instrument's improving physical complex condition.

I am Ra. You are conscientious in your endeavors. We shall be with you. We leave you now in the love and in the light of the One Infinite Creator. Rejoice, therefore, in the power and the peace of the One Infinite Creator. Adonai.

28.0   **RA** I am Ra. I greet you in the love and the light of the Infinite Creator. I communicate now.

28.1   **QUESTIONER** I may be backtracking a little bit and make a few false starts today because I think we are at possibly the most important part of what we are doing in trying to make it apparent, through questioning, how everything is one, and how it comes from one intelligent infinity. This is difficult for me to do, so please bear with my errors in questioning.

The concept that I have right now of the process, using both what you have told me and some of Dewey Larson's material having to do with the physics of the process— I have the concept that intelligent infinity expands outward from all locations everywhere. It expands outward in every direction uniformly like the surface of a balloon or a bubble, expanding outward from every point everywhere. It expands outward at what's called unit velocity, or the velocity of light. This is Larson's idea of the progression of what he calls space/time. Is this concept correct?

RA I am Ra. This concept is incorrect, as is any concept of the one intelligent infinity. This concept is correct in the context of one particular Logos, or Love, or focus of this Creator which has chosen Its, shall we say, natural laws and ways of expressing them mathematically and otherwise.

The one undifferentiated intelligent infinity, unpolarized, full and whole, is the macrocosm of the mystery-clad being. We are messengers of the Law of One. Unity, at this approximation of understanding, cannot be specified by any physics but only be activated, or potentiated, intelligent infinity due to the catalyst of free will. This may be difficult to accept. However, the understandings we have to share begin and end in mystery.

28.2   **QUESTIONER** Well, we had yesterday arrived at a point where we were considering colors of light. You said that "the nature of the vibratory patterns of your universe is dependent upon the configurations placed on the original material, or light, by the focus of Love using Its intelligent energy to create a certain pattern of . . . of illusions or densities." Then after this material you said that there's further information which you'd be happy to share, but we ran out of time. Could you complete the further information on that?

RA I am Ra. In discussing this information we then, shall we say, snap back into the particular methods of understanding or seeing that which is that the one, sound vibration complex, Dewey, offers; this being correct for the second meaning of intelligent infinity: the potential which then through catalyst forms the kinetic.

This information is a natural progression of inspection of the kinetic shape of your environment. You may understand each color, or ray, as being, as we had said, a very specific and accurate apportion of intelligent energy's representation of intelligent infinity, each ray having been previously inspected in other regards.[1]

This information may be of aid here. We speak now nonspecifically to increase the depth of your conceptualization of the nature of what is. The universe in which you live is recapitulation, in each part, of intelligent infinity. Thus you will see the same patterns repeated in physical and metaphysical areas; the rays or apportions of light being, as you surmise, those areas of what you may call the physical illusion which rotate, vibrate, or are of a nature that may be, shall we say, counted, or categorized, in rotation manner in space/time as described by the one known as Dewey; some substances having various of the rays in a physical manifestation visible to the eye, this being apparent in the nature of your crystallized minerals which you count as precious, the ruby being red and so forth.

28.3 **QUESTIONER** This Light that occurred as a consequence of vibration, which is a consequence of Love. I am going to ask if that statement is right. Is that correct?

RA I am Ra. This statement is correct.

28.4 **QUESTIONER** OK. This light then can condense into material as we know it in our density, into all of our chemical elements because of rotations of the vibration at quantized intervals, or units, of angular velocity. Is this correct?

---

[1] In this context, *apportion* may be defined as "to divide and assign according to a plan."

RA I am Ra. This is quite correct.

28.5 QUESTIONER Thank you. I am wondering, what is the catalyst, or the activator, of the rotation? What causes the rotation so that the light condenses into our physical or chemical elements?

RA I am Ra. It is necessary to consider the enabling function of the focus known as Love. This energy is of an ordering nature. It orders in a cumulative way from greater to lesser so that when Its universe, as you may call it, is complete, the manner of development of each detail is inherent in the living light, and thus will develop in such and such a way; your own universe having been well-studied in an empirical fashion by those you call your scientists, and having been understood, or visualized, shall we say, with greater accuracy by the understandings, or visualizations, of the one known as Dewey.

28.6 QUESTIONER When does individualization, or the individualized portion of consciousness, come into play? How does this individualization occur, and at what point does individualized consciousness take over in working on the basic light?

RA I am Ra. You remain carefully in the area of creation itself. In this process we must further confuse you by stating that the process by which Free Will acts upon potential intelligent infinity to become focused intelligent energy takes place without the space/time of which you are so aware, as it is your continuum experience.

The experience, or existence, of space/time comes into being after the individuation process of Logos, or Love, has been completed and the physical universe, as you would call it, has coalesced or begun to draw inward while moving outward to the extent that that which you call your sun bodies have, in their turn, created timeless chaos coalescing into what you call planets, these vortices of intelligent energy spending a large amount of what you would call first density in a timeless state, the space/time realization being one of the learn/teachings of this density of beingness.

Thus we have difficulty answering your questions with regard to time and space and their relationship to the, what you would call, original creation which is not a part of space/time as you can understand it.

28.7 **QUESTIONER** Thank you. Does a unit of consciousness, an individualized unit of consciousness, create, say, a unit of the creation? I will give an example.

Would one individualized consciousness create one galaxy of stars, the type that has many millions of stars in it. Does this happen?

RA I am Ra. This can happen. The possibilities are infinite. Thus a Logos may create what you call a star system, or it may be the Logos creating billions of star systems. This is the cause of the confusion in the term galaxy, for there are many different Logos entities or creations, and we would call each, using your sound vibration complexes, a galaxy.

28.8 **QUESTIONER** Let's take as an example the planet that we are on now, and tell me how much of the creation was created by the same Logos that created this planet?

RA I am Ra. This planetary Logos is a strong Logos creating approximately two hundred fifty billion [250,000,000,000] of your star systems for Its creation. The, shall we say, laws or physical ways of this creation will remain, therefore, constant.

28.9 **QUESTIONER** Then what you're saying is that the lenticular star system, which we call a galaxy, that we find ourself in, with approximately 250 billion other suns like our own, was created by a single Logos. Is this correct?

RA I am Ra. This is correct.

28.10 **QUESTIONER** Now, since there are many individualized portions of consciousness in this lenticular galaxy, did this Logos then subdivide into more individualization of consciousness to create these consciousnesses or divide into these consciousnesses?

RA I am Ra. You are perceptive. This is also correct, although an apparent paradox.

28.11 **QUESTIONER** Could you tell me what you mean by an apparent paradox?

RA I am Ra. It would seem that if one Logos creates the intelligent energy ways for a large system, there would not be the necessity or possibility of the further sub-Logos differentiation. However, within limits, this is precisely the case, and it is perceptive that this has been seen.

28.12 **QUESTIONER** Thank you. Could you please make the instrument cough?

RA [*Cough.*]

28.13 **QUESTIONER** Thank you. Do all of the individualized portions of the Logos, then, in our— I'll call the lenticular galaxy that we are in, 250 billion suns, or stars, I will call that the major galaxy just so we will not get mixed up in our terms.

Does all the consciousness, then, in this individualized form that goes into what we are calling the major galaxy start out and go through all of the densities in order, one, two, three, four, five, six, seven or—then to eighth—or is there, shall I say, some who start higher up the rank and go in a . . . so that there is always a mixture of intelligent consciousness in the galaxy?

RA I am Ra. The latter is more nearly correct. In each beginning, there is the beginning from infinite strength. Free Will acts as a catalyst. Beings begin to form the universes. Consciousness then begins to have the potential to experience. The potentials of experience are created as a part of intelligent energy and are fixed before experience begins.

However, there is always, due to Free Will acting infinitely upon the creation, a great variation in initial responses to intelligent energy's potential. Thus almost immediately the foundations of the, shall we call it, hierarchical nature of beings begins to manifest as some portions of consciousness, or awareness, learn through experience in a much more efficient manner.

28.14 **QUESTIONER** Is there any reason for some portions being much more efficient in learning?

RA I am Ra. Is there any reason for some to learn more quickly than others? Look, if you wish, to the function of the will . . . the, shall we say, attraction to the upward spiraling line of light.

28.15 **QUESTIONER** Now, as the major galaxy is created, and I am assuming all of its densities . . . I am assuming all— There are eight densities created when this major galaxy is created. Is this correct?

RA I am Ra. This is basically correct. However, it is well to perceive that the eighth density functions also as the beginning density, or first density—in its latter stages—of the next octave of densities.

28.16 **QUESTIONER** Are you saying, then, there are an infinite number of octaves of densities one through eight?

RA I am Ra. We wish to establish that we are truly humble messengers of the Law of One. We can speak to you of our experiences and our understandings and teach/learn in limited ways. However, we cannot speak in firm knowledge of all the creations. We know only that they are infinite. We assume an infinite number of octaves.

However, it has been impressed upon us by our own teachers that there is a mystery-clad unity of creation in which all consciousness periodically coalesces and, again, begins. Thus we can only say we assume an infinite progression, though we understand it to be cyclical in nature and, as we have said, clad in mystery.

28.17 **QUESTIONER** Thank you. Would you please make the instrument cough again?

RA [*Cough.*]

28.18 **QUESTIONER** Thank you. When this major galaxy is formed by the Logos, polarity then exists in a sense that we have electrical polarity, a gravitational effect that probably isn't polarity, I'm . . . I'll have to ask that question. We do have electrical polarity existing at that time. Is this correct?

RA I am Ra. I accept this as correct with the stipulation that what you term electrical be understood as not only the one, Larson, stipulated its meaning but also in what you would call the metaphysical sense.

28.19 **QUESTIONER** Are you saying then that we not only have a polarity of electrical charge but also a polarity in consciousness at that time?

RA I am Ra. This is correct. All is potentially available from the beginning of your physical space/time—it then being the function of consciousness complexes to begin to use the physical materials to gain experience, to then polarize, in a metaphysical sense. The potentials for this are not created by the experiencer but by intelligent energy.

This will be the last full question of this session due to our desire to foster this instrument as it slowly regains physical complex energy. May we ask if you have one or two questions we may answer shortly before we close?

28.20 **QUESTIONER** I am assuming that the process of creation, then, after the original creation of the major galaxy, is continued by the further individualization of consciousness of the Logos so that there are many, many portions of individualized consciousness then creating further items, you might say, for experience all over the galaxy. Is this correct?

RA I am Ra. This is correct, for within the, shall we say, guidelines, or ways, of the Logos, the sub-Logos may find various means of differentiating experiences without removing or adding to these ways.

28.21 QUESTIONER Thank you. And since we are out of time I'll just ask if there is anything that we can do to make the instrument more comfortable or help the contact?

RA I am Ra. This instrument is well adjusted. You are conscientious.

I am Ra. I leave you, my friends, in the love and the light of the One Infinite Creator. Go forth, then, rejoicing in the power and the peace of the One Creator. Adonai.

SESSION 29

29.0 **RA** I am Ra. I greet you in the love and in the light of the Infinite Creator. We communicate now.

29.1 **QUESTIONER** Is our sun (this planetary system) as we know it a sub-Logos, or the physical manifestation of a sub-Logos?

RA I am Ra. This is correct.

29.2 **QUESTIONER** Then I am assuming this sub-Logos created this planetary system in all of its densities. Is this correct?

RA I am Ra. This is incorrect. The sub-Logos of your solar entity differentiated some experiential components within the patterns of intelligent energy set in motion by the Logos, which created the basic conditions and vibratory rates consistent throughout your, what you have called, major galaxy.

29.3 **QUESTIONER** Then is this sub-Logos which is our sun the same sub-Logos but just manifesting in different parts through the galaxy which is . . . is it all the stars in this galaxy?

RA I am Ra. Please restate.

29.4 **QUESTIONER** What I'm saying is there are roughly 250 billion stars, or suns, something like ours in this major galaxy. Are they all part of the same sub-Logos?

RA I am Ra. They are all part of the same Logos. Your solar system, as you would call it, is a manifestation, somewhat and slightly different, due to the presence of a sub-Logos.

29.5 **QUESTIONER** Now, all of these— Let me be sure I'm right then. Then our sun is a sub-Logos of the Logos that is the major galactic Logos. Correct?

RA I am Ra. This is correct.

29.6 **QUESTIONER** Are there any sub-sub-Logos that are found in our planetary system that are "sub" to our sun?

RA I am Ra. This is correct.

29.7 **QUESTIONER** Would you tell me what one of those— Would you give me an example of one of those, I'll call sub-sub-Logos?

RA I am Ra. One example is your mind/body/spirit complex.

29.8 **QUESTIONER** Then every entity that exists would be some type of sub- or sub-sub-Logos. Is this correct?

RA I am Ra. This is correct down to the limits of any observation, for the entire creation is alive.

29.9 **QUESTIONER** Then the planet which we walk upon here would be some form of sub-sub-Logos. Is this correct?

RA I am Ra. A planetary entity is so named only as Logos if it is working in harmonic fashion with entities, or mind/body complexes, upon its surface or within its electromagnetic field.

29.10 **QUESTIONER** Okay. Do the sub-Logos, such as our sun, do any of them— in our major galaxy—do they have a metaphysical polarity, shall we say, positive or negative as we've been using the term?

RA I am Ra. As you use the term, this is not so. Entities through the level of planetary have the strength of intelligent infinity through the use of free will, going through the actions of beingness. The polarity is not, thusly, as you understand polarity. It is only when the planetary sphere begins harmonically interacting with mind/body complexes, and more especially mind/body/spirit complexes, that planetary spheres take on distortions due to the thought complexes of entities interacting with the planetary entity.

The creation of the One Infinite Creator does not have the polarity you speak of.

29.11 **QUESTIONER** Thank you. Yesterday you stated that planets in first density are in a timeless state to begin with. Can you tell me how the effect we appreciate as time comes into being?

RA I am Ra. We have just described to you the state of beingness of each Logos. The process by which space/time comes into continuum form is a function of the careful building, shall we say, of an entire, or whole, plan of vibratory rates, densities, and potentials. When this plan has coalesced in the thought complexes of Love, then the physical manifestations begin to appear; this first manifestation stage being awareness or consciousness.

At the point at which this coalescence is at the livingness or beingness point—the point, or fountainhead, of beginning—space/time then begins to unroll its scroll of livingness.

29.12 **QUESTIONER** As the Love creates the vibration— I will make this statement first. Let me say, I believe that Love creates the vibration in space/time in order to form the photon. Is this correct?

RA I am Ra. This is essentially correct.

29.13 **QUESTIONER** Then the continued application of Love—I will assume this is directed by a sub-Logos or a sub-sub-Logos—this continued application of Love creates rotations of these vibrations which are in discrete units of angular velocity. This then creates chemical elements in our physical illusion and, I will assume, the elements in the other, or what we would call nonphysical, or other densities in the illusion. Is this correct?

RA I am Ra. The Logos creates all densities. Your question was unclear. However, we shall state the Logos does create both the space/time densities and the accompanying time/space densities.

29.14 **QUESTIONER** What I am assuming is that the rotations, the quantized incremental rotations of the vibrations, show up as the material of these densities. Is this correct?

RA I am Ra. This is essentially correct.

29.15 **QUESTIONER** Well, then because of these rotations there is an inward motion of these particles which is opposite the direction of space/time progression, the way I understand it, and this inward progression then is seen by us as what we call gravity. Is this correct?

RA I am Ra. This is incorrect.

29.16 **QUESTIONER** Can you tell me how the gravity comes about?

RA I am Ra. This that you speak of as gravity may be seen as the pressing towards the inner light/love, the seeking towards the spiral line of light which progresses towards the Creator. This is a manifestation of a spiritual event or condition of livingness.

29.17 **QUESTIONER** Now, gravity we know now on our moon is less than it is upon our planet here. Is there a metaphysical principle behind this that you could explain?

RA I am Ra. The metaphysical and physical are inseparable. Thus that of which you spoke which attempts to explain this phenomenon is able to, shall we say, calculate the gravitational force of most objects due to the various physical aspects such as what you know of as mass. However, we felt it was necessary to indicate the corresponding and equally important metaphysical nature of gravity.

29.18 **QUESTIONER** I sometimes have difficulty in getting, you might say, a foothold into what I am looking for in trying to seek out the metaphysical principles, you might say, behind our physical illusion.

Could you give me an example of the amount of gravity in the third density conditions at the surface of the planet Venus? Would it be greater or less than Earth?

RA I am Ra. The gravity, shall we say, the attractive force which we also describe as the pressing outward force towards the Creator, is greater spiritually upon the entity you call Venus due to the greater degree of success, shall we say, at seeking the Creator.

This point only becomes important when you consider that when all of creation in its infinity has reached a spiritual gravitational mass of sufficient nature, the entire creation infinitely coalesces, the light seeking and finding its source, and thusly ending the creation, and beginning a new creation—much as you consider the black hole, as you call it, with its conditions of infinitely great mass at the zero point from which no light may be seen, as it has been absorbed.

29.19 **QUESTIONER** Then the black hole would be a point . . . am I correct in saying it would be a point at which the environmental material had succeeded in uniting with unity or the Creator? Is this correct?

RA I am Ra. The black hole which manifests third density is the physical complex manifestation of this spiritual, or metaphysical, state. This is correct.

29.20 **QUESTIONER** Thank you. Then when our planet Earth here gets fully into fourth density, will there be a greater gravity?

RA I am Ra. There will be a greater spiritual gravity thus causing a denser illusion.

29.21 **QUESTIONER** This denser illusion, then, I will assume would increase the gravitational acceleration above the measured 32.2 feet per second squared that we now experience. Is this correct?

RA I am Ra. Your entities do not have the instrumentation to measure spiritual gravity but only to observe a few of its extreme manifestations.

29.22 **QUESTIONER** This I know, that we can't measure spiritual gravity, but I was just wondering if the . . . the physical effect would be measurable as an increase in the gravitational constant? That was my question.

RA I am Ra. The increase measurable by existing instrumentation would, and will be, statistical in nature only and not significant.

29.23 **QUESTIONER** OK. Now, as the creation is formed, as the atoms form from rotations of the vibration which is light, they coalesce in a certain manner sometimes. They find distances, inter-atomic distances, from each other at precise distance and produce a lattice structure which we call crystalline.

I am guessing that because of the formation from intelligent energy of the precise crystalline structure that it is possible, by some technique, to tap intelligent energy and bring it into the physical illusion by working through the crystalline structure. Is this correct?

RA I am Ra. This is correct only insofar as the crystalline physical structure is charged by a correspondingly crystallized, or regularized, or balanced, mind/body/spirit complex.

29.24 **QUESTIONER** I don't wish to get off on subjects of no importance or subjects that don't lead us to a better understanding of our mechanism of growth, which lead us to things that are not transient, but it's difficult sometimes to see precisely what direction to go in. I would like to investigate a little bit more this idea of crystals and how they are used.

I'm assuming then from what you said that in order to use the crystal to tap intelligent energy, it is necessary to have a partially undistorted mind/body/spirit complex. Is this satisfactory, or do you need— Is this correct?

RA I am Ra. This is specifically correct.

29.25 **QUESTIONER** There must be a point at which the removal of distortion reaches a minimum for use of the crystal in tapping intelligent energy. Is this correct?

RA I am Ra. This is correct only if it is understood, shall we say, that each mind/body/spirit complex has an unique such point.

29.26 **QUESTIONER** Can you tell me why each mind/body/spirit complex has this unique point of distortion-ridding?

RA I am Ra. Each mind/body/spirit complex is an unique portion of the One Creator.

29.27 **QUESTIONER** Then you are saying that there is no single level of, shall we say, purity required to tap intelligent energy through crystals, but there can be a wide variation in the amount of distortion that an entity may have. But each entity has to reach his particular point of, what I might call, energizing the ability. Is this right?

RA I am Ra. This is incorrect. The necessity is for the mind/body/spirit complex to be of a certain balance, this balance thus enabling it to reach a set level of lack of distortion. The critical difficulties are unique for each mind/body/spirit complex due to the experiential distillations which, in total, are the, shall we say, violet-ray beingness of each such entity.

This balance is what is necessary for work to be done in seeking the gateway to intelligent infinity through the use of crystals or through any other use. No two mind/body/spirit crystallized natures are the same. The distortion requirements, vibrationally speaking, are set.

29.28 **QUESTIONER** I see. Then if you are able to read the violet ray of an entity, to see that ray, is it possible then to immediately determine whether the entity could use crystals to tap intelligent energy?

RA I am Ra. It is possible for one of fifth density or above to do this.

29.29 **QUESTIONER** Is it possible for you to tell me how a crystal is used by an entity who has satisfactorily achieved necessary violet-ray qualification, I will say, how it is possible for the entity to use the crystal or how he should use the crystal?

RA I am Ra. The gateway to intelligent infinity is born of, shall we say, the sympathetic vibration, in balanced state, accompanying the will to serve, the will to seek.

29.30 **QUESTIONER** But can you tell me precisely what the entity would do with the crystal to use it for the purpose of seeking the intelligent infinity?

RA I am Ra. The use of the crystal in physical manifestation is that use wherein the entity of crystalline nature charges the regularized physical crystal with this seeking, thus enabling it to vibrate harmonically, and also become the catalyst, or gateway, whereby intelligent infinity may thus become intelligent energy, this crystal serving as an analog of the violet ray of mind/body/spirit in relatively undistorted form.

29.31 **QUESTIONER** Is it possible at all for you to instruct us in specific uses of crystals?

RA I am Ra. It is possible. There are, we consider, things which are not efficacious to tell you due to possible infringement upon your free will. Entities of the Confederation have erred in this in the past. The uses of the crystal, as you know, include the uses for healing, for power, and even for the development of life-forms. We feel that it is unwise to offer instruction at this time as your peoples have shown a tendency to use peaceful sources of power for disharmonious reasons.

29.32 **QUESTIONER** I guess what we'd better get to then—now that we have traced the path of creation at least down to the crystalline structure— we'd better concentrate on the evolution of thought and its seeking path to intelligent infinity.

We have created, in the major galaxy of the Logos, a very large number of planets. As these planets develop, is it possible for you to give me an example of various planetary developments, in what I would call a metaphysical sense, having to do with the development of consciousness and its polarities throughout the galaxy? In other words, I believe that some of these planets develop quite rapidly into higher density planets and some take longer times. Can you give me some idea of that development?

RA I am Ra. This will be the final full query of this session.

The particular Logos of your major galaxy has used a large portion of Its coalesced material to reflect the beingness of the Creator. In this way there is much of your galactic system which does not have the progression of which you speak but dwells spiritually as a portion of the Logos. Of those entities upon which consciousness dwells there is, as you surmise, a variety of time/space periods during which the higher densities of experience are attained by consciousness.

Does this fulfill the requirements of your query?

29.33   **QUESTIONER** I'll study it and possibly have something tomorrow since I don't want to overtire the instrument. The instrument had a question if you have time for a short question, and I will read it.

The instrument does not desire to do physical healing work. She already does spiritual balancing by hands. Can she read the private healing material without doing physical healing? I am assuming that she means can she read it without creating problems in her life pattern? She does not wish to incur lessening of positive polarity. Can she read this material under those conditions?

RA I am Ra. We shall speak shortly due to the fact that we are attempting to conserve this instrument's vital energies during the three-month period of which we have spoken.

This entity has a[n] experiential history of healing on levels other than the so-called physical. Thus it is acceptable that this material be read. However, the exercise of fire shall never be practiced by this instrument, as it is used in the stronger form for the physical healing.

Is there any short query further before we close?

29.34   **QUESTIONER** Is there anything that we can do to make the instrument more comfortable or improve the contact?

RA I am Ra. You are conscientious. The entity is well aligned.

I am Ra. I leave you now in the love and the light of the One Infinite Creator. Go forth, therefore, rejoicing in the power and the peace of the One Infinite Creator. Adonai.

Session 30

30.0 **RA** I am Ra. I greet you in the love and in the light of the One Infinite Creator. We communicate now.

30.1 **QUESTIONER** I am going to make a statement and then let you correct it if I have made any errors. This is the statement: creation is a single entity, or unity. If only a single entity exists, then the only concept of service is service to self. If this single entity subdivides, then the concept of service of one of its parts to the other part is born. From this concept springs the equality of service to self, or to others.

It would seem that as the Logos subdivided, parts would select each orientation. As individualized entities emerge in space/time then I would assume that they have polarity. Is this statement correct?

RA I am Ra. This statement is quite perceptive and correct until the final phrase in which we note that the polarities begin to be explored only at the point when a third-density entity becomes aware of the possibility of choice between the concept, or distortion, of service to self or service to others. This marks the end of what you may call the unselfconscious, or innocent, phase of conscious awareness.

30.2 **QUESTIONER** Thank you. Would you define mind, body, and spirit separately?

RA I am Ra. These terms are all simplistic descriptive terms which equal a complex of energy focuses; the body, as you call it, being the material of the density which you experience at a given space/time or time/space; this complex of materials being available for distortions of what you would call physical manifestation.

The mind is a complex which reflects the inpourings of the spirit and the up-pourings of the body complex. It contains what you know as feelings, emotions, and intellectual thoughts in its more conscious complexities. Moving further down the tree of mind we see the intuition, which is of the nature of the mind more in contact, or in tune, with the total beingness complex. Moving down to the roots of mind we find the progression of consciousness which gradually turns from the personal to the racial memory to the cosmic influxes, and thus becomes a direct contactor of that shuttle which we call the spirit complex.

This spirit complex is the channel whereby the inpourings from all of the various universal, planetary, and personal inpourings may be funneled into the roots of consciousness, and whereby consciousness may be funneled to the gateway of intelligent infinity through the balanced intelligent energy of body and mind.[1]

You will see by this series of definitive statements that mind, body, and spirit are inextricably intertwined and cannot continue, one without the other. Thus we refer to the mind/body/spirit complex rather than attempting to deal with them separately, for the work, shall we say, that you do during your experiences is done through the interaction of these three components, not through any one.

30.3   **QUESTIONER** Upon our physical death, as we call it, from this particular density and this particular incarnative experience, we lose this chemical body. Immediately after the loss of this chemical body, do we maintain a different type of body? Is there still a mind/body/spirit complex at that point?

RA I am Ra. This is correct. The mind/body/spirit complex is quite intact; the physical body complex you now associate with the term "body" being but manifestation of a more dense, and intelligently informed, and powerful body complex.

30.4   **QUESTIONER** Is there any loss to the mind or spirit after this transition which we call death or any impairment of either because of the loss of this chemical body that we now have?

RA I am Ra. In your terms, there is a great loss of mind complex due to the fact that much of the activity of a mental nature of which you are aware during the experience of this space/time continuum is as much of a surface illusion as is the chemical body complex.

In other terms, nothing whatever of importance is lost; the character or, shall we say, pure distillation of emotions and biases, or distortions and wisdoms, if you will, becoming obvious for the first time, shall we say;

---

[1]   To see an illustration of the tree of mind metaphor, see the Resource Series.

these pure emotions and wisdoms and bias-distortions being, for the most part, either ignored or underestimated during physical life experience.

In terms of the spiritual, this channel is then much opened due to the lack of necessity for the forgetting characteristic of third density.

30.5 **QUESTIONER** I would like to know how the mind/body/spirit complexes originate. How, going back as far as necessary, does the— Do they originate by spirit forming mind and mind forming body? Can you tell me this?

RA I am Ra. We ask you to consider that you are attempting to trace evolution. This evolution is as we have previously described:[2] the consciousness being first, in first density, without movement, a random thing. Whether you may call this mind or body complex is a semantic problem. We call it mind/body complex, recognizing always that in the simplest iota of this complex exists, in its entirety, the One Infinite Creator.

This mind/body complex then in second density discovering the growing and turning towards the light, thus awakening what you may call the spirit complex, that which intensifies the upward spiraling towards the love and light of the Infinite Creator.

The addition of this spirit complex, though apparent rather than real, it having existed potentially from the beginning of space/time, perfects itself by graduation into third density. When the mind/body/spirit complex becomes aware of the possibility of service to self or other-self, then the mind/body/spirit complex is activated.

30.6 **QUESTIONER** Thank you. I don't wish to cover ground that we have covered before, but it sometimes is helpful to restate these concepts for complete clarity since words are a poor tool for what we do.

Just as a passing point, I was wondering, in . . . on this planet, during the second density, I believe there was habitation at the same time/space of bipedal entities and what we call the dinosaurs. Is this correct?

RA I am Ra. This is correct.

---

2 Previously described in 13.15–21.

30.7 **QUESTIONER** These two types of entities seem to be incompatible, you might say, with each other. I don't know. Can you tell me the reason behind both types of entities inhabiting the same space/time?

RA I am Ra. Consider the workings of free will as applied to evolution. There are paths that the mind/body complex follows in an attempt to survive, to reproduce, and to seek in its fashion that which is unconsciously felt as the potential for growth; these two arenas, or paths, of development being two among many.

30.8 **QUESTIONER** I see. A news program I saw a couple of weeks ago raised the question of why the dinosaurs vanished, you might say, from our planet suddenly. I know this is unimportant, but I just wondered what the reason was.

RA I am Ra. These entities could not feed their body complexes.

30.9 **QUESTIONER** Now, in second density the concept of bisexual reproduction first originates. Is this correct?

RA I am Ra. This is correct.

30.10 **QUESTIONER** Can you tell me the philosophy behind this mechanism of propagation of the bodily complex?

RA I am Ra. The second density is one in which the groundwork is being laid for third-density work. In this way it may be seen that the basic mechanisms of reproduction capitulate into a vast potential in third density for service to other-self and to self; this being not only by the functions of energy transfer, but also [by] the various services performed, due to the close contact of those who are, ·shall we say, magnetically attracted, one to the other; these entities thus having the opportunities for many types of service which would be unavailable to the independent entity.

30.11 **QUESTIONER** Was the basic reason, the original reason for this then to increase opportunity for experience of the One Creator? Is this correct?

RA I am Ra. This is not merely correct but is the key to that which occurs in all densities.

30.12 **QUESTIONER** Does the process of bisexual reproduction, or the philosophy of it, play a part in the spiritual growth of second-density entities?

RA I am Ra. In isolated instances this is so due to efficient perceptions upon the part of entities or species. For the greater part, by far, this is not the case in second density, the spiritual potentials being those of third density.

30.13 **QUESTIONER** I was wondering if the male cat, Gandalf, has benefited by that mechanism in some way, or by other mechanisms, in increasing spiritual potential or understanding.

RA I am Ra. We examine this information and find it harmless. The second-density entity, sound vibration Gandalf, is a rare sample of its species due first to previous individualization, secondly due to a great amount of investment in this particular life experience. This is the greatest catalyst in this entity's progress.

It is very unusual, as we have said. However, the experiences of bisexual reproduction which were of the nature of the entity Gandalf were, to a small extent, of spiritual benefit due to an unusual relationship with another entity, this also what you call a cat. This entity also being of an unusually third-density orientation, or investment, from previous life experiences. Thus the formation of what could be seen to be recognizably love did exist in this relationship.

30.14 **QUESTIONER** Thank you. Can you give me a brief history of the metaphysical principles of the development of each of our planets around the sun and their function with respect to evolution of beings?

RA I am Ra. We shall give you a metaphysical description only of those planets upon which individual mind/body/spirit complexes have been, are, or shall be experienced. You may understand the other spheres to be a part of the Logos.

We take the one known as Venus. This planetary sphere was one of rapid evolution. It is our native Earth, and the rapidity of [the progress of] the mind/body/spirit complexes upon its surface was due to harmonious interaction.

Upon the entity known to you as Mars, as you have already discussed,[3] this entity was stopped in mid-third density, thus being unable to continue in progression due to the lack of hospitable conditions upon the

---

[3] Discussed in 9.6–11, 10.6, 14.3, 18.20, 19.5, 20.17–18, 20.20, 20.26, and 21.8.

surface. This planet shall be undergoing healing for some of your space/time millennia.

The planet which you dwell upon has a metaphysical history well known to you, and you may ask about it if you wish. However, we have spoken to a great degree upon this subject.

The planet known as Saturn has a great affinity for the infinite intelligence, and thus it has been dwelled upon in its magnetic fields of time/space by those who wish to protect your system.

The planetary entity known to you as Uranus is slowly moving through the first density and has the potential of moving through all densities.

30.15 **QUESTIONER** Thank you. I was wondering if any of the other planets had a metaphysical evolution.

You stated yesterday that much of this major galactic system dwells spiritually as a part of the Logos. By that do you mean that nearer the center of this major galactic system that the stars there do not have planetary systems? Is this correct?

RA I am Ra. This is incorrect. The Logos has distributed itself throughout your galactic system. However, the time/space continua of some of your more central sun systems is much further advanced.

30.16 **QUESTIONER** Well then, could you generally say that as you get closer to the center of this major galactic system that there is a greater spiritual density, I'll use the term, or that this general spiritual quality is advanced at that area?

RA I am Ra. This will be the last full question of this session as this instrument is somewhat uncomfortable. We do not wish to deplete the instrument.

The spiritual density, or mass, of those more towards the center of your galaxy is known. However, this is due simply to the varying timelessness states during which the planetary spheres may coalesce, this process of space/time beginnings occurring earlier, shall we say, as you approach the center of the galactic spiral. We welcome any short [*tape ends*].

30.17 **QUESTIONER** The instrument would like to know if you could tell her whether or not this item which is called Sam Millar's polarizer would help her physical well-being. Can you do that?

RA I am Ra. As we scan the instrument, we find anomalies of the magnetic field which are distorted towards our abilities to find narrow-band channel into this instrument's mind/body/spirit complex. The polarizer of which you speak, as it is, would not be helpful. A careful reading of this instrument's aura by those gifted in this area, and subsequent alterations of the magnetizing forces of this polarizer, would assist the entity, Sam, in creating such a polarizer that would be of some aid to the instrument. However, we would suggest that no electrical or magnetic equipment not necessary for the recording of our words be brought into these sessions, for we wish no distortions that are not necessary.

30.18 **QUESTIONER** Thank you. Is there anything that we can do to make the instrument more comfortable or to improve the contact?

RA This instrument is well balanced, and the contact is as it should be. This instrument has certain difficulties of a distortion you would call the muscular spasm, thus making the motionless position uncomfortable. Thus we leave the instrument.

I am Ra. You are doing well, my friends. I leave you in the love and the light of the One Infinite Creator. Go forth, then, rejoicing in the power and the peace of the One Creator. Adonai.

SESSION 31

31.0   RA   I am Ra. I greet you in the love and in the light of the One Infinite Creator. We communicate now.

31.1   QUESTIONER   I would like to ask a question first for the instrument herself. She requests to know if it would be advisable for her to walk alone now that she feels better.[1]

RA   I am Ra. This is acceptable.

31.2   QUESTIONER   OK. What I'm going to do is use the information that we did at the end of the previous book that you suggested would be more appropriate for more advanced material. We will put it in the book at this point, as we are talking about bisexual reproduction, and I would like to expand on this material a little bit to get some definitions and better understandings.

> *Editor's Note: The following is the information that the Questioner referred to from 26.38 that deals with sexual energy transfers and blockages, both positively and negatively oriented:*
>
> RA   I am Ra. The first energy transfer is red ray. It is a random transfer having to do only with your reproductive system.
>
> The orange- and the yellow-ray attempts to have sexual intercourse create, firstly, a blockage if only one entity vibrates in this area, thus causing the entity vibrating sexually in this area to have a never-ending appetite for this activity. What these vibratory levels are seeking is green-ray activity. There is the possibility of orange- or yellow-ray energy transfer; this being polarizing towards the negative—one being seen as object rather than other-self; the other seeing itself as plunderer, or master of the situation.
>
> In fourth ray there are two possibilities. Firstly, if both vibrate in fourth ray there will be a mutually strengthening energy transfer, the

---

[1] Carla walked 3–5 miles per day, and it was felt that, as a safety measure, Jim should accompany her on these walks after her episode of not being able to breathe and almost fainting. In this question, Carla was asking if she could walk without Jim by her side.

negative or female as you call it, drawing the energy from the roots of the beingness up through the energy centers, thus being physically revitalized; the positive, or male polarity, as it is deemed in your illusion, finding in this energy transfer an inspiration which satisfies and feeds the spirit portion of the body/mind/spirit complex, thus both being polarized and releasing the excess of that which each has in abundance by nature of intelligent energy; that is, negative/intuitive, positive/physical energies, as you may call them; this energy transfer being blocked only if one, or both, entities have fear of possession, of being possessed, of desiring possession or desiring being possessed.

The other green-ray possibility is that of one entity offering green-ray energy, the other not offering energy of the universal love energy, this resulting in a blockage of energy for the one not green ray, thus increasing frustration or appetite; the green-ray being polarizing slightly towards service to others.

The blue-ray energy transfer is somewhat rare among your people at this time, but is of great aid due to energy transfers involved in becoming able to express the self without reservation, or fear.

The indigo-ray transfer is extremely rare among your people. This is the sacramental portion of the body complex whereby contact may be made, through the violet ray, with intelligent infinity. No blockages may occur at these latter two levels, due to the fact that if both entities are not ready for this energy, it is not visible, and neither transfer nor blockage may take place. It is as though the distributor were removed from a powerful engine.

This instrument was able, as an example of this working, to baffle the Orion group during its LSD experiences, as you call this substance, due to the fact that it effectively completely opened other-self to third-ray—we correct this instrument; it is growing low in vital energy—green-ray energy and partially open other-self to blue-ray interaction.

You speak in this material of sexual energy transfer. Could you define that energy transfer and expand upon its meaning, please?

RA I am Ra. Energy transfer implies the release of potential energies across, shall we say, a potentiated space. The sexual energy transfers occur due to the polarizations of two mind/body/spirit complexes, each of which have some potential difference, one to the other. The nature of the transfer of energy, or of the blockage of this energy, is then a function of the interaction of these two potentials. In the cases where transfer takes place, you may liken this to a circuit being closed. You may also see this activity, as all experiential activities, as the Creator experiencing Itself.

31.3 **QUESTIONER** Would this then be the primal mechanism for the Creator to experience Self?

RA I am Ra. This is not a proper term. Perhaps the adjective would be "one appropriate" way of the Creator knowing Itself, for in each interaction, no matter what the distortion, the Creator is experiencing Itself. The bisexual knowing of the Creator by Itself has the potential for two advantages.

Firstly, in the green-ray activated being there is the potential for a direct and simple analog of what you may call joy—the spiritual, or metaphysical, nature which exists in intelligent energy. This is a great aid to comprehension of a truer nature of beingness.

The other potential advantage of bisexual reproductive acts is the possibility of a sacramental understanding, or connection, shall we say, with the gateway to intelligent infinity, for with appropriate preparation, work in what you may call magic may be done, and experiences of intelligent infinity may be had. The positively oriented individuals concentrating upon this method of reaching intelligent infinity, then, through the seeking or the act of will, are able to direct this infinite intelligence to the work these entities desire to do, whether it be knowledge of service, or ability to heal, or whatever service to others is desired.

These are two advantages of this particular method of the Creator experiencing Itself. As we have said before, the corollary of the strength of this particular energy transfer is that it opens the door, shall we say, to the individual mind/body/spirit complex's desire to serve in an infinite number of ways an other-self, thus polarizing towards positive.

31.4 **QUESTIONER** Can you expand somewhat on the concept that this action not only allows the Creator to know Itself better but also creates, in our density, an offspring or makes available the pathway for another entity to enter the density?

RA I am Ra. As we have previously said, the sexual energy transfers include the red-ray transfer which is random and which is a function of the second-density attempt to grow, to survive, shall we say. This is a proper function of the sexual interaction. The offspring, as you call the incarnated entity which takes on the mind/body complex opportunity offered by this random act or event called the fertilization of egg by seed, causes an entity to have the opportunity to then enter this density as an incarnate entity.

This gives the two who were engaged in this bisexual reproductive energy transfer the potential for great service in this area of the nurturing of the small-experienced entity as it gains in experience.

It shall be of interest at this point to note that there is always the possibility of using these opportunities to polarize towards the negative, and this has been aided by the gradual building up, over many thousands of your years, of social-complex distortions which create a tendency towards confusion, shall we say, or baffling of the service-to-others aspect of this energy transfer and subsequent opportunities for service to other-selves.

31.5 **QUESTIONER** If a sexual energy transfer occurs in green ray—and I am assuming in this case that there is no red-ray energy transfer—does this mean it is impossible then for this particular transfer to include fertilization and the birthing of an entity?

RA I am Ra. This is incorrect. There is always the red-ray energy transfer due to the nature of the body complex. The random result of this energy transfer will be as it will be, as a function of the possibility of fertilization at a given time in a given pairing of entities.

The green-ray energy transfer occurs due to the vibratory rate of each entity being undistorted in any vital sense by the yellow- or orange-ray energies; thus the gift, shall we say, being given freely, no payment being requested either of the body, of the mind, or of the spirit. The green ray is one of complete universality of love. This is a giving without expectation of return.

31.6 **QUESTIONER** I was wondering if there was some principle behind the fact that a sexual union does not necessarily lead to fertilization. I'm not interested in the chemical, or physical, principles of it. I'm interested in whether or not there is some metaphysical principle that leads to the couple having a child or not, or is it purely random?

RA I am Ra. This is random within certain limits. If an entity has reached the seniority whereby it chooses the basic structure of the life experience, this entity may then choose to incarnate in a physical complex which is not capable of reproduction. Thus we find some entities which have chosen to be unfertile. Other entities, through free will, make use of various devices to insure nonfertility. Except for these conditions, the condition is random.

31.7 **QUESTIONER** Thank you. In the material earlier you mentioned "magnetic attraction." Could you define and expand upon that term?

RA I am Ra. We used the term to indicate that in your bisexual natures there is that which is of polarity. This polarity may be seen to be variable according to the, shall we say, male/female polarization of each entity, be each entity biologically male or female. Thus you may see the magnetism when two entities with the appropriate balance, male/female versus female/male polarity, meeting and thus feeling the attraction which polarized forces will exert, one upon the other.

This is the strength of the bisexual mechanism. It does not take an act of will to decide to feel attraction for one who is oppositely polarized sexually. It will occur in an inevitable sense, giving the free flow of energy a proper, shall we say, avenue. This avenue may be blocked by some distortion towards a belief/condition which states to the entity that this attraction is not desired. However, the basic mechanism functions as simply as would, shall we say, the magnet and the iron.

31.8 **QUESTIONER** We have what seems to be an increasing number of entities incarnate here now who have what is called a homosexual orientation in this respect. Could you explain and expand upon that concept?

RA I am Ra. Entities of this condition experience a great deal of distortion due to the fact that they have experienced many incarnations as biological male and as biological female. This would not suggest what you call homosexuality in an active phase were it not for the difficult vibratory condition of your planetary sphere. There is what you may call great aura infringement among your crowded urban areas in your more populous countries, as you call portions of your planetary surface. Under these conditions the confusions will occur.

31.9 **QUESTIONER** Why does density of population create these confusions?

RA I am Ra. The bisexual reproductive urge has as its goal, not only the simple reproductive function, but more especially the desire to serve others being awakened by this activity.

In an over-crowded situation where each mind/body/spirit complex is under a constant bombardment from other-selves, it is understandable that those who are especially sensitive would not feel the desire to be of service to other-selves. This also would increase the probability of a lack of desire or a blockage of the red-ray reproductive energy.

In an uncrowded atmosphere this same entity would, through the stimulus of feeling the solitude about it, then have much more desire to seek out someone to whom it may be of service thus regularizing the sexual reproductive function.

31.10 **QUESTIONER** Roughly how many previous incarnations, shall we say, would a male entity in this incarnation have had to have had in the past as a female to have a highly homosexual orientation in this incarnation? Just roughly.

RA I am Ra. If an entity has had roughly 65% of its incarnations in the sexual/biological body complex, the opposite polarity to its present body complex, this entity is vulnerable to the aura infringement of your urban areas, and may, perhaps, become of what you call an homosexual nature.

It is to be noted at this juncture that although it is much more difficult, it is possible in this type of association for an entity to be of great service to another in fidelity and sincere green-ray love of a nonsexual nature, thus adjusting or lessening the distortions of its sexual impairment.[2]

31.11 **QUESTIONER** Timothy Leary, doing research, wrote that at the time of puberty, and up through that time, there is an imprint occurring on the DNA coding of an entity and that, for instance, sexual biases are

---

[2] To read an essay examining the meaning of these Q&As regarding homosexuality, see the Resource Series.

imprinted due to early sexual experiences or some of the first sexual experiences of the entity. Does anything like this actually happen?

RA I am Ra. This is partially correct. Due to the nature of solitary sexual experiences, it is in most cases unlikely that what you call masturbation has an imprinting effect upon later experiences.

This is similarly true with some of the encounters which might be seen as homosexual among those of this age group. These are often, instead, innocent exercises in curiosity.

However, it is quite accurate that the first experience in which the mind/body/spirit complex is intensely involved will indeed imprint upon the entity, for that life experience, a set of preferences.

31.12 **QUESTIONER** Does the Orion group use this, shall we say, as a gateway to impressing upon entities, shall we say, preferences which could create negative polarization?

RA I am Ra. Just as we of the Confederation attempt to beam our love and light whenever given the opportunity, including sexual opportunities, so the Orion group will use an opportunity, if it is negatively oriented, or if the individual is negatively oriented.

31.13 **QUESTIONER** Is there any emotional bias that has nothing to do with male/female sexual polarity that can create sexual energy buildup in an entity?

RA I am Ra. The sexual energy buildup is extremely unlikely to occur without sexual bias upon the part of the entity. Perhaps we did not understand your question, but it seems obvious that it would take an entity with the potential for sexual activity to experience a sexual energy buildup.

31.14 **QUESTIONER** I was thinking more of the possibility of the Orion group having influenced, say, certain members of the Third Reich who I have read reports of having sexual gratification from the observation of the, in some cases, the gassing and killing of entities in the gas chambers.

RA I am Ra. We shall repeat: these entities had the potential for sexual energy buildup. The choice of stimulus is certainly the choice of the entity. In the case of which you speak, these entities were strongly polarized orange ray, thus finding the energy blockage of power over others, the putting to death being the ultimate power over others; this then being expressed in a sexual manner, though solitary.

In this case the desire would continue unabated and be virtually unquenchable.

You will find, if you observe the entire spectrum of sexual practices among your peoples, that there are those who experience such gratification from domination over others either from rape or from other means of domination. In each case this is an example of energy blockage which is sexual in its nature.

31.15 **QUESTIONER** Would the Orion group then be able, shall we say, to impress on entities this orange-ray effect? Or did they— Is this the way that this came about, is what I'm trying to get at. Is this the way these concepts came about on this planet? Because if we go back to the beginning of third density, there must be a primal cause of this.

RA I am Ra. The cause of this is not Orion. It is the free choice of your peoples. This is somewhat difficult to explain. We shall attempt.

The sexual energy transfers and blockages are more a manifestation, or example, of that which is more fundamental than the other way about. Therefore, as your peoples became open to the concepts of bellicosity and the greed of ownership, these various distortions then began to filter down through the tree of mind into body complex expressions, the sexual expression being basic to that complex. Thus these sexual energy blockages, though Orion influenced and intensified, are basically the product of the beingness chosen freely by your peoples.

This will be the final question unless we may speak further upon this question to clarify, or answer any short queries before we close.

31.16 **QUESTIONER** I just need to know if this then works through the racial memory to infect the entire population in some way. Does that sort of thing happen?

RA I am Ra. The racial memory contains all that has been experienced. Thus there is some, shall we say, contamination even of the sexual, this showing mostly in your own culture as the various predispositions to adversary relationships—or, as you call them, marriages—rather than the free giving one to another in the love and the light of the Infinite Creator.

31.17 **QUESTIONER** That was precisely the point which I was trying to make. Thank you very much. Not to tire the instrument, I will just ask, then, if there is anything we can do to make the instrument more comfortable or to improve the contact?

RA I am Ra. Please be aware that this instrument is somewhat fatigued. The channel is very clear. However, we find the vital energy low. We do not wish to deplete the instrument. However, there is a, shall we say, energy exchange which we feel an honor/duty to offer when this instrument opens itself. Therefore, counsel we this instrument to attempt to assess the vital energies carefully before offering itself as open channel.

All is well. You are conscientious.

I am Ra. I leave this instrument, and you, in the love and in the light of the One Infinite Creator. Go forth, then, rejoicing in the power and the peace of the One Creator. Adonai.

32.0 **RA** I am Ra. I greet you in the love and the light of the One Infinite Creator. We communicate now.

32.1 **QUESTIONER** I have a little question I will throw in at this point from Jim. I will read it.

"The instrument's physical complex is now in the process of recovery from taking a chemical. She was ignorant of the opening that she was creating. How can each of the three of us present be more aware of how such openings may be created in our actions and thoughts? Is it possible that we could make such openings innocently as we question in certain areas during these sessions? And then, what can we do to protect ourselves from distorting influences in general? Is there any ritual or meditation that we could use?"

RA I am Ra. Although we are in sympathy with the great desire to be of service exemplified by this question, our answer is limited by the distortion of the Way of Confusion. We shall say some general things which may be of service in this area.

Firstly, when this instrument distorted its bodily complex towards low vital energy due to this occurrence, it was a recognizable substance which caused this. This was not a, shall we say, natural substance, nor was the mind/body/spirit complex enough aware of its distortion towards physical weakness. The natural ways of, shall we say, everyday existence in which the entity without the distortions caused by ingestion of strongly effective chemicals may be seen to be of an always appropriate nature. There are no mistakes, including the action of this instrument.

Secondly, the means of protection against any negative, or debilitating, influence for those upon the positive path was demonstrated by this instrument to a very great degree. Consider, if you will, the potentials that this particular occurrence had for negative influences to enter the instrument. This instrument thought upon the Creator in its solitude, and in actions with other-self continually praised and gave thanksgiving to the Creator for the experiences it was having.

This, in turn, allowed this particular entity to radiate to the other-self such energies as became a catalyst for an opening and strengthening of the other-self's ability to function in a more positively polarized state. Thus we see protection being very simple. Give thanksgiving for each moment. See the self and the other-self as Creator. Open the heart. Always know the light and praise it. This is all the protection necessary.

32.2   QUESTIONER Thank you very much. I will now continue with the material from day before yesterday. Our subject is how sexual polarity acts as a catalyst in evolution and how to best make use of this catalyst. Going back to that material, I will fill in a few gaps that we possibly don't understand at this point too well.

Can you tell me the difference between orange- and yellow-ray activation? I am going to work up from red ray right on through the violet, and we covered red ray, so what's the difference between orange- and yellow-ray activation?

RA I am Ra. The orange ray is that influence, or vibratory pattern, wherein the mind/body/spirit expresses its power on an individual basis. Thus power over individuals may be seen to be orange ray. This ray has been quite intense among your peoples on an individual basis. You may see in this ray the treating of other-selves as non-entities, slaves, or chattel, thus giving other-selves no status whatever.

The yellow ray is a focal and very powerful ray, and concerns the entity in relation to, shall we say, groups, societies, or large numbers of mind/body/spirit complexes. This orange—we correct ourselves—this yellow-ray vibration is at the heart of bellicose actions in which one group of entities feel the necessity and right of dominating other groups of entities and bending their wills to the wills of the masters.

The negative path, as you would call it, uses a combination of the yellow ray and the orange ray in its polarization patterns. These rays, used in a dedicated fashion, will bring about a contact with intelligent infinity. The usual nature of sexual interaction, if one is yellow or orange in primary vibratory patterns, is one of blockage and then insatiable hunger due to the blockage. When there are two selves vibrating in this area, the potential for polarization through the sexual interaction is begun, one entity experiencing the pleasure of humiliation and slavery, or bondage, the other experiencing the pleasure of mastery and control over another entity. In this way a sexual energy transfer of a negative polarity is experienced.

32.3 **QUESTIONER** From the material that you transmitted February 17th you stated: "In third ray there are two possibilities. Firstly, if both vibrate in third ray there will be a mutually strengthening energy transfer." What color is third ray in this material?

RA I am Ra. The ray we were speaking of in that material should be properly the green ray or fourth ray.

32.4 **QUESTIONER** So I should change that third to fourth?

RA I am Ra. This is correct.[1] Please continue to scan for errors having to do with numberings, as you call them, as this concept is foreign to us and we must translate, if you will, when using numbers. This is an ongoing weakness of this contact due to the difference between our ways and yours. Your aid is appreciated.

32.5 **QUESTIONER** OK. Thank you. I believe that for the time being we've amply covered green ray, so I am going to skip over green ray and go to blue ray.

Could you tell me the difference that occurs between green and blue with the emphasis on blue ray?

RA I am Ra. With the green-ray transfer of energy you now come to the great turning point sexually as well as in each other mode of experience. The green ray may then be turned outward, the entity then giving rather than receiving. The first giving beyond green ray is the giving of acceptance, or freedom, thus allowing the recipient of blue-ray energy transfer the opportunity for a feeling of being accepted, thus freeing that other-self to express itself to the giver of this ray.

It will be noted that once green-ray energy transfer has been achieved by two mind/body/spirits in mating, the further rays are available without both entities having the necessity to progress equally. Thus a blue-ray vibrating entity or indigo-ray vibrating entity whose other ray vibrations are clear may share that energy with the green-ray other-self, thus acting as catalyst for the continued learn/teaching of the other-self. Until an

---

[1] A footnote has been added to 26.38.

other-self reaches green ray, such energy transfers through the rays is not possible.

32.6 **QUESTIONER** My next question had to do with indigo ray. Is there any difference between indigo and blue-ray energy transfer?

RA I am Ra. The indigo ray is the ray of, shall we say, awareness of the Creator as self; thus one whose indigo-ray vibrations have been activated can offer the energy transfer of Creator to Creator. This is the beginning of the sacramental nature of what you call your bisexual reproductive act. It is unique in bearing the allness, the wholeness, the unity in its offering to other-self.

32.7 **QUESTIONER** And then finally, the violet ray. What is the difference between violet ray and the others?

RA I am Ra. The violet ray, just as the red ray, is constant in the sexual experience. Its experience by other-self may be distorted, or completely ignored, or not apprehended by other-self. However, the violet ray, being the sum and substance of the mind/body/spirit complex, surrounds and informs any action by a mind/body/spirit complex.

32.8 **QUESTIONER** Do the energy transfers of this nature occur in fourth, fifth, sixth, and seventh density? I mean, of all the rays?

RA I am Ra. The rays, as you understand them, have such a different meaning in the next density, and the next, and so forth, that we must answer your query in the negative. Energy transfers only take place in fourth, fifth, and sixth densities. These are still of what you would call a polarized nature. However, due to the ability of these densities to see the harmonies between individuals, these entities choose those mates which are harmonious, thus allowing constant transfer of energy and the propagation of the body complexes which each density uses.

The process is different in the fifth and the sixth density than you may understand it. However, it is in these cases still based upon polarity. In the seventh density there is not this particular energy exchange as it is unnecessary to recycle body complexes.

32.9 **QUESTIONER** I am assuming from what we have previously looked at . . . we have on Earth today, and have had in the past, fourth-, fifth-, and sixth-density wanderers. As they come into incarnation in the physical of this density for a period as a wanderer, what types of polarizations with respect to these various rays do they find affecting them? Can you tell me that?

RA I am Ra. I believe I grasp the thrust of your query. Please ask further if this answer is not sufficient.

Fourth-density wanderers, of which there are not many, will tend to choose those entities which seem to be full of love or in need of love. There is the great possibility/probability of entities making errors in judgment due to the compassion with which other-selves are viewed.

The fifth-density wanderer is one who is not tremendously affected by the stimulus of the various rays of other-self and, in its own way, offers itself when a need is seen. Such entities are not likely to engage in the, shall we say, custom of your peoples called marriage and are very likely to feel an aversion to childbearing and child-raising due to the awareness of the impropriety of the planetary vibrations relative to the harmonious vibrations of the density of light.

The sixth density, whose means of propagation you may liken to what you call fusion, is likely to refrain, to a great extent, from the bisexual reproductive programming of the bodily complex and instead seek out those with whom the sexual energy transfer is of the complete fusion nature insofar as this is possible in manifestation in third density.

32.10 **QUESTIONER** Can you expand a little bit on what you mean by "complete fusion nature?"

RA I am Ra. The entire creation is of the One Creator. Thus the division of sexual activity into simply that of the bodily complex is an artificial division, all things thusly being seen as sexual equally—the mind, the body, and the spirit—all of which are part of the polarity of the entity. Thus sexual fusion may be seen, with or without what you may call sexual intercourse, to be the complete melding of the mind, the body, and the spirit in what feels to be a constant orgasm, shall we say, of joy and delight each in the other's beingness.

32.11 **QUESTIONER** Would then many wanderers of the higher densities have considerable problems with respect to incarnation in third density because of this different orientation?

RA I am Ra. The possibility/probability of such problems, as you call them, due to sixth density incarnating in third is rather large. It is not necessarily a problem if you would call it thusly. It depends upon the unique orientation of each mind/body/spirit complex having this situation or placement of vibratory relativities.

32.12   **QUESTIONER** Can you give me an idea how the different colors . . . this is a difficult question to ask. I hardly have any words.

What I'm trying to get at is how the different colors, I might say, originate as these functions . . . or the essence, you might say, of the origin of these colors as functions for these different expressions in consciousness. I don't know if this question is sufficient.

RA I am Ra. This question is sufficiently clear for us to attempt explanation of what, as you have observed, is not easily grasped material for the intellectual mind. The nature of vibration is such that it may be seen as having mathematically strait or narrow steps. These steps may be seen as having boundaries. Within each boundary there are infinite gradations of vibration or color.

However, as one approaches a boundary, an effort must be made to cross that boundary. These colors are a simplistic way of expressing the boundary divisions of your density. There is also the time/space analogy which may be seen as the color itself in a modified aspect.

32.13   **QUESTIONER** Thank you. Is it possible for an entity in third-density physical to vary widely across the entire band of colors, or is the entity pretty well zeroed in on one color?

RA I am Ra. This will be the last full question of this working. Please restate for clarity.

32.14   **QUESTIONER** I just meant was it possible, say, for a green-ray . . . when we're talking about green-ray activation and energy transfers, is it possible for a green-ray person who is primarily green-ray activation to vary on both sides of green ray a large or a small amount in energy activation, or does he stay primarily green-ray?

RA I am Ra. We grasp the newness of material requested by you. It was unclear, for we thought we had covered this material. The portion covered is this: the green-ray activation is always vulnerable to the yellow or orange ray of possession, this being largely yellow ray but often coming into orange ray. Fear of possession, desire for possession, fear of being possessed, desire to be possessed: these are the distortions which will cause the deactivation of green-ray energy transfer.

The new material is this: once the green ray has been achieved, the ability of the entity to enter blue ray is immediate and is only awaiting the efforts of the individual. The indigo ray is opened only through considerable discipline and practice largely having to do with acceptance of self, not only as the polarized and balanced self but as the Creator, as an entity of infinite worth. This will begin to activate the indigo ray.

32.15 **QUESTIONER** Thank you.

RA I am Ra. Do you have any brief queries before we close?

32.16 **QUESTIONER** I think anything would be too long. I'll just ask if there's anything we can do to make the instrument more comfortable or make the contact better?

RA I am Ra. All is well. We caution not only this instrument but each to look well to the vital energies necessary for non-depletion of the instrument and the contact level. You are most conscientious, my friends. We shall be with you.

I leave you now in the love and in the light of the One Infinite Creator. Go forth, then, rejoicing in the power and the peace of the One Infinite Creator. Adonai.

SESSION 33

33.0 RA I am Ra. I greet you in the love and in the light of the One Infinite Creator. I communicate now.

33.1 QUESTIONER In our last session you cautioned "each to look well to the vital energies necessary for non-depletion of the instrument and the contact level." Did that mean that we should . . . that Jim and I should look at the instrument's . . . or be careful of the instrument's vital energies or be careful of our own vital energies?

RA I am Ra. Each entity is responsible for itself. The mechanics of this process taking place involve, firstly, the use of the physical bodily complex of third density with its accompanying physical material in order to voice these words. Thus this instrument needs to watch its vital energies carefully, for we do not wish to deplete this instrument.

Secondly, the function of the supporting group may be seen to be, firstly, that of protection for this contact; secondly, that of energizing the instrument and intensifying its vital energies.

This supporting group has always, due to an underlying harmony, been of a very stable nature as regards protection in love and light, thus ensuring the continuation of this narrow-band contact. However, the vital energies of either of the supporting members being depleted, the instrument must then use a larger portion of its vital energies, thus depleting itself more than would be profitable on a long-term basis.

Please understand that we ask your apology for this infringement upon your free will. However, it is our distortion-understanding that you would prefer this information rather than, being left totally to your own dedication-distortions, deplete the instrument or deplete the group to the point where the contact cannot be sustained.

33.2 QUESTIONER Can you give us advice on how to maintain the best possible condition for maintaining contact?

RA I am Ra. We have given information concerning the proper nurturing of this channel. We, therefore, repeat ourselves only in two ways in general.

Firstly, we suggest that rather than being, shall we say, brave and ignoring a physical-complex-weakness distortion, it is good to share this distortion with the group and thus, perhaps, shall we say, remove one opportunity for contact which is very wearying to the instrument in order that another opportunity might come about in which the instrument is properly supported.

Secondly, the work begun in harmony may continue. Harmony, thanksgiving, and praise of opportunities and of the Creator: these are your protection. These are our suggestions. We cannot be specific, for your free will is of the essence in this contact. As we said, we only speak to this subject because of our grasp of your orientation towards long-term maintenance of this contact. This is acceptable to us.

33.3 **QUESTIONER** Thank you very much. The instrument has a device for so-called color therapy, and since we were on, in the past session, the concept of the different colors I was wondering if these, in some way, apply to the principle of color therapy in the shining of particular colors on the physical body. Does this have any beneficial effect, and can you tell me something about it?

RA I am Ra. This therapy, as you call it, is a somewhat clumsy and variably useful tool for instigating in an entity's mind/body/spirit complex an intensification of energies, or vibrations, which may be of aid to the entity. The variableness of this device is due, firstly, to the lack of true colors used; secondly, to the extreme variation in sensitivity to vibration among your peoples.

33.4 **QUESTIONER** I would think that you could achieve a true color by passing the light through a crystal of the particular color. Is this correct?

RA I am Ra. This would be one way of approaching accuracy in color. It is a matter of what you would call quality control that the celluloid used is of a varying color. This is not a great, or even visible, variation; however, it does make some difference given specific applications.

33.5 **QUESTIONER** Possibly the use of a prism breaking white light into its spectrum and then screening off all parts of the spectrum except that which you wish to pass through a slit and use would be even better. Would this be true?

RA I am Ra. This is correct.

33.6 **QUESTIONER** Thank you. I was wondering if there is a programming of experiences that causes an individual to get certain catalyst in his daily life. For instance, as we go through our daily life there are many things that we can experience. We look at these experiences as occurring by pure chance or by a conscious design of ours, like making appointments or going places. I was just wondering if there was a behind-the-scenes, I might call it, programming of catalyst to create the necessary experiences for more rapid growth in the case of some entities. Is this . . . does this happen?

RA I am Ra. We believe we grasp the heart of your query. Please request further information if we are not correct.

The incarnating entity which has become conscious of the incarnative process and thus programs its own experience may choose the amount of catalyst or, to phrase this differently, the number of lessons which it will undertake to experience and to learn from in one incarnation. This does not mean that all is predestined, but rather that there are invisible guidelines shaping events which will function according to this programming. Thus if one opportunity is missed, another will appear until the, shall we say, student of the life experience grasps that a lesson is being offered and undertakes to learn it.

33.7 **QUESTIONER** Then these lessons would be reprogrammed, you might say, as a life experience continues. Let's say that an entity develops a bias that he actually didn't choose to develop prior to incarnation. It is then possible to program experiences so that he will have an opportunity to alleviate this bias through balancing. Is this correct?

RA I am Ra. This is precisely correct.

33.8 **QUESTIONER** Thank you. Then from this I would extrapolate to the conjecture, I will say, that the orientation in mind of the entity is the only thing that is of any consequence at all. The physical catalyst that he experiences, regardless of what is happening about him, will be a function strictly of his orientation in mind. I will use as an example [*example deleted*], this being a statement of the orientation in mind governing the catalyst. Is this correct?

RA I am Ra. We prefer not to use any well-known examples, sayings, or adages in our communications to you due to the tremendous amount of distortion which any well-known saying has undergone. Therefore, we may answer the first part of your query, asking that you delete the example. It is completely true, to the best of our knowledge, that the orientation, or polarization, of the mind/body/spirit complex is cause of the perceptions generated by each entity.

Thus a scene may be observed in your grocery store. The entity ahead of self may be without sufficient funds. One entity may then take this opportunity to steal. Another may take this opportunity to feel itself a failure. Another may unconcernedly remove the least necessary items, pay for what it can, and go about its business. The one behind the self, observing, may feel compassion, may feel an insult because of standing next to a poverty-stricken person, may feel generosity, may feel indifference.

Do you now see the analogies in a more appropriate manner?

33.9 **QUESTIONER** Yes, I do. Then from this I will extrapolate the concept which is somewhat more difficult because, as you have explained before, even fourth-density positive has the concept of defensive action, but above the fourth density the concept of defensive action is not in use. The concept of defensive action and [*chuckles*] offensive action are very much in use in this, our present experience.

I am assuming that if an entity is polarized strongly enough in his thought in a positive sense, defensive action is not going to be necessary for him because the opportunity to apply defensive action will never originate for him. Is this correct?

RA I am Ra. This is unknowable. In each case, as we have said, an entity able to program experiences may choose the number and the intensity of lessons to be learned.

It is possible that an extremely positively oriented entity might program for itself situations testing the ability of self to refrain from defensive action, even to the point of the physical death of self or other-self. This is an intensive lesson, and it is not known, shall we say, what entities have programmed. We may, if we desire, read this programming. However, this is an infringement and we choose not to do so.

33.10 **QUESTIONER** I will ask you if you are familiar with the motion picture called *The Ninth Configuration*. Are you familiar with this?

RA I am Ra. We scan your mind complex and see this configuration called *The Ninth Configuration.*

33.11 **QUESTIONER** This motion picture brought out this point of which we have been talking. And the entity, the Colonel, had to make a decision at that point. I was just wondering, with respect to polarity, his polarization. He could have either knuckled under, you might say, to the negative forces, but he chose to defend his friend instead.

Is it possible for you to estimate which is more positively polarizing: to defend the positively oriented entity or to allow the suppression by the negatively oriented entities? Can you answer this even?

RA I am Ra. This question takes in the scope of fourth density as well as your own, and its answer may best be seen by the action of the entity called Jehoshua, which you call Jesus. This entity was to be defended by its friends. The entity reminded its friends to put away the sword. This entity then delivered itself to be put to the physical death.

The impulse to protect the loved other-self is one which persists through the fourth density, a density abounding in compassion. More than this we cannot and need not say.

33.12 **QUESTIONER** Thank you. As we near the end of this master cycle there may be an increasing amount of catalyst for entities. I am wondering if, as the planetary vibrations mismatch somewhat with the fourth-density vibrations and catalyst is increased, if this will create a slight amount of more polarization, thereby getting a slightly greater positive harvest because of this catalyst, and in the same way create a more negative polarization, and then get a slight amount more negative harvest by this mechanism of transition that is, unfortunately, somewhat more catalytic than it would be if the planet had reached a higher state of consciousness. Does this happen?

RA I am Ra. The question must be answered in two parts:

Firstly, the planetary catastrophes, as you may call them, are a symptom of the difficult harvest rather than a consciously programmed catalyst for harvest. Thus we do not concern ourselves with it, for it is random in respect to conscious catalyst such as we may make available.

The second portion is this: the results of the random catalyst of what you call the earth changes are also random. Thus we may see probability/possibility vortices going towards positive and negative. However, it will be as it will be. The true opportunities for conscious catalyst are not a function of the earth changes but of the result of the seniority system of incarnations which at the time of the harvest has placed in incarnation those whose chances of using life experiences to become harvestable are the best.

33.13 **QUESTIONER** Is this seniority system also used for the service-to-self side for becoming harvestable on that side?

RA I am Ra. This is correct. You may ask one more full question at this time.

33.14 **QUESTIONER** OK. What I would like for you to do is list all the major mechanisms designed to provide catalytic experience that do not include interaction with other-self. That's the first part of the question I'll ask.

RA I am Ra. We grasp from this question that you realize that the primary mechanism for catalytic experience in third density is other-self. The list of other catalytic influences: firstly, the Creator's universe; secondly, the self.

33.15 **QUESTIONER** Can you list any sub-headings under the self that would . . . or ways that the self is acted on catalytically to produce experience?

RA I am Ra. Firstly, the self unmanifested. Secondly, the self in relation to the societal self created by self and other-self. Thirdly, the interaction between self and the gadgets, toys, and amusements of the self/other-self invention. Fourthly, the self relationship with those attributes which you may call war and rumors of war.

33.16 **QUESTIONER** I was thinking possibly the catalyst of physical pain. How does this . . . Does this go under this heading?

RA I am Ra. This is correct, it going under the heading of the unmanifested self; that is, the self which does not need other-self in order to manifest or act.

33.17 **QUESTIONER** Do we have enough time left to ask the second part of this question, which is to list all major mechanisms designed to provide the catalyst that include action with other-self? Do we have enough time for that?

RA I am Ra. You have much time for this, for we may express this list in one of two ways. We could speak infinitely, or we could simply state that any interaction betwixt self and other-self has whatever potential for catalyst that there exists in the potential difference between self and other-self, this moderated and undergirded by the constant fact of the Creator as self and as other-self. You may ask to this question further if you wish specific information.

33.18 QUESTIONER I believe that that is sufficient for the time being.

RA I am Ra. Do you have a brief query or two before we close this working?

33.19 QUESTIONER Uh, just a minute. I don't think that anything I could ask at this time would be brief enough. Just a minute. [*Sounds of papers being handled.*]

Yes, there's one question. Is there any difference in violet-ray activity, or brightness, between entities who are at the entrance level to fourth-density positive and negative?

RA I am Ra. This is correct. The violet ray of the positive fourth-density will be tinged with the green, blue, indigo triad of energies. This tinge may be seen as a portion of a rainbow or prism, as you know it, the rays being quite distinct.

The violet ray of fourth-density negative has in its aura, shall we say, the tinge of red, orange, yellow, these three rays being muddied rather than distinct.

33.20 QUESTIONER Just as a slight appendage to that question: what would the rays of fifth and sixth density look like?

RA I am Ra. We may speak only approximately. However, we hope you understand, shall we say, that there is a distinctive difference in the color structure of each density.

Fifth density is perhaps best described as extremely white in vibration.

The sixth density of a whiteness which contains a golden quality as you would perceive it; these colors having to do with the blending into wisdom of the compassion learned in fourth density, then in sixth the blending of wisdom back into an unified understanding of compassion viewed with wisdom. This golden color is not of your spectrum but is what you would call alive.

You may ask one more question briefly.

33.21 **QUESTIONER** Then I will ask if there is anything we can do to make the instrument more comfortable or improve the contact?

RA I am Ra. This working is well. You are attempting to be conscientious. We thank you. May we say we enjoyed your vision of our social memory complex drinking one of your liquids while speaking through this instrument.

I am Ra. I leave you in the love and in the light of the One Infinite Creator. Go forth, then, rejoicing in the power and the peace of the One Infinite Creator. Adonai.

34.0   **RA** I am Ra. I greet you in the love and in the light of the One Infinite Creator. We communicate now.

34.1   **QUESTIONER** The instrument would like to know if two short exercise periods a day would be better for her than one long one?

RA I am Ra. This is incorrect. The proper configuration of the physical complex exercising during the three-month period wherein the instrument is vulnerable to physical-complex-distortion intensifications needs the strengthening of the physical complex. This may appropriately be seen to be one major period of the exercising followed late in your diurnal cycle, before the evening meditation, by an exercise period approximately one-half the length of the first. This will be seen to be wearing upon the instrument. However, it will have the effect of strengthening the physical complex and lessening the vulnerability which might be taken advantage of.

34.2   **QUESTIONER** Thank you very much. We'll start general questioning now. You stated at an earlier time that penetration of the eighth level, or intelligent infinity level, allows a mind/body/spirit complex to be harvested if it wishes at any time/space during the cycle. When this penetration of the eighth level occurs, what does the entity who penetrates this level experience? Can you tell me this?

RA I am Ra. The experience of each entity is unique in perception of intelligent infinity. Perceptions range from a limitless joy to a strong dedication to service to others while in the incarnated state. The entity which reaches intelligent infinity most often will perceive this experience as one of unspeakable profundity. However, it is not usual for the entity to immediately desire the cessation of the incarnation. Rather the desire to communicate or use this experience to aid others is extremely strong.

34.3   **QUESTIONER** Is it possible for you to tell me what I experienced, around 1964 I believe it was, when in meditation I became aware of what I would consider to be a different density and different planet, and seemed to experience moving onto that planet? Is it possible for you to tell me what experience that was?

RA I am Ra. We see some harm in full disclosure due to infringement. We content ourselves with suggesting that this entity, which is not readily able to subject itself to the process of hypnotic regression instigated by others, nevertheless, has had its opportunities for understanding of its beingness.

34.4 **QUESTIONER** Thank you. Would you define karma?

RA I am Ra. Our understanding of karma is that which may be called inertia. Those actions which are put into motion will continue, using the ways of balancing, until such time as the controlling or higher principle, which you may liken unto your braking, or stopping, is invoked. This stoppage of the inertia of action may be called forgiveness. These two concepts are inseparable.

34.5 **QUESTIONER** If an entity develops what is called a karma in an incarnation, is there, then, programming that sometimes occurs so that he will experience catalyst that will enable him to get to a point of forgiveness, thereby alleviating the karma?

RA I am Ra. This is, in general, correct. However, both self and any involved other-self may, at any time, through the process of understanding, acceptance, and forgiveness, ameliorate these patterns.

This is true at any point in an incarnative pattern. Thus one who has set in motion an action may forgive itself and never again make that error. This also brakes, or stops, what you call karma.

34.6 **QUESTIONER** Thank you. Can you give me examples of catalytic action to produce learning under each of the following headings from the last session we had . . . Can you give me an example of the self unmanifested producing learning catalyst?

RA I am Ra. We observed your interest in the catalyst of pain. This experience is most common among your entities. The pain may be of the physical complex. More often it is of the mental and emotional complex. In some few cases the pain is spiritual in complex-nature. This creates a potential for learning. The lessons to be learned vary. Almost always these lessons include patience, tolerance, and the ability for the light touch.

Very often the catalyst for emotional pain, whether it be the death of the physical complex of one other-self which is loved or some other seeming loss, will simply result in the opposite: in a bitterness, an impatience, a souring. This is catalyst which has gone awry. In these cases, then, there will be additional catalyst provided to offer the unmanifested self further opportunities for discovering the self as all-sufficient Creator containing all that there is and full of joy.

34.7 **QUESTIONER** Do what we call contagious diseases play any part in this process with respect to the unmanifested self?

RA I am Ra. These so-called contagious diseases are those entities of second density which offer an opportunity for this type of catalyst. If this catalyst is unneeded, then these second-density creatures, as you would call them, do not have an effect. In each of these generalizations you may please note that there are anomalies so that we cannot speak to every circumstance but only to the general run, or way of things, as you experience them.

34.8 **QUESTIONER** What part do what we call birth defects play in this process?

RA I am Ra. This is a portion of the programming of the mind/body complex totality manifested in the mind/body/spirit of third density. These defects are planned as limitations which are part of the experience intended by the entity totality complex. This includes genetic predispositions, as you may call them.

34.9 **QUESTIONER** Thank you. Would you give me the same type of information about the self in relation to the societal self?

RA I am Ra. The unmanifested self may find its lessons those which develop any of the energy influx centers of the mind/body/spirit complex. The societal and self interactions most often concentrate upon the second and third energy centers. Thus those most active in attempting to remake or alter the society are those working from feelings of being correct personally, or of having answers which will put power in a more correct configuration. This may be seen to be of a full travel from negative to positive in orientation. Either will activate these energy ray centers.

There are some few whose desires to aid society are of a green-ray nature or above. These entities, however, are few due to the understanding, may we say, of fourth ray that universal love freely given is more to be desired than principalities, or even the rearrangement of peoples or political structures.

34.10 **QUESTIONER** If an entity were to be strongly biased toward positive societal effects, what would this do to his yellow ray in the aura as opposed to an entity who wanted to create an empire of society and govern it with an iron fist? What would be the difference in the yellow-ray activity of these two entities?

RA I am Ra. Let us take two such positively oriented active souls no longer in your physical time/space. The one known as Albert, who went into a strange and, to it, a barbaric society in order that it might heal. This entity was able to mobilize great amounts of energy and what you call money. This entity spent much green-ray energy both as a healer and as a lover of your instrument known as the organ. This entity's yellow ray was bright and crystallized by the efforts needed to procure the funds to promulgate its efforts. However, the green and blue rays were of a toweringly brilliant nature as well. The higher levels, as you may call them, being activated, the lower, as you may call them, energy points remain, in a balanced being, quite, quite bright.

The other example is the entity, Martin. This entity dealt in a great degree with rather negative orange-ray and yellow-ray vibratory patterns. However, this entity was able to keep open the green-ray energy and due to the severity of its testing, if anything, this entity may be seen to have polarized more towards the positive due to its fidelity to service to others in the face of great catalyst.

34.11 **QUESTIONER** Could you give me the last names of Albert and Martin?

RA I am Ra. These entities are known to you as Albert Schweitzer and Martin Luther King.

34.12 **QUESTIONER** I thought that that was correct, but I wasn't sure. Can you give me the same type of information that we have been getting here with respect to the unmanifested self interacting between self and gadgets, toys, etc. . . . . inventions?

RA I am Ra. In this particular instance we again concentrate, for the most part, in the orange and in the yellow energy centers.

In a negative sense many of the gadgets among your peoples—that is, what you call your communication devices and other distractions, such as the less competitive games—may be seen to have the distortion of keeping the mind/body/spirit complex unactivated so that yellow- and orange-ray activity is much weakened, thus carefully decreasing the possibility of eventual green-ray activation.

Others of your gadgets may be seen to be tools whereby the entity explores the capabilities of its physical or mental complexes and, in some few cases, the spiritual complex, thus activating the orange ray in what you call your team sports and in other gadgets such as your modes of transport. These may be seen to be ways of investigating the feelings of power; more especially, power over others or a group power over another group of other-selves.

34.13 **QUESTIONER** What is the general overall effect of television on our society with respect to this catalyst?

RA I am Ra. Without ignoring the green-ray attempts of many to communicate via this medium such information, truth, and beauty as may be helpful, we must suggest that the sum effect of this gadget is that of distraction and sleep.

34.14 **QUESTIONER** Can you give me the same type of information that we've been working on now with respect to the self relationship with war and rumors of war?

RA I am Ra. You may see this in relationship to your gadgets. This war-and-self relationship is a fundamental perception of the maturing entity. There is a great chance to accelerate in whatever direction is desired. One may polarize negatively by assuming bellicose attitudes for whatever reason. One may find oneself in the situation of war and polarize somewhat towards the positive, activating orange, yellow, and then green by heroic, if you may call them this, actions taken to preserve the mind/body/spirit complexes of other-selves.

Finally, one may polarize very strongly third ray[1] by expressing the principle of universal love at the total expense of any distortion towards involvement in bellicose actions. In this way the entity may become a conscious being in a very brief span of your time/space. This may be seen to be what you would call a traumatic progression. It is to be noted that among your entities a large percentage of all progression has, as catalyst, trauma.

---

[1] This should be fourth ray. Ra corrected the mistake in the next answer.

34.15 **QUESTIONER** You just used the term third ray in that statement. Was that the term you meant to use?

RA I am Ra. We intended the green ray. Our difficulty lies in our perception of red ray and violet ray as fixed; thus the inner rays are those which are varying and are to be observed as those indications of seniority in the attempts to form an harvest.

34.16 **QUESTIONER** Would the red ray, an intense red ray, then be used as an index for seniority, the seniority system of incarnation, as well as the intense violet ray?

RA I am Ra. This is partially correct. In the graduation or harvesting to fourth-density positive, the red ray is seen only as that which, being activated, is the basis for all that occurs in vibratory levels, the sum of this being violet-ray energy.

This violet ray is the only consideration for fourth-density positive. In assessing the harvestable fourth-density negative, the intensity of the red as well as the orange and the yellow rays is looked upon quite carefully, as a great deal of stamina and energy of this type is necessary for the negative progression, it being extremely difficult to open the gateway to intelligent infinity from the solar plexus center. This is necessary for harvest in fourth-density negative.

34.17 **QUESTIONER** Is it possible for you to use as an example our General Patton and tell me the effect that war had on him in his development?

RA I am Ra. This will be the last full question of this working. The one of whom you speak, known as George, was one in whom the programming of previous incarnations had created a pattern, or inertia, which was irresistible in its incarnation in your time/space. This entity was of a strong yellow-ray activation with frequent green-ray openings and occasional blue-ray openings. However, it did not find itself able to break the mold of previous traumatic experiences of a bellicose nature.

This entity polarized somewhat towards the positive in its incarnation due to its singleness of belief in truth and beauty. This entity was quite sensitive. It felt a great honor/duty to the preservation of that which was felt by the entity to be true, beautiful, and in need of defense. This entity perceived itself as a gallant figure. It polarized somewhat towards the negative in its lack of understanding the green ray it carried with it, rejecting the forgiveness principle which is implicit in universal love.

The sum total of this incarnation, vibrationally, was a slight increase in positive polarity but a decrease in harvestability due to the rejection of the Law or Way of Responsibility; that is, seeing universal love, yet still it fought on.

34.18 **QUESTIONER** Do we have enough time for me to ask if the death, almost immediately after the cessation of the war, of this entity . . . could that have been so that it could be immediately reincarnated to possibly make harvest?

RA I am Ra. This is precisely correct.

34.19 **QUESTIONER** Thank you. Then I will just ask if there is anything we can do to make the instrument more comfortable or improve the contact?

RA I am Ra. All is well. We leave you, my friends, in the love and the light of the One which is All in All. I leave you in an ever-lasting peace. Go forth, therefore, rejoicing in the power and the peace of the One Infinite Creator. Adonai.

SESSION 35

35.0 **RA** I am Ra. I greet you in the love and in the light of the One Infinite Creator. We communicate now.

35.1 **QUESTIONER** I would like to say that we consider this a great privilege to be doing this work, and hope that we are going to question in a direction that will be of value to the readers of this material.

This session, I thought that possibly inspecting the effect on the rays of different well-known figures in our history might be of help in understanding how the catalyst of the illusion creates spiritual growth. I was making a list here, and the first I thought we might possibly hit the high points on (as to the effect of catalyst of the individual's working life) would be the one we know as Franklin D. Roosevelt. Could you say something about that entity?

RA I am Ra. It is to be noted that in discussing those who are well known among your peoples there is the possibility that information may be seen to be specific to one entity whereas, in actuality, the great design of experience is much the same for each entity. It is with this in mind that we would discuss the experiential forces which offered catalyst to an individual.

It is further to be noted that in the case of those entities lately incarnate upon your plane much distortion may have taken place in regard to misinformation and misinterpretation of an entity's thoughts or behaviors.

We shall now proceed to, shall we say, speak of the basic parameters of the one known as Franklin. When any entity comes into third-density incarnation, each of its energy centers is potentiated but must be activated by the self using experience.

The one known as Franklin developed very quickly up through red, orange, yellow, and green, and began to work in the blue-ray energy center at a tender age, as you would say. This rapid growth was due, firstly, to previous achievements in the activation of these rays; secondly, to the relative comfort and leisure of its early existence; thirdly, due to the strong desire upon the part of the entity to progress. This entity mated with an entity whose blue-ray vibrations were of a strength more than equal to its own, thus acquiring catalyst for further growth in that area that was to persist throughout the incarnation.

This entity had some difficulty with continued green-ray activity due to the excessive energy which was put into the activities regarding other-selves in the distortion towards acquiring power. This was to have its toll upon the physical vehicle, as you may call it.

The limitation of the non-movement of a portion of the physical vehicle opened once again, for this entity, the opportunity for concentration upon the more, shall we say, universal, or idealistic, aspects of power; that is, the non-abusive use of power. Thus at the outset of a bellicose action this entity had lost some positive polarity due to excessive use of the orange- and yellow-ray energies at the expense of green- and blue-ray energies, then had regained the polarity due to the catalytic effects of a painful limitation upon the physical complex.

This entity was not of a bellicose nature, but rather, during the conflict, continued to vibrate in green ray working with the blue-ray energies. The entity who was the one known as Franklin's teacher also functioned greatly during this period as blue-ray activator, not only for its mate but also in a more universal expression. This entity polarized continuously in a positive fashion in the universal sense while, in a less universal sense, developing a pattern of what may be called karma; this karma having to do with inharmonious-relationship distortions with the mate/teacher.

35.2 QUESTIONER Two things I would like to clear up. Then Franklin's teacher was his wife? Is this correct?

RA I am Ra. This is correct.

35.3 QUESTIONER Secondly, did Franklin place the limitation on his physical body himself?

RA I am Ra. This is partially correct. The basic guidelines for the lessons and purposes of incarnation had been carefully set forth before incarnation by the mind/body/spirit complex totality. If the one known as Franklin had avoided the excessive enjoyment of or attachment to the competitiveness which may be seen to be inherent in the processes of its occupation, this entity would not have had the limitation.

However, the desire to serve and to grow was strong in this programming, and when the opportunities began to cease due to these distortions towards love of power, the entity's limiting factor was activated.

35.4 **QUESTIONER** I would now like to ask for the same type of information with respect to Adolf Hitler. You have given a little of this already. It is not necessary to re-cover what you have already given, but if you could complete that information it would be helpful.

RA I am Ra. In speaking of the one you call Adolf we have some difficulty due to the intense amount of confusion present in this entity's life patterns as well as the great confusion which greets any discussion of this entity.

Here we see an example of one who, in attempting activation of the highest rays of energy while lacking the green-ray key, canceled itself out as far as polarization either towards positive or negative. This entity was basically negative. However, its confusion was such that the personality disintegrated, thus leaving the mind/body/spirit complex unharvestable and much in need of healing.

This entity followed the pattern of negative polarization which suggests the elite and the enslaved, this being seen by the entity to be of an helpful nature for the societal structure. However, in drifting from the conscious polarization into what you may call a twilight world where dream took the place of events in your space/time continuum, this entity failed in its attempt to serve the Creator in an harvestable degree along the path of service to self. Thus we see the so-called insanity which may often arise when an entity attempts to polarize more quickly than experience may be integrated.

We have advised and suggested caution and patience in previous communications and do so again, using this entity as an example of the over-hasty opening of polarization without due attention to the synthesized and integrated mind/body/spirit complex. To know yourself is to have the foundation upon firm ground.

35.5 **QUESTIONER** Thank you. An important example, I believe. I was wondering if any of those who were subordinate to Adolf at that time were able to polarize in a harvestable nature on the negative path?

RA I am Ra. We can speak only of two entities who may be harvestable in a negative sense, others still being in the physical incarnation: one known to you as Hermann; the other known, as it preferred to be called, Himmler.

35.6 **QUESTIONER** Thank you. Earlier we discussed Abraham Lincoln as a rather unique case.[1] Is it possible for you to tell us what the orientation was and why the fourth-density being used Abraham's body, and when this took place with respect to the activities that were occurring in our society at that time?

RA I am Ra. This is possible.

35.7 **QUESTIONER** Would it be of value for the reader to know this in your estimation?

RA I am Ra. You must shape your queries according to your discernment.

35.8 **QUESTIONER** Well in that case I would like to know the motivation for this use of Abraham Lincoln's body at that time?

RA I am Ra. This shall be the last full query of this session as we find the instrument quite low in vital energies.

The one known as Abraham had an extreme difficulty in many ways and, due to physical, mental, and spiritual pain, was weary of life but without the orientation to self-destruction. In your time, 1853, this entity was contacted in sleep by a fourth-density being. This being was concerned with the battle between the forces of light and the forces of darkness which have been waged in fourth density for many of your years.

This entity accepted the honor/duty of completing the one known as Abraham's karmic patterns, and the one known as Abraham discovered that this entity would attempt those things which the one known as Abraham desired to do but felt it could not. Thus the exchange was made.

The entity, Abraham, was taken to a plane of suspension until the cessation of its physical vehicle, much as though we of Ra would arrange with this instrument to remain in the vehicle, come out of the trance state, and function as this instrument, leaving this instrument's mind and spirit complex in its suspended state.

---

[1] Earlier discussed in 26.15–17.

The planetary energies at this time were at what seemed to this entity to be at a critical point, for that which you know as freedom had gained in acceptance as a possibility among many peoples. This entity saw the work done by those beginning the democratic concept of freedom, as you call it, in danger of being abridged, or abrogated, by the rising belief and use of the principle of the enslavement of entities. This is a negative concept of a fairly serious nature in your density. This entity, therefore, went forward into what it saw as the battle for the light, for healing of a rupture in the concept of freedom.

This entity did not gain or lose karma by these activities due to its detachment from any outcome. Its attitude throughout was one of service to others, more especially to the downtrodden or enslaved. The polarity of the individual was somewhat, but not severely, lessened by the cumulative feelings and thought-forms which were created due to large numbers of entities leaving the physical plane due to trauma of battle.

May we ask if this is the information you requested, or if we may supply any further information?

35.9   **QUESTIONER** If there are any further questions I will ask them in the next period which should occur in about four days. I do not want to overtire the instrument. I will only ask if there is anything that we can do to make the instrument more comfortable or improve the contact?

RA I am Ra. All is well. I leave you, my friends, in the love and the light of the One Infinite Creator. Go forth, therefore, rejoicing in the power and the peace of the One Creator. Adonai.

SESSION 36

36.0 **RA** I am Ra. I greet you in the love and the light of the One Infinite Creator. We communicate now.

36.1 **QUESTIONER** In previous communications you have spoken of the mind/body/spirit complex totality. Would you please give us a definition of the mind/body/spirit complex totality?

RA I am Ra. There is a dimension in which time does not have sway. In this dimension the mind/body/spirit, in its eternal dance of the present, may be seen in totality, and before the mind/body/spirit complex, which then becomes a part of the social memory complex, is willingly absorbed into the allness of the One Creator, the entity knows itself in its totality.

This mind/body/spirit complex totality functions as, shall we say, a resource for what you perhaps would call the higher self. The higher self, in turn, is a resource for examining the distillations of third-density experience and programming further experience. This is also true of densities four, five, and six with the mind/body/spirit complex totality coming into consciousness in the course of seventh density.

36.2 **QUESTIONER** Then would the mind/body/spirit complex totality be responsible for programming changes in catalyst during, say, a third-density experience of the mind/body/spirit complex so that the proper catalyst would be added, shall we say, as conditions for that complex changed during third-density experience? Is this correct?

RA I am Ra. This is incorrect. The higher self, as you call it—that is, that self which exists with full understanding of the accumulation of experiences of the entity—aids the entity in achieving healing of the experiences which have not been learned properly and assists, as you have indicated, in further life experience programming, as you may call it.

The mind/body/spirit complex totality is that which may be called upon by the higher self aspect, just as the mind/body/spirit complex calls upon the higher self. In the one case you have a structured situation within the space/time continuum with the higher self having available to it the totality of experiences which have been collected by an entity and a very firm grasp of the lessons to be learned in this density.

The mind/body/spirit complex totality is as the shifting sands and is, in some part, a collection of parallel developments of the same entity. This information is made available to the higher self aspect. This aspect may then use these projected probability/possibility vortices in order to better aid in what you would call future life programming.

36.3   QUESTIONER Out of the *Seth Material* we have a statement here: Seth says that each entity here on Earth is one aspect, or part, of a higher self, or oversoul, which has many aspects, or parts, in many dimensions, all of which learn lessons which enable the higher self to progress in a balanced manner. Am I to understand from this, is it correct that there are, shall we say, possibly many experiences similar to the one that we experience here in the third density that are governed by a single higher self? Is this correct?

RA   I am Ra. The correctness of this statement is variable. The more in balance an entity becomes, the less the possibility/probability vortices may need to be explored in parallel experiences.

36.4   QUESTIONER Do I understand from this then that the higher self, or oversoul, may break down into numerous units if the experience is required to, what we would call, simultaneously experience different types of catalyst and then oversee these experiences?

RA   I am Ra. This is a statement we cannot say to be correct or incorrect due to the confusions of what you call time. True simultaneity is available only when all things are seen to be occurring at once. This overshadows the concept of which you speak. The concept of various parts of the being living experiences of varying natures simultaneously is not precisely accurate due to your understanding that this would indicate that this was occurring with true simultaneity. This is not the case.

The case is from universe to universe, and parallel existences can then be programmed by the higher self, given the information available from the mind/body/spirit complex totality regarding the probability/possibility vortices at any crux.

36.5   QUESTIONER Could you give an example of an entity, possibly one from our historical past, possibly any entity that you might choose if you don't wish to name one, and give an example of how this type of programming by the higher self would then bring about the education through parallel experiences please?

RA I am Ra. Perhaps the simplest example of this apparent simultaneity of existence of two selves, which are in truth one self at the same time/space, is this: the oversoul, as you call it, or higher self, seems to exist simultaneously with the mind/body/spirit complex which it aids. This is not actually simultaneous, for the higher self is moving to the mind/body/spirit complex, as needed, from a position in development of the entity which would be considered in the future of this entity.

36.6 **QUESTIONER** Then the higher self operates from the future, as we understand things. In other words, my higher self would operate from what I consider to be my future? Is this correct?

RA I am Ra. From the standpoint of your space/time, this is correct.

36.7 **QUESTIONER** In that case my higher self would, shall we say, have a very large advantage in knowing precisely what was needed since it would know what . . . as far as I am concerned, what was going to happen. Is this correct?

RA I am Ra. This is incorrect, in that this would be an abrogation of free will. The higher self aspect is aware of the lessons learned through the sixth density. The progress rate is fairly well understood. The choices which must be made to achieve the higher self as it is are in the provenance of the mind/body/spirit complex itself.

Thus the higher self is like the map in which the destination is known; the roads are very well known, these roads being designed by intelligent infinity working through intelligent energy. However, the higher self aspect can program only for the lessons and certain predisposing limitations if it wishes. The remainder is completely the free choice of each entity. There is the perfect balance between the known and the unknown.

36.8 **QUESTIONER** I'm sorry for having so much trouble with these concepts, but they are pretty difficult to translate, I am sure, into our understanding and language, and some of my questions may be rather ridiculous. But does this higher self have a physical vehicle or some type of vehicle like our physical vehicle? Does it have a bodily complex?

RA I am Ra. This is correct. The higher self is of a certain advancement within sixth density going into the seventh. After the seventh has been well entered, the mind/body/spirit complex becomes so totally a mind/body/spirit complex totality that it begins to gather spiritual mass and approach the octave density. Thus the looking backwards is finished at that point.

36.9 **QUESTIONER** Is the higher self of every entity of a sixth-density nature?

RA I am Ra. This is correct. This is an honor/duty of self to self as one approaches seventh density.

36.10 **QUESTIONER** Well, let me be sure I understand this then. We have spoken of certain particular individuals. For instance, we were speaking of George Patton in a previous communication. Then his higher self at the time of his incarnation here as George Patton about forty years ago, his higher self was at that time sixth-density? Is this correct?

RA I am Ra. This is correct. We make note at this time that each entity has several beings upon which to call for inner support. Any of these may be taken by an entity to be the mind/body/spirit complex totality. However, this is not the case.

The mind/body/spirit complex totality is a nebulous collection of all that may occur held in understanding—the higher self itself a projection, or manifestation, of mind/body/spirit complex totality—which then may communicate with the mind/body/spirit during the discarnate part of a cycle of rebirth, or during the incarnation may communicate if the proper pathways or channels through the roots of mind are opened.

36.11 **QUESTIONER** These channels would then be opened by meditation, and I am assuming that intense polarization would help in this. Is this correct?

RA I am Ra. This is partially correct. Intense polarization does not necessarily develop, in the mind/body/spirit complex, the will or need to contact the oversoul. Each path of life experience is unique. However, given the polarization, the will is greatly enhanced and vice-versa.

36.12 **QUESTIONER** Let me take as an example the one you said was called Himmler. We are assuming from this that his higher self was of sixth density, and it was stated that Himmler had selected the negative path. Would his higher self then dwell in a sixth-density negative type of situation? Could you expand on this concept?

RA I am Ra. There are no [negative][1] beings which have attained the oversoul manifestation, which is the honor/duty of the mind/body/spirit complex totality of late sixth density, as you would term it in your time measurements. These negatively oriented mind/body/spirit complexes have a difficulty which, to our knowledge, has never been overcome, for after fifth-density graduation wisdom is available but must be matched with an equal amount of love. This love/light is very, very difficult to achieve in unity when following the negative path, and during the earlier part of the sixth density, society complexes of the negative orientation will choose to release the potential and leap into the sixth-density positive.

Therefore, the oversoul which makes its understanding available to all who are ready for such aid is towards the positive. However, the free will of the individual is paramount, and any guidance given by the higher self may be seen in either the positive or negative polarity depending upon the choice of a mind/body/spirit complex.

36.13 **QUESTIONER** Then using Himmler as an example, was his higher self at the time he was incarnate in the 1940s a sixth-density positively oriented higher self?

RA I am Ra. This is correct.

36.14 **QUESTIONER** Was Himmler in any way in contact with his higher self at that time while he was incarnate in the 1940s?

RA I am Ra. We remind you that the negative path is one of separation. What is the first separation? The self from the self.

The one known as Himmler did not choose to use its abilities of will and polarization to seek guidance from any source but its conscious drives, self-chosen in the life experience and nourished by previous biases created in other life experiences.

36.15 **QUESTIONER** Well, then let's say that when Himmler, for instance, reaches sixth-density negative at the beginnings of sixth-density negative, at this time would it be the case that an entity would realize that his higher self is sixth-density positively oriented and, for that reason, make the jump from negative to positive orientation?

---

[1] "Negative" is not heard in the audio, but the context indicates that it is what Ra meant.

RA I am Ra. This is incorrect. The sixth-density negative entity is extremely wise. It observes the spiritual entropy occurring due to the lack of ability to express the unity of sixth density. Thus, loving the Creator, and realizing at some point that the Creator is not only self but other-self as self, this entity consciously chooses an instantaneous energy reorientation so that it may continue its evolution.

36.16 **QUESTIONER** Then the sixth-density entity who has reached that point in positive orientation may choose to become what we call a wanderer and move back. I am wondering if this ever occurs with a negatively oriented sixth-density entity? Do any move back as wanderers?

RA I am Ra. Once the negatively polarized entity has reached a certain point in the wisdom density it becomes extremely unlikely that it will choose to risk the forgetting, for this polarization is not selfless but selfish and, with wisdom, realizes the jeopardy of such "wandering." Occasionally a sixth-density negative entity becomes a wanderer in an effort to continue to polarize towards the negative. This is extremely unusual.

36.17 **QUESTIONER** Then what is the motivation for the . . . oh, let me finish that question first.

What is the motiv— What is the mechanism that this unusual sixth-density entity would wish to gain to polarize more negatively through wandering?

RA I am Ra. The wanderer has the potential of greatly accelerating the density whence it comes in its progress in evolution. This is due to the intensive life experiences and opportunities of the third density. Thusly the positively oriented wanderer chooses to hazard the danger of the forgetting in order to be of service to others by radiating love of others. If the forgetting is penetrated the amount of catalyst in third density will polarize the wanderer with much greater efficiency than shall be expected in the higher and more harmonious densities.

Similarly, the negatively oriented wanderer dares to hazard the forgetting in order that it might accelerate its progress in evolution in its own density by serving itself in third density, by offering to other-selves the opportunity to hear the information having to do with negative polarization.

36.18 **QUESTIONER** Are there any examples of sixth-density negatively polarized wanderers in our historical past?

RA I am Ra. This information could be harmful. We withhold it. Please attempt to view the entities about you as part of the Creator. We can explain no further.

36.19 **QUESTIONER** Thank you. I was wondering if qualification for contact with Ra might include—of the type we're doing now—might include penetrating this forgetting process? Is this correct?

RA I am Ra. This is quite correct.

36.20 **QUESTIONER** Otherwise the Law of Confusion would prohibit this? Is this correct?

RA This is correct.

36.21 **QUESTIONER** I was also wondering if three was the minimum number necessary for this type of working? Is this correct?

RA I am Ra. For protection of this instrument, this is necessary as the minimum grouping, and also as the most efficient number due to the exceptional harmony in this group. In other groups the number could be larger, but we have observed in this contact that the most efficient support is given by the individual mind/body/spirits present at this time.

36.22 **QUESTIONER** I'm a little fuzzy on a point with respect to the higher self. Now we each, I am assuming, have a separate or different higher self at sixth-density positive level. Is this correct? Each of us in the room that is, here, the three of us?

RA I am Ra. This shall be the last full question of this working. We shall attempt to aim for the intention of your query as we understand it. Please request any additional information.

Firstly, it is correct that each in this dwelling place has one oversoul, as you may call it. However, due to the repeated harmonious interactions of this triad of entities, there may be seen to be a further harmonious interaction besides the three entities' higher selves; that is, each social memory complex has an oversoul of a type which is difficult to describe to you in words. In this group there are two such social memory complex totalities blending their efforts with your higher selves at this time.

36.23 **QUESTIONER** It is very difficult at times for us to even get a small percentage of understanding from some of these concepts because of our limitation of awareness here. I think some meditation on the communication today will help us in formulating questions about these concepts.

RA I am Ra. May we ask for any brief queries before we leave this instrument?

36.24 **QUESTIONER** I'll just ask one little short one that you may not be able to answer before the final . . .

The short one is: Can you tell me what percentage of the wanderers on Earth today have been successful in penetrating the memory block and becoming aware who they are, and then finally, is there anything that we can do to make the instrument more comfortable or improve the contact?

RA I am Ra. We can approximate the percentage of those penetrating intelligently their status. This is between eight and one-half and nine and three-quarters percent. There is a larger percentile group of those who have a fairly well defined, shall we say, symptomology indicating to them that they are not of this, shall we say, insanity. This amounts to a bit over fifty percent of the remainder. Nearly one-third of the remainder are aware that something about them is different.

So you see there are many gradations of awakening to the knowledge of being a wanderer. We may add that it is to the middle and first of these groups that this information will, shall we say, make sense.

This instrument is well. The resting place is somewhat deleterious in its effect upon the comfort of the dorsal side of this instrument's physical vehicle. We have mentioned this before.

You are conscientious. We leave you now, my friends.

I am Ra. I leave you in the love and in the light of the Infinite Creator. Go forth, then, rejoicing merrily in the power and the peace of the One Creator. Adonai.

SESSION 37

MARCH 12, 1981

37.0   **RA** I am Ra. I greet you in the love and in the light of the One Infinite Creator. I communicate now.

37.1   **QUESTIONER** Is Ra familiar with the results of our efforts today to publish the first book that we did?

RA I am Ra. This is correct.

37.2   **QUESTIONER** I don't know if you can comment on the difficulty we will have in making the Law of One available to those who would require it and want it. It is not something that is easy to disseminate to those who want it at this time. I am sure there are many, especially the wanderers, who want this information, but we will have to do something else in order to get it into their hands in the way of added material, I am afraid.

Is it possible for you to comment on this?

RA I am Ra. It is possible.

37.3   **QUESTIONER** Will you comment on it?

RA I am Ra. We shall.

Firstly, the choosing of this group to do some work to serve others was of an intensive nature. Each present sacrificed much for no tangible result. Each may search its heart for the type of sacrifice, knowing that the material sacrifices are the least; the intensive commitment to blending into an harmonious group at the apex of sacrifice.

Under these conditions we found your vibration. We observed your vibration. It will not be seen often. We do not wish to puff up the pride, but we shall not chaffer with the circumstances necessary for our particular contact.[1] Thus you have received, and we willingly undertake, the honor/duty of continuing to offer transmissions of concepts which are, to the best of our abilities, precise in nature and grounded in the attempt to unify many of those things that concern you.

---

[1] In this context, *chaffer* may be defined as "negotiate or haggle, particularly over terms of agreement."

Secondly, the use you make of these transmissions is completely at your discretion. We suggest the flowing of the natural intuitive senses and a minimum of the distortion towards concern. We are content, as we have said, to be able to aid in the evolution of one of your peoples. Whatever efforts you make cannot disappoint us, for that number already exceeds one.

37.4   **QUESTIONER** I have been very hesitant to ask certain questions for fear that they would be regarded, as I regard them, as questions of unimportance or too great a specificity and, thereby, reduce our contact with you. In order to disseminate some of the information that I consider to be of extreme importance—that is, the non-transient type of information, information having to do with the evolution of mind, body, and spirit—it seems almost necessary, in our society, to include information that is of little value, simply because that's how our . . . our society works and how the system of distribution appraises that which is offered for distribution.

Could you comm— Will . . . will you comment on this problem that I have?

RA I am Ra. We comment as follows: It is quite precisely correct that the level and purity of this contact is dependent upon the level and purity of information sought. Thusly, the continued requests for specific information, from this particular source, is deleterious to the substance of your purpose.

Moreover, as we scanned your mind to grasp your situation as regards the typescript of some of our words, we found that you had been criticized for the type of language construction used to convey data. Due to our orientation with regard to data, even the most specifically answered question would be worded by our group in such a way as to maximize the accuracy of the nuances of the answer. This, however, mitigates against what your critic desires in the way of simple, lucid prose.

More than this we cannot say. These are our observations of your situation. What you wish to do is completely your decision, and we remain at your service in whatever way we may be without breaking the Way of Confusion.

37.5   **QUESTIONER** We will attempt to work around these problems in dissemination of the Law of One. It will take some careful work to do this, but we will. I personally will not cease while still incarnate to attempt to disseminate this. I believe it will be necessary to write a book, most probably about UFOs, since the Law of One is connected with the phenomenon. It's connected with all phenomena, but this is the . . . seems to be the easiest entry into dissemination.

My first plan is to, using the UFO in the advertising sense that it was meant by the Confederation, use this as an entry into an explanation of the process of evolution that has gone on on this planet, and how the rest of the . . . or the Confederation has been involved in a more understandable way, shall I say, for the population who will read it, using the Ra material in undistorted form just as it has been recorded here in various places through the book to amplify and clarify what we are saying in the book. This is the only way that I can see right now to create enough dissemination for the people who would like to have the Law of One for them to be able to get it. I could just go ahead and print up the material we have off the tape recorder and publish it, but we would be unable to disseminate it very well because of distribution problems.

Will you comment on my second idea of doing a general book on UFOs including the material from the Law of One?

RA I am Ra. We shall comment. We hope that your Ra plans materialize. This is a cosmic joke. You were asking for such an example of humor, and we feel this is a rather appropriate nexus in which one may be inserted. Continue with your intentions to the best of your natures and abilities. What more can be done, my friends?

37.6 QUESTIONER In that case, we'll go ahead with the questions we have here, continuing the last session.

You said that each third-density entity has an higher self in the sixth density which is moving to the mind/body/spirit complex of the entity as needed. Does this higher self also evolve in growth through the densities beginning with the first density, and does each higher self have a corresponding higher self advanced in densities beyond it?

RA I am Ra. To simplify this concept is our intent. The higher self is a manifestation given to the late sixth-density mind/body/spirit complex as a gift from its future selfness. The mid-seventh density's last action before turning towards the allness of the Creator and gaining spiritual mass is to give this resource to the sixth-density self, moving, as you measure time, in the stream of time.

This self, the mind/body/spirit complex of late sixth density, has then the honor/duty of using both the experiences of its total living bank, or memory, of experienced thoughts and actions and using the resource of the mind/body/spirit complex totality left behind as a type of infinitely complex thought-form.

In this way you may see your self, your higher self or oversoul, and your mind/body/spirit complex totality as three points in a circle. The only distinction is that of your time/space continuum. All are the same being.

37.7   **QUESTIONER** Does each entity have an individual mind/body/spirit complex totality, or do a number of entities share the same mind/body/spirit complex totality?

RA I am Ra. Both of these statements are correct, given the appropriate time/space conditions. Each entity has its totality, and at the point at which a planetary entity becomes a social memory complex, the totality of this union of entities also has its oversoul and its social memory complex totality as resource. As always, the sum,[2] spiritually speaking, is greater than the sum of its parts, so that the oversoul of a social memory complex is not the sum of the oversouls of its member entities but operates upon the way of what we have called squares and what we grasp you prefer to call doubling.

37.8   **QUESTIONER** Thank you. Thank you for that explanation of the mathematics, too. That was bothering me.

Could you define spiritual mass?

RA I am Ra. This will be the last full question of this session.

Spiritual mass is that which begins to attract the out-moving and ongoing vibratory oscillations of beingness into the gravity, speaking in a spiritual sense, well of the Great Central Sun, core, or Creator of the infinite universes.

37.9   **QUESTIONER** Since we don't want to tire the instrument I will just ask if there is anything we can do to make the instrument more comfortable or improve the contact?

RA I am Ra. All is well. We leave you now in the love and the light of the

---

2   Ra presumably meant to say "the whole" here.

One Infinite Creator. Go forth, then, rejoicing in the power and the peace of the One Infinite Creator. Adonai.

38.0 **RA** I am Ra. I greet you in the love and in the light of the One Infinite Creator. We communicate now.

38.1 **QUESTIONER** Will you tell us if there would be any hope or any purpose in either Jim or I taking the instrument's place at the beginning of the session and attempting to replace the instrument as instrument by attempting the trance work ourselves?

RA I am Ra. This information is on the borderline of infringement upon free will. We shall, however, assume your desire to constitute permission to speak slightly beyond limits set by Confederation guidelines, shall we say.

At this space/time nexus neither the one known as Don nor the one known as Jim is available for this working. The one known as Don, by, shall we say, practicing the mechanics of contact and service to others by means of the channeling, as you call it, would in a certain length of your time become able to do this working. The one known as Jim would find it difficult to become a channel of this type without more practice also over a longer period of time. Then we should have to experiment with the harmonics developed by this practice. This is true in both cases.

38.2 **QUESTIONER** Thank you. Backtracking just a little bit today, I would like to know if the reason the nuclear energy was brought into this density forty or so years ago had anything to do with giving the entities that were here, who had caused the destruction of Maldek, another chance to use nuclear energy peacefully rather than destructively? Is this correct?

RA I am Ra. This is incorrect in that it places cart before horse, as your people say. The desire for this type of information attracted this data to your people. It was not given for a reason from outside influences; rather, it was desired by your peoples. From this point forward your reasoning is correct in that entities had desired the second chance which you mentioned.

38.3 **QUESTIONER** What was the mechanism of fulfilling the desire for the information regarding nuclear energy?

RA I am Ra. As we understand your query, the mechanism was what you may call inspiration.

38.4 **QUESTIONER** Was this inspiration a— Would an entity impress the person desiring the information with thoughts? Would this be the mechanism of inspiration?

RA I am Ra. The mechanism of inspiration involves an extraordinary faculty of desire, or will, to know or to receive in a certain area accompanied by the ability to open to and trust in what you may call intuition.

38.5 **QUESTIONER** Could you tell me how each of the rays, red through violet, would appear in a perfectly balanced, undistorted entity?

RA I am Ra. We cannot tell you this for each balance is perfect and each unique. We do not mean to be obscure.

Let us offer an example. In a particular entity—let us use this instrument—the rays may be viewed as extremely even, red, orange, yellow. The green ray is extremely bright. This is, shall we say, balanced by a dimmer indigo. Between these two the point of balance resides, the blue ray of the communicator sparkling in strength above the ordinary.

In the violet ray we see this unique spectrograph, if you will, and at the same time the pure violet surrounding the whole. This in turn, surrounded by that which mixes the red and violet ray, indicating the integration of mind, body, and spirit. This surrounded in turn by the vibratory pattern of this entity's true density.

This description may be seen to be both unbalanced and in perfect balance. The latter understanding is extremely helpful in dealing with other-selves. The ability to feel blockages is useful only to the healer. There is not properly a tiny fraction of judgment when viewing a balance in colors. Of course, when we see many of the energy plexi weakened and blocked, we may understand that an entity has not yet grasped the baton and begun the race. However, the potentials are always there. All the rays fully balanced are there in waiting to be activated.

Perhaps another way to address your query is this: In the fully potentiated entity, the rays mount one upon the other with equal vibratory brilliance and scintillating sheen until the surrounding color is white. This is what you may call potentiated balance in third density.

38.6   **QUESTIONER** Is it possible for a third-density planet to form a social memory complex which operates in third density?

RA I am Ra. It is possible only in the latter, or seventh, portion of such a density when entities are harmoniously readying for graduation.

38.7   **QUESTIONER** Could you give me an example of a planet of this nature, both a third-density service-to-others type and a third-density self-service type at this level of . . . of attainment conditions?

RA I am Ra. As far as we are aware, there are no negatively oriented third-density social memory complexes. Positively oriented social memory complexes of third density are not unheard of, but quite rare. However, an entity from the star Sirius' planetary body has approached this planetary body twice. This entity is late third-density and is part of a third-density social memory complex. This has been referred to in the previous material.[1] The social memory complex is properly a fourth-density phenomenon.

38.8   **QUESTIONER** I was wondering if that particular social memory complex from the Sirius star evolved from trees?

RA I am Ra. This approaches correctness. Those second-density vegetation forms which graduated into third density upon this planet bearing the name of Dog were close to the tree as you know it.

38.9   **QUESTIONER** I was also wondering then if, since action of a bellicose nature is impossible as far as I understand for vegetation, would not they have the advantage as they move into third density from second as to not carrying a racial memory of a bellicose nature and, therefore, develop a more harmonious society and accelerate their evolution in this nature? Is this true?

RA I am Ra. This is correct. However, to become balanced and begin to polarize properly it is then necessary to investigate movements of all kinds, especially bellicosity.

38.10   **QUESTIONER** I am assuming, then, that their investigations of bellicosity

---

[1]   Referred to in 8.21–22.

were primarily the type that they extracted from Hickson's memory rather than warfare among themselves? Is this correct?

RA I am Ra. This is correct. Entities of this heritage would find it nearly impossible to fight. Indeed, their studies of movements of all kinds is their form of meditation due to the fact that their activity is upon the level of what you would call meditation and thus must be balanced, just as your entities need constant moments of meditation to balance your activities.

38.11 QUESTIONER I believe this is an important point for us in understanding the balancing aspect of meditation since we have here its antithesis in another type of evolution. These entities moved, we are told by Charlie Hickson, without moving their legs. They . . . I am assuming they use a principle that is somewhat similar to the principle of movement of your crystal bells in moving their physical vehicles. Is this correct?

RA I am Ra. This is partially incorrect.

38.12 QUESTIONER But I am just assuming that they . . . their method of movement is not a function of mechanical leverage such as ours, but a direct function of the mind somehow connected with the magnetic action of a planet. Is this right?

RA I am Ra. This is largely correct. It is an electromagnetic phenomenon which is controlled by thought impulses of a weak electrical nature.

38.13 QUESTIONER Was their craft visible to . . . would it have been visible to anyone of our density on our planet who might have seen it or might have been in that area at that time? Is it a third-density material the same as this chair or anything we have here?

RA I am Ra. This is correct. Please ask one more full question before we close as this instrument has low vital energy at this space/time.

38.14 QUESTIONER All right, I'll just ask this one. I have here that—

Could you give me some idea of what conditions are like on a fourth-density negative, or self-service, planet? Can you do this?

RA I am Ra. The graduation into fourth-density negative is achieved by those beings who have consciously contacted intelligent infinity through the use of red, orange, and yellow rays of energy. Therefore, the planetary conditions of fourth-density negative include the constant alignment and realignment of entities in efforts to form the dominant patterns of combined energy.

The early fourth density is one of the most intensive struggle. When the order of authority has been established and all have fought until convinced that each is in the proper placement for power structure, the social memory complex begins. Always the fourth-density effects of telepathy and the transparency of thought are attempted to be used for the sake of those at the apex of the power structure.

This, as you may see, is often quite damaging to the further polarization of fourth-density negative entities, for the further negative polarization can only come about through group effort. As the fourth-density entities manage to combine, they then polarize through such services to self as those offered by the crusaders of Orion.

You may ask more specific questions in the next session of working. Are there any brief queries before we leave this instrument?

38.15 **QUESTIONER** I would just like to know if there is anything that we can do to make the instrument more comfortable or improve the contact?

RA I am Ra. All is well. We leave you in the love and light of the One Infinite Creator. Go forth rejoicing in the power and in the peace of the One Creator. Adonai.

SESSION 39

MARCH 16, 1981

39.0 **RA** I am Ra. I greet you in the love and in the light of the One Infinite Creator. I communicate now.

39.1 **QUESTIONER** The instrument was wondering if her fragile feeling was the result of the chemical ingestion of about six weeks ago?

RA I am Ra. This is correct. This instrument is now undergoing the most intensive period of physical-complex debilitation/distortion due to the doubling effects of the two ingestions. This instrument may expect this extremity to proceed for a period of fifteen to twenty of your diurnal cycles. The weakness distortions will then begin to lift, however, not as rapidly as we first thought due to this instrument's ongoing weakness distortions.

This instrument is very fortunate in having a support group which impresses upon it the caution necessary as regards these sessions at this time. This instrument is capable of almost instantaneously clearing the mental/emotional complex and the spiritual complex for the purity this working requires, but this instrument's distortion towards fidelity to service does not function to its best use of judgment regarding the weakness distortions of the physical complex. Thus we appreciate your assistance at space/times such as that in your most recent decision-making not to have a working. This was the appropriate decision, and the guidance given this instrument was helpful.

39.2 **QUESTIONER** Is there anything that the instrument could do, in addition to what she is attempting to do, to help her condition get better faster? I know that she hasn't been able to exercise because of her foot problem for the last couple of days . . . not able to walk, but we are hoping to get back to that. Is there anything else that she could do?

RA I am Ra. As we have implied, the negative entities are moving all stops out to undermine this instrument at this time. This is the cause of the aforementioned problem with the pedal digit. It is fortunate that this instrument shall be greatly involved in the worship of the One Infinite Creator through the vibratory complexes of sacred song during this period. The more active physical existence, both in the movements of exercise and in the sexual sense, are helpful. However, the requirements of this instrument's distortions towards what you would call ethics have an effect upon this latter activity.

Again, it is fortunate that this instrument has the opportunities for loving social intercourse which are of some substantial benefit. Basically, in your third-density continuum, this is a matter of time.

39.3 **QUESTIONER** From your reading of the instrument's condition can you approximate how often and the length of workings that we could plan in our future workings?

RA I am Ra. This query borders upon infringement. The information given sets up fairly followable guidelines. However, we are aware that not only can each of you not read this instrument's aura and so see conditions of the physical complex, but also the instrument itself has considerable difficulty penetrating the precise distortion-condition of its physical complex due to its constant dependence upon its will to serve.

Therefore, we believe we are not infringing if we indicate that one working each alternate diurnal period in the matinal hours is most appropriate with the possibility of a shorter working upon the free matinal period if deemed appropriate. This is so not only during this period but in general.

39.4 **QUESTIONER** I will then continue now with the general questioning, attempting to find a way into a line of questioning which will get us into an area of understanding non-transient functions which may be worked upon by us and others to raise our consciousness, and I may make several mistakes here in trying to find a way into this questioning. I apologize in advance if my questioning is misleading.

I notice that everything seems—or most of the basic things seem—to be divided into units which total seven. In looking at a transcript by Henry Puharich from The Nine, I found a statement by The Nine where they say, "If we get seven times the electrical equivalent of the human body then it would result in sevenon of the mass of electricity." Could you explain this?

RA I am Ra. To explain this is beyond the abilities of your language. We shall, however, make an attempt to address this concept.

As you are aware, in the beginning of the creations set up by each Logos, there are created the complete potentials, both electrical (in the sense of the one you call Larson) and metaphysical. This metaphysical electricity is as important in the understanding, shall we say, of this statement as is the concept of electricity.

This concept, as you are aware, deals with potentiated energy. The electron has been said to have no mass but only a field. Others claim a mass of infinitesimal measure. Both are correct. The true mass of the potentiated energy is the strength of the field. This is also true metaphysically.

However, in your present physical system of knowledge it is useful to take the mass number of the electron in order to do work that you may find solutions to other questions about the physical universe. In such a way, you may conveniently consider each density of being to have a greater and greater spiritual mass. The mass increases, shall we say, significantly, but not greatly, until the gateway density. In this density the summing up, the looking backwards—in short, all the useful functions of polarity have been used. Therefore, the metaphysical electrical nature of the individual grows greater and greater in spiritual mass.

For an analog one may observe the work of the one known as Albert who posits the growing to infinity of mass as this mass approaches the speed of light. Thus the seventh-density being, the completed being, the Creator who knows Itself, accumulates mass and compacts into the One Creator once again.

39.5   **QUESTIONER** Then in the equation that I have here on this page, would M_i refer to spiritual mass, I am assuming. Is this correct?

$$M_i = \frac{m_0 C^2}{\sqrt{1 - v^2 / c^2}}$$

RA I am Ra. This is correct.

39.6   **QUESTIONER** Thank you. Can you tell me— Can you interpret a transmission from The Nine where they say, "CH is a principle which is the revealing principle of knowledge and law?" Can you tell me what that principle is?

RA I am Ra. The principle so veiled in that statement is but the simple principle of the constant (or Creator) and the transient (or the incarnate being) and the yearning existing between the two, one for the other, in love and light amidst the distortions of free will acting upon the illusion-bound entity.

39.7 **QUESTIONER** Was the reason that The Nine transmitted this principle in this form the— Was the reason for this the First Distortion?

RA I am Ra. This is incorrect.

39.8 **QUESTIONER** Can you tell me why they gave the principle in such a veiled form then?

RA I am Ra. The scribe is most interested in puzzles and equations.

39.9 **QUESTIONER** I see. The Nine describe themselves as the "nine principals of God."[1] Can you tell me what they mean by that?

RA I am Ra. This is also a veiled statement. The attempt is made to indicate that the nine who sit upon the Council are those representing the Creator, the One Creator, just as there may be nine witnesses in a courtroom testifying for one defendant. The term principal has this meaning also.

The desire of the scribe may be seen in much of this material to have affected the manner of its presentation, just as the abilities and preferences of this group determine the nature of this contact. The difference lies in the fact that we are as we are. Thus we may either speak as we will or not speak at all. This demands a very tuned, shall we say, group.

39.10 **QUESTIONER** I sense that there is fruitful ground for investigation of our development in tracing the evolution of the bodily energy centers because these seven centers seem to be linked with all of the sevens that I spoke of previously and be central to our own development.

Could you describe the process of evolution of these bodily energy centers starting with the most primitive form of life to have them?

RA I am Ra. This material has been covered previously to some extent.[2]

---

[1] The Nine are usually referred to as "principles" rather than "principals," but since Ra refers to them as witnesses we have chosen the spelling to match.

[2] Possibly previously covered in 16.21, 27.17, and 32.12, though it is uncertain to which specific passages Ra is referring.

Therefore, we shall not repeat information upon which rays dwell in first and second density and the wherefores of this but rather attempt to enlarge upon this information.

The basic pivotal points of each level of development—that is, each density beyond second—may be seen to be as follows:

Firstly, the basic energy of so-called red ray. This ray may be understood to be the basic strengthening ray for each density. It shall never be condescended to as less important or productive of spiritual evolution, for it is the foundation ray.

The next foundation ray is yellow. This is the great stepping stone ray. At this ray the mind/body potentiates to its fullest balance. The strong red/orange/yellow triad springboards the entity into the center ray of green. This is again a basic ray but not a primary ray.

This is the resource for spiritual work. When green ray has been activated we find the third primary ray being able to begin potentiation. This is the first true spiritual ray in that all transfers are of an integrated mind/body/spirit nature. The blue ray seats the learning/teachings of the spirit in each density within the mind/body complex, animating the whole, communicating to others this entirety of beingness.

The indigo ray, though precious, is that ray worked upon only by the adept, as you would call it. It is the gateway to intelligent infinity bringing intelligent energy through. This is the energy center worked upon in those teachings considered inner, hidden, and occult, for this ray is that which is infinite in its possibilities. As you are aware, those who heal, teach, and work for the Creator in any way which may be seen to be both radiant and balanced are those activities which are indigo ray.

As you are aware, the violet ray is constant and does not figure into a discussion of the functions of ray activation in that it is the mark, the register, the identity, the true vibration of an entity.

39.11 **QUESTIONER** In order to clarify a little bit I would like to ask the question, if we have a highly polarized entity polarized towards service to others, and a highly polarized entity polarized towards service to self, what would be . . . taking each ray, starting with red, would there be a difference in the red ray of these two entities?

RA I am Ra. This shall be the last full question of this working.

There is no difference in equally strongly polarized positive and negative entities as regards red ray.

39.12 **QUESTIONER** Is this also true of all the other rays?

RA I am Ra. We shall answer briefly. You may question further at another working.

The negative ray pattern is the red/orange/yellow moving directly to the blue,[3] this being only used in order to contact intelligent infinity.

In positively oriented entities the configuration is even, crystallinely clear, and of the seven-ray description.

Are there any short queries before we leave this instrument?

39.13 **QUESTIONER** I only need to know if there is anything that we can do to make the instrument more comfortable or help the contact?

RA I am Ra. You are most conscientious. All is well. I leave you, my friends, in the love and in the light of the One Infinite Creator. Go forth, therefore, rejoicing in the power and in the peace of the One Creator. Adonai.

---

[3] In 47.4, Ra said that the negative pattern moves from red/orange/yellow directly to *indigo*. Presumably, then, Ra made a mistake in this response (39.12) when they said "blue." See 32.2, 34.16, 38.14, and 47.3–4 for other statements indicating that the blue ray is not used by the negative polarizing entity to contact intelligent infinity.

Though, interpreted in a certain light, 48.10, 75.23, and 85.11 may indicate the presence of the blue-ray in the negative entity's contact with intelligent infinity.

40.0   **RA** I am Ra. I greet you in the love and in the light of the Infinite Creator. We communicate now.

40.1   **QUESTIONER** I thought that I would make a statement and let you correct it. I'm trying to make a simple model of the portion of the universe that we find ourselves in. Starting with the Logos, or sub-Logos, our sun, we have white light emanating from this. This is made up of frequencies ranging from the red to the violet. I am assuming that this white light, then, contains the experiences through all of the densities, and as we go into the eighth density we go into a black hole which emerges on the other side as another Logos, or sun, and starts another octave of experience.

Can you comment on this part of my statement?

RA I am Ra. We can comment upon this statement to an extent. The concept of the white light of the sub-Logos being prismatically separated and later, at the final chapter, being absorbed again is basically correct. However, there are subtleties involved which are more than semantic.

The white light which emanates and forms the articulated sub-Logos has its beginning in what may be metaphysically seen as darkness. The light comes into that darkness and transfigures it, causing the chaos to organize and become reflective or radiant. Thus the dimensions come into being.

Conversely, the blackness of the black hole, metaphysically speaking, is a concentration of white light being systematically absorbed once again into the One Creator. Finally, this absorption into the One Creator continues until all the infinity of creations have attained sufficient spiritual mass in order that all form, once again, the Great Central Sun, if you would so imagine it, of the intelligent infinity awaiting potentiation by Free Will. Thus the transition of the octave is a process which may be seen to enter into timelessness of unimaginable nature. To attempt to measure it by your time measures would be useless.

Therefore, the concept of moving through the black hole of the ultimate spiritual gravity well and coming immediately into the next octave misses the sub-concept, or corollary, of the portion of this process which is timeless.

40.2 QUESTIONER Our astronomers have noticed that the light from spiral galaxies is approximately seven times less than it should be, from their calculations of what their mass should be. I was just wondering if that was due to the increase of spiritual mass in the galaxies in what we call white dwarf stars?

RA I am Ra. This is basically correct and is a portion of the way, or process, of creation's cycle.

40.3 QUESTIONER Thank you. I was also wondering if the first density corresponded somehow to the color red, the second to the color orange, the third to the color yellow and so on through the densities corresponding to the colors, in perhaps a way so that the basic vibration that forms the photon that forms the core of all atomic particles would have a relationship to that color in the density. And that that vibration would step up for second, third, and fourth density corresponding to the increase in the vibration of the colors. Is this in any way correct?

RA I am Ra. This is more correct than you have stated.

Firstly, you are correct in positing a quantum, if you will, as the nature of each density and further correct in assuming that these quanta may be seen to be of vibratory natures corresponding to color, as you grasp this word. However, it is also true, as you have suspected but not asked, that each density is of the metaphysical characteristic complex of its ray.

Thus, in first density the red ray is the foundation for all that is to come. In second density the orange ray is that of movement and growth of the individual, this ray striving towards the yellow ray of self-conscious manifestations of a social nature as well as individual; third density being the equivalent, and so forth—each density being primarily its ray plus the attractions of the following ray pulling it forward in evolution and, to some extent, coloring, or shading, the chief color of that density.

40.4 QUESTIONER Then the bodily energy centers for an individual would be, assuming that the individual evolves in a straight line from first through to eighth density . . . would each of these energy centers, centers or chakras, be activated to completion if everything worked as it should?

Would each be activated to completion and greatest intensity by the end of the experience in each density?

RA I am Ra. Hypothetically speaking, this is correct. However, the fully activated being is rare. Much emphasis is laid upon the harmonies and balances of individuals. It is necessary for graduation across densities for the primary energy centers to be functioning in such a way as to communicate with intelligent infinity and to appreciate and bask in this light in all of its purity.

However, to fully activate each energy center is the mastery of few, for each center has a variable speed of rotation or activity. The important observation to be made, once all necessary centers are activated to the minimal necessary degree, is the harmony and balance between these energy centers.

40.5 QUESTIONER Thank you. Taking as an example the transition between second and third density: when this transition takes place, does the frequency of vibration which forms the photon (the core of all particles of the density), does this frequency increase from a frequency corresponding to second density or orange, the color orange, the frequency we measure for the color orange, to the frequency we measure for the color yellow? What I am getting at is, do all the vibrations that form the density, basic vibrations of the photon, increase in a quantum fashion over a relatively short period of time?

RA I am Ra. This is correct. Then you see within each density the gradual upgrading of vibratory levels.

40.6 QUESTIONER Would— This is a guess. Would the frequency going from second to third increase from the middle orange frequency, or average orange frequency, to the middle yellow frequency, or average yellow frequency?

RA I am Ra. This query is indeterminate. We shall attempt to be of aid. However, the frequency that is the basis of each density is what may be called a true color. This term is impossible to define given your system of sensibilities and scientific measurements, for color has vibratory characteristics both in space/time and in time/space. The true color is then overlaid and tinged by the rainbow of the various vibratory levels within that density and the attraction vibrations of the next true-color density.

40.7 **QUESTIONER** How long was the time of transition on this planet between second and third density? Generation and a half, I believe. Is that correct?

RA I am Ra. This is correct, the time measured in your years being approximately one thousand three hundred and fifty [1,350].

40.8 **QUESTIONER** Then what will be the time of transition on this planet from third to fourth density?

RA I am Ra. This is difficult to estimate due to the uncharacteristic anomalies of this transition. There are at this space/time nexus beings incarnate which have begun fourth-density work. However, the third-density climate of planetary consciousness is retarding the process. At this particular nexus the possibility/probability vortices indicate somewhere between one hundred [100] and seven hundred [700] of your years as transition period. This cannot be accurate due to the volatility of your peoples at this space/time.

40.9 **QUESTIONER** Has the vibration of the basic . . . of the photon, of all our particles increased in frequency already?

RA I am Ra. This is correct. It is this influence which has begun to cause thoughts to become things. As an example, you may observe the thoughts of anger becoming those cells of the physical bodily complex going out of control to become what you call the cancer.

40.10 **QUESTIONER** What, assuming that we are, our vibration— I am assuming this vibration started increasing about between twenty and thirty years ago. Is this correct?

RA I am Ra. The first harbingers of this were approximately forty-five of your years ago, the energies vibrating more intensely through the forty-year period preceding the final movement of vibratory matter, shall we say, through the quantum leap, as you would call it.

40.11 **QUESTIONER** Starting then, forty-five years ago, and taking the entire increase in vibration that we will experience in this density change, approximately what percentage of the way through this increase of vibration are we right now?

RA I am Ra. The vibratory nature of your environment is true-color green. This is at this time heavily over-woven with the orange ray of planetary consciousness. However, the nature of quanta is such that the movement over the boundary is that of discrete placement of vibratory level.

40.12 **QUESTIONER** You mentioned that thoughts of anger now are causing cancer. Can you expand on this mechanism as it acts as a catalyst or its complete purpose?

RA I am Ra. The fourth density is one of revealed information. Selves are not hidden to self or other-selves. The imbalances or distortions which are of a destructive nature show, therefore, in more obvious ways, the vehicle of the mind/body/spirit complex thus acting as a teaching resource for self-revelation. These illnesses such as cancer are correspondingly very amenable to self-healing once the mechanism of the destructive influence has been grasped by the individual.

40.13 **QUESTIONER** Then you are saying that cancer is quite easily healed mentally and is a good teaching tool because it is quite easily healed mentally, and once the entity forgives the other-self at whom he is angry, cancer will disappear. Is this correct?

RA I am Ra. This is partially correct. The other portion of healing has to do with forgiveness of self and a greatly heightened respect for the self. This may conveniently be expressed by taking care in dietary matters. This is quite frequently a part of the healing and forgiving process. Your basic premise is correct.

40.14 **QUESTIONER** In dietary matters, what would be the foods that one would include, and what would be the foods that one would exclude, in a general way, for the most or the greatest care of one's bodily complex?

RA I am Ra. Firstly, we underline and emphasize that this information is not to be understood literally but as a link, or psychological nudge, for the body and the mind and spirit. Thus it is the care and respect for the self that is the true thing of importance. In this light we may iterate the basic information given for this instrument's diet. The vegetables, the fruits, the grains, and to the extent necessary for the individual metabolism, the animal products. These are those substances showing respect for the self.

In addition, though this has not been mentioned, for this instrument is not in need of purification, those entities in need of purging the self of a poison thought-form or emotion complex do well to take care in following a program of careful fasting until the destructive thought-form has been purged analogously with the by-products of ridding the physical vehicle of excess material. Again you see the value not to the body complex, but used as a link for the mind and spirit. Thus self reveals self to self.

40.15   **QUESTIONER** Thank you. A very important concept. Does the fact that basic vibration that we experience now is green true color, or fourth density, account for the fact that there are many mental effects upon material objects that are now observable for the first time in a mass way, like the bending of metal by mind?

RA I am Ra. This shall be the final query, in total, of this working. This is not only correct but we suggest you take this concept further and understand the great number of entities with the so-called mental diseases being due to the effect of this green-ray true color upon the mental configurations of those unready, mentally, to face the self for the first time.

Are there any brief queries before we close?

40.16   **QUESTIONER** Just two. With respect to what you just said, would then people incarnating here by seniority of vibration who incarnate for the service-to-self path be ones who would have extreme difficulty, mentally, with this green-ray vibration?

RA I am Ra. This is incorrect. It is rather the numbers who have distracted themselves and failed to prepare for this transition, yet who are somewhat susceptible to its influence, who may be affected.

40.17   **QUESTIONER** Thank you. I'll just ask if there's anything that we can do to make the instrument more comfortable or improve the contact?

RA This instrument is well. You are conscientious. The appurtenances cause this instrument greater comfort in the distortion of the warmth of the body complex.

I am Ra. I leave you, my friends, in the love and in the light of the One Infinite Creator. Go forth, then, rejoicing in the power and the peace of the One Infinite Creator. Adonai.

SESSION 41

41.0 **RA** I am Ra. I greet you in the love and in the light of the One Infinite Creator. We communicate now.

41.1 **QUESTIONER** I have one question of logistics to start with. I know it's a dumb question, but I have to ask it to be sure.

There is a possibility that we may have to move from this location to a location a thousand or more miles from here in the future. Will this have any effect at all on our contact with Ra?

RA I am Ra. This is not a foolish question. The location is meaningless, for are we not in the creation? However, the place of the working shall be either carefully adjudged by your selves to be of the appropriate vibratory levels, or it shall be suggested that the purification of the place be enacted and dedication made through meditation before initial working. This might entail such seemingly mundane chores as the cleansing or painting of surfaces which you may deem to be inappropriately marred.

41.2 **QUESTIONER** I am familiar with the Banishing Ritual of the Lesser Pentagram. I was just wondering if this ritual was of use in preparing a place for this type of working?[1]

RA I am Ra. This is correct.

41.3 **QUESTIONER** Then generally, what you're saying is that even if we moved over a thousand miles away, if we carefully prepared a place that we found, even though it had been used by others previously, it could be made satisfactory. Is this correct?

RA I am Ra. Yes.

41.4 **QUESTIONER** In trying to build an understanding from the start, you might say, starting with intelligent infinity and getting to our present condition of being, I am having some difficulty, but I think I should go

---

[1] An explanation of the Banishing Ritual can be found in various Hermetic Order of the Golden Dawn works, including as an appendix in W.E. Butler's book *The Magician, His Training, and His Work.*

back and investigate our sun since it is the sub-Logos that creates all that we experience in this particular planetary system.

Will you give me a description of the sun, of our sun?

RA I am Ra. This is a query which is not easily answered in your language, for the sun has various aspects in relation to intelligent infinity, to intelligent energy, and to each density of each planet, as you call these spheres. Moreover, these differences extend into the metaphysical, or time/space, part of your creation.

In relationship to intelligent infinity, the sun body is, equally with all parts of the infinite creation, part of that infinity.

In relation to the potentiated intelligent infinity which makes use of intelligent energy, it is the offspring, shall we say, of the Logos for a much larger number of sub-Logoi. The relationship is hierarchical in that the sub-Logos uses the intelligent energy in ways set forth by the Logos and uses its free will to co-create the, shall we say, full nuances of your densities as you experience them.

In relationship to the densities, the sun body may physically, as you would say, be seen to be a large body of gaseous elements undergoing the processes of fusion and radiating heat and light.

Metaphysically, the sun achieves a meaning to fourth through seventh density according to the growing abilities of entities in these densities to grasp the living creation and co-entity, or other-self, nature of this sun body. Thus by the sixth density the sun may be visited and inhabited by those dwelling in time/space, and may even be partially created from moment to moment by the processes of sixth-density entities in their evolution.

41.5   **QUESTIONER** In your last statement did you mean that the sixth-density entities are actually creating the manifestation of the sun in their density? Could you explain what you meant by that?

RA I am Ra. In this density some entities whose means of reproduction is fusion may choose to perform this portion of experience as part of the beingness of the sun body. Thus you may think of portions of the light that you receive as offspring of the generative expression of sixth-density love.

41.6 **QUESTIONER** Then could you say that sixth-density entities are using that mechanism to be more closely co-Creators with the Infinite Creator?

RA I am Ra. This is precisely correct as seen in the latter portions of sixth density, seeking the experiences of the gateway density.

41.7 **QUESTIONER** Thank you. What I want to do now is investigate, as the first density is formed, what happens and how energy centers are first formed in beings. Let me first ask you, does it make any sense to ask you if the sun itself has a density, or is it all densities?

RA I am Ra. The sub-Logos is of the entire octave and is not that entity which experiences the learning/teachings of entities such as yourselves.

41.8 **QUESTIONER** When the first density is formed, the— I am going to make a statement of my understanding and if you will correct me. I will . . .

I intuitively see the first density being formed by an energy center that is a vortex. This vortex then causes these spinning motions that I have mentioned before of the light, vibration which is light, which then starts to condense into the materials of the first density. Is this correct?

RA I am Ra. This is correct as far as your reasoning has taken you. However, it is well to point out that the Logos has the plan of all the densities of the octave in potential completion before entering the space/time continuum in first density. Thus the energy centers exist before they are manifest.

41.9 **QUESTIONER** Then what is the simplest being that is manifested? I am supposing it might be a single cell or something like that. And how does it function with respect to energy centers?

RA I am Ra. The simplest manifest being is light, or what you have called the photon. In relationship to energy centers it may be seen to be the center, or foundation, of all articulated energy fields.

41.10 **QUESTIONER** When first density is formed, we have fire, air, earth, and water. There is at some time the first movement, or individuation, of life into a portion of consciousness that is self-mobile. Could you describe the process of the creation of this and what type of energy center that it has?

RA I am Ra. The first, or red-ray, density, though attracted towards growth, is not in the proper vibration for those conditions conducive to what you may call the spark of awareness. As the vibratory energies move from red to orange the vibratory environment is such as to stimulate those chemical substances, which lately had been inert, to combine in such a fashion that love and light begin the function of growth.

The supposition which you had earlier made concerning single-celled entities, such as the polymorphous dinoflagellate, is correct. The mechanism is one of the attraction of upward spiraling light. There is nothing random about this or any portion of evolution.

41.11   **QUESTIONER** As I remember, the polymorphous dinoflagellate has an iron- rather than a copper-based cell. Could you comment on that?

RA I am Ra. This information is not central. The base of any metabolism, shall we say, is that which may be found in the chemical substances of the neighborhood of origin.

41.12   **QUESTIONER** I was just commenting on this because this indicates that it has the motion of our animal life with copper-based cells, yet it has the iron-based cell of plant life indicating a transition from, possibly, plant to animal life. Am I wrong? My memory is a little fuzzy on this.

RA I am Ra. It is not that you are incorrect, but that no conclusions should be drawn from such information. There are several different types of bases for conscious entities, not only upon this planetary sphere, but to a much greater extent in the forms found on planetary spheres of other sub-Logoi. The chemical vehicle is that which most conveniently houses the consciousness. The functioning of consciousness is the item of interest rather than the chemical makeup of a physical vehicle.

We have observed that those whom you call scientists have puzzled over the various differences and possible interrelationships of various stages, types, and conditions of life-forms. This is not fruitful material as it is that which is of a moment's choice by your sub-Logos.

41.13   **QUESTIONER** I didn't mean to waste time with that question, but you just happened to mention that particular single cell. Does this polymorphous dinoflagellate, then, have an orange energy center?

RA I am Ra. This is correct.

41.14   **QUESTIONER** Is this energy center, then, on a very small scale, related to the orange energy center in man?

RA I am Ra. The true color is precisely the same. However, the consciousness of the second-density beginning is primitive and the use of orange ray limited to the expression of self which may be seen to be movement and survival.

In third density, at this time, those clinging to orange ray have a much more complex system of distortions through which orange ray is manifested. This is somewhat complicated. We shall endeavor to simplify.

The appropriate true color for third density is, as you have ascertained, yellow. However, the influences of the true-color green acting upon yellow-ray entities have caused many entities to revert to the consideration of self rather than the stepping forward into consideration of other-self, or green ray.

This may not be seen to be of a negatively polarized nature, as the negatively polarized entity is working very intensively with the deepest manifestations of yellow-ray group energies, especially the manipulations of other-self for service to self. Those reverting to orange ray—and we may add these are many upon your plane at this time—are those who feel the vibrations of true-color green and, therefore, respond by rejecting governmental and societal activities as such and seek once more the self.

However, not having developed the yellow ray properly so that it balances the personal vibratory rates of the entity, the entity then is faced with the task of further activation and balancing of the self in relation to the self, thus the orange-ray manifestations at this space/time nexus.

Thus true-color orange is that which it is, without difference. However, the manifestations of this, or any ray, may be seen to be most various depending upon the vibratory levels and balances of the mind/body or mind/body/spirit complexes which are expressing these energies.

41.15 **QUESTIONER** Could you tell me the simplest and first entity to have both orange- and yellow-ray energy centers?

RA I am Ra. Upon your planetary sphere those having the first yellow-ray experiences are those of animal and vegetable natures which find the necessity for reproduction by bisexual techniques, or who find it necessary to depend in some way upon other-selves for survival and growth.

41.16 **QUESTIONER** And then what entity would be the simplest that would have red, orange, yellow, and green activation?

RA I am Ra. This information has been covered in a previous session.[2] To perhaps simplify your asking, each center may be seen to be activated potentially in third density, the late second-density entities having the capability, if efficient use is made of experience, of vibrating and activating the green-ray energy center.

The third-density being, having the potential for complete self-awareness, thus has the potential for the minimal activation of all energy centers. The fourth, fifth, and sixth densities are those refining the higher energy centers. The seventh density is a density of completion and the turning towards timelessness, or foreverness.

41.17 **QUESTIONER** Well, then would an animal in second density have all of the energy centers in some way in its being, but just not activated?

RA I am Ra. This is precisely correct.

41.18 **QUESTIONER** Now, the animal in second density is composed of light as are all things. What I am trying to get at is the relationship between the light that the various bodies of the animal are created of, and the relationship of this to the energy centers which are active, and the ones which are not active, and how this is linked with the Logos. It is a difficult question to ask.

Can you give me some kind of answer on that?

RA I am Ra. The answer is to redirect your thought processes from any mechanical view of evolution. The will of the Logos posits the potentials available to the evolving entity. The will of the entity, as it evolves, is the single measure of the rate and fastidiousness of the activation and balancing of the various energy centers.

41.19 **QUESTIONER** Thank you. In yesterday's, or the day before yesterday's session, you mentioned variable speed of rotation or activity of energy centers. What did you mean by that, speed of rotation?

RA I am Ra. Each energy center has a wide range of rotational speed, or as you may see it more clearly in relation to color, brilliance. The more

---

2   Possibly referring to 35.1.

strongly the will of the entity concentrates upon and refines, or purifies, each energy center, the more brilliant, or rotationally active, each energy center will be. It is not necessary for the energy centers to be activated in order in the case of the self-aware entity. Thusly, entities may have extremely brilliant energy centers while being quite unbalanced in their violet-ray aspect due to lack of attention paid to the totality of experience of the entity.

The key to balance may then be seen in the unstudied, spontaneous, and honest response of entities toward experiences, thus using experience to the utmost, then applying the balancing exercises and achieving the proper attitude for the most purified spectrum of energy center manifestation in violet ray.

This is why the brilliance, or rotational speed, of the energy centers is not considered above the balanced aspect, or violet-ray manifestation, of an entity in regarding harvestability; for those entities which are unbalanced, especially as to the primary rays, will not be capable of sustaining the impact of the love and light of intelligent infinity to the extent necessary for harvest.

41.20 **QUESTIONER** Could you tell me the difference between space/time and time/space?

RA I am Ra. Using your words, the difference is that between the visible and invisible, or the physical and metaphysical. Using mathematical terms, as does the one you call Larson, the difference is that between s/t and t/s.

41.21 **QUESTIONER** You mentioned in the last session that fasting was a method of removing unwanted thought-forms. Can you expand on this process and explain a little more about how this works?

RA I am Ra. This, as all healing techniques, must be used by a conscious being; that is, a being conscious that the ridding of excess and unwanted material from the body complex is the analogy to the ridding of mind or spirit of excess or unwanted material. Thus the one discipline, or denial, of the unwanted portion as an appropriate part of the self is taken through the tree of mind down through the trunk to subconscious levels where the connection is made. And thus the body, mind, and spirit, then, in unison, express denial of the excess or unwanted spiritual or mental material as part of the entity.

All then falls away, and the entity—while understanding, if you will, and appreciating the nature of the rejected material as part of the greater self, nevertheless, through the action of the will—purifies and refines the mind/body/spirit complex, bringing into manifestation the desired mind complex or spirit complex attitude.

41.22 **QUESTIONER** Then would this be like a conscious reprogramming of catalyst? For instance, for some entities catalyst is programmed by the higher self to create experiences so that the entity can release itself from unwanted biases. Would this be analogous then to the entity consciously programming this release and using fasting as the method of communication to itself?

RA I am Ra. This is not only correct but may be taken further. The self, if conscious to a great enough extent of the workings of this catalyst and the techniques of programming, may, through concentration of the will and the faculty of faith alone, cause reprogramming without the analogy of the fasting, the diet, or other analogous body complex disciplines.

41.23 **QUESTIONER** I have a book, *Initiation*,[3] in which the woman describes initiation. Are you familiar with the contents of this book?

RA I am Ra. This is correct. We scan your mind.

41.24 **QUESTIONER** Jim has read the entire book. I have only read part of it, but I was wondering if the teachings in the book with respect to balancing were your teachings, Ra's teachings?

RA I am Ra. This is basically correct with distortions that may be seen when this material is collated with the material we have offered.

41.25 **QUESTIONER** Why are the red, yellow, and blue energy centers called primary centers? I think from the previous material I understand this, but is there some tracing of these primary colors back to intelligent infinity that is more profound than what you have given us?

---

3   *Initiation*, by Elisabeth Haich

RA I am Ra. We cannot say what may seem profound to an entity. The red, yellow, and blue rays are primary because they signify activity of a primary nature.

Red ray is the foundation; orange ray the movement towards yellow ray which is the ray of self-awareness and interaction. Green ray is the movement through various experiences of energy exchanges having to do with compassion and all-forgiving love to the primary blue ray, which is the first ray of radiation of self regardless of any actions from another.

The green-ray entity is ineffectual in the face of blockage from other-selves. The blue-ray entity is a co-Creator. This may perhaps simply be a restatement of previous activity, but if you consider the function of the Logos as representative of the Infinite Creator in effectuating the knowing of the Creator by the Creator, you may perhaps see the steps by which this may be accomplished.

May we ask for one final full question before we leave this working?

41.26 QUESTIONER This may be too long a question for this working, but I will ask it, and if it is too long we can continue it at a later time.

Could you tell me of the development of the social memory complex Ra from its first beginnings, and what catalyst it used to get to where it is now in activation of rays? Is this too long a question?

RA I am Ra. The question does not demand a long answer, for we who experienced the vibratory densities upon that planetary sphere which you call Venus were fortunate in being able to move in harmony with the planetary vibrations with an harmonious graduation to second, to third, and to fourth, and a greatly accelerated fourth-density experience.

We spent much time/space, if you will, in fifth density balancing the intense compassion we had gained in fourth density. The graduation, again, was harmonious, and our social memory complex, which had become most firmly cemented in fourth density, remained of a very strong and helpful nature.

Our sixth-density work was also accelerated because of the harmony of our social memory complex so that we were able to set out as members of the Confederation to even more swiftly approach graduation to seventh density. Our harmony, however, has been a grievous source of naïveté as regards working with your planet. Is there a brief query before we leave this instrument?

41.27 **QUESTIONER** I'll only ask if there's anything that we can do to make the instrument more comfortable or improve the contact?

RA I am Ra. All is well. I leave you, my friends, in the love and in the light of the One Infinite Creator. Go forth, therefore, rejoicing in the power and the peace of the One Infinite Creator. Adonai.

42.0 **RA** I am Ra. I greet you in the love and in the light of the One Infinite Creator. We communicate now.

42.1 **QUESTIONER** I have a question on balancing. It's quite long, and we'll copy it directly into the book as it is. If you can answer it without me reading it, it would save time, otherwise I will read it.

RA I am Ra. We understand your desire to preserve your opportunity. However, a summary of the query would be well. For if we answer a mentally requested query, this query shall not be published. If you wish this answer to be for private use only, we shall proceed.

42.2 **QUESTIONER** I will just read it very rapidly, the question, then.

I am going to make a statement and ask you to comment on its degree of accuracy. I am assuming that the balanced entity would not be swayed either towards positive or negative emotions by any situation which he might confront. By remaining unemotional in any situation, the balanced entity may clearly discern the appropriate and necessary responses in harmony with the Law of One for each situation.

Most entities on our planet find themselves unconsciously caught up into every emotional situation which they come in contact with according to their own unique biases. And, because of these biases, they are unable to see clearly teach/learning opportunities and appropriate response in each emotional situation and must, therefore, through a process of much trial and error and enduring of resulting pain, repeat such situations many, many times until they become consciously aware of the need to balance their energy centers and thusly their responses and behaviors.

Once a person becomes consciously aware of the need to balance their energy centers and responses, the next step is to allow the appropriately positive or negative responses to emotional situations to flow smoothly through their being without retaining any of the emotional coloration after it has been consciously observed and allowed to flow through the being. And I am assuming that this ability to consciously observe the positively or negatively charged energy flowing through the being may be augmented by practice of the balancing exercises you have given us, with the result in balance being achieved for the entity which would allow him to remain unemotional and undistorted in regards to the Law of One in any situation, much like the objective viewer of the television movie.

Is this correct?

RA I am Ra. This is an incorrect application of the balancing which we have discussed.[1] The exercise of first experiencing feelings and then consciously discovering their antitheses within the being has as its objective not the smooth flow of feelings, both positive and negative, while remaining unswayed, but rather the objective of becoming unswayed. This is a simpler result and takes much practice, shall we say.

The catalyst of experience works in order for the learn/teachings of this density to occur. However, if there is seen in the being a response, even if it is simply observed, the entity is still using the catalyst for learn/teaching. The end result is that the catalyst is no longer needed. Thus this density is no longer needed.

This is not indifference or objectivity but a finely tuned compassion and love which sees all things as love. This seeing elicits no response due to catalytic reactions. Thus the entity is now able to become co-Creator of experiential occurrences. This is the truer balance.

42.3 **QUESTIONER** I will attempt to make an analogy.

If an animal, shall I say a bull in a pen, attacks you because you have wandered into his pen, you get out of his way rapidly, but you do not blame him. Or, you do not have much of an emotional response other than the fear response that he might damage you.

However, if you encounter another self in his territory and he attacks you, your response may be more of an emotional nature creating physical bodily responses. Am I correct in assuming that when your response to the animal and to the other-self, seeing both as the Creator, and loving both, and understanding their action in attacking you is the action of their free will, then you have balanced yourself correctly in this area? Is this correct?

RA I am Ra. This is basically correct. However, the balanced entity will see in the seeming attack of an other-self the causes of this action which

---

[1] Discussed in 5.2.

are, in most cases, of a more complex nature than the cause of the attack of the second-density bull, as was your example. Thus, this balanced entity would be open to many more opportunities for service to a third-density other-self.

42.4　**QUESTIONER** Would a perfectly balanced entity feel an emotional response when being attacked by the other-self?

RA I am Ra. This is correct. The response is love.

42.5　**QUESTIONER** In the illusion that we now experience it is difficult to maintain this response, especially if the entity's attack results in physical pain, but I assume that this response should be maintained even through physical loss of life or extreme pain. Is this correct?

RA I am Ra. This is correct and further is of a major, or principal, importance in understanding, shall we say, the principle of balance. Balance is not indifference but rather the observer not blinded by any feelings of separation but rather fully imbued with love.

42.6　**QUESTIONER** In the last session you made the statement that, "We (that is Ra) spent much time/space in the fifth density balancing the intense compassion gained in fourth density." Could you expand on this concept with respect to what we were just discussing?

RA I am Ra. The fourth density, as we have said, abounds in compassion. This compassion is folly when seen through the eyes of wisdom. It is the salvation of third density but creates a mismatch in the ultimate balance of the entity.

Thus we, as a social memory complex of fourth density, had the tendency towards compassion even to martyrdom in aid of other-selves. When the fifth-density harvest was achieved we found that in this vibratory level flaws could be seen in the efficacy of such unrelieved compassion. We spent much time/space in contemplation of those ways of the Creator which imbue love with wisdom.

42.7　**QUESTIONER** I would like to try to make an analogy for this in third density.

Many entities here feel great compassion toward relieving the physical problems of third-density other-selves by administering to them in many ways, bringing them food if there is hunger—as there is in the African nations now—bringing them medicine if they believe they require administering to them medically, and being selfless in all of these services to a very great extent.

This is creating a polarization, or a vibration, that is in harmony with green ray or fourth density. However, it is not balanced with the understanding of fifth density that these entities are experiencing catalyst, and a more balanced administration to their needs would be to provide them with the learning necessary to reach the state of awareness of fourth density than it would be to administer to their physical needs at this time. Is this correct?

RA I am Ra. This is incorrect. To a mind/body/spirit complex which is starving, the appropriate response is the feeding of the body. You may extrapolate from this.

On the other hand, however, you are correct in your assumption that the green-ray response is not as refined as that which has been imbued with wisdom. This wisdom enables the entity to appreciate its contributions to the planetary consciousness by the quality of its being, without regard to activity or behavior which expects results upon visible planes.

42.8 QUESTIONER Then why do we have the extreme starvation problem in, generally, in the area of Africa at this time? Is this . . . is there any metaphysical reason for this, or is it purely random occurrence?

RA I am Ra. Your previous assumption was correct as to the catalytic action of this starvation and ill health. However, it is within the free will of an entity to respond to this plight of other-selves, and the offering of the needed foodstuffs and substances is an appropriate response within the framework of your learn/teachings at this time which involve the growing sense of love for, and service to, other-selves.

42.9 QUESTIONER What is the difference in terms of energy center activation between a person who represses emotionally charged responses to emotionally charged situations and the person who is balanced and, therefore, truly unswayed by emotionally charged situations?

RA I am Ra. This query contains an incorrect assumption. To the truly balanced entity no situation would be emotionally charged. With this understood, we may say the following:

The repression of emotions depolarizes the entity insofar as it then chooses not to use the catalytic action of the space/time present in a spontaneous manner, thus dimming the energy centers. There is, however, some polarization towards positive if the cause of this repression is consideration for other-selves.

The entity which has worked long enough with the catalyst to be able to feel the catalyst but not find it necessary to express reactions is not yet balanced but suffers no depolarization due to the transparency of its experiential continuum. Thus the gradual increase in the ability to observe one's reactions and to know the self will bring the self ever closer to a true balance. Patience is requested and suggested, for the catalyst is intense upon your plane, and its use must be appreciated over a period of consistent learn/teaching.

42.10 **QUESTIONER** How can a person know when he is unswayed by an emotionally charged situation, or if he is repressing the flow of emotions, or if he is in balance and truly unswayed?

RA I am Ra. We have spoken to this point. Therefore, we shall briefly iterate that to the balanced entity no situation has an emotional charge but is simply a situation like any other in which the entity may or may not observe an opportunity to be of service. The closer an entity comes to this attitude, the closer an entity is to balance.

You may note that it is not our recommendation that reactions to catalyst be repressed or suppressed unless such reactions would be a stumbling block not consonant with the Law of One to an other-self. It is far, far better to allow the experience to express itself in order that the entity may then make fuller use of this catalyst.

42.11 **QUESTIONER** How can an individual assess what energy centers within its being are activated and in no immediate need of further attention, and which energy centers are not activated and are in need of immediate attention?

RA I am Ra. The thoughts of an entity, its feelings or emotions, and least of all its behavior are the signposts for the teaching/learning of self by self. In the analysis of one's experiences of a diurnal cycle an entity may assess what it considers to be inappropriate thoughts, behaviors, feelings, and emotions.

In examining these inappropriate activities of mind, body, and spirit complexes, the entity may then place these distortions in the proper vibrational ray and thus see where work is needed.

42.12 **QUESTIONER** In the last session you said, "The self, if conscious to a great enough extent of the workings of the catalyst of fasting, and the techniques of programming, may, through concentration of the will and the faculty of faith alone, cause reprogramming without the analogy of fasting, diet, or other analogous body complex disciplines."

What are the techniques of programming which the higher self uses to ensure that the desired lessons are learned or attempted by the third-density self in our third-density incarnational laboratory?

RA I am Ra. There is but one technique for this growing, or nurturing, of will and faith, and that is the focusing of the attention. The attention span of those you call children is considered short. The spiritual attention span of most of your peoples is that of the child. Thus it is a matter of wishing to become able to collect one's attention and hold it upon the desired programming.

This, when continued, strengthens the will. The entire activity can only occur when there exists faith that an outcome of this discipline is possible.

42.13 **QUESTIONER** Can you mention some exercises for helping to increase the attention span?

RA I am Ra. Such exercises are common among the many mystical traditions of your entities. The visualization of a shape and color which is of personal inspirational quality to the meditator is the heart of what you would call the religious aspects of this sort of visualization.

The visualization of simple shapes and colors which have no innate inspirational quality to the entity form the basis for what you may call your magical traditions.

Whether you image the rose or the circle is not important. However, it is suggested that one or the other path towards visualization be chosen in order to exercise this faculty. This is due to the careful arrangement of shapes and colors which have been described as visualizations by those steeped in the magical tradition.

42.14 **QUESTIONER** As a youth I was trained in the engineering sciences which include the necessity for three dimensional visualization for the processes of design. Would this be helpful as a foundation for the type of visualization that you are speaking of, or would it be of no value?

RA I am Ra. To you, the questioner, this experience was valuable. To a less-sensitized entity it would not gain the proper increase of concentrative energy.

42.15 **QUESTIONER** Then the less-sensitized entity should use a— What should he use for the proper energy?

RA I am Ra. In the less sensitized individual the choosing of personally inspirational images is appropriate whether this inspiration be the rose, which is of perfect beauty, the cross, which is of perfect sacrifice, the Buddha, which is the All-being in One, or whatever else may inspire the individual.

42.16 **QUESTIONER** I had one experience in meditation (which I spoke of before),[2] which was very profound, approximately twenty years ago, a little less. What disciplines would be most applicable to re-create this situation and this type of experience?

RA I am Ra. Your experience would best be approached from the ceremonial magical stance. However, the wanderer or adept shall have the far greater potential for this type of experience which, as you have undoubtedly analyzed to be the case, is one of an archetypal nature, one belonging to the roots of cosmic consciousness.

42.17 **QUESTIONER** Was that in any way related to the Golden Dawn in ceremonial magic?

RA I am Ra. The relationship was congruency.

42.18 **QUESTIONER** Then in attempting to reproduce this experience would I then best follow practices for the Order of the Golden Dawn in reproducing this?

RA I am Ra. To attempt to reproduce an initiatory experience is to move, shall we say, backwards. However, the practice of this form of service to

---

2 In 34.3.

others is appropriate in your case, working with your associates. It is not well for positively polarized entities to work singly. The reasons for this are obvious.

42.19 **QUESTIONER** Then this experience was a form of initiation? Is this correct?

RA I am Ra. Yes.

42.20 **QUESTIONER** Thank you. Using the teach/learning relationship of parent to its child, what type of actions would demonstrate the activation of each energy center in sequence from red through violet?

RA I am Ra. This shall be the last full query of this working.

The entity, child or adult, as you call it, is not an instrument to be played. The appropriate teach/learning device of parent to child is the open-hearted beingness of the parent and the total acceptance of the beingness of the child. This will encompass whatever material the child entity has brought into the life experience in this plane.

There are two things especially important in this relationship other than the basic acceptance of the child by the parent.

Firstly, the experience of whatever means the parent uses to worship and give thanksgiving to the One Infinite Creator should, if possible, be shared with the child entity upon a daily basis, as you would say.

Secondly, the compassion of parent to child may well be tempered by the understanding that the child entity shall learn the biases of service to others or service to self from the parental other-self. This is the reason that some discipline is appropriate in the teach/learning. This does not apply to the activation of any one energy center, for each entity is unique, and each relationship with self and other-self doubly unique. The guidelines given are only general for this reason.

Is there a brief query before we leave this instrument?

42.21 **QUESTIONER** If this is not brief enough, don't bother to answer it. But first, I just wondered if certain parts are always removed—the same parts removed—in cattle mutilations, and is that related to the energy centers, and why these parts, these particular parts, were removed. But if that is too long of an answer, I'll just ask if there's anything that we can do to make the instrument more comfortable or improve the contact?

RA I am Ra. It would be well to respond to the query at another working. The instrument is well.

I am Ra. I leave you, my friends, in the love and the light of the Infinite Creator. Go forth, then, rejoicing in the power and the peace of the One Infinite Creator. Adonai.

SESSION 43

43.0   **RA** I am Ra. I greet you in the love and in the light of the One Infinite Creator.

Before we communicate may we request the adjustment, without the touching of this instrument's physical body complex, of the item which presses upon the instrument's head. This is causing some interference with our contact.

43.1   **QUESTIONER** Is that the pillow or something else? Do you . . . do you speak of the pillow under the neck?

RA I am Ra. There is a line of interference crossing the crown of the head.

43.2   **QUESTIONER** Is it this? [*Questioner finds a two-inch fold in the sheet three inches above the instrument's head and lays it flat.*] Is that it?

RA I am Ra. This is correct. Please increase the distance from the crown of the head.

43.3   **QUESTIONER** [*Ruffles in the sheet are smoothed all along the length of the sheet next to the instrument's head.*] Is that satisfactory?

RA I am Ra. Yes.

43.4   **QUESTIONER** I am sorry that we failed to notice that.

RA We communicate now.

43.5   **QUESTIONER** I'll just try to pick up the last question left over from the last session, if you can answer it. I don't know if it is of any importance, but it just occurred to me that the parts removed in cattle mutilations are the same every time, and I just wondered if this was related to the energy centers, and why they were important if that was so?

RA I am Ra. This is basically correct if you may understand that there is a link between energy centers and various thought-forms. Thus the fears of the mass consciousness create the climate for the concentration upon the removal of bodily parts which symbolize areas of concern or fear in the mass consciousness.

43.6 **QUESTIONER** Are you saying, then, that these parts that are removed are related to the mass consciousness of the third-density human form on the planet, and this fear is being used in some way by the second-density entities, or—correction, the thought-form entities—that do the mutilations?

RA I am Ra. This is correct as latterly stated. The thought-form entities feed upon fear; thus they are able to do precise damage according to systems of symbology. The other second-density types of which you speak need the, what you call, blood.

43.7 **QUESTIONER** These other second-density types need the blood to remain in the physical? Do they come in and out of our physical density from one of the astral planes?

RA I am Ra. These entities are, shall we say, creatures of the Orion group. They do not exist in astral planes, as do the thought-forms, but wait within the earth's surface. We, as always, remind you that it is our impression that this type of information is unimportant.

43.8 **QUESTIONER** I agree with you wholeheartedly, but I sometimes am at a loss, before investigation into an area, to know whether it is going to lead to a better understanding. This just seemed to be related somehow to the energy centers that we were speaking of.

I am going to make a statement and have you comment on it for its correctness. The statement is:

When the Creator's light is split or divided into colors and energy centers for experience, then in order to reunite with the Creator the energy centers must be balanced exactly the same as the split light was as it originated from the Creator. Is this correct?

RA I am Ra. To give this query a simple answer would be nearly impossible.

We shall simplify by concentrating upon what we consider to be the central idea towards which you are striving. We have, many times now, spoken about the relative importance of balancing as opposed to the relative unimportance of maximal activation of each energy center.[1] The reason is as you have correctly surmised.

---

[1] Spoken about in 29.27, 40.4, and 41.19.

Thusly the entity is concerned, if it be upon the path of positive harvestability, with the regularizing of the various energies of experience. Thus the most fragile entity may be more balanced than one with extreme energy and activity in service to others due to the fastidiousness with which the will is focused upon the use of experience in knowing the self. The densities beyond your own give the minimally balanced individual much time/space and space/time with which to continue to refine these inner balances.

43.9 QUESTIONER In the next density, or the . . . in the fourth density, is the catalyst of physical pain used as a mechanism for experiential balancing?

RA I am Ra. The use of physical pain is minimal, having only to do with the end of the fourth-density incarnation. This physical pain would not be considered severe enough to treat, shall we say, in third density. The catalysts of mental and spiritual pain are used in fourth density.

43.10 QUESTIONER Why is physical pain a part of the end of fourth density?

RA I am Ra. You would call this variety of pain weariness.

43.11 QUESTIONER What is the— Can you even state the average lifespan in the fourth density of space/time incarnation?

RA I am Ra. The space/time incarnation typical of harmonious fourth density is approximately 90,000 of your years as you measure time.

43.12 QUESTIONER Then, is there a time/space— Are there multiple incarnations in fourth density with time/space experiences between incarnations?

RA I am Ra. This is correct.

43.13 QUESTIONER How long is a cycle of experience in fourth density, in our years?

RA The cycle of experience is approximately 30 million of your years if the entities are not capable of being harvested sooner. There is in this density a harvest which is completely the function of the readiness of the social memory complex. It is not structured as is your own, for it deals with a more transparent distortion of the One Infinite Creator.

43.14 QUESTIONER Then the big difference in harvestability between third and fourth density is that at the end of the third density the individual is harvested as a function of individual violet ray, but in fourth density, is it the equivalent of violet-ray then for the entire social memory complex that must be of a harvestable nature to go to fifth density?

RA I am Ra. This is correct although in fifth density entities may choose to learn as a social memory complex or as mind/body/spirit complexes, and may graduate to sixth density under these conditions, for the wisdom density is an extremely free density, whereas the lessons of compassion leading to wisdom necessarily have to do with other-selves.

43.15 **QUESTIONER** Then is sixth-density harvest strictly of social memory complex because, again, we have compassion blended back using wisdom?

RA I am Ra. This is quite correct.

43.16 **QUESTIONER** We know that the physical vehicle in fourth density that is used during space/time, I am assuming, is quite similar to the one that we now use in third density. Is this correct?

RA I am Ra. The chemical elements used are not the same. However, the appearance is similar.

43.17 **QUESTIONER** Is it necessary to eat food in fourth density?

RA I am Ra. This is correct.

43.18 **QUESTIONER** The mechanism of, shall we say, social catalyst due to a necessity for feeding the body then is active in fourth density. Is this correct?

RA I am Ra. This is incorrect. The fourth-density being desires to serve, and the preparation of foodstuffs is extremely simple due to increased communion between entity and living foodstuff. Therefore, this is not a significant catalyst but rather a simple precondition of the space/time experience. The catalyst involved is the necessity for the ingestion of foodstuffs. This is not considered to be of importance by fourth-density entities, and it, therefore, aids in the teach/learning of patience.

43.19 **QUESTIONER** Could you expand a little bit on how that aids in the teach/learning of patience?

RA I am Ra. To stop the functioning of service to others long enough to ingest foodstuffs is to invoke patience.

43.20 **QUESTIONER** I'm guessing that it is not necessary to ingest food in fifth density. Is this correct?

RA I am Ra. This is incorrect. However, the vehicle needs food which may be prepared by thought.

43.21 **QUESTIONER** What type of food would this be?

RA I am Ra. You would call this type of food nectar, or ambrosia, or a light broth of golden white hue.

43.22 **QUESTIONER** What is the purpose of ingesting food in fifth density?

RA I am Ra. This is a somewhat central point. The purpose of space/time is the increase in catalytic action appropriate to the density. One of the preconditions for space/time existence is some form of body complex. Such a body complex must be fueled in some way.

43.23 **QUESTIONER** Then, there is a— In third density the fueling of our bodily complex not only simply fuels the complex but gives us opportunities to learn service. In fourth density it not only fuels the complex but gives us opportunities to learn patience. In fifth density it fuels the complex, but does it teach?

RA I am Ra. In fifth density it is comfort, for those of like mind gather together to share in this broth, thus becoming one in light and wisdom while joining hearts and hands in physical activity. Thus in this density it becomes a solace rather than a catalyst for learning.

43.24 **QUESTIONER** I am simply trying to trace the, you might say, the evolution of this catalyst that then, as you say, changes in fifth density. I might as well complete this and ask if there is any ingestion of food in sixth density?

RA I am Ra. This is correct. However, the nature of this food is that of light and is impossible to describe to you in any meaningful way as regards the thrust of your query.

43.25 **QUESTIONER** In fourth density on this planet, after we're totally transitioned and the harvest is complete, fourth-density beings will be incarnate on the surface of this planet as we know it now, this particular surface. Is that correct?

RA I am Ra. The probability/possibility vortices indicate this to be most likely.

43.26 **QUESTIONER** Then will there be at that time any fifth-density and/or sixth-density beings on the surface of the planet?

RA I am Ra. Not for a fairly long measure of your time as fourth-density beings need to spend their learn/teaching space/time with their own density's entities.

43.27 **QUESTIONER** Then basically what you are saying is that at that point the teachings of fifth- or sixth-density beings would not be too well understood by the fourth density, new fourth-density entities?

RA I am Ra. Do you wish to query us upon this point?

43.28 **QUESTIONER** I guess I didn't state that correctly. Is it true that the fourth-density, new fourth-density beings then need to evolve in their thinking to reach a point where fifth-density lessons would be of value?

RA I am Ra. We grasp the thrust of your query. Although it is true that as fourth-density beings progress they have more and more need for other density teachings, it is also true that just as we speak to you due to the calling, so the information called is always available. It is simply that fifth-density beings will not live upon the surface of the planetary sphere until the planet reaches fifth-density vibratory level.

43.29 **QUESTIONER** I was wondering, then, if the mechanism of teach/learning was the same, relatively, then in fourth density. From what you say, it seems that is necessary for first the call to exist for the teach/learning of fifth density to be given to fourth, just as a call must exist here before fourth-density lessons are given to third. Is this correct?

RA I am Ra. This query is misguided, for experience in fourth density is emphatically not the same as third-density experience. However, it is correct that the same mechanism of calling predisposes the information received in a way consonant with free will.

You may ask one more full question at this working.

43.30 **QUESTIONER** You stated that the key to strengthening the will is concentration. Can you tell me the relative importance of the following aids to concentration? I have listed: silence, temperature control, comfort of body, screening as a Faraday cage would screen electromagnetic radiation, visible light screening, and a constant smell such as the use of incense for strengthening your concentration in meditation.

In other words, an isolation-type of situation. You mentioned that this was one of the functions of the pyramid.

RA I am Ra. The analogies of body complex to mind and spirit complex activities have been discussed previously.[2] You may consider all of these aforementioned aids as those helpful to the stimulation of that which, in actuality, aids concentration—that being the will of the entity. This free will may be focused at any object or goal.

43.31 **QUESTIONER** I was really trying to get at whether it would be of great importance to construct a better place for our meditations. We have distractions here of the types which I mentioned, and I know that it is our total free will as to whether we construct this or not, but I was just trying to get at the principles. For instance, the Faraday cage would be quite a big construction, and I was wondering if it would be of any real value?

RA I am Ra. Without infringing upon free will we feel it possible to state that the Faraday cage and the isolation tank are gadgets.

The surrounding of self in a sylvan atmosphere, apart from distractions, in a place of working used for no other purpose, in which you and your associates agree to lay aside all goals but that of the meditative seeking of the Infinite Creator is, shall we say, not gadgetry but the making use of the creation of the Father in second-density love and in the love and support of other-selves.

Are there any brief queries before this working is at an end?

43.32 **QUESTIONER** I'd only ask if there is anything we can do to make the instrument more comfortable or to improve the contact?

RA I am Ra. All is well. I leave you in the love and the light of the One Infinite Creator. Go forth, therefore, rejoicing in the power and the peace of the One Infinite Creator. Adonai.

---

2 Discussed previously in 40.14 and 41.21–22.

SESSION 44

44.0   RA   I am Ra. I greet you in the love and in the light of the One Infinite Creator. We communicate now.

44.1   QUESTIONER   The instrument had some question as to her vitality. We were having a hard time appraising it. Is it possible for you to comment on this?

RA   I am Ra. We scan this instrument and find that we may be of service without infringement due to this instrument's decision to abide by the most careful appraisal possible rather than the most desired.

We have been surprised that we have been able to maintain contact on a regular basis during this most intense period of negatively influenced interference. Sexual energy transfers have at some workings given this instrument additional vital resources upon which to draw. However, this is not so at this working and, therefore, the will of the instrument drives its bodily complex. This instrument has no judgment about this service. The faculty of will, while recognized as most central and valuable, could in this application cause serious distortion in bodily complex of the instrument.

May we note that martyrdom is not necessarily helpful. We ask this instrument to examine these thoughts, judge, and discriminate the possible truth of them; and if they be deemed true, we suggest this instrument release the power of judgment to the support group whose interests are balanced far more than this instrument's. Allow decisions to be made without expectation or attachment to the outcome. Our hopes, may we say, for long-term contact through this instrument depend upon its maturing ability to be of service to other-selves by accepting their help and thus remaining a viable instrument.

May we thank the questioner for allowing us to speak to this point, for we were aware of the distortions incumbent upon one whose will to serve is not regulated by knowledge of limitations of bodily-complex distortion.

44.2   QUESTIONER   Could you please terminate this contact as soon as necessary since we are not aware of the vitality of the instrument at this time?

RA I am Ra. In your way of speaking our hands are, to a certain extent, tied. This instrument has called upon inner reserves which are dearly bought. Therefore, we have the honor/duty of using this energy to the best of our ability. When it becomes low we shall most certainly, as always, express the need for ending the working. The only way of avoiding this sharing of service at whatever cost is to refrain from the working. It is a dilemma.

44.3   QUESTIONER Can you tell me what the tone was that I heard in my left ear when you started your communication?

RA I am Ra. This was a negatively oriented signal.

44.4   QUESTIONER Can you tell me how I would hear a positively oriented signal?

RA I am Ra. Two types there are of positive signal. First, in the right ear location the signal indicates a sign that you are being given some unworded message saying, "Listen. Take heed." The other positive sign is the tone above the head which is a balanced confirmation of a thought.

44.5   QUESTIONER Are there any other negatively oriented signals that I get?

RA I am Ra. This is correct. You are able to receive thought-forms, word-forms, and visions. However, you seem able to discriminate.

44.6   QUESTIONER Is there a reason that I am open to these signals of a negative nature?

RA I am Ra. Are you not all things?

44.7   QUESTIONER I think that it might be a good idea if we terminated the contact at this time to allow the instrument to gain more necessary energy before continuing. This is my decision at this time. I would very much like to continue the contact, but it seems to me, although I can't tell the instrument's level, that the instrument should not use up any more energy.

RA I am Ra. We are responding to an unasked query. However, it is most salient, and therefore we beg your forgiveness for this infringement. The energy has been lost to the instrument, dedicated to this purpose only. You may do as you will, but this is the nature of the instrument's preparation for contact and is the sole reason we may use it.

44.8 **QUESTIONER** I'm not sure I fully understood you. Could you say that a little different way? Could you explain more completely?

RA I am Ra. Each of you in this working has consciously dedicated the existence now being experienced to service to others. This instrument has refined this dedication through long experience with the channeling, as you term it, of Confederation philosophy, as you may say. Thus when we first contacted this instrument it had offered its beingness, not only to service to other-selves, but service by communication of this nature.

As this contact has developed, this dedication of beingness has become quite specific. Thus once the vital energy is dedicated by the instrument to our communications, even if the working did not occur, this vital energy would be lost to the day-by-day experience of the instrument. Thus we indicated the importance of the instrument's releasing of the will from the process of determining the times of working, for if the instrument desires contact, the energy is gathered and thus lost for ordinary or mundane purposes.

44.9 **QUESTIONER** In that case, since the energy is already lost, we might as well continue with this session, and we should very carefully monitor the instrument and be the sole judge of when the sessions should occur. Am I correct?

RA I am Ra. This is profoundly correct. This instrument's determination to continue contact during this period has already extended the low energy period.

44.10 **QUESTIONER** This is very revealing to us. Thank you.

Each of us gets the signals and dreams. I have been aware of clairaudient communication at least once in waking up. Can you suggest a method whereby we might, shall I say, nullify the effect of the influence that we don't want from a negative source?

RA I am Ra. There are various methods. We shall offer the most available or simple. To share the difficult contact with the other-selves associated with this working and to meditate in love for these senders of images and light for self and other-selves is the most available means of nullifying the effects of such occurrences. To downgrade these experiences by the use of intellect or the disciplines of will is to invite the prolonging of the effects. Far better, then, to share in trust such experiences and join hearts and souls in love and light with compassion for the sender and armor for the self.

44.11 **QUESTIONER** Can you tell me the source of the instrument's dream of this morning that she told to me as soon as she woke up?

RA I am Ra. The feeling of the dream, shall we say, was Orion-influenced. The clothing of the dream revealing more the instrument's unconscious associative patterns of symbolism.

44.12 **QUESTIONER** In meditation a number of years ago my arm started to glow, moving rapidly involuntarily. What was that?

RA I am Ra. The phenomenon was an analogy made available to you from your higher self. The analogy was that the being that you were was living in a way not understood by, shall we say, physicists, scientists, or doctors.

44.13 **QUESTIONER** What I am trying to get at in this session is any practices that we might be able to do to best revitalize the instrument, for it is going to be necessary to do all we can, to do this, in order to maintain our contacts. Can you tell us what we could best do to increase the instrument's vitality for these contacts?

RA I am Ra. Your experience was a function of your ability to contact intelligent infinity. Therefore, it does not have a direct bearing upon this instrument's vital energy.

We have spoken before of those things which aid this instrument in the vital energy: the sensitivity to beauty, to the singing of sacred music, to the meditation and worship, to the sharing of self with self in freely given love either in social or sexual intercourse. These things work quite directly upon the vitality. This instrument has a distortion towards appreciation of variety of experiences. This, in a less direct way, aids vitality.

44.14 **QUESTIONER** I was looking at the diagram of the advancement of magical practices starting from Malkuth and ending at Kether. I was wondering if these corresponded to the colors, or the densities, with Malkuth as one, Yesod as two, Hod and Netzach being three, Tiphareth four, and so on. Is this correct?

RA I am Ra. This is basically incorrect, although you are upon the correct track of thinking. Each of these stations has a complex number and shading of energy centers as well as some part in various balances; the lower, the middle, the high, and the total balance. Thus there are complex colors, or rays, and complex charges, if you will, in each station.

44.15 **QUESTIONER** Well, does the left-hand path of this represent the service-to-self path more, and the right-hand path the service-to-others?

RA I am Ra. This will be the last full query of this working.

This is incorrect. These stations are relationships. Each path has these relationships offered. The intent of the practitioner in working with these powerful concepts determines the polarity of the working. The tools are the tools.

44.16 **QUESTIONER** As an ending question I will just ask is it possible, then, for the Ipsissimus to have either positive or negative polarity, or must he be neither?

RA I am Ra. We shall respond to the meaning of this term in a specialized sense. The Ipsissimus is one who has mastered the Tree of Life and has used this mastery for negative polarization.

Is there any brief query which we may respond to as we take leave of this instrument?

44.17 **QUESTIONER** I am sorry that we got a little off the track today. I think the most important thing we accomplished is knowing how to better regulate the instrument's sessions, and I would hope that you would bear with me for my inability to select questions properly at times, since I just happen, sometimes, to probe into areas to see if there is a possible direction we may go, and once entering, I . . .

Other than that, I would just like to know if there is anything this session that we could do to make the instrument more comfortable or to improve the contact?

RA I am Ra. There are no mistakes. Be at rest, my friend. Each of you is most conscientious. All is well.

I leave you in the love and the light of the One Infinite Creator. Go forth, therefore, rejoicing in the power and in the peace of the One Infinite Creator. I am Ra. Adonai.

SESSION 45

APRIL 6, 1981

45.0   **RA** I am Ra. I greet you in the love and in the light of the One Infinite Creator. We communicate now.

45.1   **QUESTIONER** Could you give us an estimate of the instrument's physical condition for communications now that she is rested?

RA I am Ra. This instrument's condition as regards the bodily complex is extremely poor. This instrument is not rested. However, this instrument was eager for our contact.

45.2   **QUESTIONER** Did the period of abstinence from contact help the instrument's physical condition?

RA I am Ra. This is correct. The probability of this instrument's development of what you would call disease, either of the pulmonary nature or the renal nature, was quite significant at our previous contact. You have averted a possible serious physical malfunction of this instrument's bodily complex.

It is to be noted that your prayerful support was helpful, as was this instrument's unflagging determination to accept that which was best in the long run and thus maintain the exercises recommended without undue impatience.

It is to be further noted that those things which aid this instrument are in some ways contradictory and require balance. Thus this instrument is aided by rest, but also by diversions of an active nature. This makes it more difficult to aid this instrument. However, once this is known, the balancing may be more easily accomplished.

45.3   **QUESTIONER** Can you tell me if a large percentage of the wanderers here now are those of Ra?

RA I am Ra. I can.

45.4   **QUESTIONER** Are they?

RA I am Ra. A significant portion of sixth-density wanderers are those of our social memory complex. Another large portion consists of those who aided those in South America; another portion, those aiding Atlantis—all sixth density and all brother and sister groups due to the unified feeling that as we had been aided by shapes such as the pyramid, so we could aid your peoples.

45.5   **QUESTIONER** Can you say if any of the three of us are of Ra or one of the other groups?

RA I am Ra. Yes.

45.6   **QUESTIONER** Can you say which of us are of which group?

RA I am Ra. No.

45.7   **QUESTIONER** Are all of us of one of the groups that you mentioned?

RA I am Ra. We shall go to the limits of our attempts to refrain from infringement. Two are a sixth-density origin, one a fifth-density harvestable to sixth but choosing to return as a wanderer due to a loving association between teacher and student. Thus you three form a greatly cohesive group.

45.8   **QUESTIONER** Can you explain the right and left ear tone and what I call touch contact that I continually get?

RA I am Ra. This has been covered previously.[1] Please ask for specific further details.

45.9   **QUESTIONER** I get what I consider to be a tickling in my right and my left ear at different times. Is this any different as far as meaning goes as the tone I get in my right and left ear?

RA I am Ra. No.

45.10 **QUESTIONER** Why is the left ear of the service-to-self contact and the right service-to-others?

RA I am Ra. The nature of your physical vehicle is that there is a magnetic field, positive and negative, in complex patterns about the shells of your vehicle. The left portion of the head region of most entities is, upon the time/space continuum level, of a negative polarity.

---

[1] Covered previously in 44.3–6.

45.11 **QUESTIONER** Can you tell me the purpose or philosophy behind the fourth, fifth-, and sixth-density positive and negative social memory complexes?

RA I am Ra. The basic purpose of a social memory complex is that of evolution. Beyond a certain point the evolution of spirit is quite dependent upon the understanding of self and other-self as Creator. This constitutes the basis for social complexes. When brought to maturity, they become social memory complexes. The fourth density and sixth density find these quite necessary. The fifth positive uses social memory in attaining wisdom, though this is done individually. In fifth negative much is done without aid of others.

This is the last query as this instrument needs to be protected from depletion. Are there brief queries before we close?

45.12 **QUESTIONER** I just need to know if there is anything we can do to make the instrument more comfortable or improve the contact?

RA I am Ra. All is well, my brothers.

45.13 **QUESTIONER** What did you say? I couldn't hear you. [2]

RA I am Ra. All is well, my brothers. I leave you now in the love and in the light of the One Infinite Creator. Go forth, then, rejoicing in the power and the peace of the One Infinite Creator. Adonai.

---

[2] The latter part of this session was interrupted by a water delivery person knocking on the door and honking his horn. Jim writes: "We had a sign on the front door asking not to be disturbed, but the fellows who delivered drinking water to fill our cistern ignored the sign and made every effort to complete their delivery. From this session on we parked one of our cars at the bottom of the driveway so no vehicle could pass."

The constant interruptions are not included in this transcript.

46.0   **RA** I am Ra. I greet you in the love and in the light of the One Infinite Creator. We communicate now.

46.1   **QUESTIONER** Could we please first have an indication of the instrument's condition?

RA I am Ra. This instrument scans at present at extremely low physical energy and is under attack. This will continue for some of your weeks. However, the vital energy of this instrument is gradually restoring its former level.

46.2   **QUESTIONER** In that case, we'd better ask you only one question unless you deem it all right to ask any more questions than that. But the one question that is bothering us, which I got in meditation, may be an inappropriate question, but I feel it my duty to ask it because it is central to the instrument's mental condition and ours.

It has to do with the two cats which we were going to take to have worked upon today for teeth cleaning and the small growth removed from Gandalf's leg. I got the impression that there might be an inroad there for the Orion group, and I was primarily concerned about anything that we could do for protection for these two cats. I may be out of line in asking this, but I feel it my duty to ask it. Would you please give me information, all the information you can on that subject?

RA I am Ra. The entity, mind/body/spirit complex, Gandalf, being harvestable third density, is open to the same type of psychic attack to which you yourselves are vulnerable. Therefore, through the mechanism of images and dreams, it is potentially possible for negative concepts to be offered to this mind/body/spirit complex, thus having possible deleterious results. The entity, Fairchild, though harvestable through investment, does not have the vulnerability to attack in as great an amount due to a lack of the mind complex activity in the distortion of conscious devotion.

For protection of these entities we might indicate two possibilities. Firstly, the meditation putting on the armor of light. Secondly, the repetition of short ritual sentences known to this instrument from the establishment which distorts spiritual oneness for this instrument. This instrument's knowledge will suffice. This will aid due to the alerting of many discarnate entities also aware of these ritual sentences. The meditation is appropriate at the time of the activity on behalf of these entities. The ritual may be repeated with efficacy from this time until the safe return at convenient intervals.

46.3   **QUESTIONER** I'm not familiar with the ritual sentences. If the instrument is familiar you need not answer this, but which sentences do you mean?

RA [*Silence. No response from Ra.*]

46.4   **QUESTIONER** I assume the instrument is familiar?

RA I am Ra. This is correct.

46.5   **QUESTIONER** Can you tell me something of the little growth on Gandalf's leg, what caused it and if it is a danger to him?

RA I am Ra. The cause of such growths has been previously discussed. The danger to the physical body complex is slight given the lack of repeated stimulus to anger.

46.6   **QUESTIONER** At this time I would ask if we should end the session because of the instrument's low vitality, or whether this is irrelevant because of the dedication to this session already.

RA I am Ra. The latter is correct. You may proceed. We shall monitor the vital energy of this instrument.

46.7   **QUESTIONER** I was just wondering, if an entity polarizes toward the service-to-self path, would the anger have the same physical effect that it affects an entity polarized toward the service-to-others path? Would it also cause cancer, or is it just a catalytic effect working in the positively polarized entity?

RA I am Ra. The catalytic mechanisms are dependent not upon the chosen polarity of a mind/body/spirit complex, but upon the use, or purpose, to which this catalysis is put. Thus the entity which uses the experience of anger to polarize consciously, positively or negatively, does not experience the bodily catalyst but rather uses the catalyst in mental configuration.

46.8   **QUESTIONER** Not sure that I understand that. Let's take some examples. If an entity polarizing toward the negative path becomes angry . . . let's take the condition where he develops a cancer. What is the principle of that for him?

RA I am Ra. We see the thrust of your query and will respond at variance with the specific query if that meets with your approval.

46.9 **QUESTIONER** Certainly.

RA The entity polarizing positively perceives the anger. This entity, if using this catalyst mentally, blesses and loves this anger in itself. It then intensifies this anger consciously in mind alone until the folly of this red-ray energy is perceived, not as folly in itself, but as energy subject to spiritual entropy due to the randomness of energy being used.

Positive orientation then provides the will and faith to continue this mentally intense experience of letting the anger be understood, accepted, and integrated with the mind/body/spirit complex. The other-self which is the object of anger is thus transformed into an object of acceptance, understanding, and accommodation, all being reintegrated using the great energy which anger began.

The negatively oriented mind/body/spirit complex will use this anger in a similarly conscious fashion, refusing to accept the undirected, or random, energy of anger and instead, through will and faith, funneling this energy into a practical means of venting the negative aspect of this emotion so as to obtain control over other-self or otherwise control the situation causing anger.

Control is the key to negatively polarized use of catalyst. Acceptance is the key to positively polarized use of catalyst. Between these polarities lies the potential for this random and undirected energy creating a bodily complex analog of what you call the cancerous growth of tissue.

46.10 **QUESTIONER** Then as I understand it you are saying that if the positively polarizing entity fails to accept the other-self or if the negatively polarizing entity fails to control the other-self, either of these conditions will cause cancer, possibly. Is this correct?

RA I am Ra. This is partially correct. The first acceptance or control, depending upon polarity, is of the self. Anger is one of many things to be accepted and loved as a part of self or controlled as a part of self, if the entity is to do work.

46.11 **QUESTIONER** Then are you saying that if a negatively polarized or polarizing entity is unable to control his own anger, or unable to control himself in anger, that he may cause cancer? Is this correct?

RA I am Ra. This is quite correct. The negative polarization contains a great requirement for control and repression.

46.12 **QUESTIONER** A repression of what?

RA I am Ra. Any mind-complex distortion which you may call emotional, which is of itself disorganized, needs, in order to be useful to the negatively oriented entity, to be repressed and then brought to the surface in an organized use. Thus you may find, for instance, negatively polarized entities controlling and repressing such basic bodily complex needs as the sexual desire in order that in the practice thereof the will may be used to enforce itself upon the other-self with greater efficiency when the sexual behavior is allowed.

46.13 **QUESTIONER** Then the positively oriented entity, rather than attempting repression of emotion, would balance the emotion as stated in an earlier contact. Is this correct?

RA I am Ra. This is correct and illustrates the path of unity.

46.14 **QUESTIONER** Then cancer is a training catalyst operating for both polarities in approximately the same way but attempting, let's say, to create polarization in both directions, positive and negative, depending upon the orientation of the entity experiencing the catalyst. Is this correct?

RA I am Ra. This is incorrect in that catalyst is unconscious and does not work with intelligence but rather is part of the, shall we say, mechanism of learn/teaching set up by the sub-Logos before the beginning of your space/time.

46.15 **QUESTIONER** How does cancer do this learn/teaching when the entity has no conscious idea of what is happening to him when he develops cancer?

RA I am Ra. In many cases catalyst is not used.

46.16 **QUESTIONER** What is the plan for use of the catalyst of cancer?

RA I am Ra. The catalyst, and all catalyst, is designed to offer experience. This experience in your density may be loved and accepted, or it may be controlled. These are the two paths. When neither path is chosen, the catalyst fails in its design, and the entity proceeds until catalyst strikes it which causes it to form a bias towards acceptance and love or separation and control. There is no lack of space/time in which this catalyst may work.

46.17   **QUESTIONER** I am assuming that the sub-Logos' or the Logos' plan is for positively and negatively polarized social memory complexes in fourth density and above. Can you tell me the purpose of the plan for these two types of social memory complexes with respect, shall we say, to Coulomb's Law, or negative and positive electrical polarity, or any way you can?

RA I am Ra. This instrument grows weary. We shall speak with you again. We may indicate the possibility, without further harm to this instrument, of approximately two sessions per your weekly period until these weeks of potential for attack and presence of very low physical energy are passed. May we say it is good to be with this group. We appreciate your fidelity. Are there any brief queries before the end of this work time?

46.18   **QUESTIONER** Only if there is anything we can do to make the instrument more comfortable or improve the contact?

RA I am Ra. Each is supporting the instrument well, and the instrument remains steady in its purpose. You are conscientious. All is well. We ward you ware of any laxity regarding the arrangement and orientation of appurtenances.

I am Ra. I leave you, my friends, in the love and in the light of the One Infinite Creator. Go forth, therefore, rejoicing in the power and the peace of the One Infinite Creator. Adonai.

47.0 **RA** I am Ra. I greet you in the love and in the light of the One Infinite Creator. We communicate now.

47.1 **QUESTIONER** Could you first give us an indication of the condition of the instrument?

RA I am Ra. It is as previously stated.

47.2 **QUESTIONER** OK. The question that I was trying to ask at the end of the last session was:

Of what value to evolution or experience in the Creator knowing Himself are the positive and negative social memory complexes that form starting in fourth density, and why was this planned by the Logos?

RA I am Ra. There are inherent incorrectnesses in your query. However, we may answer the main point of it.

The incorrectness lies in the consideration that social memory complexes were planned by the Logos or sub-Logos. This is incorrect, as the unity of the Creator exists within the smallest portion of any material created by Love, much less in a self-aware being.[1]

However, the distortion of Free Will causes the social memory complex to appear as a possibility at a certain stage of evolution of mind. The purpose, or consideration, which causes entities to form such complexes, of these social memory complexes, is a very simple extension of the basic distortion towards the Creator's knowing of Itself, for when a group of mind/body/spirits become able to form a social memory complex, all experience of each entity is available to the whole of the complex. Thus the Creator knows more of Its creation in each entity partaking of this communion of entities.

47.3 **QUESTIONER** We chose the values of . . . or were given the values of better

---

[1] In this context, the idiom *much less* means "especially so." Though the phrase is typically used in negative contexts, it seems that Ra is saying that if the entire Creator exists in even a microscopic piece of dust, it exists all the more in a self-aware being.

than 50% service to others for fourth-density positive and better than 95% service to self for fourth-density negative social memory complexes. Do these two values correspond to the same rate, shall I say, of vibration?

RA I am Ra. I perceive you have difficulty in expressing your query. We shall respond in an attempt to clarify your query.

The vibratory rates are not to be understood as the same in positive and negative orientations. They are to be understood as having the power to accept and work with intelligent infinity to a certain degree or intensity. Due to the fact that the primary color, shall we say, or energy blue is missing from the negatively oriented system of power, the green/blue vibratory energies are not seen in the vibratory schedules or patterns of negative fourth and fifth rates of vibration.

The positive, upon the other hand, shall we say, has the full spectrum of true-color time/space vibratory patterns and thus contains a variant vibratory pattern or schedule. Each is capable of doing fourth-density work. This is the criterion for harvest.

47.4 **QUESTIONER** Did you say that blue was missing from fourth-density negative?

RA I am Ra. Let us clarify further. As we have previously stated, all beings have the potential for all possible vibratory rates. Thus the potential of the green and blue energy center activation is, of course, precisely where it must be in a creation of Love. However, the negatively polarized entity will have achieved harvest due to extremely efficient use of red and yellow/orange, moving directly to the gateway indigo bringing through this intelligent energy channel the instreamings of intelligent infinity.

47.5 **QUESTIONER** Then at fourth-density graduation into fifth is there anything like the percentages you gave for third-density graduation into fourth for polarization?

RA I am Ra. There are, in your modes of thinking, responses we can make, which we shall make. However, the important point is that the graduations from density to density do occur. The positive/negative polarity is a thing which will, at the sixth level, simply become history. Therefore, we speak in an illusory time continuum when we discuss statistics of positive versus negative harvest into fifth.

A large percentage of fourth-density negative entities continue the negative path from fourth- to fifth-density experience, for without wisdom the compassion and desire to aid other-self is not extremely well-informed. Thus, though one loses approximately two percent moving from negative to positive during the fourth-density experience, we find approximately eight percent of graduations into fifth density those of the negative.

47.6 **QUESTIONER** Well, what I was actually asking was if 50% is required for graduation from third to fourth in the positive sense, 95% is required for graduation in the negative sense, does this have to more closely approach 100% in both cases for graduation from fourth to fifth? Does an entity have to be 99% polarized for negative and maybe 80% polarized for positive graduation from fourth to fifth?

RA I am Ra. We perceive the query now.

To give this in your terms is misleading, for there are, shall we say, visual aids, or training aids, available in fourth density which automatically aid the entity in polarization while cutting down extremely upon the quick effect of catalyst. Thus the density above yours must take up more space/time.

The percentage of service to others of positively oriented entities will harmoniously approach 98% in intention. The qualifications for fifth density, however, involve understanding. This then becomes the primary qualification for graduation from fourth to fifth density. To achieve this graduation the entity must be able to understand the actions, the movements, and the dance. There is no percentage describable which measures this understanding. It is a measure of efficiency of perception. It may be measured by light. The ability to love, accept, and use a certain intensity of light thus creates the requirement for both positive and negative fourth to fifth harvesting.

47.7 **QUESTIONER** Can you define what you mean by a "crystallized entity"?

RA I am Ra. We have used this particular term because it has a fairly precise meaning in your language. When a crystalline structure is formed of your physical material the elements present in each molecule are bonded in a regularized fashion with the elements in each other molecule. Thus the structure is regular and, when fully and perfectly crystallized, has certain properties. It will not splinter or break; it is very strong without effort; and it is radiant, traducing light into a beautiful refraction giving pleasure of the eye to many.

47.8 **QUESTIONER** In our esoteric literature numerous bodies are listed. I have here a list of the physical body, the etheric, the emotional, the astral, and the mental. Can you tell me if this listing is the proper number, and can you tell me the uses and purposes and effects, etc., of each of these, or any other bodies that may be in our mind/body/spirit complex?

RA I am Ra. To answer your query fully would be the work of many sessions such as this one, for the interrelationships of the various bodies, and each body's effects in various situations, is an enormous study. However, we shall begin by referring your minds back to the spectrum of true colors and the usage of this understanding in grasping the various densities of your octave.

We have the number seven repeated from the macrocosm to the microcosm in structure and experience. Therefore, it would only be expected that there would be seven basic bodies which we would perhaps be most lucid by stating as red-ray body, etc. However, we are aware that you wish to correspond these bodies mentioned with the color rays. This will be confusing, for various teachers have offered their teach/learning understanding in various terms. Thus one may name a subtle body one thing and another find a different name.

The red-ray body is your chemical body. However, it is not the body which you have as clothing in the physical. It is the unconstructed material of the body, the elemental body without form. This basic unformed material body is important to understand, for there are healings which may be carried out by the simple understanding of the elements present in the physical vehicle.

The orange-ray body is the physical body complex. This body complex is still not the body you inhabit but rather the body formed without self-awareness, the body in the womb before the spirit/mind complex enters. This body may live without the inhabitation of the mind and spirit complexes. However, it seldom does so.

The yellow-ray body is your physical vehicle which you know of at this time and in which you experience catalyst. This body has the mind/body/spirit characteristics and is equal to the physical illusion, as you have called it.

The green-ray body is that body which may be seen in séance when what you call ectoplasm is furnished. This is a lighter body packed more densely with life. You may call this the astral body following some other teachings. Others have called this same body the etheric body. However, this is not correct in the sense that the etheric body is that body of gateway wherein intelligent energy is able to mold the mind/body/spirit complex.

The light body, or blue-ray body, may be called the devachanic body. There are many other names for this body, especially in your so-called Indian Sutras or writings, for there are those among these peoples which have explored these regions and understand the various types of devachanic bodies. There are many, many types of bodies in each density, much like your own.

The indigo-ray body, which we choose to call the etheric body, is, as we have said, the gateway body. In this body form is substance, and you may only see this body as that of light as it may mold itself as it desires.

The violet-ray body may perhaps be understood as what you might call the Buddha body, or that body which is complete.

Each of these bodies has an effect upon your mind/body/spirit complex in your life beingness. The interrelationships, as we have said, are many and complex.

Perhaps one suggestion that may be indicated is this: The indigo-ray body may be used by the healer once the healer becomes able to place its consciousness in this etheric state. The violet-ray, or Buddhic, body is of equal efficacy to the healer, for within it lies a sense of wholeness which is extremely close to unity with all that there is. These bodies are part of each entity, and the proper use of them, and understanding of them is, though far advanced from the standpoint of third-density harvest, nevertheless useful to the adept.

47.9   **QUESTIONER** Which bodies do we have immediately after physical death from this yellow-ray body that I now inhabit?

RA I am Ra. You have all bodies in potentiation.

47.10   **QUESTIONER** Then the yellow-ray body in potentiation is used to create the chemical arrangement that I have as a physical body now. Is this correct?

RA I am Ra. This is incorrect only in that in your present incarnation the yellow-ray body is not in potentiation but in activation, it being that body which is manifest.

47.11 **QUESTIONER** Then, after death from this incarnation we still have the yellow-ray body in potentiation, but then is, perhaps, say in the general case of our planetary population after death, would they then normally have the green-ray body manifested?

RA I am Ra. Not immediately. The first body which activates itself upon death is the "form-maker," or the indigo-ray body. This body remains—you have called it the "ka"—until etherea has been penetrated and understanding has been gained by the mind/body/spirit totality. Once this is achieved, if the proper body to be activated is green-ray, then this will occur.

47.12 **QUESTIONER** Let me make a statement and see if I am correct. After death, then, if an entity is unaware, he may become what is called an earth-bound spirit until he is able to achieve the required awareness for activation of one of the bodies. And it would be possible then to activate any of the bodies—would this go all the way from red through violet?

RA I am Ra. Given the proper stimulus, this is correct.

47.13 **QUESTIONER** What stimulus would create what we call an earth-bound spirit or a lingering ghost?

RA I am Ra. The stimulus for this is the faculty of the will. If the will of yellow-ray mind/body/spirit [complex] is that which is stronger than the progressive impetus of the physical death towards realization of that which comes—that is, if the will is concentrated enough upon the previous experience—the entity's shell of yellow ray, though no longer activated, cannot either be completely deactivated and, until the will is released, the mind/body/spirit complex is caught. This often occurs, as we see you are aware, in the case of sudden death as well as in the case of extreme concern for a thing or an other-self.

47.14 **QUESTIONER** Well then, does orange-ray activation, after death, occur very frequently with this planet?

RA I am Ra. Quite infrequently, due to the fact that this particular manifestation is without will. Occasionally an other-self will so demand the form of the one passing through the physical death that some semblance of the being will remain. This is orange ray. This is rare, for normally if one entity desires another enough to call it, the entity will have the corresponding desire to be called. Thus the manifestation would be the shell of yellow ray.

47.15 **QUESTIONER** What does the large percentage of the earth's population, as they pass from the physical, activate?

RA I am Ra. This shall be the last full query of this working.

The normal procedure, given an harmonious passage from yellow-ray bodily manifestation, is for the mind and spirit complex to rest in the etheric, or indigo, body until such time as the entity begins its preparation for experience in an incarnated place which has a manifestation formed by the etheric energy molding it into activation and manifestation. This indigo body, being intelligent energy, is able to offer the newly dead, as you would term it, soul a perspective and a place from which to view the experience most recently manifested.

Is there a short query we may answer at this time?

47.16 **QUESTIONER** I will only ask if there is anything we can do to make the instrument more comfortable or improve the contact?

RA I am Ra. The appurtenances are conscientiously measured by eye and spirit. You are conscientious. All is well. Observe this instrument to ensure continued building of the vital energies. It will have to work upon its own physical energies, for this weakness was brought about by free will of the self.

I am Ra. We leave you now in the love and in the light of the One Infinite Creator. Go forth, therefore, rejoicing in the power and in the peace of the One Infinite Creator. Adonai.

SESSION 48

48.0 **RA** I am Ra. I greet you in the love and in the light of the One Infinite Creator. We communicate now.

48.1 **QUESTIONER** Could you tell me of the instrument's condition and if she is improving with time?

RA I am Ra. This instrument's vital energies are improving with time, as you measure it. This instrument's physical energies are less than your previous asking.

48.2 **QUESTIONER** I have a question from the instrument that I will read: "You have suggested several times that sexual energy transfers aid the instrument's vital energy and this contact. It seems that this is not true for all people; that the sexual circuitry and the spiritual circuitry are not the same. Is this instrument an anomaly, or is the positive effect of sexual activity on spiritual energy normal for all third-density beings?"

RA I am Ra. This instrument, though not anomalous, is somewhat less distorted towards the separation of mind, body, and spirit than many of your third-density entities. The energies of sexual transfer would, if run through the undeveloped spiritual, electrical, or magnetic complex which you call circuitry, effectually blow out that particular circuit. Contrarily, the full spiritual energies run through bodily complex circuitry will also adversely affect the undeveloped circuit of the bodily complex.

Some there are, such as this instrument, who have not, in the particular incarnation, chosen at any time to express sexual energy through the bodily circuitry. Thus from the beginning of such an entity's experience the body and spirit express together in any sexual action. Therefore, to transfer sexual energy for this instrument is to transfer spiritually as well as physically. This instrument's magnetic field, if scrutinized by one sensitive, will show these unusual configurations.

This is not unique to one entity but is common to a reasonable number of entities who, having lost the desire for orange- and green-ray[1] sexual experiences, have strengthened the combined circuitry of spirit, mind,

---

[1] Ra said "green-ray," but presumably meant "yellow-ray."

and body to express the totality of beingness in each action. It is for this reason also that the social intercourse and companionship is very beneficial to this instrument, it being sensitive to the more subtle energy transfers.

48.3 QUESTIONER Thank you. If you, Ra, as an individualized entity were incarnate on Earth now with full awareness and memory of what you know now, what would be your objective at this time on Earth as far as activities are concerned?

RA I am Ra. The query suggests that which has been learned to be impractical. However, were we to again be naïve enough to think that our physical presence was any more effective than that love/light we send your peoples and the treasure of this contact, we would do as we did do. We would be, and we would offer our selves as teach/learners.

48.4 QUESTIONER Knowing what you know now about our planetary condition and methods of communication, etc., if you, yourself, as an individual, had gone through the process of incarnation here as a wanderer and now have memory of a sufficient way to have the objective that you just stated, what mechanisms would you seek out for the process of teach/learning in our present state of communication?

RA I am Ra. My brother, we perceive you have made certain unspoken connections. We acknowledge these and, for this reason, cannot infringe upon your confusion.

48.5 QUESTIONER I was afraid of that.

My lecture yesterday[2] was attended by only a few. If this had occurred during a UFO flap, as we call them, many more would have attended. But since Orion entities cause the flaps, primarily, what is Orion's reward, shall I say, for visibility in that they actually create greater chances and opportunities for dissemination of information such as mine at this time?

RA I am Ra. This assumption is incorrect. The flaps cause many fears among your peoples, many speakings, understandings concerning plots,

---

2 The lecture was titled "The Spiritual Significance of UFOs," given at Jefferson Community College on April 21, 1981. A transcript of the lecture can be found in the speeches section on www.llresearch.org.

cover-ups, mutilations, killings, and other negative impressions. Even those supposedly positive reports which gain public awareness speak of doom. You may understand yourself as one who will be in the minority due to the understandings which you wish to share, if we may use that misnomer.

We perceive there is a further point we may posit at this time. The audience brought about by Orion-type publicity is not seeded by seniority of vibration to a great extent. The audiences receiving teach/learnings without stimulus from publicity will be more greatly oriented towards illumination. Therefore, forget you the counting.

48.6 **QUESTIONER** Thank you. That cleared it up very well. A very important point.

Can you tell me how positive and negative polarizations in fourth and fifth density are used to cause work in consciousness?

RA I am Ra. There is very little work in consciousness in fourth and in fifth densities compared to the work done in third density. The work that is accomplished in positive fourth is that work whereby the positive social memory complex, having through slow stages harmoniously integrated itself, goes forth to aid those of less positive orientation which seek their aid. Thus their service is their work.

And through this dynamic between the societal self and the other-self which is the object of love, greater and greater intensities of understanding or compassion are attained. This intensity continues until the appropriate intensity of the light may be welcomed. This is fourth-density harvest.

Within fourth-density positive there are minor amounts of catalyst of a spiritual- and mental-complex distortion. This occurs during the process of harmonizing to the extent of forming the social memory complex. This causes some small catalyst and work to occur, but the great work of fourth density lies in the contact betwixt the societal self and less polarized other-self.

In fourth-density negative much work is accomplished during the fighting for position which precedes the period of the social memory complex. There are opportunities to polarize negatively by control of other-selves. During the social memory complex period of fourth-density negative, the situation is the same. The work takes place through the societal reaching out to less polarized other-self in order to aid in negative polarization.

In fifth-density positive and negative the concept of work done through a potential difference is not particularly helpful as fifth-density entities are, again, intensifying rather than potentiating.

In positive, the fifth-density complex uses sixth-density teach/learners to study the more illuminated understandings of unity, thus becoming more and more wise. Fifth-density positive social memory complexes often will choose to divide their service to others in two ways: first, the beaming of light to creation; second, the sending of groups to be of aid as instruments of light such as those whom you're familiar with through channels.

In fifth-density negative, service to self has become extremely intense and the self has shrunk or compacted so that the dialogues with the teach/learners are used exclusively in order to intensify wisdom. There are very, very few fifth-density negative wanderers for they fear the forgetting. There are very, very few fifth-density Orion members for they do not any longer perceive any virtue in other-selves.[3]

48.7   **QUESTIONER** Thank you. I would like to take as an example an entity, at birth, who is roughly high on the seniority list for positive polarization and possible harvestability at the end of this cycle, and follow a full cycle of his experience starting before his incarnation—which body is activated, process of becoming incarnate, the activation of the third-density physical body process as the body moves through this density and is acted upon by catalyst, and then the process of death, and the activation of the various bodies—so that we make a full circuit from a point prior to incarnation back around through incarnation and death and back to that position, you might say, in one cycle of incarnation in this density. Could you do that for me?

RA I am Ra. Your query is most distorted, for it assumes that creations are alike. Each mind/body/spirit complex has its own patterns of activation and its own rhythms of awakening. The important thing for harvest is the harmonious balance between the various energy centers of

---

3   It is unclear and subject to interpretation, but this information about the number of fifth-density entities comprising the Orion group may contradict information given in 7.15.

the mind/body/spirit complex. This is to be noted as of relative import. We grasp the thrust of your query and will make a most general answer stressing the unimportance of such arbitrary generalizations.

The entity, before incarnation, dwells in the appropriate, shall we say, place in time/space. The true-color type of this location will be dependent upon the entity's needs. Those entities, for instance, which, being wanderers, have the green, blue, or indigo true-color core of mind/body/spirit complex will have rested therein.

Entrance into incarnation requires the investment, or activation, of the indigo-ray, or etheric body, for this is the form maker. The young, or small, physical mind/body/spirit complex has the seven energy centers potentiated before the birthing process. There are also analogs in time/space of these energy centers corresponding to the seven energy centers in each of the seven true-color densities. Thus in the microcosm exists all the experience that is prepared. It is as though the infant contains the universe.

The patterns of activation of an entity of high seniority will undoubtedly move with some rapidity to the green-ray level which is the springboard to primary blue. There is always some difficulty in penetrating blue primary energy, for it requires that which your people have in great paucity; that is, honesty. Blue ray is the ray of free communication with self and with other-self.

Having accepted that an harvestable or nearly harvestable entity will be working from this green-ray springboard, one may then posit that the experiences in the remainder of the incarnation will be focused upon activation of the primary blue ray of freely given communication; of indigo ray, that of freely shared intelligent energy; and, if possible, moving through this gateway, the penetration of violet-ray intelligent infinity. This may be seen to be manifested by a sense of the consecrate, or hallowed, nature of everyday creations and activities.

Upon the bodily complex death, as you call this transition, the entity will immediately, upon realization of its state, return to the indigo form-maker body and rest therein until the proper future placement is made.

Here we have the anomaly of harvest. In harvest the entity will then transfer its indigo body into violet-ray manifestation as seen in true-color yellow. This is for the purpose of gauging the harvestability of the entity.

After this anomalous activity has been carefully completed, the entity will move into indigo body again and be placed in the correct true-color locus in space/time and time/space, at which time the healings and learn/teachings necessary shall be completed and further incarnation needs determined.

48.8   **QUESTIONER** Who, shall we say, supervises the determination of further incarnation needs and sets up the seniority list, shall I say, for incarnation?

RA I am Ra. This is a query with two answers.

Firstly, there are those directly under the Guardians who are responsible for the incarnation patterns of those incarnating automatically—that is, without conscious self-awareness of the process of spiritual evolution. You may call these beings angelic if you prefer. They are, shall we say, local, or of your planetary sphere.

The seniority of vibration is to be likened unto placing various grades of liquids in the same glass. Some will rise to the top; others will sink to the bottom. Layers and layers of entities will ensue. As harvest draws near, those filled with the most light and love will naturally, and without supervision, be in line, shall we say, for the experience of incarnation.

When the entity becomes aware in its mind/body/spirit complex totality of the mechanism for spiritual evolution, it, itself, will arrange and place those lessons and entities necessary for maximum growth and expression of polarity in the incarnative experience before the forgetting process occurs. The only disadvantage of this total free will of those senior entities choosing the manner of incarnation experiences is that some entities attempt to learn so much during one incarnative experience that the intensity of catalyst disarranges the polarized entity and the experience thus is not maximally useful as intended.

48.9   **QUESTIONER** An analogy to that would be a student entering college and signing up for more courses than he could possibly assimilate in the time. Is this correct?

RA I am Ra. This is correct.

48.10   **QUESTIONER** Could you tell me how the various bodies, red through violet, are linked to the energy center, centers red through violet? Are they linked in some way?

RA I am Ra. This shall be the last full query of this working.

As we have noted, each of the true-color densities has the seven energy centers, and each entity contains all this in potentiation. The activation, while in yellow ray, of violet-ray intelligent infinity is a passport to the next octave of experience.

There are adepts who have penetrated many, many of the energy centers and several of the true colors. This must be done with utmost care while in the physical body, for as we noted when speaking of the dangers of linking red/orange/yellow circuitry with true-color blue circuitry, the potential for disarrangement of the mind/body/spirit complex is great. However, the entity who penetrates intelligent infinity is basically capable of walking the universe with unfettered tread.

Is there any brief query before we leave this instrument?

48.11 **QUESTIONER** Just if there is anything that we can do to make the instrument more comfortable or improve the contact?

RA I am Ra. All is well. As we have said, this instrument is weak physically, and continued work times will lengthen this weakness. The continued contact also aids in the continued climb in vital energy of the instrument, as well as the integration and vital energy of the group as an unit. The choice is yours. We are pleased. All is well. You are conscientious. Continue so.

I am Ra. I leave you in the love and in the light of the One Infinite Creator. Go forth, then, my friends, rejoicing in the power and in the peace of the One Infinite Creator. Adonai.

49.0 **RA** I am Ra. I greet you in the love and in the light of the One Infinite Creator. We communicate now.

49.1 **QUESTIONER** Would you please first give us a reading on the instrument's condition?

RA I am Ra. It is as previously stated.

49.2 **QUESTIONER** Thank you. I have a question here from Jim first. He says:

"For the past nine years I have had what I call frontal lobes experiences in the pre-consciousness state of sleep just before I wake up in the morning. They are a combination of pleasure and pressure which begins in the frontal lobes and spreads in pulses through the whole brain and feels like an orgasm in my brain. I have had over 200 of these experiences, and often they are accompanied by visions and voices which seldom make much sense to me. What is the source of these frontal lobes experiences?"

RA I am Ra. We scan the questioner and find some pertinent information already available which regards the physiological disposition of this particular part of the brain. The experiences described and experienced are those distillations which may be experienced after a concentration of effort upon the opening of the gateway, or indigo, mind complex so that experience of a sacramental, or violet, ray may occur. These experiences are the beginnings of that which—as the body, the mind, and the spirit become integrated at the gateway, or indigo, level—may then yield not only the experience of joy but the comprehension of intelligent infinity which accompanies it. Thus the body complex orgasm and mind complex orgasm, becoming integrated, may then set forth the proper gateway for the spiritual complex integration and its use as a shuttle for the sacrament of the fully experienced presence of the One Infinite Creator. Thus there is much to which the questioner may look forward.

49.3 **QUESTIONER** [*to Jim*] Do you have any addition to that question?

JIM No. Thanks.

QUESTIONER [*to Jim*] Okay.

[*to Ra*] I was wondering—in a previous session you had mentioned the left and right ear tones—if the left and the right brain were somehow related to the polarities of service to self and service to others. Could you comment on this?

RA I am Ra. We may comment on this.

49.4 **QUESTIONER** Well, please . . . will you go ahead and comment on it?

RA I am Ra. The lobes of your physical complex brain are alike in their use of weak electrical energy. The entity ruled by intuition and impulse is equal to the entity governed by rational analysis when polarity is considered. The lobes may both be used for service to self or service to others.

It may seem that the rational, or analytical, mind might have more of a possibility of successfully pursuing the negative orientation due to the fact that, in our understanding, too much order is, by its essence, negative. However, this same ability to structure abstract concepts and to analyze experiential data may be the key to rapid positive polarization. It may be said that those whose analytical capacities are predominant have somewhat more to work with in polarizing.

The function of intuition is to inform intelligence. In your illusion the unbridled predominance of intuition will tend to keep an entity from the greater polarizations due to the vagaries of intuitive perception. As you may see, these two types of brain structure need to be balanced in order that the net sum of experiential catalyst will be polarization and illumination, for without the acceptance by the rational mind of the worth of the intuitive faculty, the creative aspects which aid in illumination will be stifled.

There is one correspondence between right and left, and positive and negative. The web of energy which surrounds your bodies contains somewhat complex polarizations. The left area of the head and upper shoulder is most generally seen to be of a negative polarization, whereas the right is of positive polarization, magnetically speaking. This is the cause of the tone's meaning for you.

49.5 **QUESTIONER** Will you expand on the positive and negative magnetic polarizations in general and how it applies to, say, individuals and planets, etc.? I think there is a correlation here, but I'm not sure.

RA I am Ra. It is correct that there is a correlation between the energy field of an entity of your nature and planetary bodies, for all material is constructed by means of the dynamic tension of the magnetic field. The lines of force in both cases may be seen to be much like the interweaving spirals of the braided hair. Thus positive and negative wind and interweave forming geometric relationships in the energy fields of both persons, as you would call a mind/body/spirit complex, and planets.

The negative pole is the south pole, or the lower pole. The north, or upper pole, is positive. The crisscrossings of these spiraling energies form primary, secondary, and tertiary energy centers. You are familiar with the primary energy centers of the physical, mental, and spiritual body complex. Secondary points of the crisscrossing of positive and negative center orientation revolve about several of your centers. The yellow-ray center may be seen to have secondary energy centers in elbow, in knee, and in the subtle bodies at a slight spacing from the physical vehicle at points describing diamonds about the entity's navel area surrounding the body.

One may examine each of the energy centers for such secondary centers. Some of your peoples work with these energy centers, and you call this acupuncture. However, it is to be noted that there are most often anomalies in the placement of the energy centers so that the scientific precision of this practice is brought into question. Like most scientific attempts at precision, it fails to take into account the unique qualities of each creation.

The most important concept to grasp about the energy field is that the lower, or negative pole, will draw the universal energy into itself from the cosmos. Therefrom it will move upward to be met and reacted to by the positive spiraling energy moving downward from within. The measure of an entity's level of ray activity is the locus wherein the south pole outer energy has been met by the inner spiraling positive energy.

As an entity grows more polarized this locus will move upwards. This phenomenon has been called by your peoples the kundalini. However, it may better be thought of as the meeting place of cosmic and inner, shall we say, vibratory understanding. To attempt to raise the locus of this meeting without realizing the metaphysical principles of magnetism upon which this depends is to invite great imbalance.

49.6 **QUESTIONER** What process would be the recommended process for correctly awakening, as they say, the kundalini, and of what value would that be?

RA I am Ra. The metaphor of the coiled serpent being called upwards is vastly appropriate for consideration by your peoples. This is what you are attempting when you seek. There are, as we have stated, great misapprehensions concerning this metaphor and the nature of pursuing its goal.[1] We must generalize and ask that you grasp the fact that this, in effect, renders far less useful that which we share. However, as each entity is unique, generalities are our lot when communicating for your possible edification.

We have two types of energy. We are attempting, then, as entities in any true color of this octave, to move the meeting place of inner and outer natures further and further along, or upward along, the energy centers. The two methods of approaching this with sensible method are first, the seating within one's self of those experiences which are attracted to the entity through the south pole. Each experience will need to be observed, experienced, balanced, accepted, and seated within the individual. As the entity grows in self-acceptance and awareness of catalyst, the location of the comfortable seating of these experiences will rise to the new true-color entity. The experience, whatever it may be, will be seated in red ray and considered as to its survival content and so forth.

Each experience will be sequentially understood by the growing and seeking mind/body/spirit complex in terms of survival, then in terms of personal identity, then in terms of social relations, then in terms of universal love, then in terms of how the experience may beget free communication, then in terms of how the experience may be linked to universal energies, and finally in terms of the sacramental nature of each experience.

Meanwhile the Creator lies within. In the north pole the crown is already upon the head and the entity is potentially a god. This energy is brought into being by the humble and trusting acceptance of this energy through meditation and contemplation of the self and of the Creator.

---

1 Stated in the previous passage, 49.5.

Where these energies meet is where the serpent will have achieved its height. When this uncoiled energy approaches universal love and radiant being the entity is in a state whereby the harvestability of the entity comes nigh.

49.7   **QUESTIONER** Will you recommend a technique of meditation?

RA I am Ra. No.

49.8   **QUESTIONER** Is it better, or shall I say, does it produce more usable results in meditation to leave the mind, shall I say, as blank as possible—let it run down, so to speak—or is it better to focus in meditation on some object or some thing for concentration?

RA I am Ra. This shall be the last full query of this work time.

Each of the two types of meditation is useful for a particular reason. The passive meditation involving the clearing of the mind—the emptying of the mental jumble which is characteristic of mind complex activity among your peoples—is efficacious for those whose goal is to achieve an inner silence as a base from which to listen to the Creator. This is an useful and helpful tool, and is, by far, the most generally useful type of meditation as opposed to contemplation or prayer.

The type of meditation which may be called visualization has as its goal not that which is contained in the meditation itself. Visualization is the tool of the adept. Those who learn to hold visual images in mind are developing an inner concentrative power that can transcend boredom and discomfort. When this ability has become crystallized in an adept, the adept may then do polarizing in consciousness without external action which can affect the planetary consciousness. This is the reason for existence of the so-called white magician. Only those wishing to pursue the conscious raising of planetary vibration will find visualization to be a particularly satisfying type of meditation.

Contemplation, or the consideration in a meditative state of an inspiring image or text, is extremely useful also among your peoples, and the faculty of will called praying is also of a potentially helpful nature. Whether it is, indeed, an helpful activity depends quite totally upon the intentions and objects of the one who prays.

May we ask if there are any brief queries at this time?

49.9 **QUESTIONER** I will just ask if there is anything we may do to make the instrument more comfortable or to improve the contact and if the two sessions per week are still appropriate?

RA I am Ra. We request your care in the placement of the neck support for this entity as it is too often careless. You are conscientious, and your alignments are well. The timing, if we may use that expression, of the sessions is basically correct. However, you are to be commended for observing fatigue in the circle and refraining from a working until all were in love, harmony, and vital energy as one being. This is, and will continue to be, most helpful.

I am Ra. I leave you in the love and in the light of the One Infinite Creator. Go forth, therefore, rejoicing in the power and in the peace of the One Infinite Creator. Adonai.

50.0   **RA** I am Ra. I greet you in the love and in the light of the One Infinite Creator. We communicate now.

50.1   **QUESTIONER** Could you please give me an indication of the instrument's condition now?

RA I am Ra. It is as previously stated.

50.2   **QUESTIONER** In the last session you made the statement that experiences are attracted to the entity through the south pole. Could you expand on that and give us a definition of what you mean?

RA I am Ra. It takes some consideration to accomplish the proper perspective for grasping the sense of the above information. The south, or negative, pole is one which attracts. It pulls unto itself those things magnetized to it. So with the mind/body/spirit complex the in-flow of experience is of the south pole influx. You may consider this a simplistic statement.

The only specific part of this correctness is that the red-ray, or foundation energy center, being the lowest, or root, energy center of the physical vehicle, will have the first opportunity to react to any experience. In this way only you may see a physical locus of the south pole being identified with the root energy center. In every facet of mind and body the root, or foundation, will be given the opportunity to function first.

What is this opportunity but survival? This is the root possibility of response and may be found to be characteristic of the basic functions of both mind and body. You will find this instinct the strongest, and once this is balanced much is open to the seeker. The south pole then ceases blocking the experiential data, and higher energy centers of mind and body become availed of the opportunity to use the experience drawn to it.

50.3   **QUESTIONER** Why do you say the experience is drawn to, or attracted to, the entity?

RA I am Ra. We say this due to our understanding that this is the nature of the phenomenon of experiential catalyst and its entry into the mind/body/spirit complex's awareness.

50.4   **QUESTIONER** Could you give an example of how an entity sets up a condition for attracting a particular experiential catalyst and how that catalyst then is provided or is learned.

RA I am Ra. Such an example may be given.

50.5   **QUESTIONER** Will you give that?

RA I am Ra. We paused to scan this instrument's consciousness for permission to use its experiential catalyst as example. We may proceed.

This is one instance, and extrapolation may be made to other entities which are aware of the process of evolution. This entity chose, before incarnation, the means whereby catalyst had great probability of being obtained. This entity desired the process of expressing love and light without expecting any return. This instrument programmed also to endeavor to accomplish spiritual work and to comfort itself with companionship in the doing of this work.

Agreements were made prior to incarnation; the first, with the so-called parents and siblings of this entity. This provided the experiential catalyst for the situation of offering radiance of being without expectation of return. The second program involved agreements with several entities. These agreements provided and will provide, in your time/space and space/time continuum, opportunities for the experiential catalyst of work and comradeship.

There are events which were part of a program for this entity only in that they were possibility/probability vortices having to do with your societal culture. These events include the nature of the living, or standard of living; the type of relationships entered into in your legal framework; and the social climate during the incarnation. The incarnation was understood to be one which would take place at harvest.

These givens, shall we say, apply to millions of your peoples: those aware of evolution and desirous in the very extreme of attaining the heart of love and the radiance which gives understanding. No matter what the lessons programmed, they have to do with other-selves, not with events.

They have to do with giving, not receiving; for the lessons of love are of this nature both for positive and negative. Those negatively harvestable will be found at this time endeavoring to share their love of self.

There are those whose lessons are more random due to their present inability to comprehend the nature and mechanism of the evolution of mind, body, and spirit. Of these we may say that the process is guarded by those who never cease their watchful expectation of being of service. There is no entity without help, either through self-awareness of the unity of creation, or through guardians of the self which protect the less sophisticated mind/body/spirit from any permanent separation from unity while the lessons of your density continue.

50.6 **QUESTIONER** Could you give an example of negative polarization sharing love of self? It would seem to me that that would deplete negative polarization. Could you expand on that concept?

RA I am Ra. We may not use examples of known beings due to the infringement this would cause. Thus we must be general.

The negatively oriented being will be one who feels that it has found power that gives meaning to its existence precisely as the positive polarization does feel. This negative entity will strive to offer these understandings to other-selves, most usually by the process of forming the elite, the disciples, and teaching the need and rightness of the enslavement of other-selves for their own good. These other-selves are conceived to be dependent upon the self and in need of the guidance and the wisdom of the self.

50.7 **QUESTIONER** Thank you. Can you expand on the concept which is this: that it is necessary for an entity to, during incarnation in the physical, as we call it, become polarized or interact properly with other entities, and why this isn't possible in between incarnations when he is aware of what he wants to do, but why must he come into an incarnation and lose memory, conscious memory, of what he wants to do and then act in a way that he hopes to act? Could you expand on that please?

RA I am Ra. Let us give the example of the man who sees all the poker hands. He then knows the game. It is but child's play to gamble, for it is no risk. The other hands are known. The possibilities are known and the hand will be played correctly but with no interest.

In time/space and in the true-color green density, the hands of all are open to the eye. The thoughts, the feelings, the troubles: all these may be seen. There is no deception and no desire for deception. Thus much may be accomplished in harmony, but the mind/body/spirit gains little polarity from this interaction.

Let us re-examine this metaphor and multiply it into the longest poker game you can imagine: a lifetime. The cards are love, dislike, limitation, unhappiness, pleasure, etc. They are dealt, and re-dealt, and re-dealt continuously. You may, during this incarnation begin—and we stress begin—to know your own cards. You may begin to find the love within you. You may begin to balance your pleasure, your limitations, etc. However, your only indication of other-selves' cards is to look into the eyes.

You cannot remember your hand, their hands, perhaps even the rules of this game. This game can only be won by those who lose their cards in the melting influence of love; can only be won by those who lay their pleasures, their limitations, their all upon the table face up and say inwardly: "All, all of you players, each other-self, whatever your hand, I love you."

This is the game: to know, to accept, to forgive, to balance, and to open the self in love. This cannot be done without the forgetting, for it would carry no weight in the life of the mind/body/spirit beingness totality.

50.8 **QUESTIONER** Thank you. How does the ability to hold visual images in mind allow the adept to do polarization in consciousness without external action?

RA I am Ra. This is not a simple query, for the adept is one which will go beyond the green ray which signals entry into harvestability. The adept will not simply be tapping into intelligent energy as a means of readiness for harvest, but tapping into both intelligent energy and intelligent infinity for the purpose of transmuting planetary harvestability and consciousness.

The means of this working lie within. The key is first, silence, and secondly, singleness of thought. Thusly a visualization which can be held steady to the inward eye for several of your minutes, as you measure time, will signal the adept's increase in singleness of thought. This singleness of thought, then, can be used by the positive adept to work in group ritual visualizations for the raising of positive energy, by negative adepts for the increase in personal power.

50.9   QUESTIONER Can you tell me how the adept then, after being able to hold the image for several minutes, what he does then to affect planetary consciousness or increase positive polarity? I still don't quite understand about this.

RA I am Ra. When the positive adept touches intelligent infinity from within, this is the most powerful of connections, for it is the connection of the whole mind/body/spirit complex microcosm with the macrocosm. This connection enables the, shall we say, green-ray true color in time/space to manifest in your time/space.[1] In green ray, thoughts are beings. In your illusion this is normally not so.

The adepts then become living channels for love and light and are able to channel this radiance directly into the planetary web of energy nexi. The ritual will always end by the grounding of this energy in praise and thanksgiving and the release of this energy into the planetary whole.

50.10   QUESTIONER I know of people who have been recently trained in meditation who, after a very short period of intense meditation, a couple of days or so, are able to cause the action at a distance effect on metal, bending it. It's my understanding that they are wearing a pyramid-shaped wire on their heads while doing this. I was invited to one of the meditation sessions a couple of years ago, but I couldn't get there. Could you comment on this process, and if they are accomplishing anything of value or not?

RA I am Ra. No. Please ask one more full query at this working.

50.11   QUESTIONER Could you give me more information on the energy fields of the body as relates to the right and left brain and if this is somehow related to the pyramid shape as far as energy focusing goes? I am a little lost at exactly how to get into this line of questioning, so I will ask that question.

RA I am Ra. We are similarly at a loss at this line of answering. We may

---

[1]   It is possible that Ra intended to say "This connection enables the, shall we say, green-ray true color in time/space to manifest in your *space/time*," but it was never corrected as an error and thus is open for speculation.

say that the pyramid shape is but one which focuses the instreamings of energy for use by entities which may become aware of these instreamings. We may say further that the shape of your physical brain is not significant as a shape for concentrating instreamings of energy. Please ask more specifically, if you may, that information you seek.

50.12 **QUESTIONER** Each of us feel, in meditation, energy on the head in various places. Could you tell me what this is and what it signifies, and what the various places that we feel it signify?

RA I am Ra. Forgetting the pyramid will be of aid to you in the study of these experiences. The instreamings of energy are felt by the energy centers which need, and are prepared for, activation. Thus those who feel the stimulation at violet-ray level are getting just that. Those feeling it within the forehead between the brows are experiencing indigo ray and so forth. Those experiencing tinglings and visual images are having some blockage in the energy center being activated, and thus the electrical body spreads this energy out and its effect is diffused.

Those not truly sincerely requesting this energy may yet feel it if the entities are not well-trained in psychic defense. Those not desirous of experiencing these sensations and activations and changes, even upon the subconscious level, will not experience anything due to their abilities at defense and armoring against change.

50.13 **QUESTIONER** Right now I'm getting two feelings simultaneously. Is this normal to get two at once?

RA I am Ra. The most normal for the adept is the following: the indigo stimulation, activating that great gateway into healing, magical work, prayerful attention, and the radiance of being; and the stimulation of the violet ray which is the spiritual giving and taking from and to Creator, from Creator to Creator.

This is a desirable configuration.

Is there a brief query before we leave this instrument?

50.14 **QUESTIONER** Is there anything that we can do to make the instrument more comfortable or improve the contact?

RA I am Ra. You are conscientious and your alignments are careful. It would be well to take care that this instrument's neck is placed carefully upon its support.

I am Ra. I leave you, my friends, in the love and the light of the One Infinite Creator. Go forth, then, rejoicing in the power and in the peace of the One Infinite Creator. Adonai.

51.0   **RA** I am Ra. I greet you in the love and in the light of the One Infinite Creator. We communicate now.

51.1   **QUESTIONER** As we begin this session, Book III of *The Law Of One,* there are a couple of questions, one of fairly non-transient importance and one which I consider to be a bit transient, that I feel obligated to ask because of communication with others.

The first is just clearing up final points about harvest for our friend Leo Sprinkle. And I was wondering if there is a supervision over the harvest, and if so, why this supervision is necessary, and how it works since an entity's harvestability is the violet ray? Is it necessary for entities to supervise the harvest, or is it automatic? Could you answer this please?

RA I am Ra. In time of harvest there are always harvesters. The fruit is formed as it will be, but there is some supervision necessary to ensure that this bounty is placed as it should be, without the bruise or the blemish.

There are those of three levels watching over harvest.

The first level is planetary and that which may be called angelic. This type of guardian includes the mind/body/spirit complex totality or higher self of an entity and those inner plane entities which have been attracted to this entity through its inner seeking.

The second class of those who ward this process are those of the Confederation who have the honor/duty of standing in the small places at the edge of the steps of light/love so that those entities being harvested will not, no matter how confused or unable to make contact with their higher self, stumble and fall away for any reason other than the strength of the light. These Confederation entities catch those who stumble and set them aright so that they may continue into the light.

The third group watching over this process is that group you call the Guardians. This group is from the octave above our own and serves in this manner as light-bringers. These Guardians provide the precise emissions of light/love in exquisitely fastidious disseminations of discrimination so that the precise light/love vibration of each entity may be ascertained.

Thus the harvest is automatic in that those harvested will respond according to that which is unchangeable during harvest. That is the violet-ray emanation. However, these helpers are around to ensure a proper harvesting so that each entity may have the fullest opportunity to express its violet-ray selfhood.

51.2 **QUESTIONER** Thank you. This next question I feel to be a transient type of question; however, it has been asked me by one whom I have communicated with who has been intensely involved in the UFO portion of the phenomenon. If you deem it too transient or unimportant we'll skip it, but I have been asked how is it possible for the craft of, shall we say, the fourth-density to get here in that it seems that, as you approach the velocity of light, mass approaches infinite. We have talked about the increase of spiritual mass, and it was just a question as to how this transition from very distant planets is made in craft. And my question would be why craft would be necessary at all? This is not an important question.

RA I am Ra. You have asked several questions. We shall respond in turn.

Firstly, we agree that this material is transient.

Secondly, those, for the most part, coming from distant points, as you term them, do not need craft as you know them. The query itself requires understanding which you do not possess. We shall attempt to state what may be stated.

Firstly, there are a few third-density entities who have learned how to use craft to travel between star systems while experiencing the limitations you now understand. However, such entities have learned to use hydrogen in a way different from your understanding now. These entities still take quite long durations of time, as you measure it, to move about. However, these entities are able to use hypothermia to slow the physical and mental complex processes in order to withstand the duration of flight. Those such as are from Sirius are of this type.

There are two other types:

One is the type which, coming from fourth, fifth, or sixth density in your own galaxy, has access to a type of energy system which uses the speed of light as a slingshot, and thus arrives where it wishes without any perceptible time elapsed, in your view.

The other type of experience is that of fourth, fifth, and sixth densities of other galaxies, and some within your own galaxy, which have learned the necessary disciplines of personality to view the universe as one being and, therefore, are able to proceed from locus to locus by thought alone, materializing the necessary craft, if you will, to enclose the light body of the entity.

51.3 **QUESTIONER** I assume that that latter type is the type that we experience with most of our landings from the Orion group. Is this correct?

RA I am Ra. The Orion group is mixed between the penultimate and the latter groups.

51.4 **QUESTIONER** Why is a vehicle necessary for this transition? When you, as Ra, went to Egypt earlier you used bell-shaped craft, but you did this by thought. Can you tell me why you used a vehicle rather than just materializing the body?

RA I am Ra. The vehicle, or craft, is that thought-form upon which our concentration may function as motivator. We would not choose to use our mind/body/spirit complexes as the focus for such a working.

51.5 **QUESTIONER** Thank you. I would like to make a statement. I'm sure I'm somewhat off with this. It's a very difficult question to ask for me, because I don't really know what I'm talking about. But it seems to me— and you can tell me where I am going wrong with this statement—that we have seven bodies, each corresponding to one of the seven colors of the spectrum. And that energy that creates these seven bodies is a universal type of energy that streams into our planetary environment and comes in through seven energy centers that we have called chakras to develop and perfect these bodies.

And this is— Each of these bodies is in somehow related to the mental configuration that we have, and the perfection of each of these bodies and the total instreaming, you might say, of this energy is a function of this mental configuration. And through this mental configuration we may block, to some extent, the instreamings of energy that create each of these seven bodies. Could you comment on where I am wrong and correct me in this that I have stated?

RA I am Ra. Your statement is substantially correct. To use the term "mental configuration" is to oversimplify the manners of blockage of instreaming which occur in your density. The mind complex has a relationship to the spirit and body complexes which is not fixed. Thus blockages may occur betwixt spirit and mind, or body and mind, upon many different levels. We reiterate that each energy center has seven sub-colors, let us say for convenience. Thus spiritual/mental blockages combined with mental/bodily blockages may affect each of the energy centers in several differing ways. Thus you may see the subtle nature of the balancing and evolutionary process.

51.6 **QUESTIONER** I am unsure as to whether this will provide an avenue of questioning or not that will be fruitful. However, I will ask this question since it seemed to me that there is possibly a connection here.

On the back of the book, *Secrets of The Great Pyramid*, there are several reproductions of Egyptian drawings or works, some showing birds flying over horizontal entities. Could you tell me what this is and if it has any relationship to Ra?

RA I am Ra. These drawings of which you speak are some of many which distort the teaching of our perception of death as the gateway to further experience. The distortions concern those considerations of specific nature as to processes of the so-called "dead" mind/body/spirit complex. This may be termed, in your philosophy, the distortion of Gnosticism: that is, the belief that one may achieve knowledge and a proper position by means of carefully perceived and accentuated movements, concepts, and symbols.

In fact, the process of the physical death is as we have described before: one in which there is aid available, and the only need at death is the releasing of that entity from its body by those around it and the praising of the process by those who grieve. By these means may the mind/body/spirit which has experienced physical death be aided, not by the various perceptions of careful and repeated rituals.

51.7 **QUESTIONER** You spoke at an earlier time of rotational speeds of energy centers. Am I correct in assuming that this is a function of the blockage of the energy center, and the less blocked it is, the higher the speed of rotation, then, indicating greater energy instreaming?

RA I am Ra. You are partially correct. In the first three energy centers, a full unblocking of this energy will create speeds of rotation. As the entity develops the higher energy centers, however, these centers will then begin to express their nature by forming crystal structures. This is the higher, or more balanced, form of activation of energy centers as the space/time nature of this energy is transmuted to the time/space nature of regularization and balancing.

51.8   **QUESTIONER** What do you mean by crystal structures?

RA I am Ra. Each of the energy centers of the physical complex may be seen to have a distinctive crystalline structure in the more developed entity. Each will be somewhat different, just as in your world no two snowflakes are alike. However, each is regular.

The red energy center often is in the shape of the spoked wheel.

The orange energy center in the flower shape containing three petals.

The yellow center again in a rounded shape, many faceted, as a star.

The green energy center sometimes called the lotus-shape, the number of points of crystalline structure dependent upon the strength of this center.

The blue energy center capable of having perhaps one hundred facets and capable of great flashing brilliance.

The indigo center a more quiet center which has the basic triangular, or three-petaled, shape in many, although some adepts who have balanced the lower energies may create more faceted forms.

The violet energy center is the least variable and is sometimes described in your philosophy as thousand-petaled, as it is the sum of the mind/body/spirit complex distortion totality.

51.9   **QUESTIONER** Right now I feel a feeling at the indigo center. If this center were totally activated and not blocked at all, would I then feel nothing there?

RA I am Ra. This query, if answered, would infringe upon the Law of Confusion.

51.10   **QUESTIONER** Immediately after the death of the physical body, you have stated that the—I believe I'm correct in saying that—primary activated body is the indigo, and you stated that it is the form-maker. Why is this so? Can you answer that?

RA I am Ra. This will be the last full query of this session of working.

The indigo body may be seen to be an analog for intelligent energy. It is, in microcosm, the Logos. The intelligent energy of the mind/body/spirit complex totality draws its existence from intelligent infinity, or the Creator. This Creator is to be understood, both in macrocosm and microcosm, to have, as we have said, two natures: the unpotentiated infinity which is intelligent—this is all that there is.[1]

Free Will has potentiated both the Creator of us all and our selves as co-Creators with intelligent infinity which has will. This will may be drawn upon by the indigo, or form-making, body, and its wisdom used to then choose the appropriate locus and type of experience which this co-Creator, or sub-sub-Logos you call so carelessly a person, will take.

I am Ra. This is the time for any brief queries.

51.11 **QUESTIONER** Is there anything that we can do to make the instrument more comfortable or improve the contact?

RA I am Ra. All is well. You are conscientious. I leave you now, my brothers, in the love and in the light of the One Infinite Creator. Go forth, then, rejoicing in the power and the peace of the One Infinite Creator. Adonai.

---

[1] Ra says, "This Creator is to be understood, both in macrocosm and microcosm, to have, as we have said, two natures," indicating that a list of two items (presumably the potential and kinetic aspects of intelligent infinity) will follow. However, it is unclear whether the second paragraph constitutes the second item in that list.

Session 52

52.0 **RA** I am Ra. I greet you in the love and in the light of the One Infinite Creator. We communicate now.

52.1 **QUESTIONER** In the previous session you stated that "the other type of experience is the fourth, fifth, and sixth densities of other galaxies, and some within your own galaxy, which have learned necessary disciplines of personality to view the universe as one being, and, therefore, are able to proceed from locus to locus by thought alone, materializing the necessary craft."

I would like to ask you when you say that "fourth, fifth, and sixth densities of other galaxies, and some within your own galaxy," are you stating here that more of the entities in other galaxies have developed the abilities of personality than have in this galaxy for this type of, shall I say, travel? I am using the term galaxy with respect to the lenticular shape of 250 billion stars.

RA I am Ra. We have once again used a meaning for this term, galaxy, that does not lie within your vocabulary at this time, if you will call it so. We referred to your star system.

It is incorrect to assume that other star systems are more able to manipulate the dimensions than your own. It is merely that there are many other systems besides your own.

52.2 **QUESTIONER** Thank you. I think that possibly I am on an important point here because it seems to me that the great work in evolution is the discipline of personality, and it seems that we have two types of moving around the universe, one stemming from disciplines of personality, and the other stemming from what you call the slingshot effect. I won't even get into the sub-light speeds because I don't consider that too important. And I only consider this material important with respect to the fact that we are investigating discipline of the personality.

Does the use of the slingshot effect for travel—is that a what you might call an intellectual, or a left brain, type of involvement of understanding rather than a right brain type?

RA I am Ra. Your perception on this point is extensive. You penetrate the outer teaching. We prefer not to utilize the terminology of right and left brain due to the inaccuracies of this terminology. Some functions are repetitive or redundant in both lobes, and further, to some entities the functions of the right and left are reversed. However, the heart of the query is worth some consideration.

The technology of which you, as a social complex, are so enamored at this time is but the birthing of the manipulation of the intelligent energy of the sub-Logos which, when carried much further, may evolve into technology capable of using the gravitic effects of which we spoke. We note that this term is not accurate, but there is no closer term.

Therefore, the use of technology to manipulate that outside the self is far, far less of an aid to personal evolution than the disciplines of the mind/body/spirit complex resulting in the whole knowledge of the self in the microcosm and macrocosm.

To the disciplined entity, all things are open and free. The discipline which opens the universes opens also the gateways to evolution. The difference is that of choosing either to hitchhike to a place where beauty may be seen, or to walk, step by step, independent and free in this independence to praise the strength to walk, and the opportunity for the awareness of beauty.

The hitchhiker, instead, is distracted by conversation and the vagaries of the road and, dependent upon the whims of others, is concerned to make the appointment in time. The hitchhiker sees the same beauty, but has not prepared itself for the establishment, in the roots of mind, of the experience.

52.3   **QUESTIONER** I would ask this question in order to understand the mental disciplines and how they evolve. Do fourth-, fifth-, and sixth-density positive, or service-to-others orientated, social memory complexes use both the slingshot and the personality discipline type of effect for travel, or do they use only one?

RA I am Ra. The positively oriented social memory complex will be attempting to learn the disciplines of mind, body, and spirit. However, there are some which, having the technology available to use intelligent energy forces to accomplish travel, do so while learning the more appropriate disciplines.

52.4 **QUESTIONER** Then I am assuming in the positively oriented social memory complexes that a much higher percentage of them use the personality disciplines for this travel. Is this correct?

RA I am Ra. This is correct. As positive fifth density moves into sixth there are virtually no entities which any longer use outer technology for travel or communication.

52.5 **QUESTIONER** Could you give me the same information on the negatively oriented social memory complexes as to the ratios, how they use the slingshot or other effect, personality disciplines?

RA I am Ra. The fourth-density negative uses the slingshot gravitic light effect, perhaps 80% of its membership being unable to master the disciplines necessary for alternate methods of travel. In fifth-density negative approximately 50% at some point gain the necessary discipline to use thought to accomplish travel. As the sixth density approaches, the negative orientation is thrown into confusion and little travel is attempted. What travel is done is perhaps 73% of light/thought.

52.6 **QUESTIONER** Is there any difference then, at, say, close to the end of fifth density in the disciplines of personality required for this travel between positive and negative orientation, higher fifth density?

RA I am Ra. There are patent differences between the polarities, but no difference whatsoever in the completion of the knowledge of the self necessary to accomplish this discipline.

52.7 **QUESTIONER** Am I correct, then, in assuming that discipline of the personality, knowledge of self, and control, shall I say, in strengthening of the will would be what any fifth-density entity would see as those things of importance?

RA I am Ra. In actuality these things are of importance in third through early seventh densities. The only correction in nuance that we would make is your use of the word, control. It is paramount that it be understood that it is not desirable or helpful to the growth of the understanding, may we say, of an entity by itself to control thought processes or impulses except where they may result in actions not consonant with the Law of One.

Control may seem to be a shortcut to discipline, peace, and illumination. However, this very control potentiates and necessitates the further incarnative experience in order to balance this control, or repression, of that self which is perfect.

Instead, we appreciate and recommend the use of your second verb in regard to the use of the will. Acceptance of self, forgiveness of self, and the direction of the will: this is the path towards the disciplined personality. Your faculty of will is that which is powerful within you as co-Creator. You cannot ascribe to this faculty too much importance. Thus it must be carefully used and directed in service to others for those upon the positively oriented path.

There is great danger in the use of the will as the personality becomes stronger, for it may be used even subconsciously in ways reducing the polarity of the entity.

52.8 **QUESTIONER** I sense, possibly, a connection between what you just said and why so many wanderers have selected harvest time on this planet to incarnate. Am I correct? This is a vague notion.

RA I am Ra. It is correct that, in the chance to remember that which has been lost in the forgetting, there is a nimiety of opportunity for positive polarization.[1] We believe this is the specific thrust of your query. Please ask further if it is not.

52.9 **QUESTIONER** Well, I would just include the question as to why time of harvest is selected by so many wanderers as time for incarnation?

RA I am Ra. There are several reasons for incarnation during harvest. They may be divided by the terms self and other-self.

The overriding reason for the offering of these Brothers and Sisters of Sorrow in incarnative states is the possibility of aiding other-selves by the lightening of the planetary-consciousness distortions and the probability of offering catalyst to other-selves which will increase the harvest.

There are two other reasons for choosing this service which have to do with the self.

---

[1] In this context, *nimiety* may be defined as "an overabundance or redundancy."

The wanderer, if it remembers and dedicates itself to service, will polarize much more rapidly than is possible in the far more etiolated realms of higher-density catalyst. [2]

The final reason is within the mind/body/spirit totality or the social memory complex totality which may judge that an entity, or members of a societal entity, can make use of third-density catalyst to recapitulate a learning/teaching which is adjudged to be less than perfectly balanced. This especially applies to those entering into and proceeding through sixth density wherein the balance between compassion and wisdom is perfected.

52.10 **QUESTIONER** Thank you. Just as something that I am a little inquisitive about, not much importance, but I'd like to make a statement I intuitively see, which may be wrong.

You were speaking of the slingshot effect, and that term has puzzled me.

The only thing I can see is that you must put energy into the craft until it approaches the velocity of light, and this, of course, requires more and more and more energy. The time dilation occurs, and it seems to me that it would be possible to, by moving at 90° to the direction of travel, somehow change this stored energy in its application of direction, or sense, so that you move out of space/time into time/space with a 90° deflection. Then the energy would be taken out in time/space, and you would re-enter space/time at the end of this energy reversal. Am I in any way correct on this?

RA I am Ra. You are quite correct as far as your language may take you and, due to your training, more able than we to express the concept. Our only correction, if you will, would be to suggest that the 90° of which you speak are an angle which may best be understood as a portion of a tesseract.[3]

52.11 **QUESTIONER** Thank you. Just a little point that was bothering me of no real importance.

---

[2] In this context, *etiolated* may be defined as "weakened; no longer at full strength; made pale or thin."

[3] In speculative mathematics a tesseract is the fourth-dimensional analog to the cube. A tesseract is to a cube as a cube is to a square.

Well, is there, then—from the point of view of an individual who wishes to follow the service-to-others path from our present position in third density—is there anything of importance other than disciplines of personality, knowledge of self, and strengthening of will?

RA I am Ra. This is technique. This is not the heart. Let us examine the heart of evolution.

Let us remember that we are all one. This is the great learning/teaching. In this unity lies love. This is a great learn/teaching. In this unity lies light. This is the fundamental teaching of all planes of existence in materialization. Unity, love, light, and joy: this is the heart of evolution of the spirit.

The second-ranking lessons are learn/taught in meditation and in service. At some point the mind/body/spirit complex is so smoothly activated and balanced by these central thoughts or distortions that the techniques you have mentioned become quite significant. However, the universe, its mystery unbroken, is one. Always begin and end in the Creator, not in technique.

52.12 **QUESTIONER** Thank you. In mentioning, in the previous session, the harvest, you mentioned the light-bringers from the octave. Am I to understand that those who provide the light for the gradation of graduation are of an octave above the one we experience? Could you tell me more about these light-bringers, who they are, etc.?

RA I am Ra. This will be the last full query of this working.

This octave density of which we have spoken is both omega and alpha, the spiritual mass of the infinite universes becoming one Central Sun, or Creator, once again. Then is born a new universe, a new infinity, a new Logos which incorporates all that the Creator has experienced of Itself. In this new octave there are also those who wander. We know very little across the boundary of octave except that these beings come to aid our octave in its Logos completion.

Is there any brief query which you have at this time?

52.13 **QUESTIONER** Only is there anything that we can do to make the instrument more comfortable or to improve the contact?

RA I am Ra. This instrument has some distortion in the area of the lungs which has been well compensated for by the position of the physical complex.

All is well.

We leave you, my friends, in the love and in the light of the One Infinite Creator. Go forth, therefore, rejoicing in the power and in the peace of the One Infinite Creator. Adonai.

SESSION 53

53.0 **RA** I am Ra. I greet you in the love and in the light of the One Infinite Creator. We communicate now.

53.1 **QUESTIONER** I would first like to know the instrument's condition and ask two questions for her. She would like to know if she can do one exercise of one hour a day, and is the pain she feels prior to a session due to an Orion attack?

RA I am Ra. The instrument's condition is as previously stated.

In answer to the question of exercise, now that the intensive period is over, this instrument may, if it chooses, exercise one period rather than two. In scanning this instrument's physical-complex distortions we find the current period of exercise at the limit of this instrument's strength. This is well in the long run due to a cumulative building up of the vital energies. In the short run it is wearying to this entity. Thus we suggest the entity be aware of our previous admonitions regarding other aids to appropriate bodily distortions.

In answer to the second query, we may say that the physical complex difficulties prior to contact with our social memory complex are due to the action of the subconscious will of the instrument. This will is extremely strong and requires the mind/body/spirit complex to reserve all available physical and vital energies for the contact. Thus the discomforts are experienced due to the dramatic distortion towards physical weakness while this energy is diverted. The entity is, it may be noted, also under psychic attack, and this intensifies pre-existing conditions and is responsible for the cramping and the dizziness as well as mind-complex distortions.

53.2 **QUESTIONER** Thank you. I would like to know if [*name*] may attend one of these sessions in the very near future?

RA I am Ra. The mind/body/spirit complex, [*name*], belongs with this group in the spirit and is welcome. You may request that special meditative periods be set aside until the entity sits with this working. We might suggest that a photograph of the one known as James Allen[1] be sent to this entity with his writing upon it indicating love and light. This held while meditating will bring the entity into peaceful harmony with each of you so that there be no extraneous waste of energy while greetings are exchanged between two entities, both of whom have a distortion towards solitude and shyness, as you would call it. The same might be done with a photograph of the entity, [name], for the one known as James Allen.

53.3 **QUESTIONER** Thank you. During my trip to Laramie certain things became apparent to me with respect to disseminating the first book of *The Law of One* to those who have had experiences with UFOs and other wanderers, and I will have to ask some questions now that I may have to include in Book I to eliminate a misunderstanding that I am perceiving as a possibility in Book I.[2] Therefore, these questions, although for the most part transient, are aimed at eliminating certain distortions of understanding with respect to the material in Book I. I hope that I am making a correct approach here. You may not be able to answer some, but that's all right. We'll just go on to some others then if you can't answer the ones I ask.

First I will ask if you could tell me the affiliation of the entities that contacted Betty Andreasson.

RA I am Ra. This query is marginal. We will make the concession towards information with some loss of polarity due to free will being abridged. We request that questions of this nature be kept to a minimum.

The entities in this and some other vividly remembered cases are those who, feeling the need to plant Confederation imagery in such a way as not to abrogate free will, use the symbols of death, resurrection, love, and peace as a means of creating, upon the thought level, the time/space illusion of a systematic train of events which give the message of love and hope. This type of contact is chosen by careful consideration of

---

[1] Also known as Jim McCarty.

[2] Don included the information from 53.6–17 in session 26 in the original publications to give readers a broader view of "close encounters." These two sessions were originally divided between Books I and III, but as they are now contained in the same volume, a footnote has simply been added to session 26 directing readers to this session in order to address Don's concern about creating a wrong impression regarding this phenomenon.

Confederation members which are contacting an entity of like-home vibration, if you will. This project then goes before the Council of Saturn and, if approved, is completed. The characteristics of this type of contact include the non-painful nature of thoughts experienced and the message content which speaks not of doom, but of the new dawning age.

53.4   **QUESTIONER** It is not necessary that I include the information that you just gave in the book to accomplish my purpose. In order to save your polarity, shall I say, I can keep that as private material if you wish. Do you wish for me to keep it unpublished?

RA I am Ra. That which we offer you is freely given and subject only to your discretion.

53.5   **QUESTIONER** I thought you would say that. In that case can you tell me anything of the "blue book" mentioned by Betty Andreasson in that case?

RA I am Ra. No.

53.6   **QUESTIONER** Thank you. Can you tell me of various techniques used by the service-to-others, or positively oriented, Confederation contacts with the people of this planet, the various forms of, and techniques of, them making contact?

RA I am Ra. We could.

53.7   **QUESTIONER** Would you do this please?

RA I am Ra. The most efficient mode of contact is that which you experience at this space/time. The infringement upon free will is greatly undesired. Therefore, those entities which are wanderers upon your plane of illusion will be the only subjects for the thought projections which make up the so-called "close encounters" and meetings between positively oriented social memory complexes and wanderers.

53.8   **QUESTIONER** Could you give me an example of one of these meetings between a wanderer and a social memory complex as to what the wanderer would experience?

RA I am Ra. One such example of which you are familiar is that of the one known as Morris.[3] In this case the previous contact which other

---

3   This refers to Case #1 in *Secrets of the UFO*, by Don Elkins with Carla L. Rueckert, Louisville, KY., L/L Research, 1976, p. 10–11.

entities in this entity's circle of friends experienced was negatively oriented. However, you will recall that the entity, Morris, was impervious to this contact and could not see, with the physical optical apparatus, this contact.

However, the inner voice alerted the one known as Morris to go by itself to another place, and there an entity, with the thought-form shape and appearance of the other contact, appeared and gazed at this entity, thus awakening in it the desire to seek the truth of this occurrence and of the experiences of its incarnation in general.

The feeling of being awakened or activated is the goal of this type of contact. The duration and imagery used varies depending upon the subconscious expectations of the wanderer which is experiencing this opportunity for activation.

53.9 **QUESTIONER** In a "close encounter" by a Confederation type of craft I assume that this "close encounter" is with a thought-form type of craft. Do wanderers within the past few years have "close encounters" with landed thought-form type of craft?

RA I am Ra. This has occurred, although it is much less common than the Orion type of so-called "close encounter." We may note that in a universe of unending unity the concept of a "close encounter" is humorous, for are not all encounters of a nature of self with self? Therefore, how can any encounter be less than very, very close?

53.10 **QUESTIONER** Well, talking about this type of encounter of self to self, do any wanderers of a positive polarization ever encounter a so-called "close encounter" with the Orion, or negatively oriented, polarization?

RA I am Ra. This is correct. The—

53.11 **QUESTIONER** [*Interrupting*] Why does this occur?

RA I am Ra. When it occurs it is quite rare and occurs either due to the Orion entities' lack of perception of the depth of positivity to be encountered or due to the Orion entities' desire to, shall we say, attempt to remove this positivity from this plane of existence. Orion tactics normally are those which choose the simple distortions of mind which indicate less mental and spiritual complex activity.

53.12 **QUESTIONER** I have become aware of a very large variation in contact with individuals. The Confederation, I am assuming, uses a form of contact to awaken, as you say, wanderers, and could you give me general examples of the methods used by the Confederation to awaken, or partially awaken, the wanderers they are contacting?

RA I am Ra. The methods used to awaken wanderers are varied. The center of each approach is the entrance into the conscious and subconscious in such a way as to avoid causing fear and to maximize the potential for an understandable subjective experience which has meaning for the entity. Many such occur in sleep, others in the midst of many activities during the waking hours. The approach is flexible and does not necessarily include the "close encounter" syndrome as you are aware.

53.13 **QUESTIONER** What about the physical examination syndrome. How does that relate to wanderers and to Confederation and Orion contacts?

RA I am Ra. The subconscious expectations of entities cause the nature and detail of thought-form experience offered by Confederation thought-form entities. Thus if a wanderer expects a physical examination, it will, perforce, be experienced with as little distortion towards alarm or discomfort as is allowable by the nature of the expectations of the subconscious distortions of the wanderer.

53.14 **QUESTIONER** Well, are both those who are taken on Confederation and Orion craft then experiencing a seeming physical examination?

RA I am Ra. Your query indicates incorrect thinking. The Orion group uses the physical examination as a means of terrifying the individual and causing it to feel the feelings of an advanced second-density being such as a laboratory animal. The sexual experiences of some are a sub-type of this experience. The intent is to demonstrate the control of the Orion entities over the Terran inhabitant.

The thought-form experiences are subjective and, for the most part, do not occur in this density.

53.15 **QUESTIONER** Then both Confederation and Orion contacts are being made, and "close encounters" are of a dual nature as I understand it. They can either be of the Confederation or Orion type of contact. Is this correct?

RA I am Ra. This is correct, although the preponderance of contacts is Orion-oriented.

53.16 **QUESTIONER** Well, we have a large spectrum of entities on Earth with respect to harvestability, both positively oriented and negatively oriented. Would the Orion target in on the ends of this spectrum, both positive and negatively oriented, for contact . . . for Earth entities, I mean?

RA I am Ra. This query is somewhat difficult to accurately answer. However, we shall attempt to do so.

The most typical approach of Orion entities is to choose what you might call the weaker-minded entity that it might suggest a greater amount of Orion philosophy to be disseminated.

Some few Orion entities are called by more highly polarized negative entities of your space/time nexus. In this case they share information just as we are now doing. However, this is a risk for the Orion entities due to the frequency with which the harvestable negative planetary entities then attempt to bid and order the Orion contact, just as these entities bid planetary negative contacts. The resulting struggle for mastery, if lost, is damaging to the polarity of the Orion group.

Similarly, a mistaken Orion contact with highly polarized positive entities can wreak havoc with Orion troops unless these Crusaders are able to depolarize the entity mistakenly contacted. This occurrence is almost unheard of. Therefore, the Orion group prefers to make physical contact only with the weaker-minded entity.

53.17 **QUESTIONER** Then, in general, I could say that if an individual has a "close encounter" with a UFO or any other type of experience that seems to be UFO-related, he must look to the heart of the encounter and the effect upon him to determine whether it was Orion or Confederation contact. Is this correct?

RA I am Ra. This is correct. If there is fear and doom, the contact was quite likely of a negative nature. If the result is hope, friendly feelings, and the awakening of a positive feeling of purposeful service to others, the marks of Confederation contact are evident.

53.18 **QUESTIONER** Thank you. I did not wish to create the wrong impression with the material that we were including in Book I, and find it necessary to add some of this material. I know that it's transient, but it, I believe, is necessary for a full understanding or, shall I say, a correct approach to the material.

I'll ask a few questions here. If you do not care to answer them we'll skip them. I would like to ask, however, if you could tell me what, for the most part—or the major portion of Confederation entities—what they look like?

RA I am Ra. The fourth-density Confederation entity looks variously depending upon the, shall we say, derivation of its physical vehicle.

53.19 **QUESTIONER** Do some of them look just like us? Could they pass for Earth people?

RA I am Ra. Those of this nature are most often fifth-density.

53.20 **QUESTIONER** I assume that the same answer would apply to the Orion group. Is this correct? As far as fourth and fifth density goes?

RA I am Ra. This is correct.

53.21 **QUESTIONER** Can you tell me why [*name*] had so many silver flecks on her?

RA I am Ra. This is infringement. No.

53.22 **QUESTIONER** Thank you. Could you tell me why I got sick during Carl Raschke's talk?

RA I am Ra. We scan your thoughts. They are correct and, therefore, we do not infringe by confirming them. The space/time of your allotted speaking was drawing near, and you came under Orion attack due to the great desire of some positively oriented entities to become aware of the Law of One. This may be expected, especially when you are not in a group lending strength to each other.

53.23 **QUESTIONER** Thank you. Can you comment on my, and the instrument, if she approves, so-called ball of lightning experience as a child?[4]

---

4   Carla wrote: "When I was about one year old, I was sleeping in a cradle that was placed at some distance from the open window. There was a storm going on. Mom came in to close the window. She saw a ball of lightning come into the room and circle around the cradle one-and-a-half times and then go out again. When I told

RA I am Ra. This will be the last query of this working.

You were being visited by your people to be wished well.

Is there any other query of a brief nature we may answer?

53.24 **QUESTIONER** No. I apologize for asking many transient questions during this session. I hope that we did not cause any problem for you, especially with respect to loss of polarity and that one question, but I felt it necessary to include some of this material so that those wanderers and others reading the first book of *The Law of One* would not get the wrong impression with respect to their experiences in contacts. I am sorry for any problems that I might have caused.

I will just ask if there is anything that we can do to improve the contact or aid the instrument?

RA I am Ra. The instrument is well. Please guard your alignments carefully. We leave you now, my friends, in the love and in the light of the One Infinite Creator. Go forth, therefore, rejoicing in the power and the peace of the Infinite Creator. Adonai.

---

the story to Don, he said that the same thing had happened to him when he was an infant. His mother didn't elaborate on it, so that's all he knew."

SESSION 54

54.0   **RA** I am Ra. I greet you in the love and in the light of the One Infinite Creator. We communicate now.

54.1   **QUESTIONER** First, I would like to ask of the instrument's condition.

RA I am Ra. It is as previously stated.

54.2   **QUESTIONER** I have a question from Jim about an experience he had when he first moved to his land in which he was told, "The key to your survival comes indirect, through nervousness." The entity was Angelica. Can you give him information with respect to this?

RA I am Ra. Yes.

54.3   **QUESTIONER** Would you please do that?

RA I am Ra. As we have noted, each mind/body/spirit complex has several guides available to it.[1] The persona of two of these guides is the polarity of male and female. The third is androgynous and represents a more unified conceptualization faculty.

The guide speaking as sound vibration complex, Angelica, was the female polarized persona. The message may not be fully explicated due to the Law of Confusion. We may suggest that in order to progress, a state of some dissatisfaction will be present, thus giving the entity the stimulus for further seeking. This dissatisfaction, nervousness, or angst, if you will, is not of itself useful. Thus its use is indirect.

54.4   **QUESTIONER** Thank you. I would like to trace the energy that I assume comes from the Logos. I'm going to make a statement and let you correct me on the statement and expand on my concept.

From the Logos comes all frequencies of radiation of light. These frequencies of radiation make up all of the densities of experience that are created by that Logos. I am assuming that the planetary system of our sun, in all of its densities, is the total of the experience created by our sun as a Logos. Is this correct?

---

[1]   Noted in 12.14 and 18.8–9, and 36.10.

RA I am Ra. This is correct.

54.5 **QUESTIONER** Now, I am assuming that the different frequencies are separated, as we have said, into the seven colors; that each of these colors may be the basic frequency for a sub-Logos of our sun-Logos; and that a sub-Logos or, shall we say, an individual may activate any one of these basic frequency or colors and use the body that is generated from the activation of that frequency or color. Is this correct?

RA I am Ra. If we grasp your query correctly, this is not correct in that the sub-sub-Logos resides not in dimensionalities but only in co-Creators, or mind/body/spirit complexes.

54.6 **QUESTIONER** What I meant was that a mind/body/spirit complex then can have a body activated that is one of these seven rays. Is this correct?

RA I am Ra. This is correct in the same sense as it is correct to state that any one may play a complex instrument which develops an euphonious harmonic vibration complex such as your piano, and can play this so well that it might offer concerts to the public, as you would say.

In other words, although it is true that each true-color vehicle is available, potentially, there is skill and discipline needed in order to avail the self of the more advanced or lighter vehicles.

54.7 **QUESTIONER** Now, I have made these statements just to get to the basic question I wish to ask. It is a difficult question to ask.

We have, coming from the sub-Logos we call our sun, intelligent energy, which then forms—and we'll take as an example a single sub-sub-logos which is a mind/body/spirit complex. This intelligent energy is somehow modulated or distorted, so that it ends up as a mind/body/spirit complex with certain distortions of personality that it is necessary for the mind/body/spirit complex, or the mental portion of that complex, to undistort in order to conform once more precisely with the original intelligent energy.

First, I want to know if my statement on that is correct. And, secondly, I want to know why this is the way that it is; if there is any answer other than the first distortion of the Law of One for this?

RA I am Ra. This statement is substantially correct. If you will penetrate the nature of the First Distortion in its application of self knowing self, you may begin to distinguish the hallmark of an infinite creator: variety. Were there no potentials for misunderstanding and, therefore, understanding, there would be no experience.

54.8   **QUESTIONER** OK. Once a mind/body/spirit complex becomes aware of this process, it then decides that in order to have the abilities, the full abilities of the creation and the Creator (of which it is a small part yet at the same time, all of), in order to have the abilities that go with the entire creation, it is necessary to reunite its thinking or reharmonize its thinking with the Original Creative Thought in precise vibration, or frequency of vibration I will say. In order to do this it is necessary to discipline the personality so that it precisely conforms to the Original Thought, or Original Vibration, and this is broken into seven areas of discipline, each corresponding to one of the colors of the spectrum. Is this correct?

RA I am Ra. This statement, though correct, bears great potential for being misunderstood. The precision with which each energy center matches the Original Thought lies not in the systematic placement of each energy nexus, but rather in the fluid and plastic placement of the balanced blending of these energy centers in such a way that intelligent energy is able to channel itself with minimal distortion.

The mind/body/spirit complex is not a machine. It is rather what you might call a tone poem.

54.9   **QUESTIONER** Do all mind/body/spirit complexes in the entire creation have the seven energy centers once they have reached full development or development to the point where they can have seven energy centers?

RA I am Ra. These energy centers are in potential in macrocosm from the beginning of creation by the Logos. Coming out of timelessness, all is prepared. This is so of the infinite creation.

54.10 **QUESTIONER** Then I will assume that the Creator, in Its intelligent appraisal of a way of knowing Itself, created the concept of the seven areas of knowing. Is this correct?

RA I am Ra. This is partially incorrect. The Logos creates Light. The nature of this Light thus creates the nature of the catalytic and energetic levels of experience in the creation. Thus it is that the highest of all honor/duties, that given to those of the next octave, is the supervision of

Light in its manifestations during the experiential times, if you will, of your cycles.

54.11 **QUESTIONER** I will make another statement. The mind/body/spirit complex may choose, because of the First Distortion, a mental configuration that is sufficiently displaced from the configuration of the intelligent energy in a particular frequency or color of instreaming energy so as to block a portion of instreaming energy in that particular frequency or color. Is this statement correct?

RA I am Ra. Yes.

54.12 **QUESTIONER** This question may be no good, but I'll ask it. Can you give me an idea of the maximum percentage of this energy it's possible to block in any one color, or does that make any sense?

RA I am Ra. There may be, in an entity's pattern of instreaming energy, a complete blockage in any energy, or color, or combination of energies, or colors.

54.13 **QUESTIONER** OK. Then I assume that the First Distortion is the, shall I say, motivator or what allows this blockage. Is this correct?

RA I am Ra. We wish no quibbling but prefer to avoid the use of terms such as the verb, to allow. Free will does not allow, nor would predetermination disallow, experiential distortions. Rather the Law of Confusion offers a free reach for the energies of each mind/body/spirit complex.

The verb, to allow, would be considered pejorative in that it suggests a polarity between right and wrong, or allowed and not allowed.

This may seem a minuscule point. However, to our best way of thinking it bears some weight.

54.14 **QUESTIONER** Thank you. It bears weight to my way of thinking also, and I appreciate what you have told me.

Now, I would like to then consider the origin of catalyst in— First we have the condition of mind/body/spirit complex which, as a function of the First Distortion, has reached a condition of blockage, or partial blockage, of one or more energy centers. I will assume that catalyst is necessary only if there is at least partial blockage of one energy center. Is this correct?

RA I am Ra. No.

54.15 **QUESTIONER** Could you tell me why?

RA I am Ra. While it is a primary priority to activate or unblock each energy center, it is also a primary priority at that point to begin to refine the balances between the energies so that each tone of the chord of total vibratory beingness resonates in clarity, tune, and harmony with each other energy.

This balancing, tuning, and harmonizing of the self is most central to the more advanced or adept mind/body/spirit complex. Each energy may be activated without the beauty that is possible through the disciplines and appreciations of personal energies, or what you might call the deeper personality, or soul identity.

54.16 **QUESTIONER** Let me make an analogy that I have just thought of. A seven-stringed musical instrument may be played by deflecting each string a full deflection and releasing it and getting a note. Or—once the strings are capable of being deflected through their full deflection (producing a note)—instead of producing the notes this way, taking the individual creative personality and deflecting each the proper amount in proper sequence to produce the music. Is this correct?

RA I am Ra. This is correct. In the balanced individual the energies lie waiting for the hand of the Creator to pluck harmony.

54.17 **QUESTIONER** I would like then to trace the evolution of catalyst upon the mind/body/spirit complexes and how it comes into use and is fully used to create this tuning. I assume that the sub-Logos that formed our tiny part of the creation, using the intelligence of the Logos of which it is a part, provides, shall I say, the base catalyst that will act upon mind/body complexes and mind/body/spirit complexes before they reach the state of development where they can begin to program their own catalyst. Is this correct?

RA I am Ra. This is partially correct. The sub-Logos offers the catalyst at the lower levels of energy, the first triad; these have to do with the survival of the physical complex. The higher centers gain catalyst from the biases of the mind/body/spirit complex itself in response to all random and directed experiences.

Thus the less developed entity will perceive the catalyst about it in terms of survival of the physical complex, with the distortions which are preferred. The more conscious entity, being conscious of the catalytic process, will begin to transform the catalyst offered by the sub-Logos into catalyst which may act upon the higher energy nexi.

Thus the sub-Logos can offer only a basic skeleton, shall we say, of catalyst. The muscles and flesh—having to do with the, shall we say, survival of wisdom, love, compassion, and service—are brought about by the action of the mind/body/spirit complex on basic catalyst so as to create a more complex catalyst which may, in turn, be used to form distortions within these higher energy centers.

The more advanced the entity, the more tenuous the connection between the sub-Logos and the perceived catalyst until, finally, all catalyst is chosen, generated, and manufactured by the self, for the self.

54.18 **QUESTIONER** Which entities incarnate at this time on this planet would be of that category, manufacturing all of their catalyst?

RA I am Ra. We find your query indeterminate but can respond that the number of those which have mastered outer catalyst completely is quite small.

Most of those harvestable at this space/time nexus have partial control over the outer illusion and are using the outer catalyst to work upon some bias which is not yet in balance.

54.19 **QUESTIONER** In the case of service-to-self polarization, what type of catalyst would entities following this path program when they reach the level of programming their own catalyst?

RA I am Ra. The negatively oriented entity will program for maximal separation from, and control over, all those things and conscious entities which it perceives as being other than the self.

54.20 **QUESTIONER** I meant— I understand how a positively oriented entity would program catalyst such as that would result in physical pain if it . . . I'm assuming that an entity could program something that would give it the experience of physical pain if it did not follow the path that it had selected. Is this correct?

RA I am Ra. Please restate query.

54.21 QUESTIONER A positively oriented entity may select a certain narrow path of thinking and activities during an incarnation and program conditions that would create physical pain if this path were not followed. Is this correct?

RA I am Ra. This is correct.

54.22 QUESTIONER Would a negatively oriented entity do anything like this? Could you give me an example?

RA I am Ra. A negatively oriented individual mind/body/spirit complex will ordinarily program for wealth, ease of existence, and the utmost opportunity for power. Thus many negative entities burst with the physical-complex distortion you call health.

However, a negatively oriented entity may choose a painful condition in order to improve the distortion toward the so-called negative emotive mentations such as anger, hatred, and frustration. Such an entity may use an entire incarnative experience honing a blunt edge of hatred, or anger, so that it may polarize more towards the negative, or separated, pole.

54.23 QUESTIONER Now, it seems that we have prior to incarnation, in any incarnation, as an entity becomes more aware of the process of evolution and has selected a path, whether it be positive or negative, at some point the entity becomes aware of what it wants to do with respect to unblocking and balancing energy centers. At that point it is able to program for the life experience those catalytic experiences that will aid it in its process of unblocking and balancing. Is that correct?

RA I am Ra. That is correct.

54.24 QUESTIONER The purpose then, seen from previous-to-incarnation, of what we call the incarnate physical state seems to be wholly, or almost wholly, that of experiencing at that point the programmed catalyst and then evolving as a function of that catalyst. Is that correct?

RA I am Ra. We shall restate for clarity. The purpose of incarnative existence is evolution of mind, body, and spirit. In order to do this it is not strictly necessary to have catalyst. However, without catalyst the desire to evolve and the faith in the process do not normally manifest, and thus evolution occurs not.

Therefore, catalyst is programmed, and the program is designed for the mind/body/spirit complex for its unique requirements. Thus it is desirable that a mind/body/spirit complex be aware of and hearken to the voice of its experiential catalyst, gleaning from it that which it incarnated to glean.

54.25 **QUESTIONER** Then it seems that those on the positive path, as opposed to those on the negative path, would have precisely the reciprocal objective in the first three rays; red, orange, and yellow. Each path would be attempting to utilize the rays in precisely opposite manners. Is this correct?

RA I am Ra. It is partially, and even substantially, correct. There is an energy in each of the centers needed to keep the mind/body/spirit complex, which is the vehicle for experience, in correct conformation and composition. Both negative and positive entities do well to reserve this small portion of each center for the maintenance of the integrity of the mind/body/spirit complex. After this point, however, it is correct that the negative will use the three lower centers for separation from and control over others—by sexual means, by personal assertion, and by action in your societies.

Contrary-wise, the positively oriented entity will be transmuting strong red-ray sexual energy into green-ray energy transfers and radiation in blue and indigo, and will be similarly transmuting selfhood and place in society into energy transfer situations in which the entity may merge with and serve others and then, finally, radiate unto others without expecting any transfer in return.

54.26 **QUESTIONER** Can you describe the energy that enters any of these energy centers? Can you describe its path from its origin, its form, and its effect? I don't know if this is possible, but can you do that?

RA I am Ra. This is partially possible.

54.27 **QUESTIONER** Would you please do that?

RA The origin of all energy is the action of Free Will upon Love. The nature of all energy is Light. The means of its ingress into the mind/body/spirit complex is duple.

Firstly, there is the inner light which is Polaris of the self, the guiding star. This is the birthright and true nature of all entities. This energy dwells within.

The second point of ingress is the polar opposite of the North Star, shall we say, and may be seen, if you wish to use the physical body as an analog for the magnetic field, as coming through the feet from the earth and through the lower point of the spine.

This point of ingress of the universal light energy is undifferentiated until it begins its filtering process through the energy centers. The requirements of each center, and the efficiency with which the individual has learned to tap into the inner light, determine the nature of the use made by the entity of these instreamings.

54.28 **QUESTIONER** Does experiential catalyst follow the same path? This may be a dumb question.

RA I am Ra. This is not a pointless question, for catalyst and the requirements, or distortions, of the energy centers are two concepts linked as tightly as two strands of rope.

54.29 **QUESTIONER** Then, you had mentioned in an earlier session that the experiential catalyst was first experienced by the south pole and appraised with its respect to survival, etc. That's why I asked the question, and I— Can you expand on that concept?

RA I am Ra. We have addressed the filtering process by which in-coming energies are pulled upwards according to the distortions of each energy center and the strength of will, or desire, emanating from the awareness of inner light. If we may be more specific, please query with specificity.[2]

54.30 **QUESTIONER** I'll make this statement which may be somewhat distorted and let you correct it. We have, coming through the feet and base of the spine, the total energy that the mind/body/spirit complex will receive in the way of what we call light. Each energy center as it is met filters out and uses a portion of this energy, red through violet. Is this correct?

---

2   Addressed in 49.5–6 and 54.27.

RA I am Ra. This is largely correct. The exceptions are as follows: The energy ingress ends with indigo. The violet ray is a thermometer, or indicator, of the whole.

54.31 **QUESTIONER** As this energy is absorbed by the energy centers, at some point it is not only absorbed into the being but radiates through the energy center outwardly. I believe this begins with the blue center and . . . and also occurs with the indigo and violet? Is this correct?

RA I am Ra. Firstly, we would state that we had not finished answering the previous query and may thus answer both in part by stating that in the fully activated entity, only that small portion of instreaming light needed to tune the energy center is used, the great remainder being free to be channeled and attracted upwards.

To answer your second question more fully we may say that it is correct that radiation without the necessity of response begins with blue ray; although the green ray, being the great transitional ray, must be given all careful consideration, for until transfers of energy of all types has been experienced and mastered to a great extent, there will be blockages in the blue and indigo radiations.

Again, the violet emanation is, in this context, a resource from which, through indigo, intelligent infinity may be contacted. The radiation thereof will not be violet ray but rather green, blue, or indigo depending upon the nature of the type of intelligence which infinity has brought through into discernible energy.

The green-ray type of radiation in this case is the healing, the blue-ray the communication and inspiration, the indigo that energy of the adept which has its place in faith.

54.32 **QUESTIONER** What if a mind/body/spirit complex feels a feeling in meditation at the indigo center, what is he feeling?

RA I am Ra. This will be the last full query of this working.

One who feels this activation is one experiencing instreamings at that energy center to be used either for the unblocking of this center, for its tuning to match the harmonics of its other energy centers, or to activate the gateway to intelligent infinity.

We cannot be specific, for each of these three workings is experienced by the entity which feels this physical-complex distortion.

Is there a brief query before we leave this instrument?

54.33 **QUESTIONER** I just would ask if there is anything that we can do to make the instrument more comfortable or improve the contact?

RA I am Ra. Please be aware of the need for the support of the instrument's neck. All is well.

I leave you, my friends, in the love and in the light of the One Infinite Creator. Go forth, then, rejoicing in the power and the peace of the One Infinite Creator. Adonai.

55.0 **RA** I am Ra. I greet you in the love and in the light of the One Infinite Creator. I communicate now.

55.1 **QUESTIONER** I would first like to ask as to the condition of the instrument, please?

RA I am Ra. This instrument is experiencing physical distortions toward weakness of the bodily complex occurring due to psychic attack. This instrument's vital energies have not been affected, however, due to the aid of those present in healing work. This instrument will apparently be subject to such weakness distortions due to incarnative processes which predispose the body complex towards weakness distortions.

55.2 **QUESTIONER** Is there any specific thing that we can do that you have already told us? Or otherwise to alleviate this psychic attack or to help the instrument the most?

RA I am Ra. We scan this instrument and find its distortion towards appreciation of each entity and each entity's caring, as you may call it. This atmosphere, shall we say, offers the greatest contrast to the discomfort of such psychic attacks, being the reciprocal, that is, the atmosphere of psychic support.

This each of you do as a subconscious function of true attitudinal, mental, emotional, and spiritual distortions towards this instrument. There is no magic greater than honest distortion toward love.

55.3 **QUESTIONER** Thank you. I want to ask a couple questions about previous material that I didn't understand. I'm hoping that this will clear up my understanding, somewhat, with respect to the mental configurations with which we have been dealing.

In the session before last you stated, "However, this is a risk for the Orion entities due to the frequency with which the harvestable negative planetary entities then attempt to bid, or order, the Orion contact, just as these entities bid planetary negative contacts." Can you explain the mechanisms that affect polarization in consciousness with respect to this statement?

RA I am Ra. The negative polarization is greatly aided by the subjugation or enslavement of other-selves. The potential between two negatively polarized entities is such that the entity which enslaves the other or bids the other gains in negative polarity.

The entity so bidden or enslaved, in serving an other-self, will necessarily lose negative polarity, although it will gain in desire for further negative polarization. This desire will then tend to create opportunities to regain negative polarity.

55.4   **QUESTIONER** Am I to understand then—just the fact that the third-density entity on this planet . . . just the fact that he calls or bids an Orion Crusader is a polarizing type of action that affects both entities?

RA I am Ra. This is incorrect. The calling mechanism is not congruent in the slightest degree with the bidding mechanism. In the calling, the entity which calls is a suppliant neophyte asking for aid in negative understanding, if you may excuse this misnomer. The Orion response increases its negative polarity as it is disseminating the negative philosophy, thereby enslaving, or bidding, the entity calling.

There are instances, however, when the contact becomes a contest which is prototypical of negativity. In this contest, the caller will attempt not to ask for aid but to demand results. Since the third-density, negatively oriented, harvestable entity has at its disposal an incarnative experiential nexus, and since Orion Crusaders are, in a great extent, bound by the First Distortion in order to progress, the Orion entity is vulnerable to such bidding, if properly done.

In this case, the third-density entity becomes master, and the Orion Crusader becomes entrapped and can be bid. This is rare. However, when it has occurred the Orion entity or social memory complex involved has experienced loss of negative polarity in proportion to the strength of the bidding third-density entity.

55.5   **QUESTIONER** You mentioned that this will work when the bidding is properly done. What did you mean by "when the bidding is properly done?"

RA I am Ra. To properly bid is to be properly negative. The percentage of thought and behavior involving service to self must approach 99% in order for a third-density negative entity to be properly configured for such a contest of bidding.

55.6   **QUESTIONER** What method of communication with the Orion entity would a negative bidder of this type use?

RA I am Ra. The two most usual types of bidding are: One, the use of perversions of sexual magic; two, the use of perversions of ritual magic. In each case the key to success is the purity of the will of the bidder. The concentration upon victory over the servant must be nearly perfect.

55.7   **QUESTIONER** Can you tell me, in the polarizations in consciousness, if there is any analogy with respect to what you just said in this type of contact with respect to what we are doing, right now, in communicating with Ra?

RA I am Ra. There is no relationship between this type of contact and the bidding process. This contact may be characterized as one typical of the Brothers and Sisters of Sorrow wherein those receiving the contact have attempted to prepare for such contact by sacrificing extraneous, self-oriented distortions in order to be of service.

The Ra social memory complex offers itself also as a function of its desire to serve. Both the caller and the contact are filled with gratitude at the opportunity of serving others.

We may note that this in no way presupposes that either the callers or those of our group in any way approach a perfection, or purity, such as was described in the bidding process. The calling group may have many distortions and be working with much catalyst, as may those of Ra. The overriding desire to serve others, bonded with the unique harmonics of this group's vibratory complexes, gives us the opportunity to serve as one channel for the One Infinite Creator.

Things come not to those positively oriented, but through such beings.

55.8   **QUESTIONER** Thank you. You stated at an earlier time "until transfers of energy of all types have been experienced and mastered to a great extent, there will be blockages in the blue and indigo radiations." Could you explain that more fully?

RA I am Ra. At this space/time we have not covered the appropriate intermediate material. Please re-question at a more appropriate space/time nexus.

55.9 **QUESTIONER** OK. I'm sort of hunting around here for an entry into some information. I may not be looking in a productive area.

But you had stated that "we (that is, Ra) had been aided by shapes such as the pyramid, so that we could aid your people with a shape such as the pyramid." These shapes have been mentioned many, many times, and you have also stated that the shapes themselves aren't of too much consequence. I see a relation between these shapes and the energies that we have been studying with respect to the body, and I would like to ask a few questions on the pyramid to see if I might get an entry into some of this understanding.

You stated, "You will find the intersection of the triangle which is at the first level on each of the four sides forms a diamond in a plane which is horizontal." Can you tell me what you meant by the word, intersection?

RA I am Ra. Your mathematics and arithmetic have a paucity of configurative descriptions which we might use. Without intending to be obscure, we may note that the purpose of the shapes is to work with time/space portions of the mind/body/spirit complex. Therefore, the intersection is both space/time and time/space oriented and thus is expressed in three dimensional geometry by two intersections which, when projected in both time/space and space/time, form one point.

55.10 **QUESTIONER** I have calculated this point to be one-sixth of the height of the triangle that forms the side of the pyramid. Is this correct?

RA I am Ra. Your calculations are substantially correct, and we are pleased at your perspicacity.[1]

55.11 **QUESTIONER** This would indicate to me that in the Great Pyramid at Giza, the Queen's Chamber, as it is called, would be the chamber for initiation. Is this correct?

RA I am Ra. Again, you penetrate the outer teaching.

---

[1] In this context, *perspicacity* may be defined as "acuteness of sight or discernment."

The Queen's Chamber would not be appropriate or useful for healing work as that work involves the use of energy in a more synergic configuration rather than the configuration of the centered being.[2]

55.12 **QUESTIONER** Then would the healing work be done in the King's Chamber?

RA I am Ra. This is correct. We may note that such terminology is not our own.

55.13 **QUESTIONER** Yes, I understand that. It is just the common naming of the two chambers of the Great Pyramid. I don't know whether this line of questioning is going to take me to a better understanding of the energies, but until I have explored these concepts there is nothing much that I can do but ask a few questions.

There is a chamber below the bottom level of the pyramid, down below ground, that appears to be roughly in line with the King's Chamber. What is that chamber?

RA I am Ra. We may say that there is information to be gained from this line of querying.

The chamber you request to be informed about is a resonating chamber. The bottom of such a structure, in order to cause the appropriate distortions for healing catalyst, shall be open.

55.14 **QUESTIONER** The book, *Life Force in the Great Pyramid*, they have related the ankh shape with a resonance in the pyramid. Is this a correct analysis?

RA I am Ra. We have scanned your mind and find the phrase "working with crayons." This would be applicable. There is only one significance to these shapes such as the crux ansata; that is the placing in coded form of mathematical relationships.

55.15 **QUESTIONER** Is the 76° 18′ angle at the apex of the pyramid a critical angle?

RA I am Ra. For the healing work intended, this angle is appropriate.

---

[2] In this context, *synergic* may be defined as "working together."

55.16 **QUESTIONER** Why does the King's Chamber have the various small chambers above it?

RA I am Ra. This will be the last full query of this working.

We must address this query more generally in order to explicate your specific question. The positioning of the entity to be healed is such that the life energies, if you will, are in a position to be briefly interrupted, or intersected, by light.

This light then may, by the catalyst of the healer with the crystal, manipulate the aural forces, as you may call the various energy centers, in such a way that if the entity to be healed wills it so, corrections may take place. Then the entity is re-protected by its own, now less distorted, energy field and is able to go its way.

The process by which this is done involves bringing the entity to be healed to an equilibrium. This involves temperature, barometric pressure, and the electrical charged atmosphere. The first two requirements are controlled by the system of chimneys.

55.17 **QUESTIONER** Does this healing work by affecting the energy centers in such a way that they are unblocked so as to perfect the seven bodies that they generate and, therefore, bring the entity being healed into proper balance?

RA I am Ra. This entity tires. We must answer in brief and state simply that the distorted configuration of the energy centers is intended to be temporarily interrupted, and the opportunity is then presented to the one to be healed to grasp the baton, to take the balanced route, and to walk thence with the distortions towards dis-ease of mind, body, and spirit greatly lessened.

The catalytic effect of the charged atmosphere and the crystal directed by the healer must be taken into consideration as integral portions of this process, for the bringing back of the entity to a configuration of conscious awareness would not be accomplished after the reorganization possibilities are offered without the healer's presence and directed will.

Are there any brief queries before we leave this instrument?

55.18 **QUESTIONER** Only is there anything we can do to make the instrument more comfortable or improve the contact?

RA I am Ra. All is well. You are conscientious. I now leave this working.

I am Ra. I leave you, my friends, in the love and in the light of the One Infinite Creator. Go forth, then, rejoicing in the power and in the peace of the One Infinite Creator. Adonai.

Session 56

56.0   **RA**   I am Ra. I greet you in the love and in the light of the One Infinite Creator. We communicate now.

56.1   **QUESTIONER**   Would you first please give me an indication of the condition of the instrument?

RA   I am Ra. This instrument is severely distorted towards weakness of the mental and physical complexes at this time, and is under psychic attack due to this opportunity.

56.2   **QUESTIONER**   Would it be better to discontinue the contact at this time?

RA   I am Ra. This is entirely at your discretion. This instrument has some energy transferred which is available. However, it is not great due to the effects as previously stated.

We, if you desire to question us further at this working, will as always attempt to safeguard this instrument. We feel that you are aware of the parameters without further elaboration.

56.3   **QUESTIONER**   In that case, I will ask how does the pyramid shape work?

RA   I am Ra. We are assuming that you wish to know the principle of the shapes, angles, and intersections of the pyramid at what you call Giza.

In reality, the pyramid shape does no work. It does not work. It is an arrangement for the centralization, as well as the diffraction, of the spiraling upward light energy as it is being used by the mind/body/spirit complex.

The spiraling nature of light is such that the magnetic fields of an individual are affected by spiraling energy. Certain shapes offer an echo chamber, shall we say, or an intensifier for spiraling prana, as some have called this all-present, primal distortion of the One Infinite Creator.

If the intent is to intensify the necessity for the entity's own will to call forth the inner light in order to match the intensification of the spiraling light energy, the entity will be placed in what you have called the Queen's

Chamber position in this particular shaped object. This is the initiatory place and is the place of resurrection.

The off-set place, representing the spiral as it is in motion, is the appropriate position for one to be healed; as in this position an entity's vibratory magnetic nexi are interrupted in their normal flux. Thus a possibility/probability vortex ensues: a new beginning, shall we say, is offered for the entity in which the entity may choose a less distorted, weak, or blocked configuration of energy-center-magnetic distortions.

The function of the healer and crystal may not be over-emphasized, for this power of interruption must needs be controlled, shall we say, with incarnate intelligence; the intelligence being that of one which recognizes energy patterns; which, without judging, recognizes blockage, weakness, and other distortion; and which is capable of visualizing, through the regularity of self and of crystal, the less distorted other-self to be healed.

Other shapes which are arched, groined, vaulted, conical, or as your tepees are also shapes with this type of intensification of spiraling light. Your caves, being rounded, are places of power due to this shaping.

It is to be noted that these shapes are dangerous. We are quite pleased to have the opportunity to enlarge upon the subject of shapes such as the pyramid, for we wish, as part of our honor/duty, to state that there are many wrong uses for these curved shapes; for with improper placement, improper intentions, or lack of the crystallized being functioning as channel for healing, the sensitive entity will be distorted more rather than less in some cases.

It is to be noted that your peoples build, for the most part, the cornered or square habitations, for they do not concentrate power. It is further to be noted that the spiritual seeker has, for many of your time periods of years, sought the rounded, arched, and peaked forms as an expression of the power of the Creator.[1]

56.4   QUESTIONER Is there an apex angle that is the angle for maximum efficiency in the pyramid?

RA I am Ra. Again, to conserve this instrument's energy, I am assuming

---

[1] To see a diagram of the operation of the three spirals in and through the pyramid, see the Resource Series.

that you intend to indicate the most appropriate angle of apex for healing work. If the shape is such that it is large enough to contain an individual mind/body/spirit complex at the appropriate off-set position within it, the 76° 18', approximate, angle is useful and appropriate. If the position varies, the angle may vary. Further, if the healer has the ability to perceive distortions with enough discrimination, the position within any pyramid shape may be moved about until results are effected.

However, we found this particular angle to be useful. Other social memory complexes, or portions thereof, have determined different apex angles for different uses, not having to do with healing but with learning. When one works with the cone or, shall we say, the silo type of shape, the energy for healing may be found to be in a general circular pattern unique to each shape as a function of its particular height and width and, in the cone shape, the angle of apex. In these cases there are no corner angles. Thus the spiraling energy works in circular motion.

56.5   **QUESTIONER** I will make a statement that you can correct. I intuitively see the spiraling energy of the Giza pyramid being spread out as it moves through the so-called King's Chamber and then refocusing in the so-called Queen's Chamber. I am guessing that the spread of energy in the so-called King's Chamber is seen in the spectrum of colors, red through violet, and that the energy centers of the entity to be healed should be aligned with this spread of the spectrum so that the spectrum matches the various energy centers. Can you correct this statement?

RA I am Ra. We can correct this statement.

56.6   **QUESTIONER** Would you please do that?

RA The spiraling energy is beginning to be diffused at the point where it goes through the King's Chamber position. However—although the spirals continue to intersect, closing and opening in double spiral fashion through the apex angle—the diffusion or strength of the spiraling energies, red through violet color values, lessens if we speak of strength, and gains if we speak of diffusion until at the peak of the pyramid you have a very weak color resolution useful for healing purposes.

Thus the King's Chamber position is chosen as the first spiral after the centered beginning through the Queen's Chamber position. You may visualize the diffusion angle as the opposite of the pyramid angle, but the angle being less wide than the apex angle of the pyramid, being somewhere between 33 and 54°, depending upon the various rhythms of the planet itself.

56.7 **QUESTIONER** Then I assume if I start my angle at the bottom of the Queen's Chamber, and make a 33 to 54° angle from that point, so that half of that angle falls on the side of the centerline the King's Chamber is on, that will indicate the diffusion of the spectrum, starting from the point at the bottom of the Queen's Chamber; let's say if we were using a 40° angle, we would have a 20° diffusion to the left of the centerline, passing through the King's Chamber. Is that correct?

RA I am Ra. This will be the last full question of this session.

It is correct that half of the aforementioned angle passes through the King's Chamber position. It is incorrect to assume that the Queen's Chamber is the foundation of the angle. The angle will begin somewhere between the Queen's Chamber position and thence downward towards the level of the resonating chamber, off-set for the healing work.

This variation is dependent upon various magnetic fluxes of the planet. The King's Chamber position is designed to intersect the strongest spiral of the energy flow regardless of where the angle begins. However, as it passes through the Queen Chamber position this spiraling energy is always centered and at its strongest point.

May we answer any brief queries at this time?

56.8 **QUESTIONER** I will just ask if there is anything that we can do to make the instrument more comfortable or improve the contact?

RA I am Ra. All is well, my friends. It is well, however, to be conscious of the limitations of this instrument. We feel the alignments are excellent at this time.

I am Ra. I leave you in the love and in the light of the One Infinite Creator. Go forth, therefore, rejoicing in the power and in the peace of the One Infinite Creator. Adonai.

[The remaining Ra contact sessions, #57–106, are contained in *The Ra Contact: Teaching the Law of One,* Volume 2.]

PHOTO GALLERY

Unless otherwise noted, all of the photographs in the following gallery were taken on June 9, 1982, before or after the Ra contact session. Of all the photos taken that day, some were printed in the original Book I of *The Law of One*. (aka *The Ra Material.*) The photos in this gallery include those that were not printed in the original *Law of One* books.

Don and Ra discuss taking photographs of the Ra contact in the following passages (contained in Volume 2 of *The Ra Contact: Teaching the Law of One*):

88.10 **QUESTIONER** Our publisher requests pictures for the book, *The Law of One*, that is going to press at this time. Would you comment on the advisability, benefit or detriment, magical or otherwise, of us using pictures of this particular setup, the instrument, and the appurtenances in the book?

RA I am Ra. The practical advisability of such a project is completely a product of your discrimination. There are magical considerations.

Firstly, if pictures be taken of a working, the visual image must needs be that which is; that is, it is well for you to photograph only an actual working and no sham nor substitution of any material. There shall be no distortions which this group can avoid any more than we would wish distortions in our words.

Secondly, it is inadvisable to photograph the instrument or any portion of the working room while the instrument is in trance. This is a narrow-band contact, and we wish to keep electrical and electromagnetic energies constant when their presence is necessary, and not present at all otherwise.

88.11 **QUESTIONER** From what you . . . I'm sorry. Go ahead. If you meant to continue, continue. If not, I'll ask a question.

RA I am Ra. We wished to state, thirdly, that once the instrument is aware that the picture-taking will be performed, that during the entire picture-taking, whether before or after the working, the instrument be required to continuously respond to speech, thus assuring that no trance is imminent.

88.12 **QUESTIONER** From what you have told me, then, I have planned the following: We will, after a session is complete and the instrument has been awakened, before moving the instrument, have the instrument continually talk to us while I take pictures of the configuration the instrument is in at this time. In addition to this, I will take some other pictures of the instrument in the other room, and probably ourselves, too, just for additional pictures of us as requested by the publisher. Is this the optimal or one of the optimal fillings of this requirement?

RA I am Ra. Yes. We ask that any photographs tell the truth, that they be dated and shine with a clarity so that there is no shadow of any but genuine expression which may be offered to those which seek truth.

We come as humble messengers of the Law of One, desiring to decrease distortions. We ask that you, who have been our friends, work with any considerations such as above discussed, not with the thought of quickly removing an unimportant detail, but, as in all ways, regard such as another opportunity to, as the adept must, be yourselves and offer that which is in and with you without pretense of any kind.

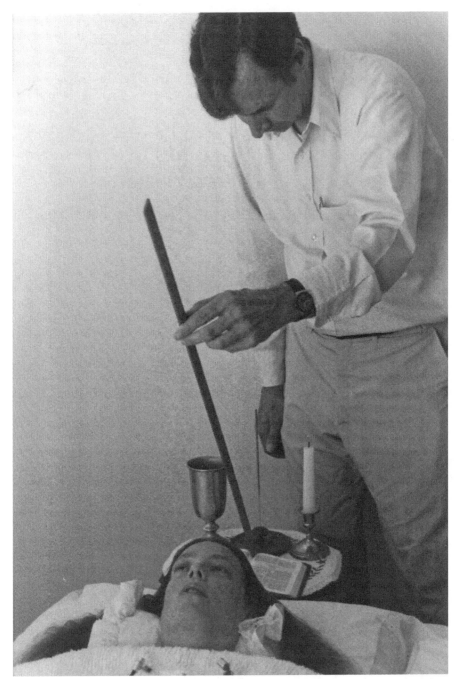

Above: Before the session with Ra, Don aligns the appurtenances: Bible opened to the Gospel of John, Chapter 1, chalice, incense, and white candle.

Above: The appurtenances that energized and nourished the instrument placed at Carla's head for each Ra session.

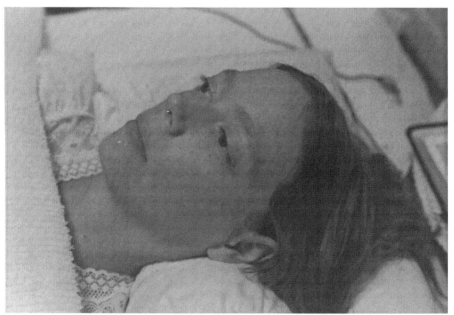

Above: Calm, courageous, fearless, serene: Carla awaits the unknown.

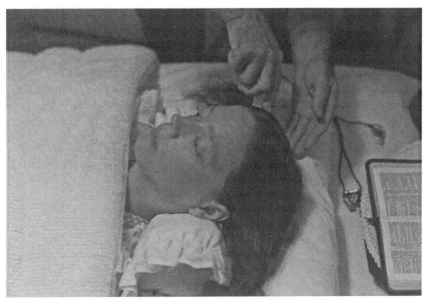

Above: Carla being lovingly attended to by Jim before beginning a session with Ra.

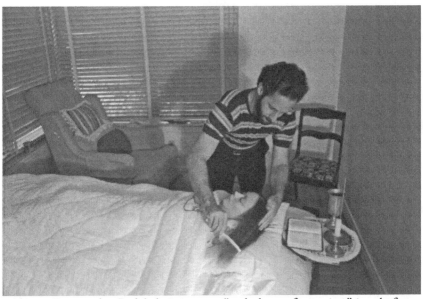

Above: Jim combs Carla's hair into an "orderly configuration" just before beginning a session with Ra. (69.0 & 75.33)

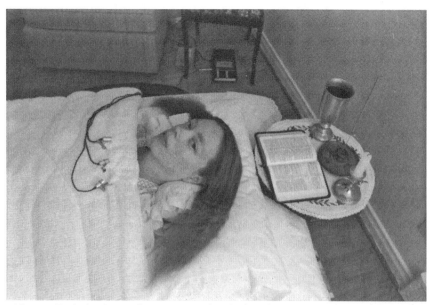

Above: Carla looks to the picture-taker before beginning a session with Ra. Jim's chair in the background.

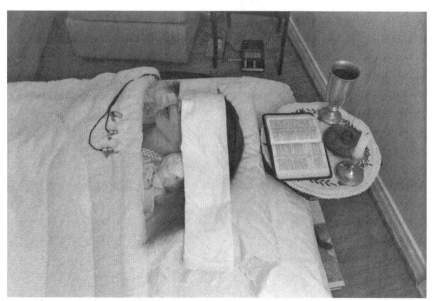

Above: Carla with three microphones attached to record the session with Ra. Carla's energy had an adverse effect upon electronics that necessitated three recorders.

Above: Notebook full of questions for Ra in his lap, Don observes
Carla singing "Amazing Grace" to be sure that she doesn't go
into trance while the pictures were being taken.

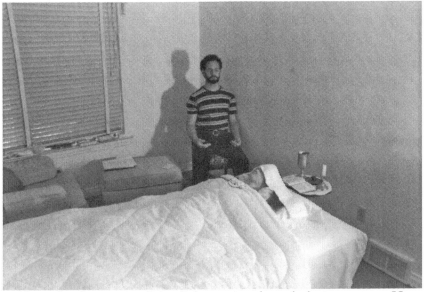

Above: Jim begins visualizing light moving through the instrument. He
will sustain this meditation with single-pointed attention throughout
the entire session, breaking only to flip the cassettes.

Above: Don checks his questions while Carla lies prone with microphones attached and eyes covered before beginning a session with Ra.

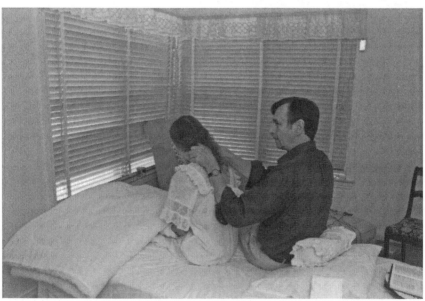

Above: Don rubs Carla's very sore and stiff shoulders after completing a session with Ra. The weariness, Ra said, was the equivalent of "many, many hours of harsh physical labor."

Fearless Carla L. Rueckert. Though we operated as a group, Carla alone would face the risk of serving as the instrument and entering into trance. Ra said also that she took the "brunt" of the greeting.

Above: Carla, her glow subdued by significant fatigue, sits beside the driveway of our house with our flower garden and kitchen windows behind her.

Above: Don in the L/L office at the Watterson Trail house. Joey Wackerbath sits on his desk while Chocolate Bar rests in the foreground. Gandalf and Fairchild are elsewhere.

Above: Jim at work in the office with Chocolate Bar in the foreground and Joey Wackerbath in the background.

Above: The corner room of our Watterson Trail house which served as the Ra session room.

Above: Carla, near her 84 lb. channeling weight for the Ra contact, handing Jim a bouquet of marigolds as they enjoy the afternoon in the little orchard behind the Watterson Trail house.

Above: Carla dances in the leaves while Jim sits on the porch of our Lake Lanier house where we had session #106, our last conversation with Ra.

Above: Don on the phone in the L/L office at the Watterson Trail house where 105 sessions took place.

Above: Carla poses for a picture, her steady determination showing.

Above: Jim sitting in the living room of the Watterson Trail house.

Above: We three posing in the driveway of the Watterson Trail house on a beautiful summer's day for one of only two pictures ever taken of us together.

THE RELISTENING REPORT

Preface from L/L Research

The following is Tobey Wheelock's "Relistening Report" written in March, 2012, soon after the completion of the Relistening Project, an effort that produced what he called The Relistened and the Lightly Edited Versions.

As the text of The Ra Contact *book comes directly from the Lightly Edited Version, the great majority of the changes to the Relistened and Lightly Edited Version—that Tobey reports about below—have been carried into this book. However, additional refinements were made to the text for* The Ra Contact. *These are detailed in the following "Addendum to the Relistening Report."*

We extend our heartfelt gratitude to Tobey for his dedication to this project and for allowing us to reprint his summary of his journey here.

Introduction

The Relistening Project started in the fall of 2004. I was interested in understanding where the Book V material fit into the sessions from which it had been removed. It turned out that the only way to find out where the material belonged was to listen to copies of the original tapes. Once I started listening, I realized that there was information that had never been published before, and I decided that it would be worth listening carefully to each session in order to produce a new, more accurate version of this amazing material.

I listened to sessions 1–98 in much the way that Jim McCarty, the original scribe, had: by playing cassettes on a small portable tape recorder. In 2006, Gary Bean at L/L Research created digital copies of the original tapes, and in 2007 and 2008 Terry Hsu carefully listened to mp3s of sessions 75–106. Terry eventually decided that, since English is not his native language, he was not the best person for the job, but his infectious enthusiasm carried me through many a dry spell in my relistening efforts.

Eventually, I realized that the digital copies were better than the cassette copies I had been using, so I switched to them for sessions 99–106. In 2010, I asked L/L if they could arrange for volunteers to verify the transcripts I had created, and Gary recruited a volunteer for the job. The volunteer began with the later sessions and worked his way back to session 31. Time constraints made it impossible for him to continue, but we were quite fortunate, because a different volunteer (who also wishes to remain anonymous) picked up the baton, verified sessions 1–30, and then worked her way through the later sessions, too.

I wanted to create as accurate a transcription as possible, but I did not want to lose the readability of the original books. My solution has been to produce three versions, which I call Original, Relistened, and Lightly Edited. The Relistened is the text version that represents what is actually on the audio as exactly as possible, stutters and all. The Lightly Edited is the version with *light* edits in order to retain readability.

Update 2018: The Lightly Edited was later refined by Jim McCarty, Gary Bean, and Austin Bridges for *The Ra Contact*. The default version at Lawofone.info is now *The Ra Contact*. For more information about the different versions and a way to identify the differences between them, please see: http://www.lawofone.info/versions.php

Most significant changes

Dropped lines restored
One of the most interesting discoveries was that segments of a number of answers were dropped in publication, many possibly due to typesetting errors. In some cases, they clarified what had been puzzling answers from Ra. Here is a list:

Complete list of restored lines:
- . . . You are part of a thought. You are dancing in a ballroom in which there is no material. You are dancing thoughts. - 1.0
- . . . We, too, have our place. We are not those of the Love or of the Light. - 1.1
- . . . This is not so with many of the entities of the Confederation. We found it was not efficacious. - 1.1
- . . . Some of these landings are of your peoples . . . - 7.12
- . . . Other sightings are due to the inadvertent visualization by your peoples' optical mechanisms of your own government's weaponry. - 12.9
- . . . a premature aging process. We were attempting to aid in giving the mind/body/spirit complexes of third density . . . - 14.10
- . . . always stating the prerequisite of meditation, contemplation . . . - 15.14

- . . . The free will of your future is not making this available. We shall speak on one item. There is a fairly large percentage, approximately thirty-five percent of the intelligent planets, which do not fit in the percentiles. These mysteries are of sixth and seventh density and are not available for our speaking. - 16.27

- . . . The errors which have occurred have occurred due to the occasional variation in the vibrational complex of this instrument due to its ingestion of a chemical substance. - 18.1

- Go forth, therefore, rejoicing in the power and the peace of the One Creator. - 20.45

- . . . at what you would call a later period in your time measurement. - 27.1

- Does this fulfill the requirements of your query? - 29.32

- . . . The green-ray energy transfer occurs due to the vibratory rate of . . . - 31.5

- . . . entity to radiate to the other- . . . - 32.1

- . . . service. You will find an infinite array of contradictory requests for . . . - 67.11

- . . . A great deal of the answer you seek is in this sentence. - 74.8

- . . . This is for the purpose of refinement of the one original thought. - 82.10

- . . . loss to the conscious mind of the . . . - 86.18

- . . . flight, and messages, and movement, and in some cases, protection. The folded wing in this image is intended to suggest . . . - 91.24

- . . . vibrations. We suggest that you then request of this living entity that it now be welcoming and absorbent for the . . . - 95.4

New questions and answers
There were also a number of questions and answers that had never been published before, not even in Book V. The most interesting ones: the benefits of service to others in maintaining youthful appearance (15.6), confederation aid in 2D to 3D harvest (19.7), sex life of the cat Gandalf (30.13), answers to unasked questions can't be published (42.1), and the effects of a pyramid built of rods (58.16). In addition, several new paragraphs in regards to healing and Carla's energy center balance were added to an answer from session 12 (12.31).

Complete list of new questions and answers:

- (inaudible) - 1.5

- (Orion/our own UFOs) - 7.13

- Not completely new, but several new paragraphs about Carla in question about wanderers healing themselves - 12.31

- (visitor to evening session) - 13.27

- (youthful appearance) - 15.6

- (Orion contacts) - 16.13–14; (cattle mutilations) - 16.43–46; (Orion techniques) - 16.58

- (Confederation aid in 2D/3D harvest) - 19.7

- (Maldek) - 21.5–7; (history of Orion contacts) - 21.21–23; (Lemuria) - 21.24–27

- (Just "Thank you.") - 23.18

- (Coughing requests, for the most part) - 24.2–24.3, 24.5, 24.7, 24.15, 24.21, 24.22

- (coughing requests) - 26.9, 26.14, 26.29, 26.35, 26.37, 26.39

- (Coughing requests) - 28.12, 28.17

- (dinosaur extinction) - 30.8; (spiritual side of the cat Gandalf's sex life) - 30.13

- (instrument's condition) - 31.1

- (will moving affect Ra contact?) - 41.3

- (difference between mentally requested and spoken questions; question about balancing) - 42.1–2; (cattle mutilations) - 42.21

- (instrument's condition) - 46.1; 46.6 (whether to end session) - 46.6

- (what would Ra do if incarnate now) - 48.4

- (metal bending wearing pyramid hats) - 50.10

- (instrument's condition) - 54.1; 54.20 (programming catalyst) - 54.20

- (rod-sided pyramid vs. solid-sided) - 58.16

- (instrument's condition) - 60.1

- (number of wanderers) - 64.3

- (instrument's condition) - 69.1–2; (Esmerelda Sweetwater) - 69.20–21

- (sexual energy transfer) - 72.16

- (correction about miracles infringing on free will) - 73.15
- (galactic evolution) - 78.14
- (sexual energy transfer) - 79.3
- (Thank you) - 79.44
- (analogy of flying in a simulator to life pre-veil) - 83.8
- (Clarification) - 94.17
- (Billy Meier contact) - 100.4–5

Less significant changes

There were many tweaks to Ra's answers and many, many changes to Don's questions. A few examples are shown below (Original Version first).

Lawofone.info has functionality to review the changes between the texts side-by-side for closer and more extensive review.

- The pyramids which we thought/built were constructed thought-forms created by our social memory complex.

   The pyramids which we thought/built were constructed **from** thought-forms created by our social memory complex. - 3.11

- . . . thus bringing with them in totally latent form many skills and understandings . . .

   . . . thus bringing with them in **sometimes** totally latent form many skills and understandings . . . - 4.9

- The exercise is to consciously **see** that love in awareness and understanding distortions.

   The exercise is to consciously **seek** that love in awareness and understanding distortions. - 10.14

- to recapitulate a learning/teaching which is adjudged to be less than **perfect**.

   to recapitulate a learning/teaching which is adjudged to be less than perfectly **balanced**. - 52.9

- Firstly, that exercise of which we have spoken called the exercise of fire: this is, **through** physical energy transfer, not that which is deeply involved in the body complex combinations.

   Firstly, that exercise of which we have spoken called the exercise of fire: this is, **though** physical energy transfer, not that which is deeply involved in the body complex combinations. - 73.22

- ... intended to be studied as individual concept **complexes** as Matrix, Potentiator, etc., in viewing mind/body/spirit connections and in pairs with . . .

  ... intended to be studied as individual concept **complexes;** as Matrix, Potentiator, etc. in viewing mind/body/spirit connections; and in pairs with . . . - 89.19

- ... that is, to put value in a fatal action and die or to put value on consciousness of the creation of the One Creator and, thereby, live.

  ... that is, to put value in a fatal action and die or to put value on consciousness of the creation **and** of the One Creator and, thereby, live. - 103.4

Unediting questions sometimes made Ra's answers clearer. Example:

- Questioner: The crown of three stars, we are guessing, **would represent the balancing** of the mind, body, and spirit. Is this in any way correct?

  Questioner: The crown of three stars, we are guessing, **indicates mastery and balancing** of the mind, body, and spirit. Is this in any way correct?

  Ra: I am Ra. This device is astrological in origin and the interpretation given somewhat confusing. - 100.10

Sometimes answers became less clear, for example:

- The mind/body/spirit complex known **as** Adolf

  The mind/body/spirit complex known Adolf - 11.7

- If it is **a** contemplative general daydream . . .

  If it is contemplative general daydream . . . - 16.54

Possible misstatements

There are a few answers where Ra may have misspoken. It's hard to know for sure because Don didn't follow up on these; however, they were changed in the originally published books. Previously published versions shown first; actual transcripts second.

- There are no **negative** beings which have attained the Oversoul manifestation . . .

There are no beings which have attained the Oversoul manifestation . . . - 36.12

- . . . common to a reasonable number of entities who, having lost the desire for orange- and **yellow**-ray sexual experiences . . .

  . . . common to a reasonable number of entities who, having lost the desire for orange- and **green**-ray sexual experiences . . . - 48.2

- You may see the air and **fire** of that which is chaos as literally illuminating and forming the formless

  You may see the air and **water** of that which is chaos as literally illuminating and forming the formless - 78.29

Edited and unedited answers

Edited answers

For the most part, the Lightly Edited Version, which is the default version on Lawofone.info, uses the answers from the Relistened Version. The exceptions include the possible misstatements above and other minor tweaks:

- . . . already closely aligned with **a[n]** **all-embracing** belief in the liveness or consciousness of all. - 2.2

- This Council is located in the octave, or **eight[h]** dimension, of the planet Saturn . . . - 6.8

- The mind/body/spirit complex known **[as]** Adolf . . . - 11.7

- The . . . memory . . . then **become[s]** known to the social complex . . . - 11.17

- The balancing pyramidal structures could **[be]** and were used for individual initiation. - 14.10

- ~~tape blank~~ LSD - 18.3

- ~~has/is/will experienced/experiences/experiences~~ has/is/will experienced/experiencing/experience

- . . . the impression that they had given to those who called them **[was]** that these entities were an elite group . . .

- . . . this being not only by the functions of energy transfer but also **[by]** the various services performed . . . - 30.10

- There are no **[negative]** beings which have attained the Oversoul manifestation . . . - 36.12

- If those who desired to be healers [were] of a crystallized nature and . . . - 57.17
- The initiation of [the] Queen's Chamber has to do with the abandoning of self . . . - 57.24
- . . . those things most holy . . . [were] placed. - 60.17
- ~~Logois~~ Logoi - 78.19
- However, in that mystic or prophet [who] desires to serve, such service will increase the entity's polarity. - 86.12
- ~~The loss to the conscious mind of~~ - 86.18
- the more carefully polarized of negative **mind/body/spirits*** - 89.44
- **mind/body/spirits*** undergoing Its care - 90.23
- ~~D   Due~~ Due to the first misperception - 92.17
- . . . **this entity** . . . [**has**] done substantial work . . . and [**has**] indeed developed maturity and rationality. - 94.9
- **Each** of the images . . . [**has**] the increasing intensity . . . −95.27

Answers that could be edited but aren't currently
These answers were edited in the original five books published by L/L Research. However, they are shown in the Lightly Edited and Relistened Versions as they were recorded in the audio:

- . . . in which case you have done **you/they** little or no good. - 1.9
- Please **check your eye** to make fine correction. - 3.4
- One item which may be of interest is that a healer asking to learn must take the distortion understood as responsibility for that ask/receiving, **thus healing**. - 4.20
- This is **a honor/duty** . . . - 4.20
- This entity has **a experiential history** of healing - 29.33
- . . . as it passes through **the Queen Chamber** position . . . - 56.7
- moves ever more **fairly** into the green ray. - 85.16

Editorial Changes

In the course of creating and editing the Relistened Version, I made some changes to paragraphing, spelling, etc.

Paragraphing changes
- 47.15

- 52.2
- 55.18
- 63.9
- 65.23

Spelling changes
- affect(ed)/effect(ed) (3.1, 6.1, 96.2, 96.3, 97.10)
- lightening/lightning (17.27)
- principles/principals (39.9)
- dynaflagallate/dinoflagellate (41.10, 41.11, 41.13)
- effect/affect (48.2, 49.8)
- naval/navel (57.10, 57.11)
- its self/itself (60.3, 72.15, 74.11, 77.6)
- in so far/insofar (72.8, 106.23)
- your self/yourself (74.11, 85.4)
- one's self/oneself (90.9)
- accouterments/accoutrements (94.30)
- waved/waived (96.13)
- Added accents to words that Ra pronounced with two syllables: wingèd (91.24, 93.10, 97.5, 97.7), blessèd (106.7), markèd (67.21, 106.12).
- Added accents to séance, naïveté, naïve.

Hyphenation changes
- being-ness → beingness
- rock-ness → rockness
- third density entity → third-density entity
- in third-density → in third density
- green ray transfer → green-ray transfer
- the green-ray is → the green ray is
- the path of service-to-others → the path of service to others
- the service to others path → the service-to-others path
- the path of service-to-self → the path of service to self
- the service to self path → the service-to-self path

- true color green → true-color green
- requestion → re-question
- over-ride → override

Capitalization changes
- Secrets Of The Great Pyramid → Secrets of the Great Pyramid - 51.6
- THE LAW OF ONE → The Law of One - 53.24
- The Life Force Of The Great Pyramid → The Life Force in the Great Pyramid - 55.14

Notes

- **Session 26.** In Book I, session 26 included a number of questions that were actually from session 53. Those questions have been removed from the versions of session 26 shown at Lawofone.info [and in *The Ra Contact*]. Also, a question about sexual energy transfer that was actually asked during this session, 26.38, was not published until Book II (originally published as 31.1).

- **Session 50.** In Book II, session 50 was published somewhat out of order. (The poker analogy was not really at the end of the session.) It is shown in the order in which it was recorded in the Edited and Relistened Versions [and in *The Ra Contact*].

- **Session 75** was also originally published out of order and has also been restored.

- There were four sessions in which Don asked Ra to cause Carla's body to cough: 24, 26, 28, 97 (97 was already marked as such).

- In the original books, individual's names were shown as "(name)." For the most part we have continued to leave names out, except where the individuals mentioned gave permission or have since passed away. Jim and Carla have given permission to use their names and Don's wherever they occurred, and we have also included the names of two well-known UFO contactees that Ra was asked about: Betty Andreasson and Billy Meier.

- Corrections. When Ra or Don noticed that incorrect information had been given, they corrected that information. In the originally published books, the incorrect questions or answers were edited. In the "Edited" and "Relistened" versions, the incorrect information is shown as recorded, but the correct information is noted below it.

Observations

This project has deepened and enriched the already profound respect I had for the individuals involved and for those of Ra. I was previously aware that Don, Carla, and Jim had made significant sacrifices in order to put themselves in a position to channel Ra. Listening to the sessions made real to me that the sacrifices were ongoing and the commitment on all parts quite unequivocal. It increased my respect for all involved:

- for Carla, because the toll it took on her was quite apparent in the sound of her voice when she returned to her body after each session, and because of her incredible accuracy as a channel in session one, which was not in trance but reads very nearly the same as the other sessions, when she was;

- for Don because of his ability to stay tuned into Ra's lengthy and uninflected answers and follow up with intelligent and focused questions, and for the love and concern for Carla and respect and friendship for Jim that he showed throughout the sessions;

- for Jim for the quiet power that he demonstrated during the times it was necessary to re-walk the Circle of One and in flipping the tapes (really!) and for the accuracy of his original transcriptions;

- for Ra — their faithfulness in answering, as precisely and completely as possible whatever was asked of them, even though it was apparent, from the tone of voice they sometimes used (for example in their answers to questions about the archetypical mind), that they did actually have significant preferences as to the type of information they wanted to share.

Some of the most poignant moments in the sessions occur at the end of each session. After Ra had given their final statement, Don would call Carla back to her body by quietly and persistently saying his nickname for her, "Alrac" (Carla backwards). "Alrac ... Alrac ... Alrac ... " Sometimes it took quite a while before Carla replied. "Yeah?" she'd say, and then Don would ask, "How do you feel?" Often the audio ended at that point, but sometimes you'd hear Carla's response: "OK," or "Tired," or "Mmmph." Often her voice sounded incredibly weary.

I had always wondered how Don could speak with no false starts. In fact, he did false start, but not too often. Sometimes, Ra picked up on parts of his questions that were later edited out. Example: 88.17 ("condense the archetypes"). Don was remarkably good at telling when Ra was done with an answer, but occasionally they would start talking at the same time. Other times Ra would wait patiently until Don realized that he had only made a statement, not asked a question, and appended "Is that correct?" or something similar to his statement. Several times it's possible to hear Don chuckling or reacting, such as after Ra answered a complicated question in one word ("No.") (65.18)

In general, there was very little background noise, the amazing exception being session 45, when water truckers attempted to make a delivery. Other exceptions: a phone ringing in session 1; Jim unloading groceries in session 1, occasional cat purrs and meows.

Ra spoke q u i t e   s l o w l y and in a mostly monotone voice except when the group discussed the archetypes—then Ra's enthusiasm came through. In the first session, as mentioned above, Carla was not in trance, and her intonations sound like we expect "normal" spoken conversation to sound. Some of the other sessions are especially monotone; it seems to have to do with how deeply in trance Carla was. The first session is the only time you hear the opening "I am Ra," because in all other sessions Don and Jim waited until Ra began speaking before they began recording.

After the first session, L/L recorded each session on three cassettes, which they staggered so as not to lose any information. Sessions 1–17 are fairly faint, especially the questions, but the quality of the rest of the recordings is relatively good. In each session, after about 45 minutes, one can hear the sound of a cassette tape stopping and being flipped and restarted.

In conclusion, I think that it's been worth it. The original purpose was to reintegrate the Book V material into each session, and I think that reading the sessions with Book V material restored does indeed add to the experience. In many ways, the Book V material is the heart of the Ra contact, and it's nice to be able to read it in context. In addition, the new material, not previously published anywhere, is interesting to read and in some cases quite valuable. Finally, the model of dedicated service exemplified in the sessions by Carla, Don, Jim, and Ra has been an inspiration to me personally.

Acknowledgments

Many thanks to Don Elkins, for his lifelong quest to learn, to understand, and to pursue his learning wherever it took him. The Ra contact was the culmination of a life of seeking. Thanks to Carla Rueckert, fearless channel, who put her life and her soul's freedom on the line to bring this information through the veil, and to Jim McCarty, the engine who made it all go. And thanks to Ra for their light, their precision and power with words, and their faith that we humans are worth the investment.

Much appreciation, also, to Gary Bean, [then] admin at L/L Research, who provided the initial batch of tapes to get this project started and who has responded to my every request with humor and grace; to Terry Hsu of Taipei, Taiwan, who provided unflagging encouragement (and occasional well-timed reminders) that greatly helped me to renew and maintain my commitment to this project; to the unnamed volunteer mentioned above, who faithfully and persistently re-relistened to sessions 31–106, catching many discrepancies between my transcripts and the actual recordings; and to the second volunteer, who has taken over the re-relistening with great gusto and diligence. I could not have completed this project without any of them.

Finally, all thanks to my beloved wife, Jennifer, and children, Elijah and Elise, who have listened, with good humor and sometimes even with interest, to many more quotes from Ra than any wife or children should ever have to.

Tobey Wheelock
March, 2012

ADDENDUM TO RELISTENED REPORT

The Lightly Edited Version described by Tobey was further refined for publication in this book. While these two versions are not drastically different, there have been changes and additions worth noting.

Transcript of a Conversation

The balance between accuracy and readability in depicting this cosmic conversation was considered in the creation of the Lightly Edited Version and further refined for the version printed in this book. In striving for the balance, some standards and methods were applied:

- As anyone who has transcribed spoken word will know, people do not speak with perfect grammar. Many imperfections were retained in editing to preserve the conversational nature of this transcript. For the most part mistakes were only corrected if retaining them would result in confusion or misunderstanding. Thus, you will see both Don and Ra making some grammatical mistakes.

  In instances where changes or clarifications *were* made to Don's speech, they were simply edited in the transcript without identifying marks. (Great effort was made to ensure that the intended meaning of each thought was retained). Whenever changes or clarifications were made to Ra's speech, brackets or footnotes were meticulously used to indicate each instance.

- As noted by Tobey, Don had many false starts and fragmented thoughts as he navigated the difficult concepts being introduced by Ra while formulating complex questions. Many of these were retained, using the em dash plus space (—) to indicate an abrupt shift in Don's thinking and suspension points (. . .) to indicate a pause or trailing off.

Punctuation

Perhaps the most intensive and significant refinement was in punctuation. Punctuating transcribed word is an innately difficult task that was made more difficult by the manner in which Ra spoke through Carla. Mechanically manipulating her vocal cords from a distance, they spoke slowly at a set cadence with little inflection. This made punctuating this transcript a sometimes creative and interpretive endeavor. Some points of note regarding punctuation include:

- Additional paragraph breaks and various punctuation marks indicating a pause have been added (or removed) to help clarify or deepen the intended meaning of a statement.

- In addition to the already-used commas and semi-colons, em dashes (—) were introduced to help break up and add clarity Ra's sentences containing many clauses.

- General refinement to the placement of punctuation such as commas has hopefully helped the readability of the text. Sometimes the strict rules of punctuation have been bent in order to aid this readability.

- In almost all cases, changes to punctuation did *not* result in a change of meaning. There were some instances, however, where a deeper reading of Ra's reply necessitated a change in punctuation in order to reflect what we felt was Ra's actual intended meaning. One example follows:

   57.17, Lightly Edited - Ra: If those who desired to be healers [were] of a crystallized nature and were all supplicants, those wishing less distortion, the pyramid would be, as always, a carefully designed set of parameters to distribute light and its energy so as to aid in healing catalyst.

   57.17, *The Ra Contact* - Ra: If those who desired to be healers [were] of a crystallized nature, and were all supplicants those wishing less distortion, the pyramid would be, as always, a carefully designed set of parameters to distribute the light and its energy so as to aid in healing catalyst.

In the former, the punctuation fails to differentiate between healer and supplicant. It indicates that, for the pyramid to act in its intended design, healers must be "of a crystallized nature" *and* acting as "supplicants wishing less distortion."

After we realized that the supplicant is the one to be healed (the patient), it was clear that healer and supplicant were two different entities present in healing. The following, then, became its own clause: "and were all supplicants those wishing less distortion." Meaning: when the healers are of a crystallized nature, and when all patients are those wishing less distortion (healing), *then* the pyramid would function according to its design.

Footnotes

Various footnotes have been added to aid readers and expand certain topics, including:

- Additional definitions of words so unusual (sometimes because archaic) that they would not be recognized by most English readers.
- Notes from Jim giving context and insight for some passages.
- References given for when Ra refers to previously discussed material.
- Clarifications and corrections of errors Ra identified, or of very strongly presumed errors that were not identified by Ra.

Capitalization

Some new capitalization standards were implemented in hopes to create consistency and clarity for certain context. For instance, terms describing the beginning cosmology of the Law of One that are read like proper nouns were capitalized, including First, Second, and Third Distortions; along with Free Will, Love, and Light when they refer to those primal three distortions. One Infinite Creator, of course. All Laws and their synonyms: Ways. Great Central Sun. The seven categories of archetypes: Matrix, Potentiator, Catalyst, Experience, Significator, Transformation, Great Way, and The Choice.

Some terms that were capitalized inconsistently, such as wanderer and higher self, were made consistent in their capitalization. Guardians seemed to be used in three different ways, including in the top tier those entities from the next octave, in the middle tier those of this octave who watch over and facilitate harvest, and those of the lower tier who are our personal guardians. The first two categories were capitalized.

These standards are necessarily arbitrary but were considered heavily.

Hyphenating Distortion

Ra qualifies *a lot* of things as "distortions," from a thought, to a person, to Free Will itself. Sometimes distortion was the operative word. Often they used it almost as if it were an add-on, something appended to a noun to qualify that noun as a distortion. In such instances where "distortion" wasn't necessary to use, but used in such a way so as to form a compound with the noun, hyphens were added. For instance:

- . . . in your projections of mind-distortion at this time/space . . . - 2.0
- . . . for all understanding-distortions are available . . . - 11.17
- . . . entertain the thought-distortion towards this entity . . . - 86.2

Five Books of the Law of One vs. The Ra Contact

The following chart depicts the differences in the journey of the two transcriptions, highlighting what makes each unique.

Original cassette recordings ↓	Original cassette recordings ↓
First transcript • Questioner's questions edited for clarity • Q&As intentionally omitted due to transient or personal nature • 55 Q&As accidentally missed. (Not discovered until Relistening Project. See next column.) • Occasional mistakes in transcription made ↓	**New Re-Listened Transcript** • Cassettes relistened to in order to produce new transcript • Exact transcript of recordings: no edits • Omitted material restored • New Q&As discovered • Q&A numbers added. (eg "1.13") • New footnotes ↓
Original published books • Titled: *The Ra Material* or *Law of One* • 50-page Introduction • Five books • All features listed above • Intentionally omitted Q&As published 15 years later in Book V • Jim and Carla's commentary included in Book V	**Lightly Edited Transcript** • All features listed above + *light* edits for improved comprehension ↓ **New Books** • Titled: *The Ra Contact: Teaching the Law of One* • 2 Volumes featuring above plus: • Further, mostly grammatical refinements to editing • More Footnotes • New photo gallery, Introduction, Foreword, Epilogue, Afterword, massive Index • No Book V Commentary

The Final Text

All of the various changes listed were made in the hope of producing a more readable, clear, and consistently presented transcript of this conversation. It is inevitable that any written representation of a recorded conversation may introduce distortion to the intended meaning for each statement made. Each decision was made with the ultimate consideration of Ra's and Don's intention, attempting always to preserve the purity of the conversation as it was spoken, and, when in doubt, erring on the side of retaining authenticity.

This book represents our final and best effort to present a transcript with minimal distortion. It is a continuation of the Lightly Edited Version that attempts to capture in text a representation of the conversation between Don and Ra with minimal distortion and refinements made only when necessary.

You can listen to the original audio of that conversation online from www.llresearch.org or www.lawofone.info.

Austin Bridges
Gary Bean
Jim McCarty
January, 2018

GLOSSARY

Adept – One who devotes the self to seeking the Creator using the disciplines of the personality in the work of faith and spirit. After having adequately balanced the preceding energy centers, the adept proceeds into indigo-ray to make contact with intelligent infinity. The adept may bring intelligent energy through the indigo gateway in order to heal, teach, and work for the Creator in ways that are both radiant and balanced. Whatever the outer service, though, the adept's primary work is not that of doing, but of being.

Archetypal Mind – The architecture of the nature of the evolution of mind, body, and spirit, containing all facets which may affect mind or experience. It is a resource within the deep mind that is of great potential aid to the adept. The archetypal mind is not specifically a *plan* for evolution but is rather, when penetrated lucidly, a blueprint without distortion of the builded structure of all energy expenditures and all seeking.

Bodies (Seven) – One of the preconditions for space/time existence is some form of body complex. Each body offers a vehicle for learning, movement, and experience in a particular environment. Including the present physical body, there are seven basic bodies.

> **Red Ray:** The unconstructed material of the body, the elemental body without form, the chemical body. Not, however, the biological system of bone, tissue, organs, muscle, nerves, hormones, electrochemical impulses and so forth that is the human physical body. This basic unformed material body is important to understand for there are healings which may be carried out by the simple understanding of the elements present in the physical vehicle.

> **Orange Ray:** This purely physical body complex formed without self-awareness, the body in the womb before the spirit/mind complex enters. This body may live without the inhabitation of the mind and spirit complexes. However, it seldom does so.

> **Yellow Ray:** The body that is in activation within third-density incarnation; the physical vehicle as we now know it that is integrated with mind and spirit.

The following higher bodies—often referred to as subtle bodies—are available to the third-density entity, but there is skill and discipline needed in order to avail the self of the more advanced or lighter vehicles. They are not necessary for third-density work but are useful to the adept.

Green Ray: A lighter body packed more densely with life, called by some teachings the astral body. It is the body that will be activated and enjoyed by those in the fourth-density cycle of experience.

Blue Ray: A body of light which may also be called the devachanic body. There are many other names for this body, especially in the Indian Sutras as those of that culture have explored the regions available to the blue-ray body.

Indigo Ray: The etheric, or gateway, or form-maker body, described both as the "analog for intelligent energy" and "being intelligent energy." In this body, form is substance; it would be perceptible to our eyes only as light, as it may mold itself as it desires.

This is the first body activated upon what we call death (the cessation of the yellow-ray body). The indigo body also plays a critical role in health and healing, adopting the desired configuration and manifesting it in the yellow-ray body.

Violet Ray: The violet-ray body may perhaps be understood as what we might call the Buddha body or *that body which is complete*. It is also the body activated during the anomalous moment of harvest in order to gauge the harvestability of the entity.

Catalyst – A neutral instigator that, when used, offers learning (especially of pre-incarnatively chosen lessons), facilitates evolution, develops will and faith, precipitates experience, and polarizes the third-density entity. Essentially all that reaches the senses and everything that comes before the notice of an entity is catalyst, though other-selves are the primary mechanism of catalyst, serving as mirrors that offer reflections of the fruit of beingness.

The Choice – The primary function of the very intense, very short third-density experience is the making of the Choice: to choose and dedicate the self to the positive path of service to others or the negative path of service to self. If the catalyst of third density is successfully used to make the Choice, that is, to polarize and bias the consciousness (measured in vibratory rate of 51% for service to others and 95% for service to self), then, at the time of harvest, the entity will graduate from third to fourth density.

Complex – A term used by Ra essentially as a noun in the same fashion as Merriam-Webster defines it: "A whole made up of complicated or interrelated parts." Ra speaks of it this way in context of the archetypes: "A *concept complex* is a complex of concepts just as a molecule is a complex structure made up of more than one type of energy nexus or atom."

Some examples include: mind/body/spirit complex, mind complex, body complex, spirit complex, social memory complex, sound vibrational complex, and many more.

It may also mean a complex *of* something. When used this way, it may denote either a whole made of up interrelated parts (as in the above definition), or an assortment of multiple things, e.g.: "a complex of thought, ideas, and actions."

Confederation (of Planets In the Service of the Infinite Creator) – The Confederation of Planets (often called the "Confederation" for shorthand) is a group consisting of approximately fifty-three civilizations, comprising approximately five hundred planetary consciousnesses, along with entities from Earth's inner planes and graduates from Earth's third density. It is a true Confederation in that its members are not alike but are all allied in service according to the Law of One. In this Confederation each of the constituent social memory complexes voluntarily place their collective data in a central repository that becomes available to all members.

There are many Confederations in the galaxy, but in almost all cases this term refers to the one currently serving Earth.

Whereas their counterpart, the Orion Empire, calls itself to conquest, the Confederation of Planets awaits the call to service.

Crystallization (Crystallize, Crystallized Being) – Used in reference to energy centers or entities themselves. As Ra describes it, when a crystalline structure is formed of physical material, the elements present in each molecule are bonded in a regularized fashion with the elements in each other molecule. Thus the structure is regular and, when fully and perfectly crystallized, has certain properties. It will not splinter or break; it is very strong without effort; and it is radiant, traducing light into a beautiful refraction giving pleasure of the eye to many.

Through consistent work in consciousness over a period of time (aka: the "discipline of the personality"), energy centers themselves become crystalline, forming unique crystal structures described in 51.8.

Density – One of seven (or eight, depending on the perspective) dimensions or cycles of evolution in an octave of experience. It is called "density" because each successive density is more *densely* packed with light. Akin to a musical scale, seven densities are grouped together in an octave, where the eighth density begins the first of the next octave in an infinite string of octaves. Each density represents a quantum vibrational spectrum or portion of intelligent energy, and each density cycles, or moves to the next density, according to the predetermined clock-like rhythms of intelligent energy.

Designed by the Logos, each density of experience offers its own set lessons and parameters that must be learned and understood in order to cross the threshold and graduate from one density to the next. Each density has seven sub-densities. Each sub-density has seven sub-sub densities. And so on, infinitely. The core vibrations of the seven densities have correspondence to the seven true colors and the seven energy centers.

Disciplines of the Personality – The paramount work of any who have become consciously aware of the process of evolution. The heart of the discipline of the personality is threefold: One, know yourself. Two, accept yourself. Three, become the Creator.

The discipline of the personality results, eventually, in the whole knowledge of the self in micro- and macrocosm, and in a finely tuned compassion and love which sees all things as love.

Distortion – The second definition given for "distort" in Merriam-Webster is "to twist (something) out of a natural, normal, or original shape or condition." In a similar sense, Ra uses the term "distortion" to convey the twisting, modification, misrepresentation, or *concealment* of the un-differentiated, un-potentiated intelligent infinity in its pure form, i.e., the Creator.

Everything in the universe, then, is a distortion, beginning with the First Distortion of Free Will, moving to Love, then to Light, then to the created universe, including stars, planets, people, space, time, etc.

"Distortion" can have any value assigned to it ("good," "bad," "beautiful," "terrible,") but ultimately lacks positive and negative connation. It is used as a strictly neutral term to indicate that everything experienced within creation is a distortion of the One Creator.

Dual-Activated (Bodies, Entities) – Entities harvested from other third-density planets who have incarnated in Earth's third density to make the transition with this planet into fourth density. These entities are not wanderers in the sense that this planetary sphere *is* their fourth-density home planet. They are the pioneers or forerunners of Earth's fourth density.

They incarnate with a third-density/fourth-density double body in activation. This transitional body is one which will be able to appreciate fourth-density energies as the instreaming increases without the accompanying disruption of the third-density body. (If a third-density entity were electrically aware of fourth density in full, the third-density electrical fields would fail due to incompatibility.)

The purpose of such combined activation is that such entities are to some extent consciously aware of those fourth-density understandings which third density is unable to remember due to the forgetting. Thus fourth-density experience may be begun with the added attraction of dwelling in a troubled third-density environment and offering its love and compassion. It is a privilege to be allowed this early an incarnation as there is much experiential catalyst in service to other-selves at this harvesting.

At the time of the Ra contact, dual-activated entities were limited to those harvested from other planets. It is possible that entities harvested from Earth have since joined their ranks.

Energy Centers – The seven rays or centers of consciousness that filter and process the love/light energy of the One Creator, drawn in through both the south and north poles of the energy system. Each energy center (or ray, or chakra) represents a stage or modality of consciousness with its own expressions, lessons, and aspect of the overall identity of self.

Arranged sequentially in hierarchical, ROYGBIV structure, all life experienced is processed through the sequence of energy centers.

Harvest, General (Graduation) – The point of transition between the densities within an octave that operates according to what might be perceived as a three-dimensional clock-like face stretched across the entire galaxy. As the galaxy revolves or spirals, each constituent solar system and planet moves through the scheduled density of experience. The cycles move precisely as a clock strikes the hour. Upon completing a density, or cycle therein, those who have successfully learned the lesson of that cycle are harvested in order that they may ascertain whether they are ready to graduate to the next density. This is perhaps somewhat analogous to passing a final exam at the end of a grade in school in order to move onto the next grade.

Higher Self (Oversoul) – A being beyond polarity in the mid-sixth density that exists with full understanding of the accumulation of experiences of the entity. Operating from what we would consider our future, the higher self is you at mid-sixth density: the end result of all the development experienced by you up to that point. Every entity—whether positive, negative, or undecided—has a higher self. Whatever guidance is received from the higher self may be interpreted in a positive or negative light depending upon the polarity of the seeker, though the negative entity, separated from itself, is not likely to seek such guidance.

The higher self also works closely with the entity in between incarnations, aiding the entity in achieving healing of the experiences which have not been learned properly, and assisting in further life experience programming. Whatever its activity, though, the free will of the incarnate entity is paramount in the service it offers.

Honor/Responsibility, Honor/Duty, and vice versa – Each responsibility is an honor; each honor, a responsibility. Responsibilities and duties are not seen as chores or obligations to which one is shackled in a pejorative sense; rather, the seeker has the freedom to accept the responsibility or duty as an honor, and freedom to fulfill the responsibility or duty as a service. (It is Ra's honor/responsibility to stay with those of planet Earth to eliminate the distortions given to the Law of One.)

Initiation – A person will move through multiple initiations during the course of their incarnation. Each initiation may be characterized generally by stating that a threshold is crossed that delineates the former experience from the newer. This may transpire in a moment or over a long period of time. There is often a challenge or difficulty associated with the crossing of the threshold, and some measure of will and faith needed. For some this may manifest as a dark night of the soul.

Ra speaks of initiation as a process and means whereby the mind/body/spirit complex becomes a purified or initiated channel for the Law of One. The mind, the body, the spirit, or all of the above may move through an initiation. Such an initiated person may then channel the love/light of the One Infinite Creator through the gateway in order to be of service, whether that service be radiance of being alone, or the magical work of indigo ray, the communication of blue ray, or the healing of green ray.

Inner Light – The energy which dwells within an entity, that which is the entity's heart of being, the birthright and true nature of all entities. Drawn by the strength of the inner light, the upward spiraling light enters the red ray and moves northward through the energy centers of an entity to be met and reacted to by the inner light, indicating the level of an entity's progression. The strength of the inner light equals the strength of will to seek the light.

Inner Planes – Whereas humans in their physical bodies experiencing incarnation in the physical world are in space/time or *outer planes*, the non-physical portion of the third-density experience is in time/space, or *inner planes*. The inner planes are also experienced in between incarnations in the review and healing of the previous incarnation and the planning of the coming incarnation. They are also entered in the dreaming state and in other modes of non-ordinary consciousness.

Karma – Ra likens karma to inertia: those actions which are put into motion will continue using the ways of balancing until such time as the controlling or higher principle, which may likened unto braking or stopping, is invoked. This stoppage of the inertia of action may be called forgiveness. These two concepts are inseparable. In forgiveness lies the stoppage of the wheel of action, or what you call karma. Actions undertaken in a consciously unloving manner with other beings are those which may generate karma.

Law of One – Beyond the limitations of language, the Law of One may be approximated by stating that all things are one, that there is no polarity, no right or wrong, no disharmony, but only identity. You are every thing, every being, every emotion, every event, every situation. You are unity. You are infinity. You are love/light, light/love. You are.

To state that another way: All is one. That one is love/light, light/love, the Infinite Creator. This is the Law of One.

Law of Responsibility – A law or way which begins to be effectuated by the increasing ability of entities to grasp the lessons to be learned in this density. If a quickened or increased rate of learning is sought, the Law of Responsibility requires that the greater understanding be put into practice in the moment to moment experience of the entity. Likewise, the closer to the light one seeks to stand, the more the Law of Responsibility goes into effect. When in earlier cycles of this third-density experience the catalysts went unused, the lessons not learned, the fruits of learning not demonstrated, the life span became greatly reduced, for the ways of honor/duty were not being accepted.

Laws – Though the field of physics as it applies to the material realm (i.e., space/time) is a limited approach to understanding what Ra may mean by "Law," the definition can begin there. Scientific laws are understood to be fundamental operations of the physical universe that are not human-designed but human-discovered. Among their characteristics, scientific laws are verifiably empirically true, simple, absolute, stable, constant, and universal. Everything in the universe must in some way comply with or conform to or operate within these laws.

Ra indicates that there is actually only one law: the Law of One. Other so-called laws are *distortions of this law*, though some of them being primal and incredibly significant for evolutionary progress. Ra nevertheless does use the word "Law" when referring to the law-like *distortions* of the Law of One, such as Law of Confusion, Law of Love, Law of Light, etc. Ra indicates that the term "law" is interchangeable with "way."

Learn/Teaching (Teach/Learning) – Learn/teaching and teach/learning are inverse terms, one to the other. A teacher is a teach/learner; a student a learn/teacher. To learn is the same as to teach, unless you are not teaching what you are learning; in which case you have done you/they little or no good. One cannot learn/teach for another, but only teach/learn.

Logos (Logoi)Sub-logos – Logos is the Second Primal Distortion of the Law of One, the focusing of intelligent infinity through free will into intelligent energy, the Creative Principle, or Love. Each Creative Principle, Love, or Logos designs its own creation or system. Each Logos determines the paths of intelligent energy, designing the natural laws and ways of expressing them mathematically and otherwise. This energy is of an ordering nature which creates its patterns in holographic style.

The mind/body/spirit complex, or human being, once sufficiently awakened, is itself a Logos—or, more technically, a sub-sub-sub-Logos.

Sub-logos (Sub-Logoi) – The One Great Logos (Primal Logos, Great Central Sun) that creates the octave (universe, creation) is the Logos. Ra also commonly uses the term "Logos" to refer to the galactic Logoi, thus using the term "sub-Logos" to refer to the solar Logoi (sun body) and "sub-sub-Logos" to refer to mind/body/spirit complexes. All levels of sub-Logoi, like the Logos, are possessed of free will. Within the guidelines or ways of the senior Logos, the junior sub-Logos may find various means of differentiating and refining experiences without removing or adding to these ways. Every entity that exists is a sub-Logos of some order down to the limits of any observation, for the entire creation is alive. Each is also a co-Creator which, in holographic style, contains the whole.

Ra may, at times, use the "sub" prefix inconsistently, though it is always used to indicate a hierarchical architecture of the Logoi. If the one Primal Logos of the octave is seen as the first or original tier in the Logos hierarchy, and if it is thereby used as the basis for the "sub" prefixes, then *sub-Logos* could refer to the next tier (galactic Logoi), *sub-sub-Logos* to solar Logoi, and *sub-sub-sub-Logoi* referring to mind/body/spirit complexes. (92.22 may be an example of this nomenclature.)

Love/Light (Light/Love) – In the infinite universe there is only one energy: love/light or light/love or intelligent energy—the universe is made from and of love/light, light/love. It is that energy which heals, builds, removes, destroys, transforms, and forms the pathways or so-called natural laws of any particular universe. This energy comes into being as Love (the Second Primal Distortion), using Free Will, creates Light (the Third Primal Distortion), thus becoming love/light.

Love and light (like love and wisdom), are not black and white, but faces of the same coin. There is the same difference between love/light and light/love as there is between teach/learning and learn/teaching. Love/light is the enabler, the power, the energy giver. Light/love is the manifestation which occurs when light has been impressed with love.

Magic – The ability to create changes in consciousness through will, or the ability to consciously use the unconscious. Magic is the work of the adept; it is a sacramental connection undertaken at the level of the gateway, or indigo ray, which is fed by the disciplines of the personality. The heart of white magic (the positive use of magic) is an experience of the joy of union with the Creator that joins body, mind, and spirit with the One Infinite Creator and radiates throughout the life experience.

Magical Personality – When the higher self is properly and efficaciously invoked for the purpose of a working, it is called the *magical personality*. Upon this invocation, a bridge is made between space/time and time/space. As consequence, the higher self directly experiences the third-density catalyst for the duration of the working. And the third-density self takes upon itself something of a vestment of a personality of consciousness that bestows magical perception and power.

Master & Major Cycles – Third density begins and ends in the span of a master cycle, ours being approximately 75,000–76,000 years. At the end of the master cycle, all are harvested regardless of their progress. Those who have successfully polarized will transfer to a polarized fourth-density home. Those who have not made the Choice will repeat third density elsewhere. Within the master cycle are three major cycles of approximately 25,000 years.

Maldek – What we know as the asteroid belt is the remains of a former planet which was home to active first, second, and third densities. There are various names by which this planet has been identified, but in certain quarters of Earth's history (perhaps some of which have been lost) it apparently had the name of Maldek. The third-density population of Maldek had a civilization that gained much technological information and used it without care for the preservation of their planet, following the ways of warfare and service to self which was sincerely believed to be service to others. The escalating devastation wracked their biosphere and caused its disintegration.

Mars – Was once home to active first, second, and third density vibrations. The tendencies of the native third-density population toward warfare caused the atmosphere to become inhospitable before the end of its cycle. The Confederation aided these entities by transferring them at the start of Earth's third-density experience 75,000 years ago. This transfer was unusual in that their genetic material was preserved, adjusted, and, through a sort of cloning process, transferred to Earth. Consequently, the quarantine of planet Earth was instituted due to the assessment of the Guardians that the free will of those of Mars had been abridged.

Meditation – Ra describes meditation as a foundational prerequisite of the path of the spiritual seeker, for without such a method of reversing the analytical process, one could not integrate into unity the many understandings gained in such seeking. They would not endorse a best way to meditate, but described broad categories:

1. The **passive meditation** involving the clearing of the mind and emptying of the mental jumble which is characteristic of the human mind complex. This is efficacious for those whose goal is to achieve an inner silence as a base from which to listen to the Creator. It is by far the most generally useful type of meditation as opposed to contemplation or prayer.

2. **Contemplation** or the consideration in a meditative state of an inspiring image, text, or spiritual principle.

3. The faculty of will called **praying**. Whether it is indeed an helpful activity depends quite totally upon the intentions and objects of the one who prays.

4. The type of meditation which may be called **visualization** is the tool of the adept. When the ability to hold visual images in mind has become crystallized in an adept, the adept may then, without external action, do polarizing in consciousness which can affect the planetary consciousness. Only those wishing to pursue the conscious raising of planetary vibration will find visualization to be a particularly satisfying type of meditation.

Mind Complex – That aspect of an entity which contains feelings, emotions, intellectual thoughts, ideation, imagination, conceptualization, dreaming, etc. It reflects the inpourings of the spirit and the up-pourings of the body complex. The mind is referred to as "complex" due to the veiling that partitions the conscious from the unconscious mind.

Ra describes the mind as having a configuration of layers or deeper natures. The intuition conveys information to the individual mind from the deeper aspects of the racial mind, the planetary mind, the archetypical mind, and the cosmic mind. The spirit complex then funnels these roots of mind into contact with intelligent infinity.

Mind/Body/Spirit Complex – A term Ra uses to refer to entities (aka: people) of third-density or higher. (Second-density entities are referred to as mind/body complexes.) Mind, body, and spirit are inextricably intertwined and cannot continue, one without the other. The work of third density is done through the interaction of these three components, not through any one.

The nature of the mind, body, and spirit as *complex* (consisting of seemingly separate and distinct components or parts) is a result of the veiling. Pre-veil entities were simply mind/body/spirits (non-complex).

Mixed Contact – It is possible for a positively oriented but un-tuned and confused channel to receive both positive and negative communications. If the channel at the base of its confusion is oriented towards service to others, negative sources may impress messages which speak of coming doom and offer reason to fear. Many channeling contacts have been confused and self-destructive because the channels were oriented towards service to others but, in the desire for proof, were open to the deceptive information of the crusaders who were then able to neutralize the effectiveness of the channel. Tuning and challenging are always counseled for positively oriented channels.

Octave – The system of densities that the evolving entities and social memory complexes move through takes place within a larger cycle known as an octave. Each octave contains seven densities with the eighth density being the first density of the following octave. Each octave is a heartbeat that births a new universe which begins with first density and is absorbed again at the eighth density. That which is learned in one octave is carried forward in the next. Acknowledging limitations upon their knowledge, Ra assumes that there are an infinite number of octaves, the ways of the octave being without time; that is, there are seven densities in each creation, infinitely.

As the creation can be seen to have some fractal characteristics, Ra sometimes refers to individual densities, sub-densities, or even certain cycles of experience, as octaves. Octave is also synonymous with the terms *universe* and *creation*.

One Original Thought/Original Thought – All things, all of life, all of the creation is part of One Original Thought. In each octave this Original Thought contains the harvest of all experience of the Creator by the Creator from the preceding octaves. For instance, the harvest of the previous octave into our present octave was the efficiency of the male/female polarity, and the Creator of Love manifested in mind, body, and spirit.

Orion – An empire of entities and social memory complexes who have chosen the negative path. Whereas the Confederation of Planets is organized as a confederation of alliances which share power and service on the basis of the oneness of all things, the Orion Group organizes itself on the basis of power against power, establishing a pecking order with the more powerful controlling the less powerful. The Confederation teaches unity and service to others; the Orion Empire teaches separation and service to self. They do this by calling themselves to conquest, attempting to bring third-density entities and planets into their fold using various means of manipulation and enslavement. This is done by finding and establishing an elite and causing others to serve the elite. Due to the problems inherent in pitting power against power, spiritual entropy causes them to experience constant disintegration of their social memory complexes, thus their numbers are perhaps one-tenth of the Confederation's at any point.

They are referred to as Orion because social memory complexes from the Orion constellation have the upper hand and thus rule the other members. It is unclear whether there are also positive beings from the stars within the Orion constellation.

Other-Self – The term Ra uses to refer to entities other than the self, i.e. I am your other-self, and you are my other-self. It is also a term that acknowledges the unity of all things, for each is a self, and each is an other-self to a self, and each is part of one self: the One Infinite Creator.

Polarity (In Consciousness) – In order to successfully graduate from the third density, consciousness can and must become polarized toward one pole or the other: "service to others" or "service to self." The purpose of polarity is to develop the potential to do work. This work drives evolution forward and galvanizes the development of will and faith, creating a more vivid and intensive experience of the Creator knowing itself. Called the axis upon which the creation turns, the higher densities do their work due to the polarity gained in this choice until sixth density when the polarities are released.

The Law of One blinks neither at the light or the darkness, but is available for service to others and service to self. In sixth density, the density of unity, the positive and negative paths must needs take in each other for all now must be seen as love/light and light/love. This is not difficult for the positive polarity, which sends love and light to all other-selves. It is difficult enough for service-to-self polarized entities that at some point the negative polarity is abandoned.

Possibility/Probability Vortex – A term used by Ra to describe possible experiences and scenarios in the future (as we understand it). Some vortices or possibilities may be stronger than others, having a higher probability of unfolding based upon the free will choices of the entities involved and existing patterns of momentum and energy. Any possibility/probably complex has an existence due to infinite opportunity. Prophecy can be considered a viewing of various possibility/probability vortices, with the stronger vortices being more readily perceivable. The value of prophecy must be realized to be only that of expressing possibilities.

Programming (Incarnational) – Prior to an entity becoming consciously aware of the path of spiritual evolution, incarnation is automatic and catalyst is generally of a random nature. When the entity becomes aware of the mechanism for spiritual evolution (upon the activation of the green-ray energy center), the entity itself will, prior to incarnation, arrange and place those lessons and entities necessary for maximum growth and expression of polarity in the incarnative experience. Such programming may include: genetic predispositions, selection of parents and family, life circumstances, time period in which the incarnation will take place, personality characteristics, lessons of polarity, balance between love and wisdom, etc.

Psychic Greeting (Psychic Attack) – The energizing of pre-existing distortions of a third-density seeker by higher-density entities. A negative greeting may consist of the tempting of the entity or group of entities away from total polarization towards service to others and toward the aggrandizement of self or of social organizations with which the self identifies. Depending upon the vibratory nature and purpose of the greeting, the third-density entity may be energized, blocked, or its imbalances accentuated.

Quarantine – Approximately 75,000 years ago, those who Ra calls the Guardians transferred the genetic material of the third-density Mars population from its destroyed home to Earth. This was deemed to be an abridgement of free will, so a quarantine was placed around Earth by the Guardians at the start of the 75,000 year master cycle of third density. The quarantine prevents interference from entities of other densities except in two circumstances: one, the Council grants permission to break quarantine, or two, a negative entity takes advantage of the window effect.

Ra – A social memory complex that evolved upon the planet Venus, experiencing the third-density there 2.6 billion years ago, they have since left the planet and are presently at the sixth-density level of evolution. Their primary purpose is to teach the Law of One in response to the call for service issuing from this planet. They have made historical attempts of this, including interacting with the Egyptians. Their teachings, however, were distorted by the peoples of the time, thus their primary present goal is to heal those distortions given to the Law of One.

Seniority of Vibration – The preferential treatment that gives priority of reincarnation to entities who are aware of the need to bend mind, body, and spirit toward achieving harvestability. It can be likened to placing various grades of liquids in the same glass: some will rise to the top, others will sink to the bottom. Layers and layers of entities will ensue, and, as harvest draws near, those filled with the most light and love will naturally, and without supervision, be in line for the experience of incarnation.

Service to Others (Positive Path) – One of two paths of polarity chosen in third-density experience. Also called the *path of that which is*; love, acceptance, and radiance are the hallmarks of the positive path. The positive path seeks to understand the unity of all things and revolves around the understanding, experiencing, accepting, and merging of self with self and with other-self, and finally with the Creator. In the desire to serve others is the fundamental respect for the free will of all beings and thus the positive entity awaits the call to service, serving only insofar as it is requested. The best way of service to others is the constant attempt to seek to share the love of the Creator as it is known to the inner self. This path attempts to open and balance the full spectrum of energy centers.

Service to Self (Negative Path) – One of two paths of polarity chosen in third-density experience. Also called the *path of that which is not*; control, manipulation, and absorption are the hallmarks of the negative path. This path is predicated upon separation and the manipulation, infringement, and enslavement of the free will of all other selves for the benefit of the self. This necessitates an omission and denial of universal love, or the green-ray energy center. Thus lacking empathy, the service-to-self entity does not await the call to service but calls itself to conquest.

Sexual Energy Transfer – Energy transfer in general is the release of potential energy differences across a potentiated space. *Sexual energy transfer* is the transfer of energy during sexual intercourse between two sexually polarized entities depending upon the male/female principle ratio. Both positive and negative sexual energy transfers are possible. Positive energy transfer requires both entities to be vibrating at a green-ray level. In the positive transfer, the male will have offered the discharge of physical energy to the female, and the female discharges its stored mental and emotional energy. The transfer is mutually uplifting and enhancing, and offers possibility of polarization and service. With careful development this transfer also holds the possibility of opening the gateway and experiencing sacramental communion with the Creator.

Sinkhole of Indifference – The spiritual path being predicated on the choice between the positive and negative polarities, the sinkhole of indifference is the state of remaining unpolarized and not achieving the transformation afforded by making the Choice. It is a state of being less-than-conscious and without power, a blind repetition of patterns. When neither path is chosen, the entity will continue to receive catalyst until it forms a bias towards acceptance and love or separation and control.

Social Memory Complex – When a collection of related entities, called a social complex, reaches a point of one orientation or seeking, it becomes a *social memory complex*. In a social memory complex, the experience of each entity is available to the whole, this forming a group memory that becomes available to the entire social complex. This is generally achieved in fourth density by positive and negative groups. The advantages of this complex are the relative lack of distortion in understanding the social beingness and the relative lack of distortion in pursuing the direction of seeking.

Negative social memory complexes are organized in a strict pecking order on the basis of relative power, those more powerful controlling and enslaving the less. Positive social memory complexes are organized on the basis of unity, or the Creator in all things. In this arrangement, power and love are shared and free-will-respecting service is freely given.

Space/Time and Time/Space – **Space/time** is the visible, physical realm that we now experience as conscious, incarnate beings. This is the realm of physics and the proverbial five senses. **Time/space** is the invisible, metaphysical realms, also known as the inner planes. This is the realm of intention and the unconscious. The terminology is likely based upon the theories of physics of Dewey Larson, used by Don and Ra to integrate this scientific understanding with the spiritual understanding.

Space/time and time/space are complex and complete systems that form fundamental aspects of our illusion. They share an inverse relationship due to the inequality between time and space. In space/time, the spatial orientation of material causes a tangible framework for illusion. In time/space, the inequality is shifted to the property of time.

These space/time and time/space distinctions, as we understand them, do not hold sway except in third density. However, fourth, fifth, and to some extent, sixth densities, work within some system of polarized space/time and time/space.

Note: Ra also uses the term "time/space" to indicate the passage of clock and calendar time as we know it.

Spirit Complex – The fields of force and consciousness which are the least distorted of the mind/body/spirit complex (but which can be realized in many distorted and unintegrated ways by the mind and body complexes of energy fields). When the intelligent energy of mind and body are balanced, the spirit complex acts as a two-way channel, pathway, shuttle or communicator whereby 1) the inpourings from the various universal, planetary, and personal sources may be funneled into the roots of consciousness, and 2) consciousness may be funneled to the gateway of intelligent infinity. Healing is the realization and undistorted opening of the mind and body to these spiritual instreamings.

The apparent addition of the spirit complex happens as second-density entities (mind/body complexes) become self-aware, thus becoming mind/body/spirit complexes and entering third density, the first density of consciousness of spirit. This addition is *apparent* rather than real as it is simply a realization of the spirit complex which was always available in potentiation.

Spiritual Entropy – A type of loss of polarity and cohesion. This is particularly experienced by negative social memory complexes due to their tendency toward inability to act totally as one being, thus causing them to experience constant disintegration of their social memory complexes.

Tarot – A system of 22 images (The Major Arcana) first developed by Ra during their third-density experience and later passed to the Egyptians by Ra, it is used as a tool to study the archetypal mind and develop the magical personality. Ra suggests that the Major Arcana not be used as a method of divination but instead used as a means to study the archetypal mind, and to gain knowledge of the self by the self for the purpose of entering a more profoundly, acutely realized present moment.

Thought Form – A pattern or persistence of thought that in some cases can exhibit persistent metaphysical or physical characteristics separate from the original thinker. Physical characteristics may include visual or material beingness. Thought forms can be created by entities consciously (typically higher-density beings) or unconsciously, particularly by the collective unconscious mind.

Trance State/Channel – In the context of the Ra contact, the state in which the instrument's mind/body/spirit complex left the physical body and allowed Ra to speak through it in a way supposedly undistorted by the presence of the instrument's own biases. In this state the instrument was unconscious and awoke with no memory of the information which was passed through her.

Transient Information – In the context of the Ra contact, information that is of a specific nature and lacks metaphysical principle or relevance, or is not directly related to the evolution of mind, body, and spirit. The level and purity of the contact was dependent on the level and purity of the information sought. Transient and specific information, especially if emphasized, was deleterious to the working.

True Color – The frequency that is the basis of each density, every color having specific vibratory characteristics both in space/time and in time/space. It is the basic vibration of a density which is then overlaid and tinged by the various vibratory levels within that density, and the attraction to the vibrations of the next true color density.

Tuning – To bring into harmony, reminiscent of tuning a musical instrument. Includes activities such as bringing the energy centers into a harmonious balance or tuning of the self in order to match the vibration of a contact for channeling.

Unconscious – A portion of the mind complex which is outside the perception of the entity's conscious awareness. It has various levels and depths ranging from the personal mind to the cosmic mind, and may contain a differing configuration, awareness, or will than the conscious mind. The nature of the unconscious is of the nature of concept rather than word. It corresponds to the female archetypal energy, is represented by the archetype of the High Priestess, and is the Potentiator of consciousness. Ra describes the nature of penetrating the veil to the unconscious mind as being "likened unto the journey too rich and exotic to contemplate adequate describing thereof."

Unmanifested Self – The self which does not need other-self in order to manifest or act; that being which exists and does its work without reference to or aid from other-selves. Meditation, contemplation, and internal balancing of thoughts and reactions are those activities of the unmanifested self, while things such as pain or disease are the catalyst of the unmanifested self. In magic, one is working with one's unmanifested self in body, in mind, and in spirit; the mixture depending upon the nature of the working.

Upward Spiraling Light – Commonly called "prana," this light is the ever-present energy of the Creator which radiates outward from all points in space. The term "upward" is not an indication direction, but an indication of the concept of that which reaches towards the source of love and light (the Creator). It is through this light that we progress in evolution towards the Creator, and it may be called upon and attracted by use of the will to seek the light. Different geometric shapes, such as the pyramid, can harness this light for various purposes.

Veil – An aspect of consciousness and experience that could be described as the separation of the conscious and the unconscious mind, which also results in a veiling of our awareness from the true nature of the Creator. The veil exists as the result of an experiment of the early creations of the sub-Logoi. This is referred to "extending free will" and resulted in such a significant increase in free will that non-veiled entities were seen as not having free will. Prior to this implementation, non-veiled entities progressed along the path of spiritual evolution very slowly, the non-veiled condition being unconducive to polarization. The veiling was so effective at increasing polarization that it was adopted by all subsequent sub-Logoi. The conditions created by the veil resulted in what Ra refers to as the Choice, the central purpose of third-density experience.

The veil is semi-permeable, and while progressive lifting of the veil is third-density work, completely lifting the veil is not.

Vibration – A term used to refer to: densities or sub-densities; to sounds, or speaking, or names; to state of mind; to channeling contact; an entity's overall beingness, or pattern of behavior, or pattern of distortions, or progress of spiritual evolution, or thought-processes; the metaphysical state of a place; the metaphysical state of a planet and the peoples on the planet; vibration or movement in physics, particularly Dewey Larson's Reciprocal Theory. Ra indicates that everything which is manifest is a vibration, beginning with the photon itself.

Vibratory Sound Complex (Sound Vibration Complex) – Occasionally used by Ra as a term for "word," often used when referring to names.

Vital Energy – The complex of energy levels of mind, body, and spirit. Unlike physical energy, it requires the integrated complexes vibrating in an useful manner. It may be seen to be that deep love of life and the appreciation of other-selves and of beauty. Without this vital energy, the least distorted physical complex will fail and perish. With this love, or vital energy or élan, the entity may continue though the physical complex is greatly distorted. Vital energy may be used, or reserved, depleted or increased.

Wanderer (Brothers and Sisters of Sorrow) – Entities from the fourth, fifth, and sixth densities who respond to a calling of sorrow by incarnating into a third-density environment in order to be of service to others by radiating love of others. In performing this service, the wanderer becomes completely the creature of third density, and thus is subject to the forgetting which can only be penetrated with disciplined meditation and working. This decision carries the risk the wanderer will forget its mission and become karmically involved, thus needing to continue reincarnating within third density in order to balance the karma.

White Magic – Magic in general being ritual dedicated to working with the unmanifested being, white magic is directing this working toward experiencing the love and joy of union with the Creator for the purpose of service to others. This love or joy then may be both protection and the key to the gateway to intelligent infinity and will radiate throughout the life experience of the positive adept. White magic is best undertaken in a group, but it may be performed by an individual so long as it is done in the knowledge that to aid the self in polarization towards love and light is to aid the planetary vibration.

Will – Pure desire; the motivation, or impetus within an individual that becomes awakened and harnessed when directed towards service and spiritual seeking. Will could also be seen as the attraction to the upward spiraling line of light guiding spiritual evolution. It is the single measure of the rate and fastidiousness of the activation and balancing of the various energy centers. The will can be conscious or unconscious, the unconscious utilization of will possibly depolarizing the individual in their seeking. The faculty of will has been greatly enhanced by the veiling. In conjunction with faith, the seeker's will is a vital aspect of many aspects of service and seeking, from the simple utilization of catalyst for evolution to the opening of gateway to intelligent infinity.

Work – A term that generally refers to action, experience, or service done in a spiritually significant and effective sense. Such work requires polarity in consciousness, thus it is done far more efficiently—with greater purity, intensity, and variety—when an entity continuously makes the Choice, polarizing in either service to others or service to self. Examples can range from the subtle work of mental balancing to the great work of offering one's life in service as a healer.

Glossary created by Austin Bridges and Gary Bean.

These definitions are not intended to be final or authoritative.

For a more in-depth examination of these terms, see the Concept Guide in the Resource Series.

NOTES ABOUT THE INDEX

The following index is uniquely designed to enable an in-depth study of *The Ra Contact* material, and as such it departs from standard index formats in several ways.

- The reference numbers point to the particular *session* and *question* number in which the relevant information can be found rather than the page number.

- The entries are listed in alphabetical order, though some of the subentries are ordered based on their conceptual context presented in the material. (For instance, energy centers are listed from Red, to Orange, to Yellow, etc. within the Energy Center entry.)

- The listed references are not limited only to Q&As where the term was mentioned, but also Q&As that may not contain the term yet speak to the concept.

- This particular index is specific to Volume 1 of *The Ra Contact*, containing only references to the sessions contained within these pages. Volume 2 includes a similarly split index. Any entry with references contained only in the other volume is still included with a pointer to that volume. A complete and unified index listing references to all 106 sessions of the Ra contact is available as an independent booklet.

This index is as comprehensive as possible within the capabilities of the many individuals who have contributed to its creation and refinement. It contains 590 total terms (including primary, secondary, and tertiary), 81 alternative wordings, 114 "see also" associated terms, and 60 "see" references, with over 9,000 total Q&A listings. As comprehensive as it is, this index should be considered a constant work in progress and will receive subsequent updates in future editions.

Along with the volunteers, we discovered that reading every Q&A for a given term is one of the richest ways to deepen one's study of this material. We hope you find this index a useful tool in your own study of the many and varied topics discussed within the material.

INDEX

Activate

3.8	34.9	47.10-15
17.39	34.10	48.7
21.9	34.16	50.12
23.7	35.1	51.9-10
27.13	35.3	52.11
28.1	38.5	53.8
30.5	39.10	54.5-6
31.3	40.4	54.15
32.6	41.16-19	54.31-32
32.14	42.11	

Acupuncture
49.5

Adept

3.16	47.8	51.8
11.11	48.10	54.14-18
13.23	49.8	54.31
39.10	50.8-9	
42.16	50.13	

Cycle of the Adept
See Volume 2

Rituals of the Adept
See Volume 2

Services of the Adept

49.8	50.8-9

Tools of the Adept

3.16	49.8	50.8-9

Aging

14.10	15.4-5	15.8

Akashic Records
Hall of Records
14.32

Akhenaten
Ikhnaton

2.2	23.6	23.12-13

Allergy
12.30

Allopathic Healing
See "Healing, Allopathic"

American Indians
10.15

Anak

18.20	24.9

Angels

11.25	48.8	51.1
19.7		

See also "Guides"

Anger

40.9	46.5-7	54.22
40.12	46.9-11	

Ankh
Crux Ansata
55.14

Archetypes
See Volume 2

Archetypical Mind
See "Mind, Archetypal"

Ark of the Covenant
See Volume 2

Armageddon
24.6

Armor of Light

16.59	25.4	46.2

Astral Body
47.8
See also "Body Complex, Green Ray"

Astrology
19.20-21

Astronomy
See "Sciences, Astronomy"

Atlantis

10.1	22.20-21	24.4
10.15	22.27	27.1
14.4	23.1	45.4
21.28	23.6	

Attract

16.54	31.7	49.6
26.12	37.8	50.2-5
26.36	38.2	51.1
28.14	40.3	54.31
29.18	40.6	
30.10	41.10	

Aura

Aura Infringement

1.0	31.10	39.3
2.3	33.19	48.2
30.17	34.10	55.16
31.8	38.5	

Awakening

30.5	48.7	53.17
31.9	53.8	
36.24	53.12	

Balance

Balancing

General

3.1	16.5-7	31.7
4.17	21.20	33.7
7.9	22.26	34.4
14.6-11	25.6	36.7
14.20	26.20	38.10
15.4	26.27	52.7
15.8-9	26.30-31	52.9
16.2	29.29	

Balancing Exercises & Energy Centers

2.3	36.3	44.14
3.1	38.5	46.8-9
5.2	38.9-10	48.7
6.1	39.10	49.6
12.31	40.4	51.7
15.8-9	41.14	52.11
15.12-13	41.18-19	54.8
18.5	41.23-24	54.15-16
18.11	42.2-6	54.23-27
29.23	42.9-11	54.32
29.27	43.8	

Balance of the Body

5.2	12.31	51.5

Balance of the Spirit

6.1

Ball Lightning

53.23

Banishing Ritual of the Lesser Pentagram

41.2

Battle Beyond the Stars (movie)

23.19

Beingness

3.13	19.3	31.15
3.18	19.13	32.10
7.2	25.4	34.3
7.17	26.36	37.8
8.1	26.38	39.10
9.2	27.2	41.5
10.9-10	27.6	42.20
11.17	28.6	44.8
12.15	29.10-11	47.8
12.21	29.27	48.2
13.17	29.32	50.7
13.22	30.2	54.15
15.1	31.3	

Bermuda Triangle

See Volume 2

Bible

| 2.6 | 3.4 | 26.5 |
| 3.2 | | |

Bid

| 53.16 | 55.3-7 |

Bigfoot

| 9.18 | 9.21-22 | 10.4-5 |

Biology
See "Sciences, Biology"

Biorhythm
See Volume 2

Birth Defects

34.8

Black Hole

| 29.18-19 | 40.1 |

Body Complex
Physical Complex

2.3	19.13	41.12
3.16	19.20	41.21
3.8	20.3	43.22
4.17-18	23.7	46.9
5.2	26.13	47.8-10
6.4	29.19	48.2
10.14	30.2-3	48.10
11.30	30.5	49.5
14.18	31.6	51.5
15.4	31.15	54.6
15.8	36.8	54.17
18.15	39.1	54.27
18.20	40.9	56.1
18.27	40.12	
19.9-11	40.14	

Red Ray Body Complex

| 3.8 | 47.8 |

Orange Ray Body Complex

| 3.8 | 47.8 | 47.14 |

Yellow Ray Body Complex

| 3.4 | 47.8 | 47.13-15 |
| 3.8 | 47.10 | 48.10 |

Green Ray Body Complex

| 3.8 | 47.11 | 54.6 |
| 47.8 | | |

See also "Astral Body"

Blue Ray Body Complex

| 3.8 | 47.8 | 54.6 |
| 12.5 | 51.2 | |

See also "Devachanic Body"

Indigo Ray Body Complex

3.8	47.15	54.6
47.8	48.7	
47.11	51.10	

See also "Etheric Body"

Violet Ray Body Complex

| 3.8 | 48.7 | 54.6 |
| 47.8 | 48.10 | |

See also "Buddha Body"

Body Relationship with Mind and Spirit

6.1	40.14	51.5
19.20	47.8	
32.10	48.2	

Sacramental portion of the Body

| 4.18 | 31.3 | 49.2 |
| 26.38 | 32.6 | |

Balancing (and knowledge) of the Body
See "Balancing, of the Body"

Brain

| 49.2-4 | 50.11 | 52.2 |

Brothers and Sisters of Sorrow

| 12.26 | 52.9 | 55.7 |
| 23.10 | | |

See also "Wanderers"
See also "Confederation of Planets"

Buddha Body

47.8

See also "Body Complex, Violet Ray"

Calling

1.0	14.18	23.6
4.8	14.24	23.8
7.1-9	21.14-16	24.8
8.12	21.18-20	26.34
10.12-13	22.17	27.1
11.18	22.19	43.28-29
12.26	22.25	55.4
14.2	23.1	55.7

See also "Law of Squares"

Cancer

40.9	46.7-8	46.14-16
40.12-13	46.10-11	

Cassiopeia

11.12

Catalyst

4.20	33.14-17	46.7
5.1	34.6-7	46.9
17.2	34.9	46.14-16
17.18	34.12-15	47.6
19.3	36.2	48.6-8
19.12-13	36.17	49.4-6
22.5-6	40.12	50.2-5
28.1-2	40.15	52.9
28.5	41.22	54.14-24
28.13	42.2	54.24
29.30	42.9-10	54.28
33.6-9	43.9	
33.12	43.18	

Catalyst (Archetype)
See "Archetype, Catalyst" (Vol. 2)

Cats, (our)

30.13	46.2

Cattle Mutilations

16.43	42.21	48.5
16.46	43.5	

Cayce, Edgar

14.31-32	27.1

Celibacy
22.23

Cepheus
See Volume 2

Chakra
See "Energy Center"

Chaldea
See Volume 2

Challenging of Spirits
See Volume 2

Channel, Trance
Narrow Band

1.0	13.13	27.1
1.10-11	14.25	30.17
1.13	14.32	33.2
2.0	17.14	35.8
2.4	17.22	36.21
2.6	18.3	37.4
3.15	18.14	38.1
5.1	19.22	44.8
6.1	22.1-2	48.6
6.3	22.19	55.7
7.10	22.27	
12.15	26.36	

See also "Ra Contact Methodology"

Children

16.10	42.12

China
21.28

Choice, The

16.7	19.15-18	36.12
16.11	20.10-11	50.7
17.33	30.1	

See also "Polarity (in Consciousness)"

Choice, The (Archetype)
See "Archetypes, The Choice" (Vol. 2)

Christianity
See Volume 2

Cleanliness
See Volume 2

Cleansing Ritual
41.1

Colors

1.7	40.11	47.8
27.17	40.15	48.7
28.2	41.14	48.10
32.12-13	41.19	49.6
33.3	41.25	51.5
33.20	42.13	54.5-6
38.5	43.8	54.8
40.3	44.14	54.11-12
40.5-6	47.3	56.5-6

Compassion
Loving, Green Ray Love, Unconditional Love, Universal Love, Vibration of Love

1.5	23.6	42.2
4.6	25.5-6	42.6-7
4.17	27.13	42.20
15.12	32.9	43.14-15
16.50	33.8	44.10
17.30	33.11	47.5
18.5-6	33.20	48.6
18.11	34.17	52.9
22.6	41.25-26	54.17

Complex

Body Complex
See "Body Complex"

Consciousness Complex

6.24	21.9	28.19
9.18		

Mind Complex
See "Mind Complex"

Mind/Body/Spirit Complex
See "Mind/Body/Spirit Complex"

Physical Complex
See "Body Complex"

Social Complex

10.1	16.6	21.28
10.7	16.10	22.6
10.12	17.1	22.22
10.15	18.6	23.1
11.16-17	18.8	31.4
13.23	18.21	45.1
14.4	19.11	52.2
14.6	19.14	

Social Memory Complex
See "Social Memory Complex"

Sound Vibration Complex
See "Sound Vibration Complex"

Spirit Complex
See "Spirit Complex"

Concept

24.19	34.4	40.1
27.4	35.8	40.15

Conditioning
1.0

Confederation of Planets

1.0-1	12.9	19.7
2.2	12.11	20.26-28
2.4	12.15	21.5
6.24-25	12.18	21.14-20
7.1	14.13	21.17
7.6-9	14.18	22.11-12
7.12	14.28-29	22.16-21
7.15	16.8	22.11-12
8.1	16.13	24.4
8.6	16.19	25.4-10
8.12	16.22	26.20-22
8.30-31	16.32-35	26.32
10.1	17.0-9	26.36
10.12	17.11	27.1
11.21	17.22	29.3
11.25	18.13	31.12
12.3	18.23	37.5
12.5	19.5-7	(Cont. ...)

(... Cont.)	44.8	53.6
38.1	51.1	53.9
41.26	53.3	53.12-18

See also "Brothers and Sisters of Sorrow"
See also "Wanderers"

Consciousness
See "Complex, Consciousness"

Consonant with the Law of One

6.14	18.5	42.10
7.9	18.8	52.7

Contemplation
See "Prayer or Contemplation"

Control
Manipulate

11.15	32.2	52.7
11.18	46.9-12	53.14
11.20-21	46.16	54.19
12.2	48.6	54.25

Cosmic Mind
See "Mind, Cosmic"

Council of Saturn

6.7-8	14.28-30	26.32
7.8-10	22.17	39.9
7.12	23.6	53.3
8.1	23.16	
9.4	24.4	

Crowley, Aleister
18.10-11

Crucifixion of Esmerelda Sweetwater
(book)
See Volume 2

Crux Ansata
See "Ankh"

Crystallization
Crystallize, Crystalline

2.1	3.6	29.23
2.3	28.2	(Cont. ....)

(... Cont.)	34.10	49.8
29.27	39.12	51.7-8
29.30	47.7	56.3

Crystals

2.3	22.21	29.31
6.21	29.24	
14.7	29.27-28	

Crystal Healing
See "Healing, Crystals"

D'Obrenovic, Michel
See "Williamson, George Hunt"

Darkness

7.15	19.17	35.8
11.26-28	21.9	40.1
13.16	25.6	

Daydream
See "Fantasy"

Death

17.20	33.9	47.11-15
23.12	33.11	48.7
26.25-28	34.6	51.6
30.3-4	34.18	51.10
31.14	47.9	53.3

Deconsecration of a Sacred Place
See Volume 2

Deep Mind
See "Unconscious"

Defense, Magical
See "Magical Defense"

Deleterious Energy Exchange
See Volume 2

Deneb

10.15	21.28

Density

See also "Dimension"

See also "Sub-Density"

6.14-15	17.41	40.3-6
7.15-16	18.5-7	40.5-6
9.4	19.12	41.7-8
11.3	26.24	41.15-18
13.8	27.16-17	41.26
13.13	28.4	43.22
13.20-23	28.13-16	45.7
15.25	29.2	45.11
16.2	29.13-14	47.3-6
16.21-30	29.32	48.1
16.33	30.2	48.10
16.38	32.8-9	51.2
16.51	32.12	52.3-7
16.53	36.1	52.12
17.1	39.4	54.4
17.18	40.1	

First Density

11.4	28.15	41.7-8
13.15-18	29.11	41.10
16.21	30.5	
28.6	40.3	

Second Density

9.14-15	19.5-9	34.7
9.17-19	19.13-15	38.8
10.3-4	20.1-4	40.3
10.15	20.18	41.10
13.17-21	20.20	41.14-18
13.21	30.5-7	41.17
14.1-3	30.9-10	46.2
16.21	30.12-13	53.14
19.2-3	31.4	

Third Density

See "Third Density"

Fourth Density

6.14-19	13.20	16.39-40
11.3	13.22-23	16.50
11.5-6	14.17	17.1-2
11.8-16	15.20	17.15
11.12	16.11-12	17.18
12.16-17	16.21	17.22-24
12.28	16.32	(Cont. ....)

(... Cont.)	35.6-8	43.26
17.34	36.1	45.11
20.8	38.7	47.2-6
20.27-28	38.14	47.3
20.36	40.8-11	47.6
25.9-10	40.9	48.6
26.12	40.12	50.7-9
26.34	40.15	50.9
27.13	41.4	51.2
29.19-20	41.16	52.3-7
32.8-9	42.6-7	52.5
33.9-12	43.9-14	53.18
33.19-20	43.16-19	
34.16	43.25-29	

Fifth Density

6.6	33.20	43.23
13.20	36.1	45.11
16.21	36.12	47.3
16.41	41.4	48.6
17.11-21	41.16	51.2
25.9-11	42.6-7	52.3-7
29.28	43.14	52.4
32.8-9	43.20-29	53.19-20

Sixth Density

1.1	32.11	43.14-15
6.4-7	33.20	43.15
6.6	36.1	43.24-27
6.23	36.7-17	45.4
8.20	36.8	45.11
12.28	36.12	48.6
13.20	36.15-16	51.2
14.19-21	36.22	52.3-7
16.21-22	37.6	52.9
25.9-10	41.4-6	
32.8-9	41.16	

Seventh Density

13.20	36.1	41.4
14.19	36.8-9	41.16
16.21-23	37.6	
32.8	39.4	

Eighth Density

6.8	16.32	40.1
14.32	28.15	51.1
16.21	36.8	52.12

Devachanic Body

47.8

See also "Body Complex, Blue Ray"

Devachanic Planes

17.36-37

Diaspora

24.17	25.4

Diet

40.14	41.22	42.12

Dimension

3.8	10.16	17.18
4.2	11.12	17.31
4.4-5	13.8	20.7
4.9	13.17	20.36
5.2	14.4	21.5
6.4	14.17	26.24
6.6-8	15.18	27.2
6.13	16.2	36.1
6.15-16	16.5	36.3
6.18	16.22	40.1
6.24-25	16.25	52.1
10.1	16.32	54.5
10.3	16.43	
10.6	17.1	

See also "Density"

Dinosaur

30.6-8

Disciplines of the Body

3.16	5.2	41.21-22
4.17-18		

Disciplines of the Mind

3.16	41.21-22	52.2
4.17	44.10	
5.2	46.9	

Disciplines of the Personality

4.8	51.2	54.8
11.20	52.1-7	54.15-16
42.2	52.11	

Disciplines of the Spirit

4.17-19	41.21-22	52.3
6.1	42.12	52.11

Disease

23.13-15	40.15	45.2
34.7		

Distortion

1.1	15.9	40.12
1.5	15.21	43.13
1.7	17.33	44.13
1.10	18.6	46.2
3.4	18.22	46.12
4.9	20.32	47.2
4.19	21.3	48.2
8.31	22.6	51.6
9.9	22.19	54.8
10.10	27.7	54.22
11.17	29.25-27	54.28
13.12	31.7-8	54.32
14.10	34.12	55.2

Primal Distortion

3.14	13.12	19.21
4.20	14.10	21.14
7.15	14.18	22.27
9.10	14.28	27.12
10.12	15.21	56.3
11.20	18.5-6	
13.8	19.12	

First Distortion

Finity, Free Will, Awareness

2.2	13.6-8	18.20
3.14	13.12-13	18.24
4.20	13.16	19.12
6.26	15.13	19.16-17
7.1	15.20-21	20.11
7.12	15.25	20.26
7.17	16.1-9	20.32
8.1	16.27	21.4
9.9	16.30	21.8-9
10.12	17.1	21.14
11.18-19	18.1	21.18-20
12.5	18.5-6	(Cont. ...)

(... Cont.)

22.2	30.7	43.29-31
22.17	30.11	47.2
24.8	31.6	47.16
25.1	31.15	48.8
26.13	33.1-2	51.9-10
26.36	33.9	53.3
27.5	36.7	53.7
27.8-10	36.12	54.3
27.12-13	36.20	54.7
28.1	38.1	54.11
28.6	39.6-7	54.13-14
28.13	40.1	54.18
29.10	41.4	54.27
29.31	41.25	55.4
	42.3	

See also "Law of Confusion"

Second Distortion

Logos, Love, Co-creator, Primal Co-creator, Creative Principle

9.10	28.5-11	41.25
13.7-9	28.20	46.14
13.13	29.2-13	47.2
13.15-16	29.32	51.10
14.10	30.1	52.2
15.9	30.14-15	52.11-12
15.21-22	39.4	54.4-5
18.6	40.1	54.7-10
19.12	41.4	54.17
27.11-17	41.7-8	54.27
27.17	41.12	
28.1-3	41.18	

Third Distortion

Light, Photon

6.14	27.16-17	40.5
12.5	28.2-5	40.9
13.9	28.7-8	41.9
13.16-17	29.12	47.8
15.4	29.16	52.11-12
15.9	32.12	54.4
15.21	39.6	54.10
17.18	40.1	54.27
27.13-14	40.3	56.3

See also "Light, Downward Spiraling"
See also "Light, Upward Spiraling"
See also "Prana"

Divination
See Volume 2

Doubling

7.2-5	11.11	37.7
7.7	22.27	39.1
10.13-14	26.40	

See also "Law of Squares"

Downward Spiraling Light
See "Light, Downward Spiraling"

Dreaming

14.25-26	44.10-11	46.2

Dual Activated
Bodies, Individuals

17.1

Earth Changes

1.9	24.4	33.12
17.1		

See also "Harvest"

Earth's Population

6.13	20.18-22	47.15
10.6	21.11	

Easter Island, Heads of

20.30-35	20.37

Ectoplasm

47.8

Eden
See Volume 2

Ego

15.10-12	18.5

Egypt

1.3	22.21-22	24.4
1.5	23.1-2	24.6
2.2	23.6	27.1
14.4-5	23.8	51.4
14.26	23.13-14	51.6

Egyptian Tarot
See Volume 2

Einstein, Albert

| 17.8-9 | 26.20 | 39.4 |

Eisenhower, Dwight D.

| 24.19 | 26.33 |

Elder Race

| 15.15 | 15.17-20 |

Electricity

19.19-20	31.2	49.4
20.9	38.12	55.16
25.5	39.4	
28.18-19	48.2	

Elemental

| 16.43-46 | 17.37 |

Elements
Fire, Wind, Water, Earth

1.12-13	13.16	29.33
6.1	13.18	49.5
6.7	15.12	54.27
9.5	20.42	

Energy Center

15.7	41.14	49.5-6
15.9	41.16	50.2
15.12	41.18-19	50.12
17.39	42.9-11	51.5
21.9	42.20	51.7-8
32.12-14	43.5	54.8-9
35.1	43.8	54.14-17
38.5	44.14	54.25-32
39.10	47.4	55.16
39.12	47.8	56.3
40.4	48.7	
41.8-9	48.10	

Energy Center Blockage

31.9	38.5	51.5
31.14-15	41.25	51.7
32.2	50.2	54.11-12
32.14	50.12	(Cont. ...)

| (...Cont.) | 54.31-32 | 56.3 |
| 54.14-15 | | |

Primary Energy Centers

39.10	41.25	49.5
40.4	47.3	
41.19	48.7	

Red Ray Energy Center

15.12	41.25	54.17
26.38	46.9	54.25
31.4-5	47.8	54.27
34.15-16	50.2	
39.10-11	51.8	

Orange Ray Energy Center

15.12	34.9	47.8
26.38	34.12	47.14
31.5	34.16	49.6
31.14	41.10	51.8
32.2	41.13-14	54.17
32.14	41.25	54.25

Yellow Ray Energy Center

15.12	34.12	47.10
26.38	34.16	47.13-14
31.5	39.10	49.5-6
32.2	41.14-15	51.8
32.14	41.25	54.17
34.9-10	47.8	54.25

Green Ray Energy Center

12.31	32.14	47.8
15.12	34.9-10	47.11
21.9	34.12-15	48.7
26.38	34.17	49.6
31.3	39.10	50.8
31.5	41.16	51.8
31.10	41.25	54.17
32.3	42.7	54.25
32.5	47.3-4	54.31

Blue Ray Energy Center

15.12	41.25	49.6
26.38	47.3-4	51.8
32.5	47.8	54.17
32.14	48.7	54.25
39.10	48.10	54.31

Indigo Ray Energy Center

11.8	47.4	51.8
15.12	48.7	54.17
26.38	49.2	54.25
32.5-6	49.6	54.31-32
32.14	50.13	

Violet Ray Energy Center

11.8	33.19	49.2
12.31	34.15-16	49.6
14.14	38.5	50.12-13
15.12	39.10	51.1
19.20	41.19	51.8
26.38	47.8	54.27
29.27-30	48.7	54.30-31
32.7	48.10	

Eighth Energy Center

11.8	14.32	34.2

Energy Transfer

General

31.2	39.10	54.31
32.5	54.25	55.8

Sexual Energy Transfer

25.1	31.11-15	48.2
26.38	32.2	54.25
30.10	32.5-10	54.31
31.2-7	39.10	
31.9	44.1	

Enlightenment

Illumination

1.10	17.2	48.5
2.1	17.37	49.4
4.8	18.5	52.7
15.13	23.10	

Error

Mistake, Misstep, Incorrect

4.13	17.17	32.9
8.6	18.1	34.5
12.24	18.23	44.17
14.34	23.16	53.16
17.0	32.1	
17.12	32.4	

Error in Transmission

17.0	18.1	32.3-4
17.12		

Etheric Body

47.8	47.15	48.7
47.11		

See also "Body Complex, Indigo Ray"

Evolution

Physical Evolution

See "Sciences, Evolution"

Evolution of Spirit

28.13-14	37.3	47.2
30.1	39.10	48.8
30.5	40.3	50.5
30.7	41.4	51.5
30.14	41.10	52.2
36.15	41.18	52.11
36.17	45.11	54.24

Exercise, Physical (for the Instrument)

18.27	34.1	53.1
25.2	39.2	

Experience (Archetype)

See "Archetype, Experience" (Vol. 2)

Faith

3.9	41.22	54.24
16.18	42.12	54.31
27.4	46.9	

See also "Intelligent Infinity"

Fantasy

16.54-57

Fasting

40.14	41.21-22	42.12

Faults

See Volume 2

Female/Male

5.2	31.7-10	54.3
26.38		

Food

4.22	21.12-13	42.7-8
18.4	23.14	43.17-24
18.27	25.2	
19.22	40.14	

Forgetting, The
See "Veil of Forgetting"

Forgiveness

17.20	34.4-5	41.25
18.12	34.17	50.7
26.30	40.13	52.7

Form-maker Body

47.11	48.7	51.10

See also "Body, Indigo Ray"

Franklin, Benjamin
26.15-16

Free Will
See "Distortion, First"

Frontal Lobes (of the brain)

49.2-4	52.5

Frye, Daniel
8.30

Fusion

32.9-10	41.4-5

Games

19.17	34.12	50.7

Garlic
See Volume 2

Gateway to Intelligent Infinity
See "Intelligent Infinity, Gateway to"

Genghis Khan

11.9-15	17.25

Ghosts (Lingering Spirits)
47.12-14

Gnosticism
51.6

Goering, Hermann
35.5

Golden Dawn
42.17-18

Graduation

10.4	20.18	38.14
10.9	30.5	40.4
11.6	34.16	41.26
19.5	36.12	47.5-6
20.3	38.6	52.12

See also "Harvest"

Gravity

20.7	37.8	52.2-5
29.15-22	40.1	

Great Pyramid at Giza

3.6	4.6	51.6
3.12	23.6	55.11-16
3.15	23.8	56.3-6

See also "Pyramids"

Great Record of Creation
See Volume 2

Great Way (Archetype)
See "Archetype, Great Way" (Vol. 2)

Great Work

6.1	48.6	52.2

Greeting, Psychic
See "Psychic Greeting"

Guardians

7.9	20.28	50.5
9.6-9	21.8	51.1
9.18	21.14	52.12
12.3-5	24.4	54.10
16.1	30.14	
16.5-6	48.8	

See also "Protection"

Guides
Guidance System

12.14	18.8-9	54.3
14.18	36.12	

See also "Angels"

Hair

19.9	20.6	49.5
19.13		

Hall of Records
See "Akashic Records"

Harmony

1.1	29.30	42.2
2.0	30.14	42.7
4.13	32.8-9	43.11
7.9	33.1-2	47.6
7.14-15	36.1	47.15
15.24-25	36.17	48.6-7
16.5	36.21-22	49.9
17.18	37.3	50.7
18.6	38.1	53.2
18.11	38.6	54.6
20.13	38.9	54.15-16
22.3	40.4	54.32
29.9-10	41.26	55.7

Harvest

1.9	13.22-23	19.1-11
6.11	14.4	20.1-2
6.13-15	14.14-20	20.20
6.19	15.14-20	20.27-29
7.16-17	16.11	21.13-14
8.2	16.13	21.28
8.6	16.39-41	22.7-16
8.25	16.61	24.8
10.9	17.1	26.12
11.3	17.15	26.28
11.6	17.22-25	26.34
11.8	17.29	33.12-13
11.19	17.31-34	34.2
12.27-28	17.41-43	(Cont. ...)

(... Cont.)	43.25	51.1
34.15-18	45.7	52.8-9
35.4-5	46.2	52.12
40.7-11	47.3-8	53.16
41.19	48.6-8	54.18
42.6	49.6	55.3-4
43.8	50.5	
43.13-15	50.8	

See also "Earth Changes"

Harvestable

17.15	38.14	47.8
21.28	40.4	48.7
30.13	41.19	49.6
34.16-17	47.3	50.8
35.4	47.6	54.18

Hawk

23.1

Healing

2.2-4	18.10-11	34.10
3.14-15	21.3	35.8
4.5-20	21.5	36.2
5.1-2	21.7	38.5
6.1	21.9	39.10
9.3	22.6	40.12-14
10.9	22.21-23	41.21
11.7	22.28	47.8
12.31	23.6-7	48.7
14.4	23.12	50.13
14.6	26.26-31	54.31
14.10-11	27.1	55.1
15.14	29.31	55.11-17
17.18	29.33	56.3-7

Allopathic Healing
See Volume 2

Crystal Healing

2.2-4	23.6	55.16-17
14.4	27.1	56.3
14.7	29.23-31	
22.21-23	33.3-5	

Healing Through Fasting

40.14	41.21-22

Hebrew
See Volume 2

Heraclitus
25.4

Hickson, Charlie

8.15-22	38.10-11

Higher Self

35.3	41.22	51.1
36.1-15	42.12	54.3
36.22	44.12	
37.6-7	48.8	

See also "Guides"
See also "Protection"

Himmler, Heinrich

35.5	36.12-15

Hiroshima
26.23-31
See also "Nuclear Energy"

Hitler, Adolph

7.14	11.7	35.4-5

Hole (in spirit energy field)
6.1

Holograph

13.8	13.13	26.23

Holy Communion (Christian)
See Volume 2

Homosexuality
31.8-10

Honor/Duty
Honor/Responsibility

2.2	16.18	22.26
3.6	16.41-42	23.10
4.20	17.25	23.16
5.2	18.6-8	31.17
10.8	22.5	(Cont. ...)

(... Cont.)	36.9	44.2
33.1	36.12	51.1
34.17	37.3	54.10
35.8	37.6	56.3

Horus
23.1

Humor

21.9	37.5	53.9

Hypnosis
See Volume 2

Ikhnaton
See "Akhenaten"

Illness
25.1

Imhotep
23.8-9

Impatience

5.2	34.6	45.2

In Potentiation

30.5	38.5	47.9-11
35.1	41.17	48.10

Incarnation
See "Reincarnation"

Industrial Revolution

11.29	26.13

Infinity/Infinite (adjective)

3.8-9	10.15-16	16.51
4.2	11.26	16.53
4.18	12.26	17.35
5.2	13.7-13	18.1
7.8	14.28	18.6
7.12	15.7	19.1
7.16	15.12	19.3
9.14	16.21	19.17
10.10	16.36	20.27
10.13	16.38	(Cont. ...)

(... Cont.)	29.18	37.8
26.36	30.14	39.10
27.15	31.3	41.4
28.7	32.12	51.2
28.13	33.17	52.12
28.16	37.6	54.9

Initiation

2.3-4	17.18	42.18-19
3.15-16	22.22	55.11
4.1-8	23.6	56.3
14.6	23.16	56.6-7
14.10	41.23-24	

Inner Earth
See Volume 2

Inner Light
Inner Nature, Inward Fire, Polaris of Self, Guiding Star

29.6	54.27	56.3
49.6	54.29	

Inner Planes

6.11	17.1	25.6
7.9	17.36-39	26.22
10.1	18.10-11	26.25
11.7	20.26	43.7
12.14	21.5	47.8
14.30	21.7	47.15
16.44	23.6	51.1
16.48	25.4	

Innocence

8.15	21.9	31.11
19.15	30.1	32.1

Insanity

35.4	36.24

Inspiration

14.25	26.38	49.8
17.2	38.2-4	52.2
22.21	42.13	54.31
23.10	42.15	

Intelligent Energy

3.8	19.20	36.7
4.14	21.13	39.10
8.2	22.3	41.4
9.4	26.22	47.4
10.15	26.24	47.8
12.31	26.38	47.15
13.7-9	27.2	48.7
13.13-15	27.5-7	50.8
14.32	27.12	51.5
15.9	27.17	51.10
15.12	28.2	52.2-3
15.21	28.6	54.7-8
16.5	28.11	54.11
17.18	28.13	54.19
18.6	28.19	54.23
18.15	29.2	54.27
19.1	29.23-30	54.31
19.3	30.2	
19.12	31.3	

Intelligent Infinity
Infinity, One Infinite Creator, Unity

1.7	12.31	29.32
3.8-9	13.5-9	30.2
4.2	13.12-17	30.14
4.5	14.16	31.3
4.8	14.28	32.2
4.13-14	14.32	34.2
4.17-18	15.7	34.16
4.20	15.12	36.7
4.23	16.21	38.14
5.1-2	16.49	39.10
6.1	17.2	39.12
6.7	17.17-19	40.1
7.15	17.25	41.4
7.17	17.33	41.19
8.2	18.1	41.25
8.30	19.1	44.13
9.4	26.38	47.3-4
10.15	27.2-13	48.7
11.8	28.1-2	48.10
11.10	28.6	49.2
11.20	29.10	50.8-10
12.2	29.27	51.10
12.26	29.29-30	(Cont. ....)

(... Cont.) | 52.12 | 54.31-32

See also "Faith"
See also "One Infinite Creator"

Gateway to Intelligent Infinity

4.2	15.12	39.12
4.13	16.21	40.4
6.1	17.2	41.6
7.12	17.18	47.8
7.17	17.25	48.7
8.2	17.33	48.10
9.4	29.27-30	49.2
11.8	30.2	50.13
11.10-11	31.3	52.2
11.20	34.16	54.31-32
14.16	39.4	
14.32	39.10	

Negative Contact with Intelligent Infinity

| 11.8 | 38.14 | 47.3-4 |
| 34.16 | 39.12 | |

Instrument, The

Dedication/Purity

| 21.1 | 44.7-8 | 46.6 |
| 22.1 | | |

Martyrdom
44.1

See also "Psychic Greeting"
See also "Ra Contact"

Intention

7.14	37.5	56.3
18.1	47.6	
24.4	49.8	

Intuition

19.11	30.2	49.4
19.13	37.3	
26.38	38.4	

Investment

Evolutionary Investment

| 13.12 | 14.1-2 | 46.2 |
| 13.21 | 30.13 | |

Jefferson, Thomas
26.15-16

Jesus
of Nazareth, Jehoshua

| 17.10-12 | 17.16-22 | 33.11 |

"Second Coming"
17.22

Judaism
17.20

Judas Iscariot
17.17

Judgment

| 5.2 | 26.8 | 38.5 |
| 7.9 | 32.9 | 44.1 |

Ka
47.11
See also "Indigo Ray Body"

Karma

9.2	12.28-29	34.4-5
9.18	16.61	34.17
10.1	17.20	35.1
10.4	18.12	35.8

King, Martin Luther
34.10-11

Knot of Fear (Maldek)

| 10.1 | 10.7 | 21.5 |

Kundalini

11.10	42.11	52.11
17.39	49.5-6	54.27
34.2	50.2	54.29-31
42.9	52.7	

Larson, Dewey B. (Physics of)

20.6	28.1	41.20
20.7	28.18	
27.14	39.4	

Law of Confusion
Way of Confusion

3.14	16.9	27.10
11.19	20.26	36.19-20
16.1-2	21.9	48.4
16.6-7	26.36	54.13

See also "First Distortion"

Law of One

1.0-1	11.28	18.1
1.5	12.3	18.5-6
1.7	12.5	18.8
1.9	12.7	18.21
1.10	12.13	19.1
2.1-4	12.24-25	20.36
2.6	13.4	22.6
3.6	13.8	22.21
3.9	13.12	22.27
3.10	14.7-8	23.6
3.14	14.10-11	23.10
4.13-14	14.18	23.12
4.17	14.20	23.15
4.19-20	14.23-26	23.19
6.10	14.28	24.9
6.14	14.34	25.4
6.24-25	15.5-6	26.4-9
7.1	15.7	26.12
7.9	15.8	27.8
7.12	15.12	27.10
7.15	15.14	27.13
7.17	15.21-22	28.1
8.19	16.18-21	28.16
8.25	16.24	37.6
9.9-10	16.28-29	41.4
10.11-12	16.38-41	42.10
10.14	17.2	49.6
11.12	17.15	52.7
11.18	17.33	52.11
11.21	17.43	

Law of Responsibility

20.17	23.15	34.17
22.5-6		

Law of Squares
(Doubling/Empowerment)
Law of Service, Law of Seeking

7.1-7	17.2	26.40
7.9	17.30	29.29
10.12-14	18.13	37.77
11.11	22.25	39.1
14.18	22.27	
15.6-7	24.8	

See also "Calling"

Laws of Foreverness

3.10	27.10

Laws of Light

3.10	16.50

Laws of Love

3.10	14.10	22.21
9.10		

Laws (Natural)

13.13	27.17	41.4
13.15-16	28.1	41.8
17.18	28.5	46.14
18.6	28.8	47.2
19.12	29.2	54.17
22.27	29.11	
27.15	29.16	

Learn/Teaching

1.10	17.25	41.7
2.1	17.38	42.2
3.6	17.43	42.8-9
4.10	20.24	42.20
5.2	20.26	43.26
6.1	22.5	46.14-15
9.3	26.13	48.7
14.10	27.1	52.9
15.13	28.6	52.11
15.22	32.5	56.4
16.48	39.10	

See also "Teach/Learning"

Lemuria

Mu

| 10.15 | 21.24-25 | 24.6 |
| 14.4 | 21.27-28 | |

Lesser Banishing Ritual of the Pentragram

See "Banishing Ritual of the Lesser Pentagram"

Light

See also "Distortion, Third"

<u>Downward Spiraling Light</u>

Inner Light

4.5	12.31	54.29
4.18	49.5-6	54.31
6.1	54.27	56.3

<u>Upward Spiraling Light</u>

4.18	19.3	50.2
6.1	28.14	54.27
9.14	29.16	54.29
13.15	29.18	54.31
13.17	30.5	56.3-4
13.23	41.10	56.6-7
14.2	49.5-6	

Light Touch

| 18.6 | 34.6 | 50.7 |

Light/Love

1.7	7.17	15.22
3.4	12.3	16.21
3.15	14.20	29.16
4.20	15.4	51.1
6.14	15.9	52.11

See also "Love/Light"

Lincoln, Abraham

| 26.15 | 35.6 | 35.8 |
| 26.17-19 | | |

Logos

13.7	18.6	28.6-7
13.16	19.12	28.9-11
15.21	28.1	(Cont. ...)

(... Cont.)	30.15	41.25
28.13	39.4	47.2
28.18	41.4	51.10
28.20	41.8	52.12
29.2-5	41.12	54.4-5
29.13	41.18	54.9-10

<u>Love</u>

13.7	27.11-17	47.2
15.21	28.1-6	47.4
18.6	29.11-13	54.27

<u>Local Sub-Logos</u>

28.20	40.1	41.12
29.1	41.4	54.7
30.14	41.7	54.17

<u>Milky Way (Galactic) Logos</u>

13.15-16	28.18	30.15-16
15.21	29.2	41.7-8
19.12	29.4	52.12
28.8-10	29.32	

<u>Sub-Logos/Logoi</u>

28.10-11	40.1	51.10
28.20	41.4	52.2
29.1-2	41.7	54.5
29.4-7	41.12	54.17
29.9	46.14	54.27
29.13	47.2	

<u>Logoic Bias</u>

| 16.30-31 | 55.7 |

<u>Local Sun Body (physical)</u>

See "Solar System, Sun"

Love

See "Compassion" and "Distortion, Second" and "Logos"

Love/Light

1.7	10.12	15.25
2.3	12.5	16.21
2.6	12.7	17.37
3.4	13.13	18.5-6
3.15	14.20	23.6
4.20	15.9	36.12
7.17	15.12	48.3
10.9	15.22	52.11

See also "Light/Love"

LSD

6.1	19.22	26.40
18.3	25.1	

Magic

11.11	25.5	50.8-9
12.14	31.3	50.13
16.54-57	42.13	55.2
12.14	42.16	55.6
18.5	42.17	
22.2	49.8	

White Magic

42.13-19	49.8	55.2
44.14-15		

See also "Magical Defense"

Magical Defense/Protection

32.1	44.10	63.5

Magical Personality

See Volume 2

Magnetism

4.18	48.2	56.3
30.10	49.4-6	
31.7	50.2	

Major Cycle

6.14-15	20.27	22.14
9.4		

Maldek

See "Solar System, Maldek"

Male/Female

5.2	31.7-8	54.3
26.38	31.10	

Manhattan Project

11.23	26.20

Manipulate

See "Control"

Marijuana

19.22

Marriage

31.16	32.9

Mars

See "Solar System, Mars"

Martyrdom

42.6	44.1

Master Cycle

9.4	16.61	21.13
9.14	19.8	21.25
14.4	20.12	33.12
15.18	21.6-9	

Masturbation

31.11

Matrix (Archetype)

See "Archetypes, Matrix" (Vol. 2)

Meditation

10.14	25.2	46.2
12.1	38.10	49.6-8
15.14	41.1	50.12
17.40	42.13-16	52.11
19.13	43.31	54.32
21.3	44.10	
23.16	44.13	

Memory

4.2	16.22	36.24
6.20	21.3	37.6
6.23	30.2	38.9
11.10	31.16	50.7

Men In Black

12.20-23

Mental Illness

40.15-16

Mesopotamia

See Volume 2

Metal-Bending

40.15	50.10

Metaphor by Ra

19.17	54.6	54.16
50.7	54.8	

Mind

Cosmic Mind

22.1	30.2	49.5

Archetypal (Archetypical) Mind

16.49	30.2	42.16

See also "Tarot"

Planetary Mind
Racial Mind, Mass Mind

2.4	10.8	40.8
3.10	14.32	40.11
5.2	30.2	41.14
7.16	31.16	43.5-6
10.6	38.9	

See also "Akashic Record"

Roots/Trunk of the Mind

10.14	22.1	42.16
11.17	30.2	50.2
16.49	36.10	52.2
20.33	41.21	

See also "Unconscious"

Unconscious/Subconscious Mind
See "Unconscious"

Mind Complex

Mind

3.1	19.20	40.14
3.16	19.22	41.21
4.17	20.33	46.2
5.2	22.1-2	46.9
6.1	23.7	46.12
10.3	26.13	49.4-5
10.8	30.2	49.8
10.14	30.4-5	51.5
11.17	31.15	52.2
16.48-49	32.10	53.11
18.19	35.8	56.1
19.11	36.10	
19.13	39.1	

Mind/Body

2.2	18.18-22	30.7
4.18	19.20	31.4
9.4	20.3	39.10
10.1	29.9	46.9
13.21	30.5	

Mind/Body/Spirit Complex

1.7	18.6	41.21
3.8	18.15	43.14
3.16	19.7	43.30
4.9	19.20	46.2
4.10	20.24	47.8
6.1	20.32	48.2
8.16	21.9	48.7-10
10.6	26.23	49.5-6
10.9	26.38	50.2-3
11.8	28.13-14	50.9
11.10	29.7	51.1
11.17	29.10	51.4-6
12.10	29.23-27	51.8
12.31	30.2-5	51.10
13.21-22	30.7	52.2
15.9	31.2	52.11
15.10	32.7	54.3
15.12	33.8	54.5-9
15.14	34.8-9	54.11
16.59	36.1-2	54.13-17
17.1	36.4-9	54.24-25
17.15	36.11-12	54.27
17.18	37.6	54.30
17.30	40.12	
17.38	41.14	

Mind/Body/Spirit Complex Totality

9.2	36.4	50.7
10.9-10	36.8	51.1
12.10	36.10	51.8
16.22	36.12	51.10
34.8	37.6-7	52.9
35.3	47.11	
36.1-2	48.8	

Mind/Body/Spirits

32.5	47.2	50.7
36.21		

Mind/Spirit (Spirit/Mind)

15.12	35.8	47.8
17.38		

Mixed Contacts

12.5-9	16.18-19	24.8-16
12.15	18.24	26.34
14.13	21.20	26.36

Money

11.28	23.15	34.10
22.5		

Mu
See "Lemuria"

Muhammad
2.2

Mummies
See Volume 2

Mystery, The

1.10	18.1	28.16
13.13	22.21	52.11
16.21	27.7	
16.27	28.1	

See also "Intelligent Infinity"
See also "One Infinite Creator"
See also "Unity"

Third-Density Variety

3.14	7.12	24.9
6.25	17.2	26.21

Nagasaki
26.23-31
See also "Hiroshima"
See also "Nuclear Energy"

Narrow Band Channel
See "Channel, Trance"

Narrow Band Vibration

1.0	18.1	33.1
15.1-2	30.17	

Natural Laws
See "Laws, Natural"

Nazca (Lines of)
20.39-43

Negative Contact with Intelligent Infinity
See "Intelligent Infinity, Negative Contact With"

Negative Path
Left-Hand Path

7.17	32.5	50.6
17.32-33	35.4-5	54.9
19.15	36.12-14	54.22-23
20.29	46.7-12	54.25
32.2	47.5	55.3-6

See also "Service to Self"

Ninety Degree Deflection (tesseract)
52.10

Nothingness
See "Plenum"

Nuclear Energy
Nuclear War, Nuclear Device

7.12	17.3-9	38.2-3
9.18-19	24.4	
11.23	26.21-31	

See also "Hiroshima"

Oahspe (book)

14.28	17.31

Octave

6.8	16.21	47.8
6.14	16.38	48.10
7.17	16.51	49.6
9.14	28.15-16	51.1
13.20	36.8	52.12
14.32	40.1	54.10
15.4	41.7-8	

One Infinite Creator

26.36	39.2	55.7
29.10	43.13	56.3
30.5	49.2	

One Creator

12.5	16.9	18.13
13.13	16.11	19.7
15.7	17.22	19.20

Infinity

1.7	13.5	29.18
3.8	13.6	39.4
6.25	16.37	52.12
7.12	16.54	
10.13	22.12	

Intelligent Infinity

3.9	13.7	31.3
4.2	13.8	32.2
4.5	13.9	34.2
4.8	13.12-17	34.16
4.13	14.16	36.7
4.14	14.32	38.14
4.17	15.12	39.10
4.20	16.49	39.12
5.1	17.2	40.1
5.2	17.17-19	40.4
6.1	17.25	41.4
6.7	17.33	41.19
7.15	26.38	41.25
7.17	27.2-8	44.13
8.2	27.10	47.3
8.30	27.12-13	47.4
9.4	28.1-2	48.7
10.15	28.6	48.1
11.8	29.10	49.2
11.10	29.27	50.8
11.20	29.29	50.9
12.2	29.30	51.10
12.26	29.32	54.31-32
12.31	30.2	

Unity

1.1	3.10	7.9
1.5	6.7	15.4
1.7	7.2	(Cont. ...)

(... Cont.)

15.7	27.12-13	46.13
15.25	27.15	47.2
16.21	28.1	47.8
18.1	28.16	48.6
22.21	29.19	50.5
25.5	30.1	52.11
27.5	32.6	53.9
27.7	36.12	
	36.15	

One Original Thought

1.0	1.7	54.8
1.10	52.11-12	

Orion

Orion Constellation

11.12	62.16

Orion Empire

Orion Group

7.12-15	16.15-19	25.10
8.12-14	16.57-61	26.19
11.12-13	17.0	26.33-34
11.18	17.16-17	31.12
11.21	18.20-22	31.15
11.31	18.24-25	38.14
12.2	20.29-35	43.7
12.9	21.21-23	48.6
12.14-15	24.6	51.2-3
12.18-22	24.8	53.10-11
14.13	24.11-14	53.14-17
16.2	24.16-17	53.22
16.8-10	25.1	55.4-6
16.13	25.4-6	

Other-Self

5.2	20.26	32.9
12.13	20.36	33.9
14.5	25.1	33. 11
15.4	26.34	33. 14-17
16.5	26.38	34.5-6
17.2	30.10	36.15
17.3	30.5	38.5
18.5	31.3	40.13
18.6	32.1	41.4
18.12	32.5-7	41.14
19.5	32.7	(Cont. ...)

(... Cont.)	46.12	50.7
42.10	46.9	52.9
42.20	47.5	55.3
42.3-4	47.13-14	56.3
45.1	48.6-7	
46.10	48.7	

Oversoul (Group)

| 7.16 | 37.7 | 52.9 |
| 36.22 | | |

Parallel Existence

| 11.3 | 36.2-5 |

Paranormal Ability

6.1

Patton, General George

| 34.17 | 36.10 |

Perfect

4.20	30.5	47.7
10.15	36.7	51.5
12.31	38.5	52.7
15.8	42.4	52.9
19.20	42.15	55.6-7

Imperfect

| 4.20 | 8.10 |

Pericles

25.4

Personality

1.10	17.15	52.7
2.2	35.4	54.15
3.16	51.2	
12.30	52.2-3	

Magical
See "Magical Personality"

Peru

10.15

Pets

| 14.1 | 20.3 |

Philadelphia Experiment

26.20

Physics
See "Sciences, Physics"

Plane

17.38

Astral Plane (Green)

10.1	16.50	43.7
11.7	17.36-37	47.8
16.44	26.25	

Devachanic Plane (Blue)

| 17.36-37 | 47.8 |

Etheric Plane (Indigo)

| 15.4 | 47.8 | 47.11 |
| 17.1 | | |

Earth Plane

| 15.20 | 20.34 | 25.4 |
| 18.7 | | |

Inner Plane
See "Inner Planes"

Planetary Consciousness

Planetary Entity

2.4	13.15-16	25.7-8
6.15	15.20	29.9-10
6.24-25	16.25	30.14
8.15	16.32	37.7
9.4	16.61	53.16
11.18	20.26	
11.26-27	21.17	

Planetary Healing

2.4	26.27-28	50.9
14.7	26.30-31	
14.10	30.14	

Planetary Sphere
Planetary Body

2.2	6.6	6.16
2.3	6.10	8.7
2.4	6.13	(Cont. ....)

(... Cont.)	15.4	21.17
9.2	15.9	21.27
9.7	16.1	21.28
9.13	16.6	24.4
9.18	16.13	26.20
10.1	16.25	26.27-28
10.4	16.30	26.30-31
10.6-7	16.33	28.6
11.3	16.59	29.9-10
11.4	17.0	30.14
11.18	17.1	30.16
11.26	17.11	31.8
13.9	18.6	41.4
13.15	19.4	41.12
13.22-23	19.7	41.15
14.3	19.12	41.26
14.7	20.13	43.28
14.10	20.19	48.8
14.23	20.20	49.5
14.32	21.5	

Planetary Vibration
Planetary Aura, Electromagnetic Field, Energy Web

2.3	14.7	42.7
4.6	14.10	49.5
8.7	15.4	49.8
12.7	15.9	50.8-9
12.30	22.11	
13.23	41.4	

Planets (Inhabited)

16.24-25

Plenum

Nothingness

6.7

Polarity (in Consciousness)

8.12	17.23	25.5
12.25	17.33	26.34
16.6-9	19.15-19	26.38
16.15-20	20.9-11	27.1
16.59	20.17	28.18-19
17.1	20.26-27	29.10
17.16-17	22.5	29.33
17.19	25.1	(Cont. ...)

(... Cont.)	35.4-5	46.16
30.1	35.8	47.4-6
31.2-4	36.11-12	48.6-8
31.7	36.14	49.3-4
31.12	36.16-17	49.8
31.14	38.9	50.6-9
32.1-2	38.14	52.7-9
32.14	41.14	53.16
33.8-9	42.7	54.19
33.11-12	42.9	54.22
34.10	42.18	55.3-4
34.14	44.15-16	55.7
34.17	46.7-12	
35.1	46.14	

See also "Service to Others"
See also "Service to Self"

Polarity (General)

1.1	24.8	32.10
1.5	25.4	36.18
1.7	25.6	39.4
2.2	27.6-7	39.11
4.10	28.18	45.10
4.20	29.32	49.5
5.2	26.38	52.6
8.7	31.2	53.3-4
10.1	31.7	53.10
11.20	32.8	53.24
19.16	31.10	54.13
19.20	31.13	
20.29	32.10	

Polarization

See "Polarity (in Consciousness)"

Positive Path

1.0	32.1-2	52.7
10.11-12	43.8	52.11
15.14	46.13	54.21
17.33	46.16	54.25
18.5	49.6	55.7
18.12	50.8-9	
19.17	52.2	

See also "Service to Others"

Possibility/Probability Vortex

See "Probability/Possibility Vortex"

Potentiate
Potentiation

28.1	38.5	41.4
31.2	39.4	48.6-7
35.1	39.10	51.10
36.12	40.1	52.7

Potentiator (Archetype)
See "Archetypes, Potentiator" (Vol. 2)

Power

1.1	17.7	30.3
2.2	17.17	31.14
3.8-11	19.18	32.2
3.10	20.30	34.9
6.1	20.32	34.12
7.15	20.40-41	35.1
8.2	22.23	35.3
8.6	22.28	38.14
8.11	23.3	44.1
10.13-14	23.6	44.15
11.19-20	23.12	47.3
11.26	23.15	49.8
11.31	24.17	50.6
12.5	24.19	50.8-9
15.12	25.1	52.7
15.14	25.5-6	54.22
15.22	27.13	56.3
17.5	29.31	

Prana

14.2	41.10	56.3

See also "Light, Upward Spiraling"
See also "Distortion, Third"

Prayer or Contemplation

10.14	21.3	49.6
12.1	22.2	49.8
15.14	42.6	

Pre-incarnative choices
See "Reincarnation, Pre-incarnative choices"

Pre-veil
See "Veil of Forgetting, Pre-veil"

Primal Distortion
See "Distortion, Primal"

Primary Energy Center
See "Energy Center, Primary"

Probability/Possibility Vortex
Possibility/Probability Vortex

11.3	17.5	40.8
11.6	19.21	43.25
16.53-54	33.12	50.5
16.56	36.2-4	56.3

Probert, Mark
7.10-11

Programming, Incarnational

8.21	34.5	41.22
10.1	34.8	42.12
17.1	34.17	48.7-9
17.11	35.1	50.4-5
21.9-11	35.3	54.19
23.12	36.1-2	54.21-24
31.6	36.4	55.1
33.6-7	36.6-7	
33.9	36.10	

Prophecy
See Volume 2
See also "Divination"

Protection

19.9	33.11	45.11
32.1	36.21	46.2
33.1-2	44.10	

See also "Guardians"
See also "Higher Self"
See also "Psychic Greeting/Attack"

Protection of the Ra contact
See "Ra Contact, Methodology"

Those Who Offer Protection

6.7	30.14	50.5

Violet-Ray Shell Protection
See Volume 2

Psychic Greeting/Attack

25.1	53.1	56.1
44.10-11	53.22	
46.1-2	55.1-2	

See also "Protection"

Psychic Sensitivity

44.3-6	44.10-12

Puharich, Dr. Andrija

7.10-11	21.3-4	39.6-9
12.1	23.11	
12.10	39.4	

Purity

4.8	25.6	39.1
10.9	26.36	40.4
12.28	29.27	41.19
17.11	30.4	41.21
21.17	37.4	55.5-7
23.7	38.5	

Pyramids

2.2	14.4	23.10
3.6-8	14.6-11	27.1-2
3.10-16	22.21	45.4
4.1-8	23.6-8	

See also "Great Pyramid at Giza"
See also "Metaphysics of the Pyramids"
essay in the Resource Series

Angles

55.15	56.4

Caution

4.6	4.8	56.3

Chamber: King

55.11-12	56.3	56.5-6
55.16-17		

Chamber: Queen

55.10-11	56.3	56.6

Chamber: Resonating

3.16	55.13

Purpose

2.4	23.16	55.9
3.14		

Focusing the Spirals

50.11	56.3

Geometry
4.7

Healing
23.7
See also "Pyramids, Chamber: King"

Initiation

3.15-16	4.5	4.7
4.2		

Positive Use: Energizing
See Volume 2

Positive Use: Meditation
56.3

Spiral, Zero
See Volume 2

Spiral, First
56.7

Spiral, Second
See Volume 2

Spiral, Third
See Volume 2

Quarantine (of Earth)

6.25	12.3	21.8
7.8	12.5-7	23.16
7.12	16.1-7	24.8
8.15	16.13	26.34
9.9	17.27-28	

Questioner, The

4.13	37.3	42.14
11.12	38.1	44.12

Ra

Limits of Ra's Knowledge
See Volume 2

Ra's Communication

1.1	15.1	23.16
1.10	15.13	28.16
2.0-2	17.2	37.4
3.6	18.1	48.3
8.31	21.1	55.7
9.3	22.26-27	

Ra's Form

6.4	23.6	27.2
8.20	23.16	41.4-6

Ra's History

1.1	2.4	14.19-22
1.3	6.4-5	16.21
1.5	6.7	41.26
2.2	6.21-23	

Ra's Work on Earth

1.0-1	6.7	23.1-10
1.3	6.21-22	26.10-11
1.5	14.4-6	26.21-25
2.2	14.18	48.3
2.4	14.20	
6.4	14.23-27	

Ra Contact

Energizing the Instrument/Contact

1.11-13	17.44	33.1
3.4	18.4	55.1
5.3	18.26-27	56.2
11.2	19.22	
15.23	22.29	

Energizing the Instrument through Sexual
Energy Transfer

39.2	44.13	48.2
44.1		

Maintenance

3.17	24.7	26.37
6.27-29	24.15	26.39
13.26	24.18	28.12
18.4	24.21	28.17
21.29	25.2-3	30.17
22.2	26.9	31.1
24.2-3	26.14	34.1
24.5	26.29	(Cont. ....)

(... Cont.)	44.13	46.6
44.1-2	45.1-2	
44.7-9	45.12	

See also "Harmony"

Methodology

1.11-13	3.18	6.26
2.0	5.1	55.7
2.6	5.3	
3.1-5	6.3	

See also "Channel, Trance"

Pre-Requisites

1.11	12.1	37.3-5
2.0-1	14.25	39.9
6.20	36.21	53.2

Racial Mind
See "Mind, Racial"

Random

6.1	22.17	41.10
7.14	23.7	42.8
8.15	24.8	46.9
13.8	26.38	50.5
13.16-17	30.5	54.17
16.4-5	31.4-6	
17.27-28	33.12	

Reincarnation

4.9	17.1	33.6-7
6.11	17.41	33.12
6.13	18.15	34.17-18
9.2	19.9	35.1
9.7	20.12	40.16
9.21	21.9-10	43.11-12
10.1	21.28	48.7-8
10.4	22.6	50.5
10.12	22.15	50.7
10.15	23.12	52.7
11.11	31.4	54.23-24
11.29	31.8	
15.20	31.10	

See also "Seniority of Vibration"

Automatic Reincarnation

21.9	21.11	48.8

Between Incarnations

10.12	22.6	48.7
21.9	43.12	50.7

Pre-incarnative Choices

8.21	50.5	55.1
31.6	53.1	
35.3	54.21-22	

Religion(s)

1.5	16.15-20	22.15
2.2	17.15	23.1
14.1	17.20	42.13
14.28	17.22	47.8

Repression

41.19	46.11-13	52.7
42.9-10		

Reproduction

Cloning

18.15	18.20	24.6

Bisexual Reproduction

18.15-18	30.7	31.9
18.20	30.9-13	32.6-8
26.38	31.2-7	41.15

See also "Sexuality"

Responsibility

1.1	10.12	23.10
2.2	16.33	24.6
4.20	16.42	33.1
5.2	18.7-8	48.8
7.9	22.26	

See also "Honor/Responsibility"

Responsibility, The Law or Way of
See "Law of Responsibility"

Rhythm of Reality

27.6-7	27.13

Robot

12.18-20

Roosevelt, Eleanor

35.1-3

Roosevelt, Franklin

35.1-3

Russia

8.6	17.3-5	21.24
10.15	17.7	

Sacrifice

37.3	42.15	55.7

Human Sacrifice
23.16
Price

35.1	44.2

Saints Teresa, Augustine, Francis

22.15

Salt Cleansing
See Volume 2

Sanskrit
See Volume 2

Sasquatch
See "Bigfoot"

Schweitzer, Albert

34.10-11

Sciences

Astronomy

11.4	29.1-5	40.2
16.24-30	29.18-19	41.4
16.37-38	29.32	
28.6-11	30.15-16	

Biology

18.15	20.24	41.11-12
18.20	21.13	49.4
19.9-11	23.13	
20.12-17	31.6	

Evolution

9.4	16.28-29	27.8-9
9.16-17	16.37-38	28.6
13.16-21	21.13	(Cont. ....)

(... Cont.)	30.5-16	45.11
28.10-11	36.15	47.2
28.13-16	36.17	48.8
28.19-20	37.3	50.5
29.2	39.4	51.5
29.6-8	40.1-11	52.2
29.9-11	41.4	52.11
29.13	41.8-10	54.24
29.18-20	41.12	
30.1	41.18	

Physics

20.6-8	29.1	40.5-6
27.6	29.12	40.9-11
27.14-17	29.14-23	40.15
28.1-5	29.30	41.4-5
28.8	39.4-5	41.9
28.18	40.1-3	41.20

Scientists

8.6	17.8-9	39.4
9.16	26.20	41.12
11.22-29	28.5	44.12

Scribe, The

| 7.10 | 38.1 | 54.2-3 |
| 11.2 | | |

Seeker

| 7.17 | 17.30 | 56.3 |
| 15.13 | 50.2 | |

See also "Seeking"

Seeking

1.0	11.28	20.27
1.7	12.14	22.17
2.2	14.14	23.1
2.4	14.19	23.8
2.6	14.26-27	23.10
3.4	15.7	26.8
3.9-10	15.12-14	26.38
4.14	16.11	27.13
7.15	16.22	29.16
7.17	16.32	29.18
8.1	17.2	29.27
10.12-14	17.20	29.29-30
11.17	17.30	30.7
11.20	18.5	(Cont. ...)

(... Cont.)	41.6	51.1
31.3	41.14	53.8
31.9	43.31	54.3
32.9	48.6	56.3
36.14	49.6	
37.4	50.11	

See also "Seeker"

Self

1.10	16.50	34.6
3.10	16.56	34.9
5.2	17.2	36.5
10.14	17.18	40.12-15
11.28	17.30	41.21
11.31	17.43	42.11
12.10	18.6-7	48.6-7
12.31	18.12	53.9
13.21	21.9	54.7
14.14	26.38	54.27
15.7	32.14	
15.14	33.14-17	

Self-Acceptance

5.2	22.2	46.10
13.16	22.6	47.2
15.2	25.2	47.8
15.3	32.14	49.6
16.21	40.3	52.7
18.5	41.25	

See also "Self-Worth"

Self-Conscious

Self-Consciousness, Self-Aware, Self-Awareness

13.21	30.1-2	41.16
14.1	34.14	41.19
15.12	35.4	41.21
19.3	36.14	48.8
19.11	40.3	50.5
20.4	41.10	

Self-Worth

| 12.31 | 15.12 | 32.14 |
| 15.10 | | |

See also "Self-Acceptance"

Seniority of Vibration

17.41-43	33.12-13	48.5
26.13	34.15-16	48.7-8
31.6	40.16	

See also "Reincarnation"

Service to Others

7.15	22.5	42.20
7.17	25.1	43.19
10.1	25.5-6	43.8
11.20	26.38	44.1
11.21	30.1	44.8
12.9	30.2	44.15
12.13	31.3	45.1
12.15	31.4	46.7
12.26	31.9	46.9-10
12.31	33.9	46.13
14.13	33.11	46.16
16.7	33.19	47.3
16.11-12	34.2	47.6
16.30-32	34.9-10	49.3-5
16.59	34.14	50.6
17.2	34.16	52.3
17.23	35.8	52.7
17.30-34	36.17	52.11
18.6	38.1	53.6
19.14-15	38.7	53.17
19.17	39.11-12	53.22
20.9-10	42.9	54.21
20.27	42.18	54.25

See also "Positive Path"
See also "Polarity (in Consciousness)"

Service to Self

7.14-15	12.9	17.17
7.17	12.13-16	17.23
8.2	14.13	17.25
8.11-12	16.2	17.30-33
10.1	16.7-9	18.21
11.3	16.11-12	19.15
11.11-12	16.15	19.17
11.15-16	16.17	20.9-10
11.18	16.30-31	20.32
11.20-21	16.57	22.5
11.31	17.1	(Cont. ....)

(... Cont.)	34.16	46.16
24.6	35.4-5	47.3-5
25.5-6	36.12	48.6
26.34	36.14	49.4
26.36	36.16-17	50.6
26.38	38.7	51.7
30.1	38.14	53.11
30.5	39.11-12	53.14
30.10	41.14	53.16-17
31.14	42.20	54.19
32.2	44.16	54.22
33.13	46.7	54.25
33.19	46.9-12	55.3-5

See also "Negative Path"
See also "Polarity (in Consciousness)"

Sexual Energy Transfer
See "Energy Transfer, Sexual"

Sexuality

19.22	32.2-11	46.12
25.1	39.2	48.2
26.38	41.5-6	53.14
30.10-13	44.1	54.25
31.2-16	44.13	55.6

Fusion

32.9-10	41.4-6

See also "Reproduction"

Signals and Personal Signs

22.1	44.3-6	44.10

Significator
See "Archetypes, Significator" (Vol. 2)

Silver Cord
See Volume 2

Silver Flecks

16.47-49	53.21

Simultaneity

36.4-5

Shockley, Paul
27.1-2

Sinkhole of Indifference

3.6	20.17	46.16
17.33	40.16	
19.18	46.9	

See also "Polarity (in Consciousness)"

Sirius

8.22	38.7-8	51.2

Slavery

8.14	24.17	35.4
11.18	25.16	35.8
16.17	26.34	50.6
24.6	32.2	55.3

Social Memory Complex

1.5	12.26	36.1
2.0	14.7	36.22
3.6	14.18	37.7
3.10	14.28	38.6-8
3.11	14.32	38.14
6.4	15.18	41.26
6.16	16.13	42.6
6.23	16.21	43.13-15
7.2	16.32	45.4
7.8-9	17.13	45.11
7.14-16	18.6	46.17
8.2	18.13	47.2-3
8.11	19.7	48.6
8.18	21.1	52.3-5
9.9	22.1	52.9
10.1	23.16	53.1
10.7	25.5	53.7-8
10.12	25.9	55.4
11.3	27.1-2	55.7
11.16-17	33.21	56.4

Society

1.5	12.18	25.5
6.16	16.31	34.9-10
6.23	19.15	34.13
8.26	20.21	35.6
10.15	22.21	36.12
11.17	23.15	(Cont. ....)

(... Cont.)	38.9	54.25
37.4		

Solar System

General

6.4	10.16-17	29.4
6.9-10	11.4	30.14
6.24	13.15	
10.1	13.23	

Maldek

6.9-10	10.6-7	21.16
6.12-13	11.3	38.2
9.18	11.5	
10.1	11.13	
10.3	21.5-6	

Mars

9.6-12	19.5	21.8
10.6	20.17-18	30.14
14.3	20.20	
18.20	20.26	

Saturn

6.8	9.4	23.16
7.8	22.17	30.14
7.12	23.6	53.3

Saturn, Council of
See "Council of Saturn"

Sun

2.2	23.6	40.1
2.6	23.16	41.4-5
10.17	29.1	41.7
11.4	29.3	54.4-5
13.5	29.5-6	54.7
16.35	29.10	
23.1	30.14	

See also "Logos, Local Sub-Logos"

Uranus
30.14

Venus

6.4-7	6.23	30.14
6.21	29.18	41.26

Soul

10.1	26.21-22	47.15
12.14	34.10	54.15
14.3	44.10	

Sound Vibration Complex
Vibratory Sound Complex

4.6	14.28	27.4
7.9		

South America

1.5	14.4	22.7
2.2	20.38	23.16
8.13	21.24	24.4
10.15	21.28	45.4

Southern Cross

11.12

Space/Time

2.2	28.2	41.8
6.9	29.11-12	41.20
12.7	29.14	43.22
13.8	29.16-17	52.10
13.22-23	29.19	54.24
19.1	29.22	55.9
26.22	30.4	
26.32	39.4	

See also "Time/Space"

Spirit Complex
General

2.3	18.11	30.4-5
3.15	18.18-19	30.12-13
4.2	19.2-3	32.10
4.17-18	19.20-21	34.6
4.20	20.24	34.12
6.1	21.9	35.8
6.14	22.2	39.1
7.15	23.7	39.10
10.8	26.21-23	40.14
10.14-15	26.38	41.21
13.21	27.6	43.9
15.12	29.16	45.11
16.59	29.33	46.2
17.18	30.2	(Cont. ...)

(... Cont.)	48.6	50.13
47.8	48.8	51.5
47.12-13	49.2	52.11
47.15	49.5	53.11
48.2	50.5	

Spirit as a Shuttle

6.1	30.2	49.2
23.7		

Spiritual Entropy

7.15	36.15	46.9

Spiritual Gravity

29.16-22	37.8	40.1

Spiritual Mass
Spiritual Density

27.6	36.8	39.4-5
29.18-19	37.6	40.1-2
30.16	37.8	52.12

Spontaneous Combustion

17.26-28

Star Wars (movie)

16.10

Starvation

42.7-8

Strength

12.31	35.1	52.2
18.19	38.5	53.22
26.38	39.4	54.29
27.15	39.10	55.4
28.13	42.12	56.6
29.10	51.1	
31.3	51.8	

Light/Dark Strength
Forces of Light/Darkness

24.8	35.8

Subconscious
See "Unconscious"

Sub-Density

16.51	17.34-35	38.6
16.53	17.38-39	
17.11-12	22.13	

See also "Plane"

Sub-Logos
See "Logos, Sub-Logos"

Sumer
See Volume 2

Surrender

54.16

Tantric Yoga
See Volume 2

Taras Bulba

11.8-10

Tarot
See "Archetypes, Tarot" (Vol. 2)

Tau Cross
See Volume 2

Teach/Learning

1.10	9.3	17.37
2.1-3	10.6	22.26
2.6	14.11	42.2
3.4	14.28	42.20
3.6	15.13	43.18-19
4.19	17.2	43.29
6.1	17.17	47.8
6.3	17.20	48.3-6

See also "Learn/Teaching"

Telepathy

12.13	20.30	38.14
14.27	26.21	

Television

34.13	42.2

Temptation

18.21	18.25

Ten Commandments

16.15	16.18	16.20

Tesla, Nikola

8.6	11.25-26	26.20

Thales

25.4

The Two Paths

16.31	39.12	54.25
19.16-19	46.10	
20.9-11	46.16	

See also "Polarity (in Consciousness)"

Third Density

6.6	18.7-9	30.10
6.15	19.4	33.9
10.3	19.9-11	36.1
11.17	19.13-15	36.17
13.21-23	20.18	38.6-7
14.3	20.21	40.7
16.2	20.24	41.14
16.21	20.26-27	41.16
16.39	21.9	42.3
17.35-38	30.1	48.6

See also "Density"
See also "Choice, The"

Third Density Life Span

14.11-12	21.9	23.13-14
20.12-17	22.3-8	43.11
20.23-25	22.28	

Thought-Form

General

3.11-14	15.4	26.20
6.14	17.1	37.6
6.23	17.17	44.5
13.23	22.1	
14.7	23.6	

See also "Daydream"
See also "Fasting"

Thought-Form Entity or Projection

2.6	17.37	51.4
7.12	24.9	43.5-7
8.30-31	24.13	53.8-9
12.9	24.19	53.13-14
12.18	26.32	
16.43-46	27.2	

See also "Bigfoot"
See also "Men in Black"

Tibet

10.15

Time/Space

See also "Space/Time"

General (e.g., moment or duration of time/space)

1.11	6.10	10.16
1.13	6.13	12.1
2.2	7.12	14.10
2.6	8.2	14.24
3.14	10.9-10	
4.2	10.12	

Time/Space Analog

32.12	48.7	51.10

Metaphysical

21.5	29.17	48.7
21.7	29.19	50.7
25.4	30.2	50.9
25.6	30.14	51.7
26.22	39.4	52.10
26.30	40.1	53.3
26.32	41.4	55.9
28.18	41.20	
29.13	43.12	

Totality, Mind/Body/Spirit Complex
See "Mind/Body/Spirit Totality"

Trance Channel
See "Channel, Trance"

Transform
Transmute

4.18	26.22	54.17
6.1	46.9	54.25
15.12	50.8	
25.6	51.7	

See also "Fasting"

Transformation (Archetype)
See "Archetypes, Transformation" (Vol. 2)

Transient Information
Unimportant information

Specific information

3.6	29.24	43.7
6.25-26	30.8	51.1-2
17.21	37.4	53.3
26.36	39.4	53.18
27.3	39.6	53.24

Tree of Life

44.16

True Color

33.3-4	41.14	48.10
40.6	47.3	49.6
40.11	47.8	50.9
40.15	48.7	54.6

Tunguska

17.3

Tuning
Attunement

1.0	12.1	42.2
3.8	15.1	54.15-17
4.6	30.2	54.31-32
10.9	39.9	

Turkey

10.15

UFOs

6.21-25	24.20	38.7-8
7.12-14	26.20-21	38.11-13
8.2-32	26.32-33	51.2-4
12.2-12	26.36	52.10
23.3	37.5	

Close Encounter

8.15-22	53.3-17

UFO Flap

12.8	48.5

UFO Mass Landing

16.8-9

Unconscious
Subconscious, Deep Mind, Deeper Mind

20.33	41.21	52.7
21.16	44.11	53.1
22.1-2	46.12	53.8
27.1	46.14	53.12-13
30.7	50.12	55.2

See also "Mind, Roots/Trunk of"

Understanding

1.7	15.18	28.5
3.8	16.32	36.10
4.19	16.38-39	47.6
5.1-2	16.59	49.5
6.14	18.6	54.7
10.8	20.24	
14.10	28.2	

Vibration of Understanding

13.23	16.50	26.12
16.32		

See also "Density, Fourth"

Unity
See "Intelligent Infinity" and "One Infinite Creator"

Unmanifested Self
Unmanifested Being

33.15-16	34.9	34.12
34.6-7		

Upward Spiraling Light
See "Light, Upward Spiraling"

Ur
See Volume 2

Urantia Book

14.30

Uranus
See "Solar System, Uranus"

Van Tassel, George

14.12-13

Veil of Forgetting

12.28	36.16-17	50.7
16.2	36.19	52.8
21.9	48.6	
30.4	48.8	

Pre-veil Conditions
See Volume 2

Venus
See "Solar System, Venus"

Vibration
See also "Narrow Band Vibration"
See also "Sound Vibration Complex"

General

2.2	27.4	54.8
2.6	54.6	

Basic or Core Vibration

20.6-7	29.11-14	40.9-11
27.14-16	29.23	40.15
28.2-4	40.3	41.8-10
29.2	40.5-6	

For Energizing

1.12-13	11.2	33.3
3.18	17.11	

Vibration of Density

1.1	6.14-16	10.4
2.2	8.15	(Cont. ....)

(... Cont.)

13.23	17.11-12	32.12
16.2	17.15	33.20
16.41	17.21	40.16
17.1	19.9	53.3
	27.13	

Vibration of One's Being

1.2	20.16-17	39.10
1.5	29.29	42.7
2.1	32.2	47.3
8.14	37.3	51.1

See also "Seniority of Vibration"

Planetary Vibration

12.27	16.61	49.8
12.30		

See also "Planetary Consciousness"

Visions
Visionary Information

14.25	44.5	49.2
25.4		

Visualization

1.13	49.8	56.3
42.13-15	50.8-9	

Vital Energy
Vitality, Vital Force

13.24	22.29	33.1
15.1	23.6	44.1-2
15.23	24.1	44.7-8
17.14	25.1-3	44.13
18.3-4	26.38	48.1-2
18.26-27	26.40	53.1
19.22	29.33	

Wanderer

2.2	16.59-61	36.24
11.25	17.8-9	37.2
11.29	17.11	42.16
12.26-30	17.18-19	45.3-7
12.32	23.6	48.7
13.23	26.13	52.8-9
14.18	26.15-16	53.7-13
15.20	32.9-11	
15.25	36.16-18	

See also "Brothers and Sisters of Sorrow"

War
Bellicose Action

8.16-17	22.5	34.12
8.19	23.15	34.14
9.10	24.4	34.17
9.18-19	24.17	35.1
10.1	25.4-11	35.8
10.15	26.25	38.9-10
18.25	32.2	
20.21-22	33.15	

Water

8.3	13.16	41.10
8.13	13.18	45.7
9.5	23.14	45.12

Blessed Water (for Cleansing or Drinking)

1.12-13	2.6	3.18

Swirling Water
See Volume 2

Weapons (Particle Beam and Psychotronic)

8.7

White Magic
See "Magic, White Magic"

Will

6.1	39.3	47.13-14
10.14	41.18-19	49.2
21.1	41.21-22	49.8
28.13-14	42.12-15	52.7
29.29	43.8	52.11
31.3	43.30-31	53.1
31.7	44.1	54.3
32.2	44.8	54.29
36.11	44.10	55.6
36.14	46.9	55.17
38.4	46.12	56.3

Williamson, George Hunt

12.1	15.18

Window Effect

12.7	17.27	26.34
16.3-7	24.8	

Wisdom

4.17	36.12	48.6
8.6	36.15-16	50.6
16.50	42.6-7	51.10
22.6	43.15	52.9
25.9	44.1	54.17
30.4	45.11	
33.20	47.5	

Work

1.0	12.1	29.27
2.3	15.12	31.3
3.15	16.32	39.10
4.14	17.1	46.10
4.17	19.19	48.6
5.1-2	20.9-10	50.5
6.1	22.29	56.3
9.2	26.38	
9.18	27.5-7	

Wrong

1.7	54.13	56.3
4.20		

Yahweh

16.14	18.14-24	24.9
17.17	24.6	

Zeta Reticuli

See Volume 2

AFTERWORD

The 106 sessions of the Ra contact represent an extraordinary subset of channeling in L/L Research's long history. During those 106 sessions the instrument was completely unconscious and, according to Ra, removed from her body. This is in contrast to the great majority of L/L's channeling undertaken with a conscious vocal instrument, awake and aware of the information coming through. That conscious channeling continues unbroken into the present day.

L/L Research makes this book, every channeling transcript, and much more available for free in its online library at the archive website www.llresearch.org.

Other recommended resources for further study of *The Ra Contact: Teaching the Law of One* include:

- The world's best Law of One study tool: www.lawofone.info
- *The Ra Contact* audiobook narrated by Jim McCarty, available at Audible.com.
- The actual recordings of the conversation with Ra, available for free listening at www.llresearch.org and www.lawofone.info, and combined with text at www.youtube.com/LLResearch.
- The Resource Series.
- Book V of the original published *Law of One* series containing Commentary of the journey of conducting the Ra contact.

We do this work for L/L Research keenly aware of the worldly context. It can sometimes seem to the sensitive seeker that the circumstances on our planet are tinged by chaos, disharmony, and suffering. But if you know where to look, and how to tune your senses, you'll see that a consciousness of love is growing all the time, inside of you, inside of others.

Our message for each wanderer we meet is the same: You are not alone. You are loved. You are here to assist with the transition to fourth density, first and foremost simply by being your truest most authentic self.

We are honored to play a small part in contributing to that blossoming awareness of love. We are grateful to help heal this planet alongside you, one open heart at a time.

ADDITIONAL L/L RESEARCH PUBLICATIONS

Living The Law of One 101: The Choice

Written with the intent of creating an entry–level, simple to read report concerning the core principles of the Law of One and Confederation philosophy in general, this book takes the reader through a discussion of Law of One principles such as unity, free will, love, light and polarity.

A Wanderer's Handbook

A reference manual for spiritual outsiders. It explores the alienation that seekers experience, the varieties of the pain of living, the healing of the incarnation, the discovery of the life's mission, and how to live a devotional life in a busy world.

Secrets of the UFO

A summary of the 25 years of philosophical study that preceded the Ra contact. The progression from physical sightings to metaphysical implications is carefully traced and, in some respects, serves as an introduction to the *Law of One* series.

A Channeling Handbook

Written for channels and those who would like to improve their channeling. Topics include: What is channeling? Why channel? Psychic greetings/attacks. Temptations and the ethics of channeling. Channeling and Christianity.

Tilting At Windmills: An Interview with Carla & Jim

The transcripts of a seven-day interview with Carla Rueckert and Jim McCarty that includes exploration of the Ra contact, the life story of L/L Research, personal biography of its three founding members, and examination of spiritual principles and philosophy.

On the L/L Research Website:

- More publications not listed above
- Over 1,500 channeling transcripts from 1974–Present
- A collection of interviews and speeches including rare gems with Don Elkins.
- The *Light/Lines* and *Gatherings Newsletter*s
- Information from various past L/L Research gatherings and workshops
- An *Origins* section including the *Brown Notebook* which opened Elkins to Confederation channeling.
- Transcripts and audio of L/L Research's podcast *In the Now*.
- Over twelve translations and more being added.
- Forums, Blogs, Chatrooms, Seeker Connector, and more.

Hardcopy versions of L/L publications are available through the online store.